Ed Bacon

THE CITY IN THE TWENTY-FIRST CENTURY

Eugenie L. Birch and Susan M. Wachter, Series Editors

A complete list of books in the series
is available from the publisher.

Ed Bacon

PLANNING, POLITICS,
AND THE BUILDING
OF MODERN PHILADELPHIA

Gregory L. Heller

PENN

UNIVERSITY OF PENNSYLVANIA PRESS

PHILADELPHIA

Published by
University of Pennsylvania Press
Philadelphia, Pennsylvania 19104-4112
www.upenn.edu/pennpress

Printed in the United States of America on acid-free paper
10 9 8 7 6 5 4 3 2 1

Library of Congress Cataloging-in-Publication Data

Heller, Gregory L.
    Ed Bacon : planning, politics, and the building of modern
Philadelphia / Gregory L. Heller.—1st ed.
        p.   cm.—(The city in the twenty-first century)
    Includes bibliographical references and index.
    ISBN 978-0-8122-4490-8 (hardcover : alk. paper)
    1. Bacon, Edmund N.   2. City planners—
Pennsylvania—Philadelphia—Biography.   3. City
planning—Pennsylvania—Philadelphia—History—20th
century.   4. Philadelphia (Pa.)—HIstory—20th
century.   I. Title.   II. Series: City in the twenty-first
century.
NA9085.B29H45   2013
711'.4092—dc23
[B]   2012037695

In memory of my father

Contents

Foreword

Alexander Garvin

Ask most people who lived in Philadelphia during the second half of the twentieth century who was responsible for downtown Philadelphia and they will answer correctly: Edmund Bacon. But when you ask them what he did and how he did it, they usually cannot answer. Ask them about his work outside downtown and even fewer have anything to say. This book, for the first time, provides the answers. This is particularly important because Bacon, like Robert Moses in New York, worked hard at creating a legend that helped him to get things done, but has muddied the waters ever since.

I was fortunate to befriend Ed Bacon during the final ten years of his life. I spent four or five days annually walking around Philadelphia with him, listening to his stories about the city he so passionately loved. Each time my visit began at his house on Locust Street. The first time he opened the door, without even saying hello, he exclaimed, "You have written about me better than anybody else, without ever even talking with me." He was referring to my book *The American City: What Works, What Doesn't*. In an astonished tone of voice, I replied, "I walked all over the city at different times of the day, in different seasons, over many years." He immediately challenged me to go for a walk. As we walked around the city, he showed me many things of which I was unaware and explained much that I had not understood. I decided to return again and again and get him to tell me everything he could remember.

During my walks and talks with Ed Bacon, he was eager to impress on me that successful planning had to be based on:

- A deep and evolving understanding of the city,
- A total vision for the city

- A public realm strategy for its improvement
- A convincing vision of a better future
- A marketing program
- Ongoing public support
- Tenacity in the pursuit of one's goals

I now understand why we went on all those walks. Without ever saying so explicitly, Ed wanted me to understand the importance of pedestrian circulation and of what I now call "the public realm approach to planning." He said he "walked and walked until I had the concept in my body."[1] He had taken me on all those walks because he wanted me also to walk and walk until I had the concept in my body.

Bacon explained that he was able to make things happen because he took "the multiplicity of wills that constitutes our contemporary democratic process" and proposed a program that could "coalesce into positive, unified action on a scale large enough to change substantially the character of the city."[2] When I asked him how he devised that program, he replied that he had what he called a "total vision of the city." He promoted ideas to achieve that total vision, but "promoted," in this instance, is a term of art because, although Ed was clearly responsible for what happened, he had no specific role within the entities that developed physical projects.

At a time when countless city dwellers were escaping to the suburbs, Bacon understood that residences were an integral part of any healthy downtown. Thus, the restoration of Society Hill as one of Philadelphia's thriving residential neighborhoods became a central feature of this total vision. He explained, "I set the concept; then it was adjusted by others as required by the realities of the situation."[3] Therein lies the explanation of Edmund Bacon's amazing ability to make things happen without actually doing anything himself. It was not, however, because he gave up any role in what happened.

As usual, Bacon was as accurate as he was misleading when he intimated that all he did was "set the concept" and left the rest to developers, property owners, lending institutions, and government officials. Persistence is as important as letting others get some of the credit for implementing an agreed-upon vision. Edmund Bacon, probably the most relentless and determined of all planners, believed that the most important and difficult thing to do was deciding what to advocate and that the trick in making that decision was selecting something that you could bring to fruition. He used to say that, once you decided that something was the right thing to do, you had to devise "your own approach" to getting it done "without giving a damn about other people's ideas."[4] That, too, was misleading because he was always concerned about developing a constituency for his proposals. That is why he also told me that, whenever he said anything, he "always thought about what it would look like as a headline in the *Philadelphia Inquirer*."[5]

Certainly, determining what Edmund Bacon thought is as difficult as discovering what he did and how he did it. We are fortunate in having this stunning biography by Gregory Heller—fortunate because he knew Ed Bacon well and spent much of the years since Ed died trying to piece together what actually happened. The result is an engrossing story explaining how modern Philadelphia took shape.

Preface

I met Edmund Bacon in the summer of 2002. I was home after my junior year of college at Wesleyan University, interning at the Philadelphia City Planning Commission, and conducting research for my thesis on city planning. I wrote Bacon a letter asking permission for an interview. He obliged my request, and afterward we went to lunch, where he shocked me by asking me to take off a year of school to help him write his memoir. I agreed, and for the next year I came to Bacon's house every day at 9:00 A.M. sharp, and we worked often late into the night. Though Bacon was physically frail, at ninety-two his mind was keen and his endurance tremendous.

At the time I had no knowledge of the string of young assistants who had come before me, or Bacon's prior attempts to record his thoughts and ideas for posterity. His home office was strewn with hundreds of pages of typed autobiographical writings—each a single fragment of a narrative he did not know how to shape or finish. I quickly learned that the book he wanted to write was not really a memoir, rather a sequel to his 1967 book *Design of Cities*.[1] Like his previous work, this one would be unorthodox— highly visual, with compelling graphics and diagrams demonstrating concepts, while the text played a secondary role.

I tape recorded dozens of interviews and discussions with Bacon, and together we met with a number of his coworkers, contemporaries, and disciples. After our year together, we completed a manuscript of the book, following which I went back to college and wrote my senior thesis on Bacon's work in Philadelphia's Far Northeast. Meanwhile he continued to tinker with the manuscript, and the Bacon family eventually privately published the book in 2005 under the title *Imagination Builds a City*.[2]

While I worked with Bacon, an endless stream of students, journalists, architects, and planners flowed through his door. He would hardly turn down anybody who wanted to meet with him. It was riveting to see a new person respond to Bacon's abrupt but passionate style. At one point we held a fascinating seminar in Bacon's home with ten planning students from the University of Pennsylvania.

While I interned at the Philadelphia City Planning Commission, I was warned that Bacon was an egomaniac who was only interested in downtown projects. The Bacon I came to know, however, was quite different. He was certainly strong-willed and argumentative, but he respected informed debate, listened carefully, and would frequently change his mind based on the arguments of others. He cared deeply about community development and income and racial integration, and had innovative ideas about those topics. He believed that it was the planner's role not just to make a plan, but also to promote that plan, and to steer it through the complex political and social networks of implementation. Bacon also believed that cities do not just naturally develop—that it takes people with ideas and the commitment to realize those ideas.

Bacon passed away in 2005, so I only knew him for a few years. Still, through that limited exposure I gained a new perspective on what city planning is and what it ought to be. Perhaps Bacon's greatest contribution was not a physical project, but his methodology for planning, where the planner is involved in envisioning as well as promoting, and implementing ideas.

It has been a great honor to write this book, and I hope that other works follow that delve more deeply into topics I necessarily could not spend enough time on here. This book is part biography, part planning history, and part case study. As a practitioner I am most interested in the latter. Bacon provides a rare and fascinating example of a planner who participated in the political process of policy implementation. By studying Bacon's life and work, policy participants today can glean important insight on how to impact the implementation process, rooted in the subtle machinations of how society makes big decisions and gradually realizes evolving ideas.

INTRODUCTION

The November 6, 1964, issue of *Time* magazine appeared on the newsstands with a cover featuring a portrait of Edmund N. Bacon—Philadelphia's chief city planner. Bacon was shown in a dark suit with neatly combed hair, a firm jaw, and steely blue eyes staring determinedly off into space. Behind him was a backdrop of the Society Hill Towers—designed by I. M. Pei and recently under construction—and an image of the faux-colonial "Franklin" street lamps installed as part of the redevelopment of the historic Society Hill neighborhood. It was an intriguing composition, reinforcing the message that Philadelphia had sought to revitalize itself, merging the past and the future, with the confident Bacon leading it all.[1]

The cover story, written by Gurney Breckenfeld and adorned with full-color photographs of gleaming construction projects, was an optimistic review of the way urban renewal—backed by massive federal funding—was transforming U.S. cities. After briefly recounting ambitious projects in cities like New York, Chicago, San Francisco, and Cleveland, Breckenfeld wrote of Philadelphia,

> Of all the cities under the planner's knife, none has been so deeply and continuously committed to renewing itself as the city where the Declaration of Independence was signed: Philadelphia. For twelve years, the nation's fourth largest city has been tearing down and digging up, burrowing, building, restoring, condemning, relocating, and spending what will amount to more than $2 billion in private, city, state and federal funds to carry out the most thoughtfully planned, thoroughly rounded, skillfully coordinated of all the big-city programs in the U.S.[2]

The article continued, "One man coordinates, advises and stimulates all this activity—and the array of civic groups, politicians, architects, builders and real estate men necessary to keep it going. Edmund Norwood Bacon."[3]

The article noted Bacon's "intensely intellectual air that hardly seems the right equipment for moving and shaking a major city," but added, "his total dedication to his special art and to his native town—plus an impressive gift of gab—is changing the look and feel of the town that was once the butt of comedians as the sleepiest city of them all."

The article described and praised the various Philadelphia redevelopment projects: Penn Center, Society Hill, Eastwick, Penn's Landing. The piece was highly complimentary of Philadelphia's progress, telling the story exactly as Bacon would have wanted—touting the right elements and glossing over those he preferred to avoid. The writer bought Bacon's pitch, while also being conscious that he was in the presence of a skilled salesman of ideas, influenced by Bacon's "highly articulate proselytizing."[4]

The cover story generated a "phenomenal response," according to *Time*'s editor, A. T. Baker, who wrote to Bacon about the issue, sharing the news that the magazine had gotten requests for 25,000 reprints.[5] Bacon received 180 letters relating to the *Time* issue from twenty-seven U.S. states and fifteen foreign countries. In addition, 144 people mailed Bacon their *Time* covers, requesting his autograph.[6]

The *Time* cover story elevated Bacon and Philadelphia's redevelopment to a new level of fame at a time when cities were in stiff competition for federal funding. Philadelphia was successful in securing the second-most federal urban renewal funds, after New York City.[7] In the mid-1960s, no city would eclipse Philadelphia's national renown for its planning and redevelopment. After Bacon's retirement in 1970, the "Bacon Era" of planning would be the topic of national and international newspaper, magazine, and journal articles.[8] The March 1976 issue of *AIA Journal* recalled that, in the 1960s, under Bacon, Philadelphia "was the undisputed urban design capital of the nation."[9]

Part of Philadelphia's renown came from the novelty of its approach. The 1949 Federal Housing Act facilitated "slum clearance," which many cities used to bulldoze and rebuild entire neighborhoods. Philadelphia's model made headlines early on for its more selective demolition, focus on preservation of existing structures, and attempts to work with community groups.[10] Bacon was instrumental in pushing back against the federal focus on wholesale slum clearance; one article just before his retirement in 1970 recounted "Bacon's Battle Against the Bulldozer."[11] Philadelphia's Society Hill renewal was groundbreaking in that it included large-scale historic preservation of existing structures. A lifelong progressive and Roosevelt

Figure 1. Photo of Bacon with model of Society Hill Towers (about 1960). Courtesy of the Edmund N. Bacon Collection, The Architectural Archives, University of Pennsylvania.

Democrat, Bacon consistently focused on affordable housing, government reform, and racial equality; an article in *Harper's* characterized him as "uncompromisingly idealistic and liberal."[12]

Another element of Philadelphia's approach that made headlines was its degree of private-sector partnership. Penn Center, remaking a massive swath of downtown, was not chiefly a federally funded project—rather relying on a private company (in this case, the Pennsylvania Railroad) redeveloping its own real estate, informed and steered by public-sector actors. Society Hill involved dozens of private individuals investing their own money to restore historic houses. The Gallery at Market East was built in partnership with James Rouse, one of the nation's foremost private shopping mall developers. Philadelphia's approach relied heavily on the public sector, strategically attracting private-sector partnerships and investment.

The final significant piece that led to the acclaim of Philadelphia's program was the impact of Bacon himself. He became the charismatic face of the new Philadelphia. As one commentator later put it, "Although not himself the originator of all the ideas that have changed Philadelphia since World War II, he often appeared to be the personification of change itself."[13]

After his death, the *Philadelphia Inquirer* credited Bacon with "reinventing Philadelphia and the American city."[14] Inga Saffron, the *Philadelphia Inquirer* architecture critic, called him "a planning visionary who dragged a declining, smoke-blackened Philadelphia kicking and screaming into the modern postindustrial age."[15] *Architectural Record* called him "the last of a generation of heavy duty planners."[16] Most city planners in America during this period did not find similar fame, relegated instead to an advisory role behind more powerful politicians and development czars. Bacon was the only planner to end up on the cover of *Time*. This fact leaves significant questions of how he was able to play such a visible role in Philadelphia and what that role actually entailed.

Bacon's ability to achieve fame and his effectiveness at influencing Philadelphia's policy decisions during the urban renewal era came largely from his abilities as a promoter and marketer of ideas, his political savvy, and his understanding of the process of policy implementation. He often portrayed himself as a physical designer, though his direct influence on the final outcome of physical projects was often fairly limited, and the planning ideas he worked to implement were often not of his own creation.

Bacon's role in several major projects of the urban renewal period in Philadelphia demonstrates both the strengths and weaknesses of such an approach. Taken together with his early career, during which he developed and honed his approach, as well as his later career, when he applied it in the corporate world and as a private citizen, it becomes evident that, though he was indeed effective in moving concepts from abstract ideas through the process of policy implementation, his overall influence in Philadelphia's development program was largely exaggerated by the media, in part because of his own self-promotion. Ultimately then, Bacon's career serves as an enlightening lens through which to view the complexities of the modern urban planning process and the planner's role therein—from design to implementation, from drafting table to city hall, from theory to practice.

A Complex Persona

Bacon reached his position of prominence in Philadelphia thanks to a diverse set of life experiences, some failures that kept him from making his career elsewhere, and the fortune of being in the right place at the right time. As a youth, he rebelled against his strict Quaker upbringing and spent his childhood split between city, suburb, and country life in and around Philadelphia. He attended Cornell University's architecture program at a time when the school was still avoiding modernism but breaking from the Beaux Arts design tradition. He found his first job as a draftsman in Shanghai in the 1930s, working for architect Henry K. Murphy, who developed a new hybrid Chinese-Western architecture style.

Bacon studied at the Cranbrook Academy of Art, in Michigan, under Eliel Saarinen, the renowned Finnish architect/planner. He was then sent on assignment to Flint, Michigan, where he got his first experiences in planning and politics, working on projects funded by the Works Progress Administration—part of President Franklin Roosevelt's New Deal legislation. There he witnessed events like the famous 1937 United Auto Workers strike that would impact labor relations in America. Ultimately, Bacon's stance in favor of publicly funded housing created conflict with the ruling elites, concluding with his post being terminated and his return to Philadelphia in 1939.

During his early career, Bacon was inspired by colleagues like Catherine Bauer and Lewis Mumford, two of the founders of the Regional Planning Association of America (RPAA), a group that focused on physical design as a cure for social ills, through better communities with "modern" housing. This group and their followers reimagined the city as an equitable place, with affordable housing for all and modern community design, influenced by the then-forward-thinking concept of separating cars and pedestrians, made popular by architect Clarence Stein in Radburn, New Jersey. Bacon became a strong proponent of affordable housing, he was friendly with the early staff of the U.S. Housing Authority, and when he returned to Philadelphia, he headed up an affordable-housing advocacy nonprofit.

Bacon joined a civic and political reform movement in Philadelphia that in the 1940s was largely responsible for creating a modern city planning commission, electing progressive mayors, and gaining the city a new charter. He served in the Navy during World War II, where he saw combat in the South Pacific. On returning home, he was one of the main designers of the Better Philadelphia Exhibition—a massive city planning show that was viewed by 385,000 visitors in 1947 and paved the way for a new public consciousness of planning in Philadelphia.

Bacon fortuitously found himself, at age thirty-nine, head of the Philadelphia City Planning Commission just prior to passage of federal acts that would provide unprecedented resources for cities across the U.S. to engage in redevelopment, and also just before Philadelphia's landmark political reform, associated with the election of Democratic mayors Joseph S. Clark and Richardson Dilworth, ending the decades-long prominence of Philadelphia's Republican political machine.

After his appointment as executive director of the Philadelphia City Planning Commission, Bacon spent the next twenty-one years, from 1949 to 1970, as part of a complex bureaucracy that shaped Philadelphia's planning and rebuilding program through four mayors, during an era of population decline, racial tension, civic unrest, and changing federal directives on how best to invest in the future of urban America. All the while Bacon was part of a community of intellectuals from across the globe that met at his colleague Oskar Stonorov's farm for lunches and parties full of scholarly discourse and debate. Bacon also went on a series of Aegean cruises convened by Greek architect Constantine Doxiadis that brought together scholars to develop ideas for a visionary urban future. He taught at the University of Pennsylvania throughout his tenure as planning director. Thus, continually, Bacon was both a pragmatic public official and active in the community of prominent theorists and intellectuals.

Though Bacon came off professionally as a hard-nosed official, privately he loved art, theater, and all manner of creative forms. One of his hobbies was building and putting on performances with Dutch-designed model puppet theaters. He was an avid bicyclist. He raised six children, all of whom led accomplished careers in various fields (including one who became a movie star). His wife, Ruth Holmes Bacon, was a respected professor of early childhood development at Community College of Philadelphia, with a successful career of her own.

At the height of his prominence, Bacon was a powerful figure with a complex persona—difficult to simplify or categorize. His tall, lanky frame towered over most people, and his blue eyes could sparkle or pierce, depending on his mood. He was known for his Quaker modesty on the one hand, always wearing conservative suits, never displaying any of his myriad awards on his office walls. At the same time, he was famous as a forceful, outspoken figure who exuded power and was not to be reckoned with. Bacon was stubborn and had a tremendous temper. When he disagreed with something, he would shout and slam his fist on the table or kick his heel into the floor. He was known by some as an egomaniac, believing fiercely in his own ideals. He was also known as a loyal public servant,

Figure 2. Bacon giving a presentation to the Philadelphia City Planning Commission (probably 1963). Courtesy of the Edmund N. Bacon Collection, The Architectural Archives, University of Pennsylvania.

ethical to a fault, never veering from the mayor's orders, even if they seemingly contradicted with his personal beliefs.

Bacon had a strong stage presence and was a convincing public speaker. One of Bacon's former Planning Commission staff members, Ralph Hirsch, explained, "I have seen him take over large public meetings from the floor, through sheer force of personality."[17] Another staff member, Richard Huffman, recalled, "He was a genius in dealing with other agency heads and bureaucrats. . . . He almost always got his way in those meetings."[18] Yet another staff member, G. Craig Schelter, recounted the first time he saw Bacon speak in public, "He came to that conference and he just rocked it on its heels. . . . You knew he was larger than life."[19]

As exemplified by his ability to sway the tenor of the *Time* magazine piece, one of Bacon's skills was as a marketer of ideas. He knew how to speak the language of different constituencies—designers, politicians, business people, the media. He was never afraid to dream big, audacious ideas, and promote them without fear of ridicule. For decades he promoted the notion of a world-class Philadelphia, on the same playing field as London, Rome, and Paris, at a time when it was not clear whether this was prognostication or wishful thinking. He consistently launched big ideas and promoted them until they finally caught hold. No idea was too big for Bacon, who, after his retirement in 1970, spent decades promoting the notion of a "post-petroleum city," imagining a sustainable urban future where the world's oil supply was exhausted, cities flourished, and private automobiles became obsolete.

Bacon had no training in economics or finance. Although he participated in the realm of politics and policy, he was assuredly a designer, and his perception of the city was through its physical reality—not numbers on paper. He told one interviewer, "City planners should not look at themselves as disembodied intellects who observe the phenomena of other people as a statistical and quantifiable entity, but as people along with everyone else."[20] He explained in another setting, "It is only through the accumulation of interactive experiences that you really encounter community values."[21] It was this preference for developing concepts by experiencing the city, rather than by analyzing numbers, that placed Bacon in a rare position among political actors of the period. He once explained, "The primary difference between the way I see a city and the way other people do is that I see it as a teeming collection of thrusts and rushes. . . . All my paradigms are kinesthetic with me rushing about."[22] To Bacon, the city was a living, breathing entity that could grow, be injured, and could heal. The solution was never to amputate but always to cure and nurture.[23]

Throughout his career, Bacon maintained a consistent and profound belief that people can shape the future. In his book *Design of Cities*, he included a page titled "The City as an Act of Will." Here he wrote,

> My hope is to dispel the idea, so widely and uncritically held, that cities are a kind of grand accident, beyond the control of the human will, and that they respond only to some immutable law. I contend that human will can be exercised effectively on our cities now, so that the form that they take will be a true expression of the highest aspirations of our civilization. . . . [W]e are in danger of losing one of the most important concepts of mankind, that the future is what we make it.[24]

Bacon served most of his career as a public official, but throughout he appears to have been stymied and frustrated by public-sector bureaucracy.

Soon after he retired from the Philadelphia City Planning Commission in 1970, he began working for a private real estate development company and explained, "the true planners of the city today are in private enterprise."[25] He spoke across the globe and gained a reputation as a visionary but at home struggled to maintain a positive legacy, constantly disputing criticisms of the projects he worked on as planning director. In his retirement, he would jump into local debates around planning and development controversies in Philadelphia, earning him both applause and disdain, characterized by some as an aging crank who did not know when to step away gracefully. An appreciation of Bacon's varied and complex persona creates the framework needed to understand his professional role and methodology.

The Planner as Policy Entrepreneur

In other cities during the urban renewal period, the key figure was a development czar like Robert Moses in New York or Edward Logue in Boston. Otherwise, it was a developer like James Rouse in Baltimore. Bacon was perhaps the only planner to become a city's primary public figure during this era. This fact makes him a fascinating case study of how he came to achieve such prominence in a position that was less visible in other cities.

Robert Moses was educated in political science, interested in good government reform. He became close with Governor Robert E. Smith, from whom he would derive a significant degree of political access. Moses's influence was also due to his own savvy in getting himself appointed to commissions that were empowered to develop public works projects. At the height of his influence, he held twelve public and quasi-public positions that gained him influence to shape public projects and access to funding through entities like the Triborough Bridge and Tunnel Authority. Moses is credited with building 658 playgrounds in New York City, 416 miles of parkways, and 13 bridges, as well as playing a major role in projects such as Jones Beach, Shea Stadium, and Lincoln Center, and bringing the United Nations to New York.[26] He was obsessed with understanding the process of getting things done and adamant that he was not a planner, a profession whose members he held in low regard and referred to as "socialists."

Edward Logue was a career public works administrator, and though he was less hostile to planners than Moses, he famously argued, "I'm not

inclined to generate plans that don't get built."[27] Logue served as administrator in New Haven, development administrator of the Boston Redevelopment Authority, president and chief executive of the New York State Urban
Development Corporation, and president of the South Bronx Development
Organization. During his career, he was responsible for major buildings
like Boston's City Hall, as well as over 33,000 units of housing in New York.
Like Moses, he gained influence through close relationships with elected
officials—most significantly Mayor John F. Collins of Boston. Like Moses
and Bacon, Logue became closely identified with a city he helped shape—in
this case, Boston.[28]

Bacon stands in contrast to Moses and Logue in that he was his city's
chief planner, rather than holding a position responsible for implementing
public works development. Still, after reading some articles on Philadelphia's 1950s and 1960s redevelopment, one could reasonably think Bacon
was chief cook and bottle washer, wielding tremendous power over Philadelphia's redevelopment agenda. The reality is more complex. The Philadelphia City Planning Commission was a relatively weak, mostly advisory
body, without direct access to federal funding. While Bacon received great
fame, other public-sector actors in Philadelphia who played equally (or
arguably more) significant roles fell into obscurity. One prime example
is William Rafsky, who served in a number of powerful roles including
development coordinator—the main official responsible for overseeing federal funds.

Rafsky was Philadelphia's closest counterpart to the role played by Robert Moses and Ed Logue elsewhere. One of Bacon's contemporaries called
Rafsky "almost as omnipresent, although by no means as omnipotent, as
Robert Moses in New York."[29] Another remarked that he "was the person
that I always thought should have been on the front cover of *Time* magazine."[30] Rafsky was not the only powerful player of the period; a slew of
important individuals were critical to Philadelphia's success and renown,
but Bacon somehow became the exclusive figurehead.

Although they played different roles, held different titles, and gained
their influence in different means, Moses, Logue, and Bacon had a unifying
element in their political astuteness and understanding of the process of
turning ideas into reality. Bacon (and arguably Moses, Logue, and others)
occupied a position akin to what John W. Kingdon, in his landmark political science book *Agendas, Alternatives, and Public Policies*, called the "policy
entrepreneur."[31] According to Kingdon, these "entrepreneurs" can be in or

outside government, and they play the critical role of doggedly promoting and guiding ideas through the process of societal decision making.

According to Kingdon, entrepreneurs are individuals who understand that ideas "float around" and become reality over long periods of time, through a subtle gestation that resembles "a process of biological natural selection."[32] Policy entrepreneurs have a grasp on this process, including several key pieces of knowledge. First, "new ideas do not suddenly appear. Instead, people recombine familiar elements into a new structure or new proposal."[33] Indeed, few of the ideas Bacon promoted were his own. Many originated years or decades earlier and were reshaped (sometimes by Bacon) to fit the times, political actors, and public sentiment.

In *Design of Cities*, Bacon dedicated a whole section to "decision making," writing about a planning process whereby "there is a continuous cyclical interaction, not just a one-way street. The leaders may influence the people and the people influence the leaders, or change them."[34] He wrote here of "cyclical feedback" and a process of "hypothesis formation and reformation" between the planner and the "community." This process appears very much in line with the process of policy creation and adoption Kingdon discusses, where ideas gestate for long periods of time, influenced by many actors, and where "feedback . . . can lead to innovation."[35]

Another important element of the policy entrepreneur according to Kingdon is the understanding that promoting ideas includes a period spent "softening up" policy makers and the public who may be "resistant to major changes" the first time around.[36] Most of Bacon's major ideas were rejected or postponed when he first tried to promote them, but he continued to push them through different venues. Kingdon explains that it takes dogged promotion of ideas, in speeches, articles, and constant repetition, to start to turn the tide and approach a point of acceptance by policy makers and the public.[37] Bacon did exactly this, repeating the same concept in numerous speeches and interviews, over and over, until the idea he was promoting began to seep into public consciousness.

According to Kingdon, once the critical point for realizing a policy idea is reached, it takes compromise and coalition building to actually attain acceptance and adoption of ideas and policy.[38] For Bacon, this often meant allowing his ideas to evolve in ways that were very different from his initial vision and allowing other stakeholders to take ownership and sometimes credit for the ideas. Bacon seems to have hated compromise but understood that strategic compromise is an important element of the policy entrepreneur's toolkit. At times he reluctantly accepted compromise as a necessity of getting things done. He was a master at understanding "what makes an idea's time come."[39] Like the policy entrepreneurs of Kingdon's book, Bacon realized that ideas do not become reality by accident.

Viewing Bacon as a policy entrepreneur is intriguing because, though there are certainly exceptions, city planners are not typically thought of as policy makers engaged heavily in implementation. Rather they are typically actors who create plans to be implemented by others. This is the reason the key individuals in other cities were typically individuals like Robert Moses or Ed Logue—whose official role was more directly connected to implementing physical public works projects.

In this regard, Bacon broke the mold—successfully playing the challenging dual role of planner-implementer. He was tenacious and stubborn, never satisfied with creating a plan and leaving it to sit on a shelf; he always involved himself in propelling the plan along a course that he felt would lead to its implementation—whether or not it was his stated responsibility to do so and though lacking direct access to financial resources. One article in the *Philadelphia Inquirer* noted, "unlike Moses, who controlled hundreds of millions of dollars and wielded the authority conferred by such wealth, Mr. Bacon achieved his stature and power from the force of his ideas and rhetoric, the clarity of his vision, the support of powerful reform-minded political patrons, and sheer stubbornness."[40]

Bacon was highly cognizant, early in his career, of the daunting challenges related to implementing planning ideas in a complex political climate, and throughout his career he learned strategies for navigating this process. One comment late in life demonstrated his keen understanding of the amorphous but moldable realm of ideas and public opinion. He explained, "I learned that you cannot make a plan, you have to grow a plan. I grew my plan in the collective unconscious of Philadelphia."[41] He used a number of tools to sell ideas. He loved the three-dimensional element of models but also relied on vivid drawings, diagrams showing complex movement systems, photo montages, films, slide shows, and compelling public presentations with dynamic visuals. He believed that telling people something was not enough; the salesman of ideas had to show a concept vividly.

Bacon was a hybrid of dreamer and pragmatist. In a 1988 interview, he said that did not want to be called a visionary because "visionaries don't get to see their ideas built."[42] His view of the designer's role differed sharply from that conventionally held by planners, architects, and designers. Renowned Philadelphia architect Louis Kahn said, "If your ideas are right, they—the businessmen and the politicians—will come to you."[43] Bacon, in contrast, believed that an effective planner had to actively promote ideas in a persuasive way. Kahn called Bacon "A planner who thinks he is a politician."[44] Kahn was largely right. However, as Bacon explained, "I never was a politician in the sense of currying political favor. . . . I understood how to wield the architectural image as a political force, without letting people know I was doing it."[45] Walt D'Alessio, of the Philadelphia Redevelopment Authority, recalled, "He was a pretty good politician. He could sense a trend and get out in front of it."[46]

Still, Bacon's entrepreneurial approach had significant challenges. His scope of influence was indeed limited; as much as he sold himself as the face of Philadelphia's development program, others arguably held much more influence, political connections, and access to federal dollars. While he often succeeded in promoting general ideas, the details of his visions were frequently distorted or altered beyond recognition.

Bacon clearly was more entrepreneurial at times than others—backing off projects that involved too much involvement with public-sector departments. He was not skilled at negotiating complex issues involving red tape and was easily frustrated by government logjam, preferring to work with private-sector actors when possible. At times he also seems to have been willing to sacrifice his ideals for the sake of simply moving a project along. While he was strong-willed on the one hand, he sometimes seems to have retreated on ideological issues surprisingly easily when it appeared that a project could become stalled.

Bacon also exhibited some degree of hypocrisy between his public views and his private ideology. A chief example was when he represented the city to community groups and the media, in the construction of the ill-fated Crosstown Expressway, while, during the same period, he privately spoke about the destruction wrought on the world by automobiles. Thus, Bacon's approach, position, and ideology were deeply complex and deserve a thorough analysis.

A Planner in a Shifting World

Bacon was active during two major periods of federal urban investment—the New Deal and urban renewal. He came of age as a Roosevelt liberal but,

Figure 3. Bacon making a presentation on television for Philadelphia
Channel 35, WHYY, on April 10, 1958. Courtesy of the Edmund N. Bacon
Collection, The Architectural Archives, University of Pennsylvania.

as planning director in Philadelphia, increasingly found himself out
of touch with emerging ideas about the role of social planning and
community-based consensus building. His ideas, once progressive, became
outdated, and he did not successfully adapt to the changing landscape of
urban trends or the shifting role of his own profession in the 1950s and
1960s.

As Bacon was promoting a rosy future for Philadelphia, racial conflict
and increasing poverty led to profound urban unrest. Meanwhile, his
approach to physical planning, so progressive in the 1930s and 1940s, was
supplanted by a focus on social planning—with emphasis on antipoverty
initiatives, education, public health, and job training.

Another even more substantial shift in the planning profession was
transforming the planner's role from expert who proposed plan concepts
to mediator, helping citizen stakeholders create plans for their own

communities. With the release of Jane Jacobs's 1961 book *The Death and Life of Great American Cities*, bolstered by subsequent writings by intellectuals like sociologist Herbert Gans and planning scholar Paul Davidoff, communities started to push back against government actors telling them how to plan, and many city planners reacted by taking a more passive role in plan creation. Bacon was highly critical of these changing priorities, commenting, "Planning has . . . been relegated into a kind of service role."[47]

Some saw Bacon as out of touch and outdated by the time he retired, with younger professionals placing greater priority on social planning and criticizing the physical planning tradition that was so progressive earlier in his career. Bacon's complex legacy involves a remarkable ability to influence public discourse and policy implementation. However, he shares the blame for projects that ultimately fell short, and he often encountered daunting challenges within city government that he had difficulty overcoming. He never was truly effective in working with communities and left his post at a time of unprecedented urban disinvestment—a frustrated and exhausted public official.

We study history to understand the past but also to glean lessons for the present and future. There is a contemporary cartoon, often circulated within the planning community, portraying a man placing a document onto a dusty shelf in a back room, with a caption that reads "implementing the plan." The image draws a laugh but also identifies a significant weakness in the planning profession: to realize the ideas it puts on paper. Despite his shortcomings, Bacon's ability to bridge the worlds of visionary and active political actor was rare in 1949 and remains perhaps rarer today.

Chapter 1

PLANNING FOR A NEW DEAL

Edmund Bacon would become known primarily for his work as planning director in Philadelphia in the 1950s and 1960s. However, Bacon's first significant experience with planning, urban housing, and public policy came in the 1930s in Flint, Michigan, where he worked for the Flint Institute of Research and Planning, carrying out a traffic study that he parlayed into a larger comprehensive planning and housing reform effort. Bacon's service in Flint came during a unique period of American history, when cities across the U.S. were starting to see the trends of urban decline and suburban flight that would exacerbate after World War II, and the nation was working to recover from the Great Depression. Many cities were experiencing deterioration of their downtowns and the need for better quality housing and services for the urban poor.

At the same time, during this period, significant federal funding was available for public works projects to combat the nation's high unemployment rate, through President Franklin Delano Roosevelt's New Deal programs like the Works Progress Administration (WPA). New federal programs were also available for supporting housing construction, via the creation of the U.S. Housing Authority. The New Deal era saw increased focus on planning through instruments like the Tennessee Valley Authority and National Resources Planning Board. Additionally, in this period, the national labor movement gained significant influence—felt especially strongly in industrial cities like Flint.

Flint in the 1930s was a major automobile manufacturing hub, a center of the nation's emerging workers-rights movement, and the site of the famous 1937 United Auto Workers strike on General Motors. At the same time, it was a city in which powerful business leaders and corporate executives exerted influence over the staunchly conservative political landscape.

This was the complex sociopolitical context in which Bacon first became professionally involved in planning and urban development.

Journey to Flint

Before arriving in Flint in 1936, Bacon had little planning or policy experience. Indeed, his professional focus was predominantly on architecture, and his life prior to that point was both provincial and worldly. Edmund Norwood Bacon was born May 2, 1910, in his family's modest three-story brick home in West Philadelphia, the third of four children of Ellis and Helen Comly Bacon. Bacon's parents were both members of the Society of Friends (known as Quakers), with lineage on his mother's side to Henry Comly, one of the Quakers who fled to the new colony of Pennsylvania established by William Penn in the seventeenth century, to escape religious persecution.[1] The young Bacon was raised in a strict Quaker household, attending meeting for worship with his parents every week.[2] Bacon's father insisted on traditions such as referring to fellow Quakers as "thee" and non-Quakers as "you."[3]

The Bacons lived in the middle-class neighborhood of Powelton Village, an area notable for its exquisite Victorian homes built for the executives of the Pennsylvania Railroad (though the Bacons' home was more modest). It was a quiet white-collar residential neighborhood with vibrant shopping streets, close to downtown, and near two major institutions of higher learning: the University of Pennsylvania and the Drexel Institute of Art, Science, and Industry. The area included a diversity of ethnicities and religions, with Quakers, Catholics, and Protestants.

Bacon's father Ellis Bacon was a man of conservative social views, rigid notions of morality, and a frequent temper. He worked as director of the Medical Department at the prominent Philadelphia publishing house J. B. Lippincott. Throughout his childhood, Bacon and his father would have a tense relationship.[4] His mother, in contrast, was a quiet woman, serving in the Women's International League for Peace and Freedom, and whose activities included running an art and literary circle.[5] Bacon grew up as part of an extended family, surrounded by relatives, who spent the summers together in Chester Heights, in the rural Pennsylvania countryside. Bacon recalled growing up with both a "city home" and a "country home." He was not a very social child, and grew up feeling like "an outsider."[6]

The young Bacon attended grade school at the Friends West Philadelphia School, a few blocks from his family's city home. The school was based on Quaker teaching philosophy, where "every situation . . . is used by the teachers to develop character."[7] He briefly attended Friends Central School, located at the time in the heart of Philadelphia's downtown, but he transferred to Swarthmore High School after his family moved to Wallingford, joining a number of Quaker families who left the city for the western suburbs in the early twentieth century.[8] Down the road from the Bacons' new home was the arts and crafts community of Rose Valley, established by architect William L. Price.[9] The Bacons became close with the other families in Rose Valley, meeting the numerous architects, artists, and artisans who lived there. Here, Bacon met William Price's son, a young architect named Bill Price, who gave Bacon his first exposure to architecture as a profession.[10]

By the time he was preparing for college, Bacon was set on studying architecture. He briefly considered the acclaimed program at the University of Pennsylvania, just down the street from his childhood home. However, he longed for a change of scenery and a life away from his parents. He fell in love with Cornell University and was admitted to the school's five-year architecture program.

Bacon began his first year at Cornell in fall 1927. He was one of about 185 architecture students taught by a faculty of twenty-three. That spring, the architecture school's Dean Francke H. Bosworth stepped down. Over his eight-year tenure, Bosworth built Cornell's architectural program into one of the nation's finest, establishing the first five-year architecture degree program in the U.S. He focused on integrating disciplines, giving students more flexibility and exposure to topics outside their field of study than was customary at other schools. He rebelled against the status quo of architectural teaching at the time and pulled Cornell out of the Society of Beaux-Arts Architects in New York.[11]

While Bosworth forged an exciting new curriculum for Cornell, he still taught his own variation of the curriculum at the École des Beaux-Arts in Paris, where he had studied. This neoclassical design philosophy was prominent in the recent City Beautiful movement in the U.S. that led to the construction of grand, European-style buildings and boulevards like Philadelphia's Museum of Art and Benjamin Franklin Parkway. By the time Bacon entered college, new modernist styles were emerging in Europe that turned their backs on the Beaux-Arts and Classical forms; however, the Beaux-Arts methodology was still prominent, even in forward-thinking

American architecture programs in the 1920s. The influence of Cornell's Beaux-Arts-inspired curriculum shaped Bacon's ideas, and throughout his career, he would often favor symmetry and formal design over modernism.

The year Bacon entered Cornell, Bosworth was replaced by Dean George Young, Jr. The new dean continued in Bosworth's footsteps, promoting the school's multidisciplinary approach. He also brought on a new faculty member to teach a course on the emerging field of city planning—a course Bacon never took. Bacon did, however, attend a lecture on designing parks and parkways by Gilmore Clarke, one of "a special series of lectures on city planning" Dean Young brought to campus.[12] Later in life Bacon asserted that this lecture was the only formal exposure to planning he received at Cornell and "the only thing I learned . . . was that city planning was impossible."[13] The college would not add planning as a major component of the curriculum until 1938.

Cornell architecture students had to create a thesis project. Most projects were individual building designs; however, Bacon took on the ambitious task of designing "A Civic Center for Philadelphia," clearly showing an early interest in planning rather than stand-alone architecture. His thesis called for replacing the city's massive Second Empire-style City Hall with a pedestrian court flanked by two small civic buildings, a war memorial, and bus platforms.[14] He planned a block-and-a-half-long tree-lined promenade terminating in a semicircular plaza, where it met the diagonal Benjamin Franklin Parkway, with a William Penn Memorial at the center. His plan also assumed the removal of the so-called "Chinese Wall," the Pennsylvania Railroad's massive viaduct that divided the western end of Philadelphia's Center City. Bacon was not the first to propose replacing the Chinese Wall, and his thesis design referenced an existing plan for developing this area.[15] Several ideas from his thesis eventually found their way into Philadelphia's urban environment during his career, including the plaza cutting off the diagonal of the Parkway.

With his thesis completed, Bacon closed out his fifth year and graduated on June 20, 1932. In summer 1932, he was faced with the daunting task of finding a job in the midst of the Great Depression. While some of his peers from Cornell struggled to begin their careers, Bacon took advantage of a $1,000 gift from his grandfather, supplemented by money he earned as art editor of *The Cornellian*, to travel around the world. He felt this traveling could be an opportunity to see firsthand the great architectural wonders and styles he had studied in college.[16]

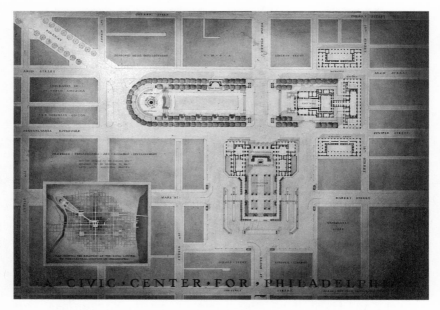

Figure 4. Plan drawing from Bacon's 1932 thesis at Cornell University,
"A Civic Center for Philadelphia." In the plan, Philadelphia's City Hall is
replaced with modern structures, a new plaza is positioned at the terminus
of the Benjamin Franklin Parkway, and reference is made to removing the
Pennsylvania Railroad tracks. Courtesy of the Edmund N. Bacon
Collection, The Architectural Archives, University of Pennsylvania.

On July 13, 1932, Bacon set sail for England, starting in London, then
traveling to Oxford, where he bought a bicycle. Over the next few months,
he biked through England, France, and Italy. He left his bicycle at the
American Academy in Rome and continued to Greece, where he went to
Athens and took a trip to Delphi, Aegina, and Corinth. From there he went
to Istanbul. Finally, Bacon traveled to Egypt so that "nearly all the cultures
important to Western civilization I shall have touched, at least."[17] He hoped
to visit Germany to see the emerging modernist architectural movement,
but never made it there, in part because it was getting cold and he was
running out of money: it was cheaper to go to Egypt than to purchase a
winter coat, he asserted.[18]

Bacon's travels shaped his appreciation and understanding of architecture and urban planning. In Bath, he wrote about his impressions of

European city planning: "I mean we diddle around with civic pride and planning—etc., but that it actually did happen was rather grand. Human intelligence dominating the design and growth of an entire city."[19] His experiences in Greece reaffirmed his love of Classical forms, first developed at Cornell. It was thrilling to observe the ancient ruins.[20] He also used his travels as an opportunity to meet important international figures in architecture and planning, such as when he found himself dining with Sir Raymond Unwin, one of the most prominent figures in architecture and town planning at the time, courtesy of a letter of introduction from Cornell. Unwin suggested that Bacon pursue city planning—an idea he politely rejected at the time.[21]

Nearly out of money and faced with the increasingly inhospitable political situation in Europe, Bacon considered his next move. Having heard of a building boom in China (and still living in Egypt), he discussed the potential for Chinese architectural employment with a former ambassador to China and a doctor who had worked there. He also traveled to Jerusalem to meet with Arthur Adamson, an American architect who had worked in Shanghai and who "definitely indicated that I could get work of some sort [in China]."[22] Expecting their son home within a month or so, Bacon's parents were surely shocked with the news that they should "send a word of greeting c/o American Express Shanghai."[23]

When Bacon arrived in Shanghai, he found a city much less foreign than he had expected. In 1933, Shanghai was already a truly international city, with tens of thousands of foreigners, many British and American, and a cityscape that resembled a Western metropolis. Shanghai was a center of international commerce, with the U.S., Great Britain, and France having access to the city's port. During the late nineteenth and early twentieth centuries, Shanghai had grown into a hub of shipping and banking industries.[24] By the time of Bacon's arrival, it had 40,000–70,000 foreign residents, from more than fifty nationalities, in addition to three million Chinese residents.[25]

Shanghai's center of industry, business, and culture was its famous riverside boulevard, the "Bund"—a wide thoroughfare lined with modern office buildings, hotels, extravagant nightclubs, restaurants, and upscale shops. Starting around 1910, the city saw a multitude of flashy modern buildings, designed by foreign architects, rise along the Bund.[26] Outside the Bund, architects were busy building eclectic homes for the foreigners, with faux Spanish, Tudor, Classical, and Italianate architecture. Known as the

"Paris of the Orient," the city was famous for its glitz, gangsters, nightclubs, racetracks, prostitution, and drugs. It bustled with commerce by day and glowed with colorful lights by night.[27]

Bacon took up residence at the YMCA in the International Settlement and, likely through a reference by Arthur Adamson, got in touch with Henry Killam Murphy, a semiretired American architect known for his groundbreaking architectural style that merged traditional Chinese and Western design.[28] Murphy helped secure Bacon a job at Realty Investment Company, a large real estate office with an architecture department, over which Murphy supervised residential development. Realty was a second-generation, missionary-owned firm that dealt in real estate outside the city, also designing homes for some clients.[29]

Murphy had a strong influence on Bacon, instilling in him an admiration of Chinese design and an appreciation of the value of harmoniously melding old and new styles. In one letter, Bacon called Murphy "the best teacher I could get."[30] Murphy spoke of China's architecture as a "living organism," a concept Bacon would embrace throughout his career.[31] He surely also inherited from Murphy his admiration for the Forbidden City in Beijing, which he later called "Possibly the greatest work of man on the face of the earth."[32]

Bacon started at Realty Investment as a draftsman, making $200 per month.[33] The bulk of his work was designing private homes and drawing iron railings, ornate doorways, and porches. The company's projects incorporated some elements of Murphy's hybrid design style but were often more conservative, imitating Western residential styles.[34] Over time Bacon received some more exciting jobs, including work on a proposed new national airport, a $2 million project billed as a "monumental gateway to the country."[35]

Bacon called China "a sort of Peter Pan country—where the dull is unknown."[36] He adapted to the rushing rickshaws and bustle of merchants and businessmen on the Bund, though, ironically, considering his future career, he wrote, "I don't like living in a city—but the profession demands it." In December 1933, he was joined in China by John Townsend, a classmate from Cornell, who struggled to find work in the U.S. before deciding an invitation from Bacon was his best prospect. The two worked and lived together for a brief period. However, after Townsend was diagnosed with polio, Bacon decided to accompany his friend back to the U.S.[37]

Figure 5. Bacon on a boat in China in 1933 or 1934, with architect Henry K. Murphy seated at center. Courtesy of the Edmund N. Bacon Collection, The Architectural Archives, University of Pennsylvania.

After almost two years away, trotting the globe and working in China, in June 1934 Bacon was living at home with his parents in suburban Wallingford, Pennsylvania. He secured a job as an assistant in the firm of architect William Pope Barney, a friend of his parents. The job paid only $10 per week—a meager sum, even during the Depression.[38] However, he learned much from the position. Barney had worked with some of Philadelphia's top designers, including Paul Cret and the firm of Zantzinger, Borie & Medary.[39] Bacon gained valuable experience working for Barney, learning the ins and outs of running an architecture shop in the U.S., creating working drawings and supervising project construction in the field. At the time, Barney was working on a public housing project called the Carl Mackley Houses in the Juniata Park section of North Philadelphia. However, he was mostly serving as architect of record; the primary architects, Germans Oskar Stonorov and Alfred Kastner, were both unregistered in the U.S.

Oskar Stonorov, a twenty-nine-year-old architect from Frankfurt, was a practitioner of the European modernist movement and a disciple of famous Swiss architect Le Corbusier. Stonorov was enamored with the concept of applying modernist architecture to create high-quality, low-cost worker housing, and he was intrigued by the opportunity for designing such housing in the Depression-stricken industrial U.S. In Philadelphia, Stonorov saw an opportunity to create a new model for cooperative housing that meshed with the city's traditional row-house architecture. He sold John Edelman, of the Full-Fashioned Hosiery Workers Union, on his idea for co-op worker housing. The project became the Carl Mackley Houses, eventually the first project to receive federal support from the Housing Division of the Public Works Administration.[40]

Stronorov and Bacon met during this project and would become long-time friends, colleagues, and compatriots. Through Stonorov, Bacon also met Catherine Bauer, a young woman already making waves as a leader of the American housing movement, and Lewis Mumford, a prominent architecture writer, scholar, and critic. Bauer and Mumford were deeply involved with the Regional Planning Association of America (RPAA), an organization committed to building partnerships among like-minded individuals to forge a new urban design paradigm. The organization had commissioned Radburn, the new town designed by RPAA founder Clarence Stein that adapted the British Garden City model to an American context.

The "Radburn principles" involved separating pedestrians from automobiles by routing vehicular through traffic away from residential enclaves and building pedestrian pathway systems.[41] Radburn allowed automobile use, while keeping pedestrians separate and dominant, with dedicated walkways away from the roads.[42] These design principles were very influential for a generation of practitioners including Stonorov, Bauer, and Bacon.

In Catherine Bauer's 1934 *Modern Housing*, she argued that better designed housing in well-planned new communities could improve the lives of working people in America by creating "a new standard for human environment, and a new technique for achieving it."[43] The Carl Mackley Houses merged some Radburn design principles with the clean lines of Stonorov's modernist architecture. Bacon had studied an antimodernist aesthetic and learned how to design buildings for the sake of beauty and aesthetics. However, through his exposure to Stonorov, Bauer, and Mumford, he first came to the stunning revelation that architecture could have a profound social value if applied properly. If Bacon's new colleagues were right, progressive architecture and community design could help house America's workers, rebuild its communities, and prevent the slums of the future.

Excited to broaden his horizons, Bacon's next opportunity came in a letter from his former dean, George Young. With Young's recommendation, he was awarded one of six full scholarships to the Cranbrook Academy of Art in Bloomfield Hills, Michigan.[44] Cranbrook was established just a few years earlier by Detroit newspaper baron George Booth and his wife Ellen as an academy to train artists and craftsmen in a bucolic setting about twenty-five miles north of Detroit. Its first president and the designer of most of its campus was Eliel Saarinen, a prominent architect-planner from Finland, who brought immediate attention to the school.[45] A handful of early pupils would go on to great acclaim in their fields, including Bacon, Harry Bertoia, Charles Eames, Florence Knoll, Eero Saarinen (Eliel's son), and Marianne Strengell.[46]

Cranbrook was a dynamic school where students had the freedom to pursue projects of interest on their own schedules. There was an endless string of activities: lectures, exhibitions, and demonstrations. While Bacon was there, Le Corbusier presented a lecture.[47] Saarinen built his own house across the street from the drafting studios, and students were always welcome to join him in his home, sit around his L-shaped couch, drink beer with their mentor, and discuss architecture and philosophy.[48]

As it turned out, Bacon would spend only about five months full time at Cranbrook. He quickly learned that Saarinen had selected him as one of two students to send on a special assignment to the nearby city of Flint, Michigan.[49] Nonetheless, Saarinen's philosophy left a strong mark on Bacon. It was likely Saarinen who inspired him to shift his thinking substantially from architecture to urban planning. Most important, like Bacon's new colleagues, Saarinen believed in the power of architecture and design to address social problems—that the architect could and must play a central role in improving social conditions in America. Saarinen wrote, "the city's 'form order' and 'social order' cannot be separated: they must be developed hand-in-hand, reciprocally inspiring one another."[50] In his application to Cranbrook, Bacon wrote, "The relation of the architect to society certainly has, and is, undergoing changes. . . . I have learned that the architect has social responsibility."[51] Saarinen likely strengthened Bacon's belief in his social duty, which would propel him to chart his own path in Flint.

Planning Meets Politics

In 1936, Flint was a small industrial city located on the Flint River about sixty miles from Detroit. The home of four General Motors plants—Chevrolet, Buick, AC Spark Plug, and Fisher Body—Flint boomed during the early the twentieth century. Although business slowed during the Great Depression, Chevrolet and AC Spark Plug remained stable, keeping much of Flint's predominantly blue-collar populace employed. But with rapid expansion came new problems like traffic congestion, aging freight rail lines, declining housing conditions, and deterioration of the downtown core. Flint had not seen any real city planning since 1920, when the city Planning Board engaged prominent New York architect-planner John Nolen to develop the city's first comprehensive plan. In summer 1935—a year before Bacon's arrival—General Motors, the city of Flint, the University of Michigan, and the local Rackham and Mott Foundations created a new program for addressing the city's planning and policy challenges. Eliel Saarinen agreed to oversee the new planning program, assisted by Cranbrook students.[52]

Bacon's assignment in Flint was at the Flint Institute of Research and Planning, a multidisciplinary organization charged with creating technical reports to inform Flint's leadership on a variety of issues, including health, child welfare, planning, housing, and recreation. The institute was created under an umbrella organization called the Flint Community Association.[53] President Roosevelt's New Deal programs provided new funding for states and cities to deal with issues of poverty, housing, and urban redevelopment. As a result, cities began engaging in "city planning well beyond traditional concepts of physical planning . . . [including] the collection of basic sociological and economic data."[54] Cities used these data to develop studies to apply for federal funding and, for the first time, truly focus on solving complex social and economic urban issues in a comprehensive manner. For Bacon, Flint offered an exciting opportunity to test some of the ideas he had learned from Saarinen, Stonorov, Mumford, and Bauer—using design to create better places that could inherently address social issues.

Bacon's first task was to oversee a downtown traffic survey, one of a number of similar studies across the nation funded through the federal WPA. This survey was intended to make recommendations for relieving traffic associated with the auto factories and recent urban development. The study was slated to begin in June 1936 and finish in December. Despite his young age, Bacon was given seemingly free rein to develop the methodology and carry out the study. He and his colleagues began the project by meeting with local civic officials, the police, and the media. He made presentations before the city's clubs and major organizations and was able

to meet with some of the city's wealthy leaders and top auto executives—
including the president of Fisher Body and the vice president of Buick.[55]
He wrote in one letter, "the curious by product of this survey is that it has
opened up access to the top industrial executives through their interest in
trucking—but it has introduced our whole concept of planning as it's [sic]
logical background." It is difficult to assess the impact of these meetings,
but Bacon hoped they would lead to broad buy-in down the line when the
study became the foundation for actual policy recommendations. These
meetings show Bacon's early awareness of the need to promote his work
and court important individuals to implement planning concepts.

Bacon made an innovative choice in his methodology for the study.
Rather than rely on the expertise of traffic engineers, he printed tens of
thousands of index cards to survey members of the public on how they
moved about the city. His crew of staff and volunteers distributed cards to
workers at the auto plants and drivers along the major roadways. The presence of the study was impossible to miss. Dozens of WPA workers, police,
Boy Scouts, and other volunteers assisted Bacon's staff in distributing cards.
By the end of August, nearly half the cards had been returned—a response
rate better than even Bacon anticipated. He came to supervise sixty men on
the field, two graduate engineers, two draftsmen, and one secretary.[56]

The study was not without its critics. At one point, officials from Washington, D.C., visited and were furious to discover Bacon's unorthodox
method of data collection, which deviated from the established guidelines
for a traffic survey. Showing surprising chutzpah for someone so early in
his career, Bacon told the officials he was the only person who understood
the methodology, that the study was too far along to start over, so there
was no choice but to let him continue. It apparently worked, and the study
moved ahead.[57]

In March 1936, Bacon presented the tentative results of the study,
including a large-scale color map showing proposed street, bridge, and rail
routes, at a public exhibition. The event was attended by Eliel Saarinen and
civic officials from Flint and was covered by the *Flint Journal*.[58] Bacon
hoped that Flint's leadership would adopt the traffic survey's findings as
the basis for making future policy decisions.

In August 1936, Bacon gained a partner in Eero Saarinen, Eliel's son.[59]
The two young planners soon had their first test as to whether their
approach would be successful, in a controversy over where to build a new
bridge over the Flint River. Prior to the traffic survey, public opinion

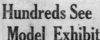

Hundreds See Model Exhibit

Model City of Future Put on Display for Public; Project Is Praised

By Ewald Pfeiffer

Several hundred Flint citizens, city commissioners and other officials and guests from Cranbrook Academy of Arts Thursday night had their first view of a new city plan designed for Flint to meet the changes brought about by the motor age.

The public display at 404 South Saginaw street, one door south of Kearsley street, was preceded at 7:30 p. m. by a preview for those directly connected with its creation. The exhibit is being continued tonight, Saturday and Saturday night.

The display, developed as a WPA traffic project at the request of the city under the technical supervision of the Flint Institute of Research and Planning and the Cranbrook Academy of Arts, consisted of 52 maps, models and charts showing a comprehensive design for the entire city of Flint and its environs as an objective toward which development over a period of years may be directed.

Cranbrook President Here

At the preview, in charge of Inspector Demaroff of the city police, Prof. Eliel Saarinen, president of Cranbrook, was introduced to the audience and brief talks were given by City Manager Findlater,

Flint's New Civic Design Exhibited—The basis of a comprehensive civic design for Flint as a continuity of the Nolen plan was explained to officials attending the opening of the public exhibit at 404 South Saginaw street Thursday night. The display will continue tonight and through Saturday night with everyone in Flint invited to see the plan for the Flint of tomorrow. In the picture, Edmund A. Bacon, technical supervisor of the display, is shown as he pointed out some of the interesting features to interested officials. In addition to Mr. Bacon, those in the picture, left to right, are Seward C. Simons, managing director of the Flint Community association; Prof. Eliel Saarinen, president of Cranbrook Academy of Arts; Inspector Robert Demaroff of the police department; Carl W. Bonbright, member of the city plan commission and chairman of the citizens' planning committee, and City Manager Findlater, later. (Journal Photo.)

Figure 6. Article from *Flint Journal*, March 26, 1936, with Bacon at far left and Eliel Saarinen third from left. Courtesy of the Edmund N. Bacon Collection, The Architectural Archives, University of Pennsylvania. Reprinted with permission from *The Flint Journal*.

seemed to be leaning toward Harrison Street as the best location. The survey recommended placing it a few blocks upriver at Clifford Street. When an influential city commissioner tried to rush through a bill for a bridge at the original Harrison Street location, Bacon and his colleagues mobilized a public education campaign attempting to change the commissioners' minds.[60] The *Flint Journal* reported approvingly on the maps and data Bacon and Saarinen used as evidence that the Clifford Street location made more sense from a planning and fiscal standpoint, and Bacon felt confident that he would prevail.[61]

Bacon wrote, "It really seems as though politics may be combated by public education."[62] However, he was naïve to the realities of politics and underestimated the extent to which the powerful auto industry influenced the City Commission. The Chamber of Commerce, City Planning Board, director of public works, city engineer, and local newspapers all supported the Clifford Street site recommended in the traffic survey. But the city commissioners were set on the original location and voted to build the bridge at Harrison Street. Soon after the vote, Harlow Curtice, president of Buick and head of the Flint Community Association, used his influence to dissolve the Association and fire its president, Seward C. Simons.[63] It was a clear message that Flint's powerful elites did not want anything to do with the Community Association and its young planners who had drummed up annoying opposition to their plans.

Bacon was blindsided and discouraged by this turn of events, writing to his parents, "I am completely stunned, and have no idea what I shall do . . . it truly revealed things as they are. . . . It amounts to an absolute, personal dictatorship, because of the economic concentration in General Motors. . . . Perhaps in the distant future of a labor government, someone will dig [my work] out of the dust of ages, brush it off and decide it is pretty good."[64] This was Bacon's first real run-in with politics. Although he had held some meetings with business executives, he clearly had not gained the alliances he needed to advance his policy agenda. This experience was a wake-up call, exposing him to the importance of figuring out how to build support and gain buy-in for policy ideas, if he wanted to be effective in implementing planning concepts.

Although the umbrella Community Association was no more, the Flint Institute continued as a bare-bones organization, supported in its limited capacity by the Community Fund. The directors of its various departments either quit immediately or began planning to leave. With his future in Flint looking dim, Bacon started to plan his next move—staying another year to complete his WPA work, then perhaps more traveling in Europe, before going to MIT to "study the technical side of city planning."[65] He was doing all right financially, supplementing his income with side jobs such as designing a prototype for Chevrolet and Ford used car lots and one hundred units of senior housing for the Genesee County Board of Supervisors.

Bacon's traffic survey report came out in January 1938, titled "A Comprehensive City Plan for Flint, Michigan: Part I—Traffic Survey and Thoroughfare Plan."[66] The title was strategic on his part, branding the study the first element of an ongoing comprehensive planning process (Bacon had previously proposed a land-use survey as a follow-up project and next piece of the plan).[67] While the cover said it was a traffic survey, Bacon had in fact created a hybrid document that also focused on his true interests of housing and community planning. In the report, he inserted a neighborhood layout for a "hypothetical location" that he explained was designed based on "the principles worked out at Radburn, New Jersey."[68] He pointed out that recent new developments in Flint were sprawling on the outskirts of the city, draining the tax base and wasting public resources. Bacon argued for the importance of investing in the downtown, while building new urban-type communities that also "meet the needs of the motor age."

In the report, Bacon argued, "Flint is facing a clear cut choice: whether this building shall be done in a disorganized, haphazard way, with regard only for immediate ends and individual considerations, or whether it shall be guided by a definite, coordinated policy for the greatest general good."[69] To frame his recommendations in terms Flint business leaders would respect and understand, he pointed to the positive impacts of attracting residents and growth for the city's tax base. In a gesture toward the auto industry, he noted that the recommendations would improve the efficiency of delivering materials to and from the factories, saving companies significant money.[70]

The report clearly showed what a profound effect Bacon's colleagues—Stonorov, Mumford, and Bauer—had on him. He was now a wholehearted disciple of the Radburn design principles as the basis for a new type of American, urban community. While he was inspired by Radburn's design principles, however, his focus was on downtown renewal rather than creation of new suburbs. Other practitioners of the period, in contrast, focused on outlying areas, "as the automobile and suburban rapid transit hastened the exodus from the congested central city to promised light and air at the urban fringe."[71] Even Bacon's teacher Eliel Saarinen wrote about "organic decentralization," planning for cities to spread into "those outlying areas which are available for growth."[72]

However, as one scholar of the period noted, this focus on "outlying communities . . . short-circuited the basic problem of replanning the cities themselves."[73] Bacon argued in the traffic report that Flint must reinvest in its downtown if the city wanted to survive. He reiterated this view in a magazine article in *Shelter* in 1939, where he attacked the trend of constructing new suburbs on the outskirts of the city and emphasized the economic and social benefits of building more compactly, closer to Flint's industrial centers.[74] This was the earliest example of an argument Bacon would make continually in Philadelphia, later in his career, for downtown renewal and urban-style development for new communities.

Bacon was thrilled finally to have the report completed and was eager to distribute it widely. He sent it to dozens of contacts in Flint, as well as municipal officials and planners across the country.[75] The report was apparently even more groundbreaking than he thought. Requests for copies flooded in from planning departments across the nation and the world, including Canada and Sweden.[76] The *Flint Journal* dedicated the entire front page of its local section to the report.[77] Suddenly, Bacon became something of a local celebrity and was in demand to serve on organizations in Flint. He was honored with the United States Junior Chamber of Commerce Distinguished Service Award for his work on the study.[78]

To top off Bacon's triumphs, on his twenty-eighth birthday, the City Commission reversed its earlier decision and voted to approve the city's new bridge at his favored Clifford Street site. Bacon wrote of the victory, "the particular commissioner with whom I had been bitterly fighting came around and was friendly, so maybe city planning is worth while after all."[79] It is unclear to what the success can be credited. However, throughout his career, Bacon confronted adversity by doggedly working to convince critical decision makers while taking his ideas to other groups and the media, gradually shifting the momentum of the situation. It is possible that the success of the traffic report convinced skeptics that the recommendations were reputable after all, not just the crazy ideas of a young upstart.

A Hurdle in Housing

In Flint, Bacon was in the midst of a divided city, ready to erupt. In December 1936, just after Roosevelt defeated Republican Kansas governor Alf Landon in the presidential election, tensions between auto workers and company executives burst into one of the seminal events in U.S. labor history—the United Auto Workers (UAW) strike of 1937. Bacon witnessed the warlike atmosphere that took over Flint, as police tried to storm the General Motors plant, occupied by striking workers, and the governor sent in the National Guard. When management eventually gave in, the UAW emerged as a strong organization with a powerful membership in Flint. This local triumph, coupled with Roosevelt's victory, created an environment strongly in favor of government intervention and workers' rights. Bacon, a strong Roosevelt supporter, witnessed the strikes firsthand and believed himself in an environment poised for progressivism and reform.[80]

On September 1, 1937, President Roosevelt signed into law the Federal Housing Act. Also known as the Wagner-Steagall Act, it created the U.S.

Housing Authority and allocated hundreds of millions of dollars of interest-free loans to local housing authorities to support low-income housing development. Bacon's colleagues Bauer, Stonorov, John Edelman (Philadelphia union leader who commissioned the Carl Mackley Houses), and William Jeanes (Carl Mackley's first manager) were influential in contributing ideas to the federal bill. Bauer was the most involved of the group, with prestige as a leader in the field of public housing elevated by her book *Modern Housing*. She was hired as an advisor to the U.S. Housing Authority as its director of information and research. Through Bauer, Bacon became friendly with the head of the Authority, Nathan Straus, and was even offered a job, which he turned down.[81]

Though viewed as an important step for advocates of publically supported housing, the federal act was controversial, attacked by critics as bad for private enterprise.[82] To those who understood Flint politics, it was clear that housing was a touchy subject. The city had serious issues regarding substandard worker housing conditions. According to one survey, some districts in Flint averaged 2.25 persons per bedroom, one-eighth of homes lacked toilets, and one-fifth lacked baths.[83] However, it had a strong real estate industry tied closely with the Republican city commissioners. Indeed, some politically connected businessmen had made their fortune developing substandard worker housing, and their interests would certainly be threatened by federal dollars for higher quality public housing. If Bacon thought the politics around the location of a bridge were daunting, he was hardly ready for the opposition the city's business elite would present when he got involved in an issue that would cut into their profits.

Bacon's supervisor in Flint, Elroy Guckert, a member of the City Planning Board, knew of Bacon's close ties with Catherine Bauer. It was likely for this reason that Bacon was appointed to the Planning Board as its secretary, so Flint could attempt to access new federal funding. The Board was an antiquated body, with limited power or influence, which had done little since overseeing the city's last master plan in 1920. Still, this opportunity allowed Bacon to pursue his interest in housing and progressive community development in an official context.

After the passage of the Wagner-Steagall Act, a number of cities engaged in early planning for new housing, positioning them to apply for federal funds. These places included Cincinnati, Detroit, Boston, Milwaukee, Toledo, Nashville, and Louisville.[84] Flint had work to do if it was to compete with its peer cities. In October 1937, several members of the Planning

Board, including Bacon and Guckert, formed an ad hoc Citizen's Housing Committee to elevate awareness of public housing issues in Flint.[85] Its chairman was Robert P. Gerholz, a respected realtor and home builder who brought the committee instant legitimacy.[86] The group started lobbying the state and city to take the necessary legal steps so Flint could receive federal funding. Here, Bacon took a new approach, trying to enlist the buy-in of powerful individuals, while simultaneously developing grassroots support. He formed a group called the Flint Housing Council, composed of forty-five diverse city and county organizations representing everything from the chamber of commerce and real estate community to women's and "negro" organizations to church groups and labor organizations.[87]

By demonstrating diverse public support, Bacon's group was successful in gaining approval for the city to create a formal housing commission— the legal organization necessary to receive the federal funds. The city commissioners created the Flint Housing Commission in September 1938, and Mayor Harold E. Bradshaw appointed its five-member board.[88] With the legal hurdles cleared, Bacon and delegates from the Flint Housing Commission traveled to Washington to meet with Nathan Straus and request earmarking $10 million in federal funds. Straus agreed to award Flint federal funding, but only $3.5 million. Though not as much as requested, it was a significant allocation for Flint, and the delegation returned home elated.[89]

Across the U.S., conservative elected officials and members of the business community were skeptical of the new housing program. The federal loans, though they had favorable terms, would still have to be repaid. Even members of the business community not specifically interested in real estate regarded the program with trepidation and associated it with Roosevelt's liberal New Deal agenda. According to one business leader, speaking on city participation in the federal housing program, "There's nothing about it that appeals to a businessman. . . . The idea appeals to those with a sympathetic heart."[90]

Due to this kind of skepticism, things would become more difficult when the Housing Commission actually settled down to do its work. The Commission would need a budget to hire staff to write the application for federal funds. In October 1938, the commissioners first made their voices known on housing issues when they refused to allocate a meager $6,500 to the Housing Commission so it could apply for federal money. The commissioners referred the matter to the city manager for further study, leaving the Housing Commission in limbo, unfunded and unable to move ahead.[91]

In response, Bacon attempted to boost the profile of the issue, demonstrate wide public support, and convince the city commissioners to allocate the funding.

Bacon had to determine the proper avenues for communicating the issue so it would resonate. The most memorable of these efforts was a competition and exhibition of photographs displaying the dismal housing situation in Flint. The photos showed gut-wrenching conditions such as dilapidated wooden shacks the size of sheds housing entire families of auto workers.[92] The grassroots Flint Housing Council held a citywide conference to discuss Flint's housing needs, gave numerous presentations to groups around the city, and issued questionnaires to gauge public opinion.[93]

While Bacon was drumming up local support and lobbying the commissioners, he remained oblivious to the discussions behind the scenes. It appears that Flint's powerful real estate leaders essentially concluded that Bacon's efforts were dangerous to their interests and long-term profits.[94] The controversy came to a head in January 1939, when the commissioners again voted down the proposal to allocate $6,500 to the Housing Commission, halting its ability to carry out any work. Interestingly, the vote was decided by a commissioner who, according to the *Flint Journal*, "last week argued in favor of the appropriation" but switched his position suddenly.[95] It was immediately evident to Bacon and his group what was going on. The decision to cripple the Housing Commission enraged groups across the city that supported the public housing efforts. UAW Local 156 threatened to drop its support of the five commissioners who voted against the funding allocation.[96]

Several members of the Housing Commission approached Mayor Harry Comins after the hearing to ask if he wanted their resignations.[97] Bacon's boss, Elroy Guckert, director of the Flint Community Fund, submitted his resignation and announced he had taken a new job in Detroit. Guckert had been one of Bacon's most important allies, keeping him employed despite the political pressure and securing him a seat on the Planning Board. With Guckert gone, there was nobody to protect Bacon from the powerful interests that increasingly saw him as a threat. Before he realized what happened, the Community Fund board voted to eliminate the City Planning Division of the Flint Institute, putting Bacon out of a job.[98]

Unknown to Bacon, there was secret support from Cranbrook for his dismissal. The Cranbrook Academy wanted to maintain a friendly relationship with Flint leadership, and word had gotten to the academy that

Bacon was making powerful political enemies. In correspondence that Bacon probably never saw, Richard Raseman, Cranbrook's executive secretary, explained, "[Bacon] became involved in politics, for which he is totally unequipped, and neglected his job. . . . His political adventures . . . alienated his prime supporters, and it was for this reason that he was dismissed."[99]

In a sense, Bacon's own efforts were used against him. He had recently gotten to know Walter Blucher, director of the American Society of Planning Officials—an outspoken advocate for establishing modern city planning commissions with regular funding and a professional staff. At Bacon's urging, the city commissioners had put a referendum on the ballot in November 1938 asking voters whether they favored amending the City Charter to create a modern planning commission.[100] The referendum passed but the commissioners did not immediately act formally to create and appoint members to the Planning Commission. The stated reason for eliminating Bacon's division at the Flint Institute was that the Planning Commission's technical staff would make the Flint Institute's City Planning Division redundant.[101] Bacon did not buy this rationale, namely because the city commissioners still had not officially created the commission, nor was there any reason to believe they would do so in the near future.[102]

Word of Bacon's dismissal quickly got around Flint and soon arrived in Washington, to the dismay of his friends at the U.S. Housing Authority.[103] But Bacon was not ready to give up. He put together a Report of the City Planning Division to lobby for keeping his job. He wrote, "If the Planning program is dropped now, much of the base material and work already done will be wasted, and the city will inevitably sink more deeply into its old haphazard methods."[104]

Meanwhile, in January 1939, Nathan Straus wrote an official letter implying that, if Flint's government did not act soon, the promised federal money would be withdrawn.[105] Of course, this was exactly what the opposition wanted. At this point, Bacon and his colleagues decided to make a last-ditch effort to appeal directly to the citizens. At the Housing Commission's request, the city commissioners agreed to submit to the voters the question of whether the city should apply for federal housing funding.[106] Bacon's group issued a letter to mobilize support from every organization that favored the housing program and produced a leaflet explaining the ballot question. The group ran a series of local newspaper ads. Catherine Bauer came from Washington to give a talk in mid-February 1939, adding the support of an established voice in the field.[107] The U.S. Housing Authority also sent materials to help convince the public of the housing program's value.

The opposition was formidable. It included Flint's real estate, banking, and business community, the Flint Real Estate Board, the Genesee County chapter of the National Small BusinessMen's Association, and a conservative businessman's group called the Taxpayers League.[108] The opponents of the housing program had, in some ways, an easier target. The financing structure used by the U.S. Housing Authority was complex and difficult to communicate to the general public. The opposition's financial resources were enormous, and no matter how many ads and pamphlets the Flint Citizens Housing Committee produced, the opposition produced more. While the Housing Committee took out quarter- and half-page advertisements, the opposition took out full double-page spreads, paid for a barrage of radio ads, and littered the city with fliers targeted at terrifying the public with threats of increased taxes.

When election day finally came on March 6, 1939, turnout was sparse— just over 10 percent. As sound as the Housing Committee arguments may have been, the media blitz and scare tactics by the real estate interests worked. The referendum was voted down by a margin of almost 2 to 1, and Bacon's last hopes for salvaging his work in Flint were shattered. After the referendum's defeat, he wrote a letter to Bauer: "The committee couldn't compete with this type of propaganda, but it did do a valiant job within its own limitations."[109]

Edmund Hoben, assistant director of the National Association of Housing Officials, explained to Bacon, "We are as disappointed over the outcome as you may well be, but we are not greatly surprised. The holding of referenda on the participation of a city in the public housing program is quite likely to lead to a negative vote due to the extreme difficulty of presenting such a complex subject with sufficient force to offset the catch word criticisms."[110] Following the election, four of the five members of the Housing Commission immediately submitted their resignations.[111] In an ironically disingenuous statement that smacked of insult to the housing supporters, Mayor Comins announced to the press, "the commission's work is just starting."[112]

After the defeat of the referendum, Bacon was out of a job, out of support, and out of hope for Flint. In September 1938, he had married Ruth Hilda Holmes, daughter of a wealthy New York publishing family. Ruth came to

Flint in summer 1938 on a volunteer work camp organized through the American Friends Service Committee, and the two married after knowing each other for less than three months.[113] Ruth would be a steadfast supporter of her husband throughout his future endeavors, while establishing her own successful career in the field of early childhood development. Ed and Ruth decided to travel to Europe with the money they had received in wedding gifts, starting April 1, 1939, before seeking a new course for their lives.

Though he did not appreciate it at the time, Bacon matured dramatically through his work in Flint. He later recalled, "I was thrown out of Flint in disgrace. But I had learned that city planning is a combination of social input as well as design."[114] He discovered that publicly confronting powerful officials and organizing a grassroots effort will not always work. He recalled that Catherine Bauer had told him, "in a political situation, jump into the middle of the politics."[115] However, it appears that he learned from Flint that it takes both grassroots efforts and insider politics to produce changes in a city. While his work in Flint did not come to fruition, his later work demonstrates that he emerged with an understanding that a planner needs to be able to sell ideas to the right stakeholders and firmly grasp the process of policy implementation. It would take years before Bacon again found himself in a similar role in Philadelphia; when he did, he would be much better prepared to understand the tools of implementation.

The New Deal era was an enlightening time for young Bacon to cut his teeth in the planning field. It was an unprecedented period of federal resources, when many cities were just starting to address comprehensive planning, while seeing the need to focus on issues like downtown reinvestment, suburban growth, and transportation infrastructure. In addition, planning became much more connected to social issues such as housing, public health, crime and safety, and poverty. According to one scholar of the period, the New Deal era expansion of planning to "keep in step with the vital problems of municipal government," led to the "re-examination of the planning function" and its role in urban government.[116]

This expanded role of planning would be the foundation for the next major period of federal investment in cities in the 1950s. The experience of practitioners like Bacon who started their careers during the New Deal era would lead to a group of progressive voices for housing and neighborhood planning that became one of several forces to shape the later urban renewal era of urban investment.

Chapter 2

TOWARD A BETTER PHILADELPHIA

After leaving Flint, Ed and Ruth Bacon traveled through Europe, Russia, and Palestine, arriving back in Philadelphia in August 1939, just weeks before Hitler would invade Poland, effectively starting World War II. Bacon was unhappy in Philadelphia, viewing his hometown as a corrupt and backward place that he sought to escape as quickly as possible. He applied for jobs all over the East Coast, but finding one was difficult.[1] He also unsuccessfully applied for a scholarship from the John Simon Guggenheim Memorial Foundation to finish his work from Flint.[2] Ruth had a trust fund that helped make ends meet—important considering that their first child, Karin, was born in 1940.

Through his contacts, Bacon obtained short-term work doing research for the National Resources Planning Board (NRPB).[3] He also had a couple of articles published in professional periodicals. In February 1940, the *Journal of Land and Public Utility Economics* published a piece by Bacon titled "A Diagnosis and Suggested Treatment of an Urban Community's Land Problems (Flint, Michigan)."[4] In April 1940, he had another article published, in the New York-based magazine *American City*, called "Tax-Delinquent Subdivisions: A Liability That Might Become a Municipal Asset."[5]

In these writings, Bacon focused on Flint, blaming suburban construction outside the city as a major force that drained the city of its residents and tax base, while the downtown deteriorated and lost population. Bacon queried, "Why is the vacant land within the city so unattractive for private building?"[6] His solution was for the city to take ownership of tax-delinquent and abandoned property, write off the owed back taxes, "clear away the neighborhood factors causing blight, replan and rehabilitate the area, and again offer it to private builders on condition that it be developed according to sound neighborhood planning principles."[7] In retrospect, it was a well-informed view of the problems cities would face even more heavily in the latter half of the twentieth century.

Oskar Stonorov and another colleague, Walter Phillips, were set on keeping Bacon in Philadelphia. After meeting at a party in Philadelphia, Phillips—then at Harvard Law School—agreed to join Bacon for a summer in Flint to learn about municipal policy work, and the two young men became good friends. Stonorov helped Bacon get a temporary job as an architect on the Clement T. Branch Village housing project in Camden, New Jersey. Phillips came from a wealthy family and inherited part of an estate in the Torresdale section of the Philadelphia, where he hired Bacon and Stonorov to design him a new home. Then Phillips secured Bacon an interview for the job of managing director of the Philadelphia Housing Association, a small nonprofit housing advocacy organization.[8] Bacon was offered the job and took the post, keeping him in Philadelphia for the immediate future.

Bacon saw his new job as an opportunity to address the same issues he had focused on in Flint—housing and planning for the poor—but in a much larger city. The Philadelphia Housing Association, founded in 1916, had the mission of developing studies and advocating for policy to "improve the housing condition in Philadelphia." In addition, the Association's mission included "securing the adoption of such features of town planning . . . as bear upon the welfare of the home."[9] Bacon would find that Philadelphia had many of the same challenges as Flint: lacking a modern city planning commission and having a need for affordable housing and urban redevelopment. Now that he was somewhat more rooted in Philadelphia, Bacon worked with Oskar Stonorov and some of his other colleagues to launch a new effort at bringing planning reform to Philadelphia.

Philadelphia's Planning Problems

The Philadelphia in which Bacon found himself had been long controlled by one of the most powerful Republican political machines in the nation's history. Up to that point, planning and development were more functions of political patronage than efforts to build a better city. Over the course of the early twentieth century, the city continually borrowed money for major construction projects, giving the contracts to the local party bosses, who made a fortune.[10] Ironically, during this period when Philadelphia had little planning, it also financed some of the most transformative public works projects of the twentieth century, such as the Benjamin Franklin Parkway. However, there were other projects that were seen as financial black holes, such as the Locust Street subway, which required enormous investment and never actually opened for service.

As debt increased, it became clear that the money that fed these projects could not continue without some sort of coordinated planning. In 1909, Mayor John E. Reyburn created a Committee on Comprehensive Plans, comprised of major civic and business leaders, which issued a report in 1911 with a list of desirable projects worthy of city investment.[11] Mayor Rudolph Blankenberg, with City Council support, created the Philadelphia Planning Board in 1912 and allocated $10,000 to support its work.[12] This board became the city's first real planning body, releasing a report in 1915 with recommended project proposals.[13] However, the budget shrank as the years went on, until in 1919 the board was effectively disbanded.[14]

That same year, the state approved a new charter for the city, creating a City Planning Commission and Zoning Commission (Philadelphia would not obtain its own "home-rule" charter until 1951, necessitating the state's approval). The Zoning Commission was appointed immediately; however, due to the lack of enthusiasm from Philadelphia's political leadership, the City Planning Commission sat dormant until 1929 when Mayor Harry Mackey finally appointed its members, including prominent and wealthy individuals such as Joseph E. Widener, banker E. T. Stotesbury, real estate mogul Albert M. Greenfield, and civic leader Eli Kirk Price.[15] This was not a planning commission in the modern sense; it had no professional staff, nor did it have a real budget or power to influence policy. The commission outlined a fifty-year plan for the city but, once the Great Depression hit, the planning process fell into a state of stagnation.[16] Another notable planning effort was the formation of the Regional Planning Federation in 1924, which released a 500-page "Tri State Philadelphia District Plan" in 1932 that also did little more than sit on a shelf.[17]

By 1940, Philadelphia was on the brink of bankruptcy. One article in *Time* magazine stated, "So many street lights had failed or been turned out in eight years that total illumination of city streets was less than one-third of what it was in 1931. Drinking water was so nauseous the mayor's office had to be provided with bottled water . . . whole sections of its [Philadelphia's] great textile industry moved south . . . [and] thousands of families [who] decided they preferred the suburbs, migrated."[18] While the region's population was booming, the city's growth slowed precipitously, sending a warning sign of the population drain that was to come after World War II.[19] Overall, the city was experiencing some distressing indicators that Bacon and others believed showed the need for serious city planning.

In April 1939, a campaign to gain a home-rule charter for the city failed in the Republican-controlled state legislature—preventing the city from being able to pass many of its own laws without state approval.[20] One of the employees of the independent Charter Committee, which sought to drum up grassroots support for the new charter, was Bacon's colleague Walter Phillips. Although he came from a wealthy and staunchly Republican family, Phillips had strong liberal leanings—a "blueblood with radical ideas."[21] After experiencing the charter movement's failure, Phillips attempted to build a new framework for civic reform by creating an organization for young, political outsiders that he called the City Policy Committee. Phillips's idea was that a group of young reformers would become "the nucleus" for building a larger group committed to civic affairs. At regular meetings held over lunch or dinner, members of the City Policy Committee would learn about the issues of the day and start to develop the basis for influencing politics and policy.[22]

Phillips's experience with the failed charter reform was similar in some ways to the political roadblocks Bacon saw in Flint, and the idea of this group was compelling to Bacon. On January 13, 1940, Phillips sent a letter to several friends and colleagues inviting them to become members of the new organization.[23] Besides Bacon, other early members included Oskar Stonorov; Bacon's and Stonorov's friend Eleanor Davis; William Jeanes, who had served as first manager of the Carl Mackley Houses; Murray H. Shusterman, a young attorney on the staff of the Bureau of Municipal Research; Roger Scattergood, Phillips's fellow Harvard alumnus, also a lawyer; and Johannes U. Hoeber, who had a Ph.D. in political science from Heidelberg University and was working at the Institute of State and Local Government.[24]

In October 1940, the City Policy Committee held its first elections; Phillips was elected president and Bacon vice president.[25] Bacon quickly convinced Phillips to make city planning a major focus of the group's agenda. While other cities across the country already had well-funded planning commissions with a department of technical staff, Philadelphia had a barely functioning commission, without staff, and with hardly any funding. According to Walter Blucher, director of the American Society of Planning

Officials, in 1941, "Philadelphia is the only big city in the country that is not doing an effective job of planning."[26] Bacon, of course, had been inspired by Blucher to push for a modern planning commission in Flint, and he believed Philadelphia needed the same remedy. He sought to make the City Policy Committee the vehicle for promoting this goal.

The second meeting of the City Policy Committee featured a panel of speakers, including Bacon, on the topic of city planning in Philadelphia.[27] Phillips also recruited Bacon to chair the organization's Planning Subcommittee.[28] In order to draft and promote legislation for the creation of a new planning commission, Phillips formed a partnership between the City Policy Committee and two other groups—the Lawyers' Council on Civic Affairs and the Junior Board of Commerce—to work together as the Joint Committee on City Planning. Phillips also enlisted the support of the Bureau of Municipal Research, a Philadelphia-based good-government think tank, of which he was on the board of directors.[29] By the 1940s, most major cities had a organization similar to the bureau, with "a professional staff able to master and advise on complex problems which even civic leaders could not take time to analyze."[30] The new Joint Committee started its work by meeting with a number of knowledgeable individuals in Philadelphia and New York and, based on these meetings, summarized its fact finding into a preliminary report. The group found that Philadelphia's current planning commission was too large to be effective. It lacked the inclusion of city department heads and was disconnected from the actual city administration. It also lacked the confidence of City Council and never was given funding for professional staff.

Based on his experiences in Flint, Bacon believed it would take more than a group of enthusiastic young reformers to get important decision makers interested, involved, and committed to this issue. He decided a good strategy would be to bring the annual National Conference on Planning to Philadelphia. Bacon felt that this tactic could sell the idea of planning on a large scale, with the top national names in the field promoting Philadelphia's need for planning, to convince the city's entrenched leadership. Thanks to Walter Blucher's support, the other national planning organizations that together comprised the conference—the American Institute of Planners, the American Planning and Civic Association, and the National Economic and Social Planning Association—agreed to host the conference in Philadelphia in 1941.[31]

Just as Bacon had hoped, the conference flooded the city with high-profile figures in the planning professions, such as Walter Blucher, Russel

Van Nest Black, Frederick A. Delano, John Nolen, Jr., and Robert A. Walker. Numerous sessions highlighted how much Philadelphia needed serious city planning.[32] At a "Philadelphia lunch" attended by Republican mayor Robert Eneas Lamberton, Henry Beerits, a young lawyer and the chairman of the Joint Committee, made an impassioned plea for the city to make city planning a priority and presented the mayor with the Joint Committee's preliminary report.[33] Much to Bacon's horror, however, Beerits's upbeat presentation was followed by a speech by Hugh R. Pomeroy, a respected public housing official, who upbraided Lamberton for rejecting $19 million from the Federal Housing Authority for low-income housing in Philadelphia.[34] Having already seen planning and housing issues lose out to a political turf battle in Flint, Bacon might have feared history would repeat itself in Philadelphia.

However, Bacon and the Joint Committee were in luck; Mayor Lamberton possessed a thicker political skin than the decision makers of Flint, and he came away from the conference supportive of the idea of creating a modern planning commission.[35] Lamberton may have embraced the idea in part out of desperation. With World War II raging, a new crisis emerged as companies converted factories to produce military supplies and the city was flooded by new workers—many in dire need of affordable housing.[36] For Bacon, the path forward was clear: Philadelphia needed a modern city planning commission with adequate staff, funding, and institutional support. But having been seasoned from the events in Flint, Bacon also realized that persuading the city's decision makers would be an uphill battle.

A Modern Planning Commission for Philadelphia

After working feverishly, the Joint Committee assembled a technical proposal for a new planning commission and drafted an ordinance for creating such a commission that could be introduced by City Council. The proposal laid out a structure for a commission that would carry out long-term planning and create a "capital program" for the city—a six-year spending plan linked to specific projects.[37] It recommended a commission consisting of five citizen members, four ex-officio members, one member of City Council, and three department heads. It also stressed the need for paid, technical staff to create studies and to inform the commission. It provided a budget with recommended salaries, based on figures from other cities.

The proposal was significantly influenced by Robert A. Walker's book *The Planning Function in Urban Government*, which discussed best practices from dozens of planning commissions and boards across the country. Walker was a major proponent for the idea that cities should replace their volunteer planning boards with formal commissions or planning departments, with a staff of professionals, headed by a paid director, and with a substantial budget to carry out their work. He also believed that these commissions or departments should be directly accountable to the mayor or chief executive.[38]

The Joint Committee mailed its proposal to Mayor Lamberton on August 15, 1941, but the excitement was to prove short lived. On the morning of August 23, they woke up to read in the morning newspaper that Mayor Lamberton had died.[39] Lamberton was replaced by City Council president Bernard Samuel, an eighteen-year political veteran and an entrenched South Philadelphia loyalist to the Republican machine. Unlike Lamberton, Samuel viewed city planning as a direct challenge to the authority of City Council and the mayor.[40] Seeing no hope at convincing Mayor Samuel, the Joint Committee turned instead to the public, releasing the details of its proposal to the media. Henry Beerits announced that the group would push City Council to add a $50,000 appropriation in the 1942 budget to support a City Planning Commission staff.[41] The situation started to have the feeling of the political tensions Bacon saw in Flint. Before it could become polarized, however, the attack on Pearl Harbor intervened, and with the nation distracted, Bacon and Phillips temporarily put their efforts on hold.

In spring 1942, Bacon decided to try again with a fresh approach that could be effective in persuading both grassroots reformers and high-level political decision makers. First, he called in a favor. One of the members of his Philadelphia Housing Association's Board of Directors, judge Nochem Winnet, agreed to speak to his friend city councilman Frederick D. Garman, chairman of City Council's Finance Committee, to ask that the Joint Committee's draft ordinance introduced into Council.[42] Garman made good on his promise, introducing the bill in April 1942, but the bill languished in committee.[43]

Councilman Garman explained that moving the ordinance out of committee would require the Joint Committee to obtain "resolutions and letters in support of the Ordinance," so that City Council and the mayor "may be aware of public support in this matter."[44] With its marching orders clear, the Joint Committee set out to drum up support for the council bill. As in Flint, Bacon hoped to assemble a large and diverse set of organizations

across the city's political geography.[45] Bacon, Phillips, and other members
of the Joint Committee met with organizations of every ilk, tailoring their
message on the importance of city planning to their specific audience. They
couched the argument for city planning in terms that ordinary citizens
could understand—comparing it to planning for a family's or organization's own budget.

The Joint Committee secured the support of fifty-five organizations,
and letters began flowing into City Council. These groups included good
government organizations, labor unions, civic associations, women's groups,
religious organizations, and others that had no clear connection to the issue
but felt it would be beneficial for the public good.[46] To solidify further these
groups' support, the Joint Committee morphed into an "Action Committee" that included members of these interest groups from the broader Philadelphia civic community—building a true broad-based coalition. By now,
Bacon knew better than to rely solely on grassroots support to influence
elected officials. He and Phillips also reached out to Edward Hopkinson,
Jr., one of the city's most prominent business leaders and a senior partner
at Drexel & Company.[47] Hopkinson was a Republican with close ties to
powerful elites, but he was also a progressive businessman who understood
the inherent value of planning for the city.

With this coalition behind the effort, Mayor Samuel became more
receptive and gave his tentative support to both the planning bill and a
budgetary allocation to fund the City Planning Commission. Working with
the city's director of public works, the Action Committee produced some
recommendations for strengthening the bill.[48] Finally, on December 1, 1942,
City Council's Committee on Planning and Zoning held a hearing on the
revised ordinance. The Action Committee brought out over one hundred
members of the public to the Council hearing, representing sixty organizations. Fifteen of these members testified, demonstrating the extraordinary
array of interests gathered in support of the bill. Hopkinson made a surprise
appearance, voicing his support.[49] To the great joy of Bacon and his group,
the committee voted to approve the bill, and it was officially adopted by the
full City Council on December 10, 1942, with unanimous approval.[50] Mayor
Samuel signed the bill into law, and City Council allocated $40,000 for the
Commission's inaugural budget. By February, Mayor Samuel had named his
appointments to the new City Planning Commission, selecting Hopkinson
as its chairman.[51] Compared to Flint, where Bacon's efforts slowly unraveled,
in Philadelphia things seemed to fall neatly into place.

In spring 1943, in order to continue to harness the momentum and interest of the Action Committee, Bacon and Phillips helped create a new organization called the Citizens' Council on City Planning, intended to serve as a direct link between the new Planning Commission and the numerous grassroots organizations that were so supportive of bringing planning to Philadelphia.[52] Phillips became the Citizens' Council's first president and Bacon its first secretary. The Citizens' Council surveyed neighborhood organizations as a starting point for the Commission's community outreach efforts and spearheaded an effort to build a "three dimensional model of a typical Philadelphia neighborhood, illustrating some of the things that could be done to make it a more livable, workable place."[53] Ironically, years later, once he became planning director, Bacon would at times find himself at odds with this very group that he had been so instrumental in creating.

A key difference between Philadelphia's old and new planning commissions was that the new one would be staffed by paid professionals. For its first executive director, Hopkinson (advised heavily by the Citizens' Council and the Fels Institute of Local and State Government at the University of Pennsylvania) chose Robert B. Mitchell, an accomplished administrator, professor, and expert in housing and urban redevelopment, who most recently had served as chief of the Urban Section of the National Resources Planning Board.[54]

Finally, after decades of stagnation, the potential for meaningful city planning had come to Philadelphia. It was not the work of one person or even a few; it was the work of an astoundingly broad and diverse coalition. As Bacon wrote, recounting the effort, "The initiation and much of the work of this move came from citizen groups. That is as it should be in a democracy."[55] While Bacon fought a quixotic battle against uncooperative elites in Flint, in Philadelphia he did a much better job understanding the people and processes for advancing his agenda. He came away from the effort well connected to Philadelphia's emerging civic leadership and with an established name for himself as an up-and-coming mover and shaker.

The Better Philadelphia Exhibition

The early years of the City Planning Commission were spent making up for lost time, working on critical but unexciting projects such as replacing sewers and utilities—long postponed. There were a few more interesting projects, such as planning for the city's new airport and Philadelphia's failed

1946 bid to attract the United Nations headquarters—which of course ended up in New York.[56]

Two federal acts in the mid-1940s shaped the direction of planning agencies across the country. In 1944, the U.S. Congress enacted the Federal-Aid Highway Act, authorizing a roadway system up to 40,000 miles in length.[57] In 1947, the City of Philadelphia was negotiating agreements with the state for eight city-state highway projects, and the Planning Commission and Department of Public Works had agreed on preliminary designs for six of these.[58] In May 1945, Congress passed the Urban Redevelopment Law, enabling cities to create redevelopment authorities to determine areas for postwar rebuilding. Philadelphia established its local Redevelopment Authority in 1946 and approved its first ten redevelopment areas in 1948.[59] These federal acts set the stage for the Planning Commission to focus heavily on Philadelphia's highway and urban redevelopment programs in the coming years.

Bacon did not get involved with the Planning Commission early on. In December 1943, he left his job at the Philadelphia Housing Association and enlisted in the U.S. navy. It was an unexpected move for a Quaker—a religion of which pacifism is a core tenet. Bacon wrote to his upset parents, "I feel that it is a privilege to be in this war, that it is right to be in it, and that being in it in no way violates the centuries long tradition of Quakerism which I inherit and respect."[60] After a tour of duty as quartermaster in the South Pacific on the U.S.S. *Shoshone*, where he was in the battles of Iwo Jima and Okinawa, Bacon returned home in December 1945.[61]

Ruth and the Bacons' now two children were living in New York at the time; however, after Bacon's discharge, the family decided to return to Philadelphia, where they lived as tenants of Oskar and Betty Stonorov. Oskar's wife Betty had inherited a sizable estate in Chester County on which Oskar would design a large modernist home called Avon Lea. Ruth and Ed Bacon moved into an old farmhouse called Little Saffron on the Stonorov estate.[62] The Bacons and Stonorovs formed a tight-knit community, along with a third family, the Crowells—Lucius Crowell was an accomplished painter, and his wife Priscilla was a friend of Ruth's from college at Bennington. The Crowells, Bacons, and Stonorovs had weekly lunches and parties in the country. The Stonorovs were wealthy and well connected, and so these lunches and celebrations attracted internationally renowned guests, including Le Corbusier, Eric Erickson, Louis Kahn, Lewis Mumford, Xanti Schawinsky, and Paolo Venini.[63] Thus, Bacon was exposed to these prominent individuals and the vibrant intellectual discourse that took place in the country, focused around the Stonorov farm.

Bacon's postwar plans were not immediately clear. He had resigned his position at the Philadelphia Housing Association to enlist, and he briefly considered going back to school for a master's degree or possibly even establishing an art school on his return.[64] Once again, however, Stonorov and Phillips had different ideas for Bacon's future. The two men had dreamed up a plan to host a major exhibition in Philadelphia—to educate the public about city planning, inspire citizens with visions for an exciting future, and provide a foundation of grassroots awareness and support for the Philadelphia City Planning Commission.[65] In partnership with the Citizens' Council, the Planning Commission, and its director Robert Mitchell, they formed a committee and started raising funds for this exhibition. Stonorov was to be the show's technical director, and he convinced Bacon to work with him in planning the exhibition. Rather than be paid through the exhibition's nonprofit corporation, Bacon was hired to the staff of the Philadelphia City Planning Commission in October 1946, where he was paid a salary of $4,600 and given the position of senior land planner, although his work was predominantly focused on designing the exhibition.[66]

The exhibition's team assembled an impressive crew of innovative and respected civic leaders to design the show, raise money, and attract the support it would need to be successful. Prominent businessman Benjamin Rush, Jr., served as corporation president. Mayor Samuel served as honorary president. Arthur C. Kaufmann, owner of Gimbels department store, was enlisted as vice president and agreed to donate floor space in his Market Street store for the exhibition. Walter Phillips also served as a vice president. Allan G. Mitchell, president of Philadelphia Electric, served as secretary, George T. Eager of the *Bulletin* chaired the Exhibition Committee, and advertising executive Al Paul Lefton chaired the Public Relations Committee.[67]

With Gimbels and Philadelphia Electric as major sponsors and with the support of the Chamber of Commerce, Edward Hopkinson, Jr., and Benjamin Rush were able to raise $200,000 from the local business community. The mayor and City Council appropriated an additional $125,000 in public funds for the exhibition.[68]

A major motivator for the exhibition was to showcase current and proposed concepts from the City Planning Commission's work and to "test the public reaction" of new and potentially controversial ideas.[69] Stonorov worked closely with Robert Mitchell to ensure that the Planning Commission's work was expressed as fully as possible, and he relied heavily on the staff of the Commission to design elements of the show. Similarly, Bacon worked with Stonorov, Mitchell, and Commission staff to develop the various elements of the exhibition. Bacon also met with individuals and groups, including the Citizens' Council on City Planning, to seek buy-in for some of the major concepts in the exhibition before they were revealed to the public.[70] Although Stonorov's business partner and prominent architect Louis I. Kahn is often mentioned in connection with the exhibition, notes from the committee meetings indicate that Kahn had little actual involvement. Apparently Kahn and Stonorov had a tense relationship during the planning, and they dissolved their firm soon after the exhibition ended.[71]

A major component of exhibition planning included generating public excitement about both the planning profession and the event itself. At one meeting, Arthur Kaufmann asserted, "If we don't feel that there's something to attract thousands of people—then call the thing off."[72] These efforts were intended not only to ensure attendance but also to educate Philadelphians about the purpose of city planning. According to a poll by the *Bulletin* in 1946, only 10 percent of Philadelphians polled had "a substantially correct idea of what the City Planning Commission does."[73] The exhibition's planners distributed car cards, window displays, posters, and billboards. They secured hundreds of columns of newspaper stories, twenty full pages of advertisements, and sixty-three major radio broadcasts.[74] Meanwhile, the Citizens' Council met with neighborhood groups across the city to spread the word and reached out to the next generation of planners by introducing city planning into the curriculum at sixteen schools across Philadelphia. Bacon and Stonorov were particularly involved in this effort, spending time in classrooms and working directly with the students, helping them learn about planning concepts and ultimately to create their own plans, models, and drawings of their neighborhoods' future.[75]

While they wanted to generate public excitement, the designers of the Better Philadelphia Exhibition also had to explain the city's profound problems. Robert Mitchell raised the issue at one planning meeting: "When a man goes to the doctor—He knows he is sick. Most people don't know there's something wrong with the city."[76] However, the show's designers knew there was something wrong. They discussed how they would address issues such as declining taxes and the rapidly growing population of poor

African American residents in a number of neighborhoods.[77] In a show about the future, how should its designers confront the very real social, economic, and racial challenges of the present?

Finally, on September 8, 1947, the Better Philadelphia Exhibition opened its doors to the public. The final price tag was about $340,000, a fairly modest cost, all things considered. Over its span, between September 8 and October 15, it attracted 385,000 visitors.[78] Admission was free. The exhibition was massive, and visitors could spend hours wandering among the maps, models, films, and light shows. It was a first-of-its-kind undertaking. The closest precedent was the Futurama exhibit at the 1939 New York World's Fair (which Oskar Stonorov had worked on). However, while Futurama was funded by General Motors, presenting a utopian and futuristic city, the Better Philadelphia Exhibition was humanistic, firmly rooted in making planning accessible and showing ideas for the attainable and practical near future.

A large metal sculpture of a hand greeted visitors, with a map of Philadelphia on its palm and large letters below the map proclaiming "A better Philadelphia . . . within your grasp." The beginning section of the show built drama, taking visitors along a mysterious dark foyer. A mirror would disappear, magically replaced by a view of a panorama of a future Philadelphia.[79] In a small circular room, cloaked in darkness, was an exhibit called "Philadelphia: Past, Present, Future," or the "Time and Space Machine," in which visitors watched four stages of edge-lit Plexiglas screens illuminated to demonstrate the history of Philadelphia's urban growth, the spread of "blight," and ways that planning could address the problem.[80]

In the next section, blown-up drawings by cartoonist Robert Osborn showed scenarios in everyday life that involved planning: a boy and his football team plotted a play, a squirrel figured out how many nuts to stow for the winter, a woman charted out her weekly finances. A window between the cartoon room and a later section contained cardboard cut-outs of people and animals standing cheerfully aside a map of Philadelphia, facing the words "We all plan." A display called "What the City Planning Commission Does" attempted to explain the origins and function of the Commission and its staff.

The following room made the case that planning, while expensive, was worth the price. Models of actual buildings and projects rolled by on a conveyor belt, with price tags hanging from them: "Nursery School—$40,000," "Health Center—$270,000," "Playfield—$300,000," "Sewage

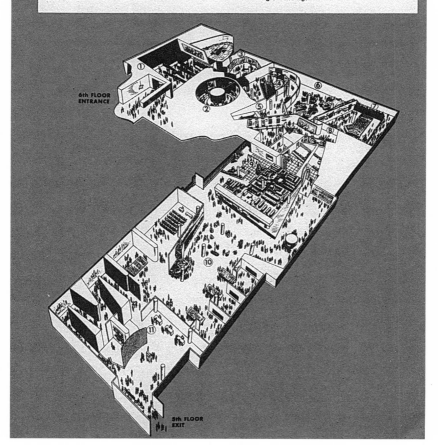

THE BETTER PHILADELPHIA EXHIBITION

. . was conceived by the Citizens' Council on City Planning and the Chamber of Commerce . . . sponsored by the City of Philadelphia . . . designed by Oskar Stonorov and Edmund N. Bacon . . . administered by Richard A. Protheroe . . . produced by the Philadelphia City Planning Exhibition . . . paid for by the City and civic-minded business and industrial firms.

Key to floor plan shown below

1. Vista of the Better Philadelphia.
2. Philadelphia: Past, Present and Future
3. Everybody Plans.
4. The City Planning Commission.
5. Progress Must be Bought and Paid For.
6. The Six-Year Plan.

7. A Better Downtown Philadelphia.
8. How City Planning Affects You and Your Family.
9. The Redevelopment Authority.
10. School Exhibits.
11. "Magic" Ending.

Figure 7. Floor plan of the 1947 Better Philadelphia Exhibition at Gimbels department store, from the show's official brochure. Personal collection of the author.

Treatment Plant—$12,000,000." This area was followed by an exhibition explaining the concept of a six-year capital program for the city. Visitors entered a large room with a massive map of the city laid horizontally, at table height, on which were over six hundred small Plexiglas flags, showing the specific location of every project that had been introduced by the Planning Commission.

The exhibit that followed, "A Better Downtown Philadelphia," would become the most compelling and memorable for many Philadelphians. Visitors entered a room with a 30- by 14-foot scale model of Center City. Every building was shown, and landmark buildings were elaborately detailed—in total 45,000 buildings, 25,000 cars and buses, and 12,000 trees. Visitors stood around the model, on a ramp and balcony, looking down as a narrated voice talked about the great promise of the city of the future.[81] Accompanied by spot lighting, the narration would call attention to a part of the current city, and then, dramatically, that area would mechanically lift up and rotate to reveal a future vision. While the map of the capital projects in the previous room was an accurate reflection of the City Planning Commission's work, the downtown model was largely a fantasy, devised by its designers.

The model did include some projects already in the works, including widened Vine Street, a highway along the Delaware River, and a three-block, tree-lined, green mall stretching north from Independence Hall. Other more visionary projects included a yacht basin at the edge of the Delaware River, a new Academy of Music and a Museum of Natural History, a federal office building, a merchandising center with underground parking at the foot of Market Street, and a new bus terminal. Perhaps the most shocking change from the current to future city was the replacement of the Pennsylvania Railroad's massive masonry viaduct and elevated tracks, known as the "Chinese Wall," with a series of commercial buildings.

After leaving the Center City model, visitors were exposed to an array of human-scale exhibits on how planning affects neighborhoods, including a full-size model of a redesigned South Philadelphia street corner. There were several models of redeveloped and new communities designed around the Radburn principles of creating residential clusters separating pedestrians and automobiles. The final section of the exhibition contained the results of the planning curriculum in the public schools, with student-designed models of shining new playgrounds, parks, and rebuilt streets with modern housing, accompanied by graphics, charts, and, in one case, a poem.[82] At the conclusion of the exhibition, visitors were handed a seem-ingly blank sheet of paper and ushered into a dark room with black lights. Magically, words appeared on the paper, revealing a note from Mayor Sam-uel: "Fellow Citizens," it read, "The exhibition suggests how to achieve a Better Philadelphia. . . . With your help, it can be done." A sign over the exit read, "What kind of Philadelphia are you going to give your children?" And with that, visitors found themselves on the bustling fifth floor of the Gimbels store, to ponder all they had seen and perhaps do some shopping.

After viewing the exhibition, visitors were asked to fill out a question-naire, and the results were encouraging, with 68 percent giving the show a favorable response.[83] Most of the exhibition went into storage after its close. However, several elements, including the Center City model with the rotat-ing panels, were installed in the City Commercial Museum as a permanent display, where they would be seen by thousands of visitors and school chil-dren (neither the model nor the museum is now in existence).[84] The model was updated over the years and would be sent around the world to such venues as the Brussels World's Fair in 1958 and to Morocco and Turkey in 1960. The city planning curriculum also continued in the Philadelphia schools, expanding the next year from sixteen to fifty schools across the city.[85]

Essentially, the show was a massive public relations tool, a strategy for selling the idea of planning to the public and gaining the grassroots support the Planning Commission would need to be effective in the coming dec-ades. Of course, the show would not have been possible without the backing of important players in government and in the business community. Unlike in Flint where Bacon played outsider politics, in Philadelphia he was learn-ing how to utilize his connections to gain access to important individuals and how to work within the political and business structure to advance his agenda for the future.

The Bacon Era Begins

One perhaps unintended result of the exhibition was the reelection of Mayor Samuel the next month. With the mayor's name all over the success-ful show and powerful Republicans like Edward Hopkinson, Jr., so crucial to making the exhibition a reality, it was a difficult time to blame the Republicans for not being progressive. An attractive young attorney and former marine named Richardson Dilworth nevertheless attempted to do so, running a campaign that one writer called "one of the most vigorous, if hopeless, reform campaigns in years."[86] Despite Dilworth's eye-opening campaign, the Republican machine would triumph again in 1947, as Dilworth was defeated by Mayor Samuel by a sizable margin. The effort for city planning reform was at an all-time high in Philadelphia, but the political reform to support a truly progressive planning agenda would have to wait.

In May 1948, Robert Mitchell left his post as executive director of the Philadelphia City Planning Commission to take a job teaching at Columbia University. Bacon's supervisor, Raymond Leonard, took over as executive director, and Bacon moved up to become chief of the Land Planning Division. Things seemed to be proceeding routinely until August 9, 1948, when Leonard died suddenly of leukemia.[87] Bacon was next in line for the directorship. However, he had not been on the Commission staff for very long and was not sure he even wanted the job. He wavered, and Hopkinson made no decision immediately. The Commission carried on without a director, and Bacon kept his title as chief of land planning.[88]

Steven Sweeney, director of the Fels Institute of Local and State Government, set up a meeting of the nation's foremost planners to identify a top candidate for executive director. Bacon was not impressed with the field of candidates and told Hopkinson that he had changed his mind and would take the job after all. On December 31, 1948, the Planning Commission issued an official press release announcing Bacon's promotion.[89] He began work as executive director of the Philadelphia City Planning Commission in the beginning of January 1949. Upon taking the job, he purchased a townhome at 2117 Locust Street for his family, where he would live for the rest of his life.

As executive director, Bacon set up the City Planning Commission to take a front-seat role in shaping Philadelphia's planning and redevelopment program. He supervised a staff of fifty-one employees in three divisions: land planning, projects, and planning analysis. The head of planning analysis was Hans Blumenfeld, formerly one of Bacon's staff at the Philadelphia Housing Association. The director of the Division of Projects was Charles A. Howland, and leading the Division of Land Planning was Paul F. Croley, a twenty-five-year municipal employee who knew the city inside and out and had strong relationships with high-ranking members of the government. Bacon quickly promoted Croley to assistant director, giving him a greater authority to steer the Commission.[90]

In the early 1950s, Bacon also started to build up the Planning Commission's staff to attract some of the nation's top young planners. In June 1953, Bacon brought Wilhelm (Willo) von Moltke to the Land Planning Division. Von Moltke had formerly worked with Eero Saarinen and was described by Bacon as "one of the outstanding architectural designers in the United States."[91] The following year, Bacon hired Irving Wasserman, a young landscape architect who recently finished graduate school at Harvard, training under the prominent landscape architect Hideo Sasaki.

Meanwhile, a political reform was brewing that would provide Bacon with greater support to promote progressive ideas. By 1949, Mayor Samuel was embroiled in a grand jury investigation into City Hall corruption. A "Committee of 15" established to identify new sources of funding for city firefighters ended up unearthing scandal and graft in City Hall, leading to several city employees committing suicide.[92] With the seeds planted for challenging the political machine, Walter Phillips steered the City Policy Committee back in the direction of charter reform, to push again for a new "home-rule" city charter.[93] Separately, two of Phillips's City Policy Committee colleagues, Richardson Dilworth and Joseph S. Clark, got behind a charter reform effort, through the Philadelphia chapter of the progressive Americans for Democratic Action (ADA).[94]

The tides had changed since the last push for a new city charter, and the Pennsylvania General Assembly soon introduced legislation to amend the State Constitution to allow Philadelphia to vote for home rule. In June 1949, City Council appointed a Charter Commission to draft the proposed new charter for the city, to be put before the voters for approval. A new and immediately influential business group, called the Greater Philadelphia Movement, was heavily recruited, with six of its directors appointed by the mayor to the Commission.[95]

A number of the individuals responsible for drafting the charter were close with Phillips and Bacon. The Greater Philadelphia Movement's paid director, Robert K. "Buck" Sawyer, was an early member of the City Policy Committee. Another of the City Policy Committee's first-generation members, Abraham Freedman, was appointed to the Charter Commission and would be one of the new charter's principal authors. Judge Nochem Winnet, Bacon's colleague who had been instrumental in getting the City Planning Commission bill introduced into City Council years earlier, was responsible for promoting the charter reform to the public.[96]

In its final form, the new charter created a "strong mayor" form of government, giving the mayor the ability to appoint most individuals to boards and commissions. At the same time, it also established a managing director, an appointed position to handle the day-to-day business of the city. It called for a City Council of seventeen members, with five of those serving at-large. The charter made many more city jobs require civil service exams, cutting down on the number of possible patronage jobs. It created a new position called the city representative, responsible for marketing Philadelphia to tourists, dignitaries, and out-of-town organizations. The new charter also created the Commission on Human Relations to ensure that, in hiring and in carrying out city business, various departments did not discriminate on the basis of race, ethnicity, or religion.[97]

Bacon worked through his friend Abraham Freedman to influence the way the charter handled the City Planning Commission.[98] In the final version of the charter, the Planning Commission remained an independent entity, advisory to the mayor and City Council. Importantly, it was given the responsibility of drafting the city's Capital Budget and six-year Capital Program, and was in charge of approving subdivisions of land. The Capital Program would be a critical tool for Bacon in putting projects into the funding pipeline years before they were on many people's radar screens. By controlling the creation of subdivisions, the Planning Commission gained the power to dictate the form of new urban development. While the Commission's power was still fairly limited, these were critical tools that would provide the foundation for the its prominent role in the coming decades.

The Home Rule Charter was approved by voters in a special election in the spring 1951, at the tail end of lame-duck Mayor Samuel's term in office. For those like Bacon, Phillips, Clark, and Dilworth who had dreamed of a new day for Philadelphia, the opportunity finally had come to pass. And things would keep looking brighter. In 1951, Joseph Clark, the Democratic Party's nominee for mayor, won handily over the Republican candidate, Rev. Daniel Poling. Clark attracted and hired likeminded, progressive people and, as it turned out, his entire cabinet comprised members of the City Policy Committee: Walter Phillips as city representative, Robert "Buck" Sawyer as managing director, Lennox Moak as finance director, and Abraham Freedman as city solicitor. Phillips's vision, originating over a decade earlier, of training the next generation of civic leaders had come to pass.

Clark hired a number of talented outsiders to fill key posts and cleaned up corruption and patronage from boards and commissions. Meanwhile,

Richardson Dilworth had been elected district attorney and rapidly began reorganizing and energizing his office. By filling city posts with qualified individuals and with a sound commitment to nondiscrimination, under Mayor Clark's administration a significant number of African Americans were hired for city jobs.[99] Clark could have replaced Bacon but chose not to, leaving him one of the few holdovers from the Samuel administration.[100] While the first three years of Bacon's tenure were under Republican Mayor Samuel, the rest of his twenty-one years as planning director would be under Democratic mayors.

In 1955, Joseph Clark was elected to the U.S. Senate, and Richardson Dilworth was elected mayor, continuing the era of good-government political reform.[101] Bacon was lucky to have ascended to the directorship of the Planning Commission just before the reform movement came to fruition. In 1952, when all his friends and colleagues were starting out in city government, Bacon had already been director for three years, allowing him to continue with his work, now supported by a more progressive government that provided greater leverage for promoting his agenda.

Chapter 3

PLANNING FOR PEOPLE

After World War II, urban leaders across America saw cities in crisis, with declining neighborhoods and infrastructure, new suburbs outside the city drawing white, middle-class families away from the urban core, and the emergence of black ghettos. The federal government under President Harry Truman passed a groundbreaking federal act, providing new instruments and significant funding sources enabling cities to undertake what became known as "urban renewal."[1] At the same time, semi-suburban parts of cities and areas outside cities saw massive new building in the post-World War II era.[2] In the early 1950s, Bacon would be involved in both types of projects—federally funded urban renewal projects and development of new tract housing by private developers.

Bacon's new position as executive director of the Philadelphia City Planning Commission, coupled with a federal focus and new funding for cities, gave him the opportunity on a larger scale than ever before in his career to attempt to apply the principles and ideology he developed in Flint, at the Philadelphia Housing Association, and through the City Policy Committee for developing housing for workers and the poor and rebuilding communities based on progressive planning principles. Bacon became a major player in shaping Philadelphia's early urban redevelopment projects such as Poplar, Temple, Eastwick, Mill Creek, and Morton, as well as the development of new communities in the city's Far Northeast section during the early 1950s.

The federal government's intended use of urban renewal funding was to demolish slums wholesale, displacing communities of people, and to facilitate rebuilding these areas by the private sector. However, Philadelphia sought a distinctly different path that used selective and targeted demolition (rather than clearing vast areas), rebuilding communities based on the

Radburn principles—with a hierarchy of streets, weaving pathways to separate pedestrians and cars, and low-rise development including garden apartments. Nationally, urban renewal became controversial for its scorched earth approach, the inherent racism of massive displacement of African American populations to attract the middle class, and questionable impacts despite enormous outlays of federal funds.[3] Cities like New York, Boston, and Pittsburgh erased entire communities and displaced huge numbers of people. While Philadelphia's program was also controversial, its application was inherently different from that of most other cities, characterized in *Architectural Forum* as "Clearing Slums with Penicillin, Not Surgery."[4]

Philadelphia's approach to urban renewal was not a clear success and was ultimately short-lived in its original form—changing dramatically after a new federal housing act passed in 1954 shifted the priorities of the renewal program from primarily a housing program to one focused on downtown and economic development projects. This act was echoed in a study by the Philadelphia Redevelopment Authority that changed the course of the local program to reflect the federal priorities.[5] After this point, Bacon would refocus his efforts on Center City projects like Penn Center and the redevelopment of the Society Hill neighborhood.

Concurrent with the early redevelopment projects, Bacon was also working to ensure that new communities in the Far Northeast section would be urban rather than suburban in style. He did this so that the houses built there would be affordable for buyers and the communities would be founded on the Radburn principles, creating dense, walkable neighborhoods. Bacon's role in the redevelopment projects and the planning of the Far Northeast highlights his strong focus on physical design, his willingness to change with the tides to follow federal funding, and his distinct preference for working with private-sector developers over public-sector bureaucracy.

A National Urban Crisis

During his time in Flint, Bacon had already seen the warning signs of urban population drain and new construction in the suburbs that would suck the life out of downtowns across the United States. This trend exacerbated after World War II, partly accelerated by the 1944 GI Bill that provided guarantees on home mortgage loans for returning veterans. New federal mortgage guarantees provided incentives for developers to build large-tract, single-family suburban projects like Levittown that redefined the American dream.[6] Meanwhile "redlining"—profiling communities based on factors like race and ethnicity—by the federal government and the mortgage industry drained the value from urban centers. By 1950, Philadelphia's African American population was surging, with the third largest black population in the U.S., at about 380,000.[7] The 1950 U.S. Census reported that more than a third of Philadelphia's nonwhite population lived in "substandard" housing.[8]

Bacon had worked in Flint during a major era of public funding for cities. After World War II would come another period of significant federal urban investment. In 1945, the federal government began to address the issues of urban decline, when Congress passed the Urban Redevelopment Law, enabling cities to create redevelopment authorities to determine areas for postwar rebuilding. Philadelphia established its Redevelopment Authority in 1946, in response to Pennsylvania's 1945 enabling law.[9] In 1949, President Truman signed into law the American Housing Act, providing unprecedented funding for subsidizing urban redevelopment, predominantly focused on rebuilding distressed, urban residential areas and providing affordable housing. The Act's famous Title I consolidated the federal government's housing agencies and created the Urban Redevelopment Authority, with the power to subsidize two-thirds of the cost of land acquisition, land clearance, and relocation of residents for federally approved redevelopment activity.[10]

Title I suddenly allowed land in the center of cities to be cleared and primed cheaply, making it economically feasible for private developers, working with redevelopment authorities, to rebuild these areas wholesale. By the nature of its design, Title I was destined to be controversial; it focused on subsidizing wholesale bulldozing of residential areas, meaning that it could facilitate the condemnation and relocation of entire neighborhoods. Additionally, Title I lacked a requirement that affordable housing must replace the cleared areas. As one scholar put it, "Too often the victims of redevelopment were the poor, because slum clearance meant removing them for the benefit of the rich and powerful."[11]

Since many poor urban areas in cities that used Title I were also heavily African American, the program took on divisive racial overtones, characterized by some as "Negro removal."[12] In cities like Pittsburgh, Boston, and Chicago, Title I led to bulldozing entire neighborhoods, displacing thousands of mostly black families.[13]

Philadelphia would also use Title I dollars, and its urban redevelopment areas would involve bulldozing and displacement. However, based on ideology promoted by Bacon and others, Philadelphia attempted to deviate from the standard pattern of urban renewal, developing what people hoped was a more humanistic approach to neighborhood redevelopment. While some redevelopment areas did end up with far less relocation of families than comparable sites in other cities, it is unclear whether the approach was truly successful as a template for neighborhood revitalization.

The Philadelphia Approach

In June 1949, Pennsylvania governor James Duff signed the Housing and Redevelopment Assistance Law, providing $150 million to be dispersed statewide for redevelopment activities, about 20 percent allocated for the Philadelphia Redevelopment Authority.[14] To adhere to federal and state regulations, in Philadelphia the Redevelopment Authority was responsible for administering federal Title I funds, while the City Planning Commission was responsible for identifying "blighted" areas, certifying them for redevelopment and creating a physical plan for each area. However, after creating the plan, the Planning Commission's role essentially ended, giving the Redevelopment Authority the responsibility of attracting private developers and guiding actual construction, including condemnation of homes and relocation of residents.

The balance of roles and responsibilities between the various agencies and individuals who dealt with planning, redevelopment, and housing was a continual struggle that would at times create friction and ambiguity. In the early years of his tenure, Bacon worked with Redevelopment Authority administrative secretary David M. Walker and its chairman, Earle Barber. In 1951, the Authority hired Francis Lammer as director. In 1953, Lammer hired his own director of planning, David A. Wallace—an individual with whom Bacon would often clash on planning issues.[15] That same year, Mayor Joseph Clark created a new position called housing coordinator and appointed his former executive secretary, William Rafsky, to the post.

Rafsky was the city's direct contact for developers; he spoke publicly for the mayor and was sent to Washington to lobby for public funds. He was one of the most powerful city officials in Philadelphia during the 1950s and

1960s. David Wallace once equated Rafsky with Robert Moses—New York's famous development czar.[16] Dorothy Montgomery of the Philadelphia Housing Association and the Redevelopment Authority board said of Rafsky, "[he] makes policy for all the public agencies and the mayor listens to no one else."[17] Rafsky became the main official in charge of implementing the city's urban renewal program.[18] Bacon's relationship with Rafsky was strained at times; in later interviews, Bacon would refer to Rafsky as "my enemy" and "like Rasputin in the royal family of Russia."[19]

Bacon had to work with a shifting cast of characters and determine how to influence policy while working with powerful individuals like Rafsky. Bacon had strong ideas about Philadelphia's approach to redevelopment, and, at least in the program's early years, it appears he was successful in convincing the other actors to adopt his views. In addition, he had a major hand in selecting designers to carry out redevelopment plans. The designers he chose included colleagues such as Oskar Stonorov and Louis Kahn—individuals who shared his design ideology for neighborhood redevelopment. Early in the redevelopment program, Bacon seems to have been heavily involved in ensuring that the neighborhood designs took on Radburn-esque elements of separating pedestrians and cars, garden pathways, a hierarchy of streets, and lower-density dwelling units, including garden apartments. The designs of the earliest redevelopment projects very much mirror those from the Better Philadelphia Exhibition for rebuilding neighborhoods.

Bacon seems to have disagreed on a basic level with the federal vision for urban renewal as a program to subsidize wholesale bulldozing of "slum" areas.[20] He wanted to see a more humanistic approach that focused on rebuilding neighborhoods, with only selective demolition.[21] He warned that attacking urban blight would not be successful if tearing down houses meant merely "the transfer of the basic problem associated with blight to other areas."[22] Bacon was lucid on his thinking at a presentation to the National Planning Conference in Cleveland Ohio in October 1949, where he explained, "The direct facilities offered by the federal redevelopment legislation are curiously negative in character. They provide only for the clearance of areas for tearing buildings down." He continued, "I recognize that the spectacular approach of huge clearance areas will be more impressive in the beginning, but in the long run it alone will fall short of the mark."[23]

Bacon suggested, "First, we should approach the problem of planning for redevelopment, not in terms of individual projects, but in terms of the whole neighborhood structure, its people and its institutions."[24] Additionally, "Rehabilitation should be used wherever appropriate, closely tied in with clearance and new building. . . . The plan should recognize existing community institutions and should use them as a point of departure in its design."[25] The Planning Commission's 1950 Annual Report elaborated on this point: "Rather than propose the complete clearance and rebuilding of extensive areas, the commission develops plans for . . . a series of relatively small and closely integrated projects which together remove blighted spots and provide needed neighborhood facilities."[26]

Bacon also spoke about the need for community participation as a critical piece of the planning process: "we should involve the people of the neighborhood in the planning process itself. Only through *participation* can they fully understand the plan, adopt it as their own, realize that it relates to the entire neighborhood structure."[27] Although the Planning Commission struggled to find the right methodology, it did make continuous attempts to empower community groups. Bacon described a community planning process he felt was effective, in which the Commission worked with a local committee representing "business, industry, church, school, social work, labor, and local residents."[28] Through a series of meetings where the Planning Commission helped the community visualize its ideas on paper, "The plan evolves slowly as a joint effort, and the representatives justly consider themselves as its co-creator." Bacon continued, "In this way the plan itself is better than it otherwise would be, and it becomes a part of local thinking."[29] As he described it in 1949, this approach sounds like a rudimentary model of the "charrette" process used widely in the twenty-first century to empower neighborhood stakeholders.

The Planning Commission and Redevelopment Authority attempted this form of citizen participation in several redevelopment areas. According to a report from the Philadelphia Housing Association, Mill Creek's planning was "developed by the joint effort of a resident's planning committee . . . and the staffs of the Redevelopment Authority and Planning Commission."[30] In the Morton area, "The Morton Neighborhood Council, through a planning committee and with block committees, drew up a plan for the area, undertook voluntary rehabilitation, and carried on a number of projects for improvement of the community, including a tot-lot."[31] Other redevelopment areas that included citizen planning committees included Whitman and Haddington.[32]

The approach to urban renewal in Philadelphia that emerged was distinctive. The elements that came to define it included a focus on selective rather than wholesale demolition; progressive, Radburn-esque design principles implemented by modernist designers such as Louis Kahn and Oskar Stonorov, including separated pedestrian pathways and garden apartments; partnerships with private sector and nonprofit organizations; and citizen participation in the planning efforts via citizen planning councils. However, the program would only exist in its original form for a few years before federal and local political forces led to a change in course.

Early Redevelopment Projects

Within the framework of this experimental approach to redevelopment, the Philadelphia City Planning Commission approved its first ten redevelopment areas in 1948: Aramingo, Passyunk Square, Mill Creek, Old City, Southeast Central, Temple, Triangle, University, Lower Eastwick, and Poplar.[33] By 1960, twenty-seven redevelopment areas were certified by the Commission.

The first to see a completed redevelopment plan would be the Poplar area of North Philadelphia, characterized as "some of the city's worst slums."[34] The area was first discussed in late 1947, when the American Friends Service Committee—a national Quaker organization based in Philadelphia—approached the Redevelopment Authority with a pilot program for housing people of moderate means, in a block of what they saw as the most viable of the proposed redevelopment sites. They called the concept a "self-help" project because the families who would live in the homes would take part in the construction, using their sweat equity to offset some of the labor costs.[35] The proposal involved a combination of new home construction, houses sold to single families, lease-to-purchase agreements, elderly housing, and a program for relocating people outside the city who wished for a more rural lifestyle.[36]

Bacon suggested to the Redevelopment Authority that Poplar should "take priority over the plan for any other redevelopment area."[37] He had high hopes, believing that "This area would become a demonstration that would be a model for the entire country."[38] His colleague Walter Blucher told Bacon in one letter, "This experiment will be watched with interest by the entire country."[39] Stonorov was hired to develop the preliminary

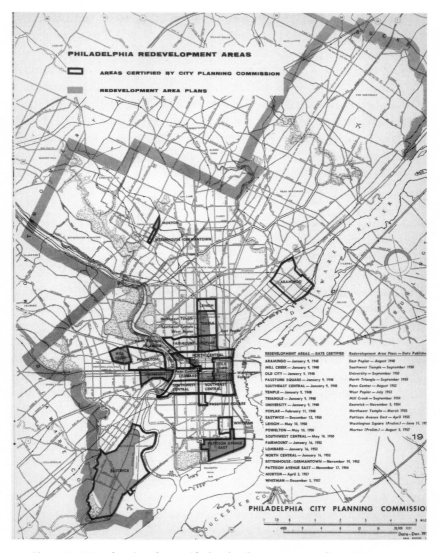

Figure 8. Map showing the certified redevelopment areas, from City Planning Commission, 1957 Annual Report. Courtesy of the Edmund N. Bacon Collection, The Architectural Archives, University of Pennsylvania.

design, which included the progressive design elements he and Bacon had included in the Better Philadelphia Exhibition.[40] The redevelopment of Poplar focused heavily on rehabilitation of existing homes, with selective demolition, the weaving of a "greenbelt" and pedestrian pathways through the site, and new construction sympathetic with the existing buildings.[41] The plans called for 2,727 dwelling units and ten acres of parkland.

In June 1951, Poplar took a major step forward, making Philadelphia the first city in the nation to have a project ready for federal loan and grant funds through the Federal Housing Act.[42] Initially Washington did not look favorably on Poplar, as it took an approach different from the "slum clearance" model.[43] Still, Bacon was committed to his approach and kept pushing Washington to become more receptive. Poplar was a complex project that involved the American Friends Service Committee, Redevelopment Authority, and Philadelphia Housing Authority—each responsible for a piece of the development process. Relocation of families would be a major hurdle, but one that fell on the Redevelopment Authority rather than the Planning Commission. About 778 families would have to be relocated.[44]

The project site was separated into three types of redevelopment: a rehabilitated section of American Friends Cooperative Homes, the Penn Towne apartments that used Title I monies to clear and reconstruct several blocks, and 203 "low-rent homes" built by the Housing Authority. Penn Towne was completed in 1952, hailed by the Planning Commission as the first residential redevelopment project in the nation under the federal program.[45] As construction moved ahead and it became clear that Philadelphia was trying to remake an urban community without wholesale bulldozing, the Poplar area started to gain wide attention. Researchers came from around the world to see the progress, even a Japanese prince, interested in Philadelphia's compassionate alternative to wholesale slum clearance and rebuilding.[46] However it was unclear if the experiment would truly work.

Another major redevelopment project was Mill Creek, a predominantly low-income, historically racially mixed area in West Philadelphia, selected by the Philadelphia Housing Authority as a site for a high-rise housing project.[47] The Philadelphia Real Property survey of 1934 gave the neighborhood the lowest possible rating of "D," leading to the redlining of the area and its subsequent residential decline.[48] In addition to Mill Creek's deteriorating housing stock, the land itself was in bad repair: part of the southeast section of the area was a vacant, diagonal tract where, in 1945, an underground sewer had collapsed, destroying the homes of 135 residents.[49]

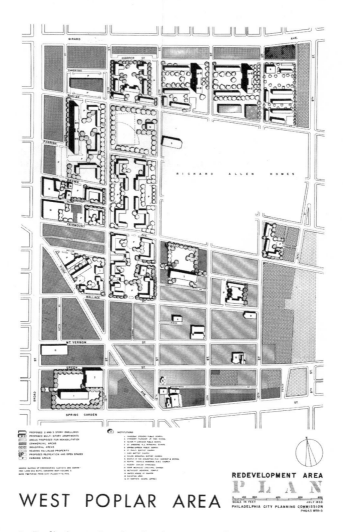

Figure 9. Preliminary site plan for the West Poplar Redevelopment Area, showing a Radburn-inspired design, with an empty area for the Philadelphia Housing Authority development. From Philadelphia City Planning Commission, July 1953, "West Poplar Redevelopment Area Plan." Courtesy of the Edmund N. Bacon Collection, The Architectural Archives, University of Pennsylvania.

In Mill Creek, Bacon approved hiring a design team that called themselves Associated Architects, including Louis Kahn.[50] Kahn would work on
a number of Philadelphia's redevelopment plans and was highly influential
in shaping the city's design approach. In fact, an article in *Architectural
Forum* that listed the six major participants in Philadelphia's redevelopment
program in order of importance put Kahn first, ahead of Bacon.[51] The
design team was later given the contract by the Philadelphia Housing
Authority to design the public housing towers, in addition to the broader
plan for overall neighborhood redevelopment.

The design concept for Mill Creek called for a new roadway system with
a hierarchy of streets: major through streets and "loop streets" that fed only
residential areas.[52] The plan incorporated a variety of housing types, parks,
and clustered commercial activity in shopping centers, as well as pedestrian-only "greenways."[53] Again the Housing Authority, Redevelopment
Authority, and Planning Commission worked together closely, in separate
but intertwined roles. Unfortunately Mill Creek would have to be rebuilt
again after the collapse of another underground sewer in 1961, killing at
least three people, injuring many others, forcing the city to condemn 104
homes, and displacing at least 500 people.[54]

By far the largest redevelopment project was Eastwick, an area of Southwest Philadelphia containing 3,000 acres, some of it densely populated by
small rowhouse communities, much of it vacant marshland. One report
characterized Eastwick as "marked by spotty development, substandard
housing, a low average elevation resulting in periodic flooding and wide
spread tax delinquency."[55] The population of the area prior to redevelopment was about 19,000.[56] A survey found that the Eastwick area had neighborhoods of white residents and pockets of "Negro population," with a
small, sparsely developed area that was "about evenly [racially] divided."[57]

Bacon and the Planning Commission forged a concept of a "city within
a city" that would contain a wide range of housing and commercial opportunities for a variety of income groups. Bacon began marketing Eastwick as
the largest redevelopment project in the country.[58] The Planning Commission and Redevelopment Authority put out a call for proposals from consultants to take on the bulk of the planning work and retained a team
of consultant firms that named themselves Eastwick Planners. The team
comprised Henry S. Churchill and W. Wilson Horst, with consultants Car-
roll, Grisdale & Van Alen; Montgomery & Bishop; and Oskar Stonorov.

In the meantime, Bacon worked with the Eastwick consultants to develop a large-scale community plan that reflected his design ideology.[59] The plan included a mixture of housing: single-family, twin, rowhouses, and garden apartments. Some roads were reconfigured to create residential enclaves. Commercial uses were situated in shopping centers, some with primarily smaller businesses and others with larger anchor stores, like supermarkets. Limited industrial uses were zoned for areas around the freight rail lines. In addition, the various stakeholders discussed building a new high-speed passenger rail line. The city had recently invested $10 million in its subway-surface system in West Philadelphia, and a connection to Eastwick seemed like a natural next investment.[60] The design was presented to urban renewal officials in Washington, D.C., to great interest from the feds.[61] On November 3, 1954, the City Planning Commission approved the Eastwick Redevelopment Area Plan, clearing the way for the Redevelopment Authority to begin property condemnation and acquisition.[62]

In 1960, the Redevelopment Authority selected a development team called the New Eastwick Corporation, comprised of Philadelphia builders Samuel and Henry Berger, with the Reynolds Aluminum Service Corporation as a principal investor.[63] Reynolds saw housing as the new frontier for innovative uses of aluminum products and wanted to spearhead this application with a major urban redevelopment project.[64] For the architect, the developers brought on Constantine A. Doxiadis, a well-known Greek designer. One of the features that most gratified Bacon was the fact that the Doxiadis plan for Eastwick would be based on the Radburn principles of separating cars and pedestrians.[65] In September 1961, Eastwick finally broke ground.[66]

Falling Short of the Mark

Early on, Philadelphia's redevelopment program gained attention for its unconventional model that deviated from the federal slum clearance formula and the scorched earth approach of most other cities. An April 1952 article in *Architectural Forum* titled "The Philadelphia Cure: Clearing Slums with Penicillin, Not Surgery," lauded Philadelphia's program, explaining, "Philadelphia, is attacking the problem of blight in a startling new way for a big U.S. city—conservatively. . . . Philadelphia's small [land] takes involve a minimum of dislocation of present inhabitants. . . . By holding meetings

Chapter 3

in the local areas before drawing any plans, Philadelphia's planning commission has preserved democracy and good feeling."[67]

However, over time significant challenges in Philadelphia's redevelopment program bred divisiveness, slowed the program, and jeopardized the long-term viability of the initial approach. A 1964 *Harper's* article explained, "On the scene of some of these projects, one is caught up in the enthusiasm of the planners and administrators and staff workers (many of them Negro); and it is impossible not to come away dazzled by hope. But around these spots of euphoria lies a sea of troubles."[68] As in cities across the country, Philadelphia's program did not live up to the hype, in part because over time Congress reduced the funding that would be allocated to cities.[69] However, lack of cash was only part of the story. Although Philadelphia's approach sought to minimize clearance and displacement of residents, these activities indeed took place and, as in other American cities, met opposition and criticism. The *Harper's* article explained, "Bulldozers have destroyed whole neighborhoods with all their ties and associations."[70] Much of the redevelopment was lower-density than the neighborhoods it replaced, creating a serious net loss of housing units for those displaced by urban renewal.

This latter issue was especially problematic, leading to the need to rehouse thousands of people and a lack of places to relocate them. In fact, in the early days of Eastwick's planning, in August 1949, David Walker, at the Redevelopment Authority, asked Bacon to "give very serious consideration" to using the Eastwick redevelopment area for housing persons relocated from redevelopment projects in other parts of the city.[71] In short, Walker wanted to turn this area of Southwest Philadelphia into a dumping ground for the victims of urban renewal. While there is no evidence of how Bacon felt about this particular plan, using Eastwick to house displaced persons was opposed by the Human Relations Commission, and the Redevelopment Authority abandoned it.[72]

The city never truly solved its problem of where to put displaced persons, and dislocation, understandably, became a major point of conflict in a number of redevelopment areas. This component fell on the Redevelopment Authority rather than the Planning Commission, so Bacon was able to stay somewhat insulated from the actual relocation process.

Bacon's perspective on urban renewal was complex. He supported the basic idea of investing public money to "restore blighted areas to the condition of the functioning usefulness and desirable living for the citizen."[73]

Furthermore, he was not opposed to displacing residents for public works projects. In one press release, he wrote about displacement of residents in the path of an expressway: "with adequate notice and fair compensation it is believed that readjustments can be made to make way for progress in the development of our city."[74]

However, as evidenced by projects like Poplar and Mill Creek, his view on neighborhood renewal clearly favored approaches that sought to reduce the amount of residential clearance and displacement of residents. In large part thanks to Bacon, Philadelphia took a different course from the scorched earth approach applied in other cities. Bacon noted, "The taking of a person's home is not an action to be treated lightly."[75] Additionally, there is evidence that, in some projects, he fought behind the scenes and expended political capital to reduce the number of homes that were torn down and residents displaced. For example, in the case of the construction of the Roosevelt Boulevard Extension, Bacon successfully pressured the state to alter the highway plans, resulting in five hundred fewer people who would have to be relocated.[76] Still, while Bacon's outlook on displacement was less heavy-handed than that of many policy makers across the country, he was certainly one of the actors who shaped Philadelphia's urban renewal approach, and residential displacement—forcing people out of their homes—was very much a component of that approach.

The issue of dislocation of residents was perhaps most contentious in Eastwick because of the scale of the project. In all, Eastwick involved relocation of 2,377 families, scheduled in three phases.[77] The Citizens' Council on City Planning stepped in and arranged public meetings to provide an organized venue for opposition to the Redevelopment Authority's plans.[78] One well-funded citizens' group in Eastwick purchased a barrage of newspaper advertisements—some in other cities' papers—railing against the project.[79] May and June 1958 were very heated, as the Citizens' Council and Commission on Human Relations worked to forge a solution that could address the public concerns relating to Eastwick's redevelopment plans.[80]

The Planning Commission and Redevelopment Authority tried to learn from their mistakes by undertaking some projects in the second and third wave of redevelopment areas that included still less demolition and relocation. A key example was the Morton area in the Germantown section, certified by the Planning Commission in 1957. The plan included building 187 homes, with significant input by the Morton Neighborhood Council—a team of residents who were empowered to create a plan for the area and mobilize the community around small-scale projects.[81] The new homes were scattered, to fill in vacant holes in the neighborhood fabric, with tasteful architecture, and with restoration of existing houses.[82] In addition, consultants Henry Magaziner and Preston Andrade developed an ambitious vision of closing the area's major avenue to vehicular traffic and making it a pedestrian and trolley-only street, focused on the neighborhood's colonial-era historic sites.[83] Morton was lauded as "a fine example of what might be called hand-crafted slum rehabilitation."[84] The great success of Morton was that it ultimately became invisible, blended in with the urban landscape. However, the project was expensive and too late to influence substantially the overall course of Philadelphia's redevelopment program.

In many cities, urban renewal and residential dislocation came with racial overtones, in large part because many of the communities in the path of the redevelopers' bulldozers were primarily occupied by African American residents. Philadelphia saw its share of racial tension in its urban renewal projects. However, the administration of Mayor Clark was, in fact, fairly committed to empowering black citizens and communities, starting by instating "minority-group leaders as his [Mayor Clark's] aides and administrators in his new government."[85] A 1964 article characterized this period in Philadelphia's history as a "racial renaissance."[86] The article went on to cite the impact of city planning in using Philadelphia's urban renewal to create new opportunities for upwardly mobile African American residents. It specifically cited Bacon as a supporter of this "racial renaissance," calling him "uncompromisingly idealistic and liberal." Bacon's racial tolerance is not surprising considering his track record in advocating for affordable housing and working with racially diverse organizations in Philadelphia and Flint. While Philadelphia would erupt in race riots in the late 1960s, there were distinct signs in the 1950s that African Americans were being given new opportunities for mobility and that the government was seriously focusing on racial diversity as a priority in some urban renewal projects.

In the early to mid-1950s, Philadelphia's poor black communities were located mainly in and around the urban core, with the largest concentration in the "jungles" of North Philadelphia, surrounded by what approximated a ring of more stable, white areas—dubbed by Mayor Richardson Dilworth a "white noose."[87] In a number of redevelopment areas, housing for middle-class African Americans and racial integration was a stated priority, with the specific goal of creating opportunities for middle-class blacks and attracting middle-class whites back into the city. Again, Eastwick is a key example. As the project evolved, it became branded as a future multiracial, middle-class community.[88] The Redevelopment Authority commissioned a study from the independent Commission on Race and Housing— which from 1955 to 1958 applied scientific research to the problems of housing inequality—to evaluate the demand for housing units in Eastwick.[89] The group commended Eastwick as "the first large-scale effort to market single family homes without discrimination by reason of race, religion, or national origin."[90] At the time, an interracial development was rare, and the Planning Commission took a risk by labeling the development as such.[91]

Despite the effort to market Eastwick as a mixed-race community, it did not succeed to expectations, failing to attract white families, and was criticized later because "the much-publicized integration is not all that it should be."[92] Attracting the white middle class became a major hurdle in redevelopment projects. In one very candid remark in 1958, Mayor Dilworth said, "What we're doing now . . . is deliberately making non-Negro apartments for older whites, pricing them out of the Negro range. We're designing the Eastwick project (2,500 acres, 12,000 units, in southwestern Philadelphia) the same way. We hope that no more than 10 percent of Eastwick will be Negro. We have to give the whites confidence that they can live in town without being flooded."[93] Such challenges to attract middle-class whites surely led to subsequent efforts, namely, Society Hill, to market city living in a way that would appeal specifically to middle-class and affluent whites.

However, some redevelopment projects found great success in creating opportunity for middle-class African Americans. The key example of this success was Yorktown, part of the Temple redevelopment area, with housing constructed by developer Norman Denny. The project was located in the middle of the so-called jungles of North Philadelphia—considered the city's most racially charged slums. The idea was to use this project to diversify the area economically and create a physical and social force for revitalizing deteriorated nearby residential areas. Bacon laid out a scheme in the redevelopment plans that resembled his other Radburn-inspired concepts, with rowhouses and separated residential and through streets.[94] In the early 1960s, Denny constructed this 280-home project on nine blocks of deteriorated twentieth-century rowhouses for factory workers, acquired and cleared with Title I dollars. As with the majority of the renewal projects, the rebuilt housing was far less dense than what it replaced. The project was almost immediately successful at attracting middle-class blacks and was quickly recognized as the first of its kind in the nation.

Bacon thought that Yorktown was a compelling model, showing that redevelopment in the worst sections of the city was truly possible. In one correspondence, he remarked, "It is extremely exciting to see such a large group of Negro families and families of mixed marriage as home owners moving into part of an area referred to as 'the jungle'."[95] He argued to the mayor, "The Denney [sic] project, Yorktown, has demonstrated that builders can sell houses in former slum areas where there is extensive clearance on a several block basis."[96] On its forty-year anniversary in 1996, an article in the *Philadelphia Inquirer* lauded Yorktown as a "Model for Urban Renewal," a successful project that remained a stable and desirable neighborhood, decades later.[97]

However, Yorktown did not realize the vision of building a mixed-race community; instead, it was "a completely Negro middle-class growth in the very center of a sea of Negro slums."[98] It was criticized for its "commercialism, cheap advertising approach, and architectural frills; and above all, for its segregation."[99] None of the urban redevelopment projects succeeded in creating mixed-race/mixed-income environments. According to one article on Philadelphia's urban renewal, "For the great upsurge of the Negro population into respectable living, there has been erected, piecemeal, a sort of rickety, gap-toothed ladder of hope."[100] Philadelphia's trend of segregated neighborhoods persisted, building a situation that would ultimately become explosive in the 1960s.

Another challenging aspect of Philadelphia's redevelopment program was the relationship between the Planning Commission, Redevelopment Authority, and Housing Authority. While the Planning Commission and Redevelopment Authority had clearly defined roles in the redevelopment program, the Housing Authority—responsible for building and maintaining public housing—was working on a parallel but somewhat separate track. Some of the redevelopment areas included public housing projects, but they were clearly separate from the rest of the plan. As an illustration of this separation, a 1953 redevelopment plan of the West Poplar area showed a blank shape cut out on a drawing, indicating where the Housing Authority project would go, but providing no indication of what the buildings would look like or where and how the buildings would be sited.[101]

Another issue had to do with the form of the public housing projects as dense, high-rise towers. While these types of projects drew criticism across the country, they appeared even more jarring in Philadelphia, a city whose predominant housing was individual rowhouses—not mid-rise or high-rise apartments.[102] In 1950, nine public housing sites were approved by the Housing Authority with a total of 4,200 units.[103] Bacon would be constantly frustrated during the 1950s in trying to convince the Housing Authority to lower the density of its developments.[104] In the 1960s, he spearheaded an alternative approach that scattered public housing units, rather than grouping them in dense developments.[105] In projects like Mill Creek, the high-rise public housing projects created divisiveness within a program where the Planning Commission was attempting to implement a more sympathetic and humanistic approach.

Changing Course

The federal government, under President Dwight Eisenhower, passed a new housing act in 1954 that significantly altered how cities could use federal money for urban renewal. The new federal policies would have a major impact on Philadelphia's strategy for urban investment and on Bacon's focus and priorities moving forward.

The forces that crafted American urban renewal were largely ideological, with liberal advocates for public housing on one side and conservatives focusing on business growth and private enterprise on the other. The 1949 act was a hybrid, passed under a Democratic president, Harry Truman, and carrying strong influence from the Roosevelt New Deal era. However, in Washington it was a controversial piece of legislation that divided Congress.[106] When the act's next iteration was debated several years later, there were already stories of controversy and failure from cities whose redevelopment programs fell short of the mark or garnered local opposition. With Republican President Eisenhower in office and a Republican majority in both houses of Congress in 1953, it would be difficult for public housing advocates to combat the forces that sought to reduce government investment in urban areas.

The 1954 Housing Act maintained federal investment in cities but substantially changed the focus to one that was more business-centric. According to one scholar, "The Housing Act of 1954 transcended the acrimonious divide between liberals and conservatives, forging a new consensus that emphasized commercial redevelopment instead of public housing as the answer to central-city decline."[107] The act did not eliminate funding for public housing, but it did significantly reduce the amount of dollars available, and public housing production saw a sharp decrease from its peak of

58,000 units produced nationally in 1952 to just 24,000 units in 1964.[108] This refocusing on commercial development and investment in downtowns and in universities and hospitals would continue in the 1959 and 1961 federal housing acts.[109] In addition, in 1956, Congress passed the Federal-Aid Highway Act, providing massive amounts of funding to state governments for the completion of roadway segments that were approved as part of the interstate highway system.[110] This act further redirected spending in urban areas, providing new resources for state governments to invest heavily in metropolitan highway networks.

Urban business leaders were naturally enthusiastic about the new federal approach, as were a number of big-city mayors.[111] It is notable that Philadelphia's Mayor Clark was not among the supporters, publicly voicing opposition to the shift away from housing.[112] The supporters of the new approach created a formidable force that substantially weakened the national commitment to neighborhood investment and public housing and ended up "leaving liberal public housers alone, weak, and isolated."[113]

At the same time that the federal government was shifting its priorities, Philadelphia's Redevelopment Authority saw a need to reassess the way the city carried out its redevelopment program—viewing the current approach as too haphazard and scattered, too focused on physical design, and too little informed by social and economic analysis. Backed by powerful voices on its board, such as former senator Francis J. Meyers and head of the Philadelphia Housing Association Dorothy Montgomery, in early 1954 the agency commissioned a study of the redevelopment program that came to be called the Central Urban Redevelopment Area (CURA) study.[114] It was surely not a coincidence that the study was commissioned the same year as the federal housing act; no doubt the leadership at the Redevelopment Authority wanted to develop an approach that was more in line with the new federal priorities.

A first draft of the CURA study was released in 1956, citing the failings of the city's approach to redevelopment and outlining new strategies.[115] When Richardson Dilworth became mayor in 1956, he kept Bill Rafsky as housing coordinator to implement the recommendations of the CURA study. In 1957, Rafsky unveiled the city's new redevelopment approach, which (not surprisingly) mirrored the activities supported by the 1954 act. The new local approach involved significant investment in downtown, universities, and industrial areas, to build a stronger core and yield economic development impacts. Meanwhile, the city would stop investing in the "most blighted" areas, and, when it did undertake residential redevelopment, it would be focused on relatively stable outlying areas, mainly occupied by whites. Redevelopment projects already underway would continue, but new ones that focused on blighted areas would be few and far between.[116]

The 1954 act did not eliminate Philadelphia's public housing investment—though the dollars available were reduced and progress would be slowed due to racial tension over new projects. Much of Dilworth's early mayoralty would be clouded by angry meetings with white residents who vehemently opposed the intrusion of public housing projects and black residents in their neighborhoods.[117] This racially charged atmosphere would come to shape much of Philadelphia's history over the following decade.

The story of Philadelphia's pre-1954 redevelopment program is significant in a discussion of Bacon's role because it seems to have marked a philosophical turning point for him and his entrepreneurial approach to planning and development. It would have seemed natural for Bacon to also be vocally opposed to this shift in policy—with his background as a Roosevelt liberal and his career advocating for affordable housing in Flint and at the Philadelphia Housing Association. However, he does not appear to have taken a public stance on the issue; instead, he seems to have withdrawn from actively focusing his energy on the redevelopment program at this point.

Bacon did not entirely depart from community planning and housing projects, but reduced his involvement in those that were part of the federally funded urban renewal program. During the 1950s, he focused significant energy on planning for new communities in Philadelphia's Far Northeast, section, where he was given the chance to use his entrepreneurial approach, demonstrating his predilection for working with projects in which the public sector was less involved and he could negotiate directly with private-sector developers.

Building New Communities in the Far Northeast

Concurrent with planning the redevelopment areas, Bacon was working on a fundamentally different type of community development. While the redevelopment areas involved incorporating new ideas into existing communities, in Philadelphia's Far Northeast, he had the opportunity to introduce a complete new community design for a sparsely developed area.

The Far Northeast comprised 16,000 acres separated from the rest of the city by Pennypack Creek. Along with a number of other areas, it had been consolidated into the city in 1854. By the early 1950s, the Far Northeast represented about one-fifth of Philadelphia's land area but only 1.8 percent of the population. The area just to the south, in contrast, was built out with block after block of modest brick rowhouses, constructed as worker housing to accommodate a steady flow of newcomers who manned the factories and shipyards.

The postwar housing boom was about to push rapidly beyond Pennypack Creek, with industrious tract developers seeking to make a profit by building on this open territory. Between 1940 and 1950, the number of dwelling units in the Far Northeast had already increased from 1,917 to 5,156, with an 81 percent population increase.[118] By the early 1950s, the question was not whether the Far Northeast would be developed but how quickly and, more important for Bacon, what the new neighborhoods would look like. He was not the only one thinking about this. The Philadelphia development community was used to building rowhouses, but some developers had shifted to tracts of single-family homes with a front lawn and a garage—the new American dream.

Neither approach appealed to Bacon. He believed it would be a mistake to build suburbia in the city. Likewise, he believed the city needed a different model of urban development from Philadelphia's traditional layout of rectilinear gridded streets.[119] He thought there was a better way to build communities that were distinctly urban but adapted the Radburn principles to provide a better quality of life. Bacon and Oskar Stonorov had proposed a new vision for the Far Northeast in the Better Philadelphia Exhibition, laid out so as to separate pedestrians and vehicular traffic around looping streets, with stores, schools, parks, and other community institutions in easy walking distance. Bacon learned how revolutionary this concept was when he invited Clarence Stein, the designer of Radburn, to Philadelphia: Stein was stymied by the idea of using the Radburn principles in a relatively dense, urban context.[120]

However, Bacon persisted. For the Far Northeast, he proposed a variation on the traditional grid street pattern, planning blocks of rowhouses but set along curving loop streets that would fit into the natural topography, wrapping around the stream valleys. A grid pattern would have enclosed the streams in underground sewers, as was the custom in other newly developed parts of the city. Bacon wanted to respect the topography and allow future residents to enjoy the region's natural resources (not to mention that the city wanted to avoid more sewer collapses). Housing clusters would be connected to each other and to the downtown with both highways and transit lines. This concept essentially borrowed the best elements of the urban grid system—rowhouses, walkability, sense of community, predictable system of streets—and combined them with new planning principles that limited traffic flow in residential areas and preserved the natural environment.

The first hurdle for Bacon was selling his concept to Frederick Thorpe, chairman of the Board of Surveyors—a powerful bureaucrat in charge of any changes in the way the city laid out land or utilities. Bacon had to make Thorpe comfortable with the idea of the Planning Commission having a role in dealing with subdivision of land. Starting in 1948, he worked with Thorpe on a number of different sites, slowly testing his ability to give the Planning Commission a foothold with Thorpe.[121] After feeling comfortable enough with their working relationship, he took his concept for the Far Northeast to Thorpe. Bacon recalled, "I showed him the idea, instead of arbitrarily imposing a preconception on land where it was not appropriate, you would derive the idea from the land itself."[122] Thorpe was apparently intrigued by the concept. Perhaps the most compelling element of Bacon's plan was that it made sound financial sense. It was expensive to level land and to bury stream beds in sewers—not to mention the cost of dealing with several major sewer collapses.[123]

Bacon was able to convince Thorpe to try his experimental new design on a 350-acre section of the Far Northeast, bordered by Roosevelt Boulevard, Holme Avenue, and Ashton, Willits, and Welsh Roads. In May 1949, Bacon and the Planning Commission announced the public release of this trial plan. When completed, the planned area would hold roughly 1,247 housing units. Bacon became the project's spokesperson. The *Bulletin* quoted him: "This will be a new type of community in which children and automobiles can exist happily and safely together. This is not just 'dream stuff'."[124]

Unlike the redevelopment areas, this land was not publicly owned. Private developers did not have to gain title through the Redevelopment Authority or use federal subsidies. In the Far Northeast, the Planning Commission was designing for private enterprise. For many developers, this was a new concept—one that was not necessarily immediately palatable. The Planning Commission staff would create new subdivision plans, showing developers how and where they could build. A Board of Subdivision

Review, comprised of members of various city departments, evaluated the plans. Once the Board signed off, the plans went to the Planning Commission for final approval. By the end of 1951, the Commission staff had developed nine final subdivision plans for 381 acres and six preliminary site plans for 667 acres.[125]

While the Planning Commission was trying to sell developers on the concept that they had to adhere to predesigned site plans, Bacon also had to deal with a brewing fight between residents in the Far Northeast and the development community. The residents did not want to see their semirural area become urban and were pushing for suburban-style, single-family homes. The developers, in contrast, wanted to develop rowhouse blocks, mainly because it was what they knew and rowhouses were far cheaper to construct. Bacon favored rowhouses, but for the reason of providing affordably priced housing, rather than exclusive suburban growth. This support, however, also had the consequence of aligning him with private developers and putting him at odds with local community groups. Bacon demonstrated his focus on providing affordable housing units in one instance when he wrote to Mayor Clark about public opposition to rezoning for the Planning Commission design concept, stating, "If proposal is turned down I think one of Philadelphia's best chances for really progressive housing for middle income group will have been lost."[126]

Bacon seized on one particular confrontation between a community in the Rhawnhurst section and developer A. P. Orleans as a test case for his new concept. He first convinced Orleans to build his new housing in conformity with the Radburn-inspired curving street pattern.[127] Next, Bacon believed he could create a solution to the conflict between Orleans and the community by introducing a new type of zoning that would be "more acceptable to those who oppose D-Residential [rowhouse] type construction, and would make best use of a better street pattern than the gridiron system."[128] During this same period, he was pushing for a major overhaul of the city's zoning code, so that zoning decisions would not have to be made on a case-by-case basis.[129] However, for the Far Northeast, he did not have time to wait for such an overhaul.

In drafting new zoning, Bacon worked closely with Orleans, as well as with Aaron Levine and John Bodine at the Citizens' Council on City Planning and Dorothy Montgomery at the Philadelphia Housing Association. As it evolved, the new zoning classification would permit rowhouse blocks but limited to ten houses per row, with a "breezeway" between the blocks, providing an easement allowing all residents access to the open space and stream valleys. Bacon sought to appease the opponents of rowhouse development by calling the new zoning C-1, giving the impression that it was more similar to semidetached C zoning than to rowhouse D zoning.[130]

The C-1 zoning ordinance was introduced into City Council on November 20, 1952. However, despite the clever name, decrease in density, and increase in open space the new zoning would achieve, it still permitted rowhouses and thus did not satisfy the community group in Rhawnhurst. John S. Schultz, head of the Rhawnhurst Civic Association, praised Bacon's street layout designs but vehemently opposed the new zoning. Schultz explained, "it seems a pity that the benefits of city planning on site and street arrangement must be accompanied by the construction of downgraded housing."[131] This statement reflected a perception that modern housing should be suburban and that rowhouses would attract less affluent residents.

The C-1 bill did not have the support it needed to get out of committee in City Council, and it seemed unlikely the Orleans development in Rhawnhurst would move ahead without the new zoning. Bacon believed that, if he could get one development built with the curving street pattern and rowhouse zoning, it would convince both the public and the developers of the merits of this new form of community design.[132] To find this model project, he turned his attention to a proposal by Albert M. Greenfield on 300 acres called the "Morrell Tract." Bacon supported Greenfield in his attempt to rezone the property for rowhouses, on the condition that Greenfield would simulate the principles of C-1 zoning. He also got a promise from Greenfield to adhere to the curving street design.[133]

Despite continued community opposition, City Council voted for approval. Bacon lobbied Mayor Clark to sign the ordinance, but Clark vetoed it.[134] The mayor was concerned about the precedent of rezoning part of the Far Northeast for rowhouses, without the proposed C-1 provisions that would make the development less dense and provide access to open space. Clark also wanted to see the Planning Commission create a master plan for the Far Northeast, rather than working project by project. Bacon regrouped and had his staff begin a series of public outreach programs, working with the Citizens' Council to educate residents of the Far Northeast and seek their buy-in.[135] Based on feedback from these community meetings, the revised C-1 zoning bill allowed either single-family or duplex homes, with a maximum of ten to a group and a minimum lot width of 18 feet. The bill also required generous rear yard space, and 12-foot side yard breezeways between the groupings of rowhouses.[136] In late February 1954, City Council passed the C-1 ordinance, and it was signed into law in early March.

The next step in the process for Bacon was to develop a subdivision ordinance for the city—a set of ground rules for developers wanting to split up land for multiple dwelling units—as permitted in the Home Rule Charter. Developed between October 1952 and March 1954, the subdivision ordinance would bolster the Planning Commission's authority substantially, requiring developers of more than three units to adhere to the Commission's designs and submit final plans to the Commission for approval.[137] The ordinance laid out some basic criteria for new development, clearly influenced by Bacon's concepts for the Far Northeast. For example, the document explained that "Streets shall be logically related to the topography" and that "Residential streets shall be so laid out as to discourage through traffic."[138]

Now, however, it was the housing developers who protested the new rules they saw as onerous. To navigate this impasse, Bacon enlisted the support of Bill Rafsky to act as broker between the Planning Commission and the developers.[139] Bacon did not have the right political connections to handle this issue effectively, so he stepped away as Rafsky and Bacon's deputy, Paul Croley, worked over the next two weeks to tweak the ordinance and successfully convince the developers to withdraw their opposition.[140] The effort was successful, and City Council adopted the ordinance in June 1954.[141]

The next step, now that the C-1 zoning and subdivision ordinance were approved by City Council, was for the Planning Commission to come up with a complete physical development plan, showing in detail where and how C-1 zoning would be applied in the Far Northeast. Bacon continued to struggle with disagreements over rezoning among City Council, the Citizens' Council, and his own City Planning Commission. Bacon's staff, led by chief of land planning Willo von Moltke, drafted a master plan for a limited area of the Far Northeast, covering about 1,500 acres and providing for about 13,000 homes. It clearly reflected the total concept Bacon had devised for these new rowhouse communities. It included a series of clusters of residential loop streets tied together by a system of arterial streets. Bacon explained, "Since the only traffic using the loop streets will be that destined for the houses on it, the streets will be quiet and safe."[142] At the center of each cluster was to be a shopping center, so that they were in easy walking distance. The shopping areas were supposed to be distinctly urban, intentionally planned to avoid the construction of suburban strip malls, referred to by the Planning Commission as "undesirable ribbon development."[143]

Each cluster was to be connected with bus lines and linked to the downtown through an integrated transit system. Bacon noted that emphasis was placed on planning "a pedestrian circulation system and bicycle pathways, leading to the schools and the recreation areas."[144] He touted the fact that these design principles had never been planned for an urban area. He explained, "The plan as proposed would establish a new type of neighborhood development, and would provide one of the largest and most significant planned neighborhoods ever to be constructed by private builders in this country." By the end of 1954, the preliminary plan was finished.

Another new element in the Far Northeast, not expressly required by C-1 or the subdivision ordinance, was the layout of the homes and position of the garages. Philadelphia rowhouses typically had garages with access from the back alley. However, in the Better Philadelphia Exhibition, Bacon and Stonorov showed a new concept of a rowhouse with a front garage and backyard patio. The idea seems to have come from Dorothy Montgomery, who wanted to introduce rear yards to urban working-class housing, not to mention that a paved rear driveway would have ruined the idea of preserving backyard stream valleys in the Far Northeast.[145] This parking issue was seen as such an important element that John Bodine of the Citizens' Council argued that front garages should be required in the C-1 zoning.[146] In the end, however, the configuration of the street patterns made rear-access parking impractical, and most Northeast developers adopted the front garage concept on their own.

Bacon was highly cognizant of the developers' opposition to the idea of the Planning Commission telling them what to build. As such, Bacon billed the plan as "preliminary," framing it as the basis for dialogue with builders and the community, rather than an unchangeable document.[147] He worked with the Citizens' Council on City Planning and also with Walter Phillips—now city representative and city commerce director—to hold public meetings on the plan.[148] Hundreds of residents packed community halls for these presentations.[149]

The Planning Commission was prepared to move ahead and work with the crowded field of developers anxiously waiting to build. In summer

1954, Irving Wasserman of Bacon's staff worked almost exclusively on the Far Northeast. The developers had to come to the Planning Commission, where Wasserman would sit down with them and show them the detailed plans for what they were required to build. Wasserman later explained, "Other planning commissions sit back and passively redline other drawings. We in the [Philadelphia] Planning Commission did the drawings."[150]

Finally, in April 1956, Bacon got what he had been seeking for years: one approved design for a complete community with C-1 zoning and loop streets. Greenfield decided to pull out of the Morrell project and sold his land to two small-time builders who agreed to go along with exactly what the Planning Commission prescribed.[151] The Morrell Park homes went up quickly and sold for $10,990 apiece. Viewed from the air, it looked like a strange and orderly community: concentric circles, with a neat weaving of loop streets. From the street level, it had the appearance of an urban neighborhood, with dense blocks of rowhouses.

However, by this point the concept had changed in a significant way: the developers opposed commercial centers in their new developments. Despite the ordered streets and dense rowhouses, without shopping and amenities within walking distance, the idea of a new urban community could not fully be realized. The mass transit connections also never materialized, and the Far Northeast became automobile-dependent. Several years later, Larry Smith, one of the nation's foremost market analysts, released a report that stated, "Virtually all shopping trips will be by automobile. . . . [The Far Northeast] is, and will continue to be an auto-oriented community similar to other suburban areas."[152]

Much to Bacon's dismay, the Zoning Board of Adjustment granted variances to numerous developers, allowing them to deviate from C-1.[153] Wasserman had to redesign some of the residential clusters that did not fit exactly as planned, cutting loops into half loops and compromising the clarity of the original design.[154] He also had different design preferences from Bacon. He recalled, "I preferred the cul-de-sacs, and the reason I preferred them was they leant themselves more to the geometry of the rowhouse . . . and the introduction of a center island for parking or planting is not possible in the loop street."[155]

With the cul-de-sacs and auto-oriented design, major components of Bacon's original concept were tossed by the wayside. Part of this fact had to do with pressure from the developers, part with Bacon's desire to get

Figure 10. Aerial photo of Morrell Park (date unknown), a completed development in Philadelphia's Far Northeast and the best-built example of Bacon's concept for new communities in this part of the city, with rowhouses and a hierarchy of streets set within the geographical constraints of existing stream valleys. Courtesy of the Edmund N. Bacon Collection, The Architectural Archives, University of Pennsylvania.

projects quickly on the ground. Part surely had to do with the allure of the suburban model that was drawing so many middle-income Philadelphians out of the city. As a result of these factors, the new developments in the Far Northeast were a strange hybrid, with rowhouses and small yards but suburban strip malls and highways. The area was neither urban nor suburban, and it failed at attaining the benefits of either paradigm. One visitor to Philadelphia wrote to Bacon about his trip to the Far Northeast: "I saw nothing but ugliness. . . . Yet the Northeast is the newest part of the City and as such I would assume should be the showcase of city living."[156]

Despite how far the final product had strayed from Bacon's vision, he continued to call the development of the Far Northeast a success. Others, too, saw its virtues. In 1959, William H. Whyte, Jr., prominent urbanist, author, and associate editor of *Fortune* magazine, wrote, "For years planners have been warning about the economic evils of the creeping artificial blight commonly known as urban sprawl, but nobody did anything about it."[157] He credited Bacon as one of the very few who did. The Urban Land Institute *Community Builders Handbook* touted the Far Northeast as a model of how the public sector could take the lead to guide the private sector toward better planned subdivisions.[158]

In fact, Bacon did achieve at least two of his key aims. The Far Northeast was developed with affordable rowhouses rather than more expensive single-family homes, keeping the area a working- and middle-class section of the city. Also, the natural stream valleys were preserved.[159] Bacon was ahead of his time in this regard. In the coming decades, as planners started to focus more on natural land preservation, it became clear that the dedication of a vast network of streams across 16,000 acres in the Far Northeast was an achievement that never would have occurred without Bacon and the Planning Commission playing a strong role. In 1968, Whyte discussed the Far Northeast in *The Last Landscape*:

> The result is not a showpiece. For so advanced a plan, what one sees on the ground is disappointingly ordinary. . . . But the plan works. . . . The houses in the cluster neighborhoods have been just as profitable for the builders, no more expensive for the homeowners, yet they are complemented by a magnificent stream-valley network that cost the city nothing and will one day be priceless.[160]

Despite the mixed results, Bacon exerted a lot of time and energy in the Far Northeast. It is a case study of his entrepreneurial approach to planning and policy implementation—working dynamically with various players and attempting new concepts when one proved ineffective. While he was heavily involved in the early planning of Philadelphia's redevelopment program, he seems to have become far less committed over time and certainly did not bring the same doggedness and entrepreneurism to the fore as he did in the Northeast.

This fact surely had to do in part with the shifting priorities from the federal government as a result of the 1954 federal housing act, as well as the local response via the CURA study that dramatically altered Philadelphia's own approach. He did speak out when it was clear that the Redevelopment Authority and Bill Rafsky were shifting away from investing in the neediest areas after the CURA study. In 1957 Bacon said, "we do not think the difficulties attendant upon the efforts in the more blighted sections should lead us to a policy that abandons these areas altogether for any sustained period, but rather to a policy in which a portion of our energy is directed toward developing new solutions to these older areas which overcome the major problems revealed by our old approach."[161]

Still, Bacon would spend much of the rest of his tenure focusing on downtown projects like Penn Center, Market East, and Society Hill. This change of focus was in line with the shifting federal and local investment priorities. Bacon's colleague Walt D'Alessio said, "He could sense a trend and get out in front of it."[162] Bacon was surely smart enough to see where the priorities and money were leading urban redevelopment and to do what it took to harness those resources. However, there is likely more to the story. He seems to have also been frustrated by other public-sector actors and bureaucratic processes getting in the way of things moving forward the way he wanted. He explained, "it must be clear that the key person in the whole [redevelopment] process must be the planner. No person approaching this problem . . . from the legal or administrative side can possibly put into the situation what I'm talking about. Only the planner, through his background, is capable of mastering the total concept of the human, of the building, and of the neighborhood itself."[163]

However, as the redevelopment program unfolded, it was clear that Bacon was outranked by Bill Rafsky and had limited influence to affect the redevelopment area plans beyond the preliminary design. In the Far Northeast, in contrast, there were also bureaucratic hurdles, but because the projects were private ventures and not eligible for urban renewal dollars, there was much less involvement and interference from the Redevelopment Authority and other public-sector departments. This fact left Bacon free to work directly with private developers.

Bacon seems to have had a strong preference for working with private-sector actors and building dynamic public-private partnerships. This element would play a key role in his entrepreneurial style as he focused his energy on downtown reinvestment. In Center City Philadelphia, his first prime focus would be the site of the "Chinese Wall," the Pennsylvania Railroad's massive viaduct that cut Center City in half. The redevelopment of this site, which became known as Penn Center, would become one of the defining elements of Bacon's career and a key example of his entrepreneurship in forging public-private partnership.

Chapter 4

THE ARCHITECT PLANNER

By the time he became executive director of the Philadelphia City Planning Commission in 1949, Bacon seems to have grasped that the success of city planning depended on bringing together politicians, business people, civic groups, developers, and communities to support a vision of development. Nothing could be achieved without building a team that could carry through that design in all its complexity—and inspiring that team to come together around a shared set of goals.

The process of convincing stakeholders, the media, and the public was the psychological side of the planning process that fascinated Bacon—the way that ideas evolved in the city's collective consciousness, how they seduced powerful people and institutions, and how they could be choreographed so as ultimately to make their way into reality. Bacon learned that, to be successful, he would have to understand the nature of ideas in the landscape of Philadelphia's power structure and in the larger societal context. In the coming years, he would dedicate himself to the process of garnering support for his ideas in a subtle, politically astute way, influencing a process that most people did not realize was going on, harnessing a force that few recognized even existed.

Bacon called the core physical concept of a project the "design idea."[1] He understood that the design ideas inevitably changed during the process of enlisting developers and communities. These and other stakeholders would reject or change certain key elements of an initial plan. Budget constraints and city politics also left their mark on every project. Still, the results that emerged in the Far Northeast raised the question of whether a design idea could be altered beyond recognition.[2] The Far Northeast, as it was built, was vastly different from Bacon's original vision. The completed project retained the dense rowhouses looping around preserved stream valleys in his design, but other key elements like the commercial centers and transit connections were lost. In the end, the Far Northeast earned mixed reviews as an urban-suburban hybrid. Could Bacon have done more to keep his original concept intact? Was his vision truly better than what was actually built? The answers were unclear.

During the same period that Bacon was working on the Far Northeast, he would grapple with these questions in the heart of Philadelphia, dealing with completely different issues and stakeholders. Still, Bacon's keynote downtown project—to be known as Penn Center—was similar to the Far Northeast in that it required public-private partnership, working within a complex web of stakeholders, and being willing to push for a vision, while making compromises in the name of advancing the project. In the end, however, Penn Center would also stray from Bacon's original "design idea," and the finished product would garner significant criticism.

Penn Center: Building a Team to Build the Project

Penn Center—the development that replaced the Pennsylvania Railroad's "Chinese Wall" viaduct—would become one of the projects most closely associated with Bacon's career. This was decidedly a plan for developing private real estate. It might have seemed inappropriate for the city planning director to advise a private corporation on how to treat its own land. However, to Bacon, the railroad's property in the center of town was just too important to leave to the whim of the corporation's board of directors. Bacon believed this property had the potential to become a new civic center—creating a fresh and modern presence that could shape Philadelphia's national image. The situation also presented an opportunity to work directly with the business community and to seek influence in the amorphous aura of public opinion, without having to navigate government bureaucracy. Bacon's challenge was to figure out how to sell his ideas so that, rather than falling on deaf ears, they would become an integral force in shaping the physical future of the city.

What became known to Philadelphians as the Chinese Wall had its start as elevated railroad tracks erected in 1881 to carry commuter trains into the Pennsylvania Railroad's Broad Street Station in Center City. In the 1890s, the celebrated Philadelphia architect Frank Furness designed the wall and the ornate Broad Street Station. The tracks terminated in an elevated train shed, while pedestrians passed under the wall through archways at the

Figure 11. Photo taken in 1950 from City Hall tower of the tracks on the Pennsylvania Railroad's "Chinese Wall" viaduct, with Broad Street Station visible at the bottom. Photo by Lawrence Williams. Courtesy of the Edmund N. Bacon Collection, The Architectural Archives, University of Pennsylvania.

street level. The Chinese Wall stretched ten blocks along Filbert Street, cutting across the western end of Center City.

The Chinese Wall was an imposing physical and visual barrier, and over time it blighted development to its north and south. By the late 1940s the area on the south side of Market Street, across from the Chinese Wall and just next to City Hall, included rows of shoddy, low buildings, parking lots, and abandoned structures, cheap bars, dance halls, and pornographic shows.[3] On the north side of the wall were old industrial buildings and storage rental facilities. After a fire devastated the train shed, the Pennsylvania Railroad made an agreement with the city, in 1925, to bury its tracks and tear down the wall, freeing up significant land for development and construction of a new "Pennsylvania Boulevard." However, the Great Depression stalled this plan, and by the 1940s, to many it seemed that the wall would probably stay standing forever. So long as the wall remained, the railroad paid no taxes on the property.[4]

However, many in the architecture community saw the potential of redeveloping the site as a grand civic center. Bacon's former employer W. Pope Barney was part of a team with the firm of Zantzinger, Borie, and Medary that produced a 1930 vision concept for replacing the wall with two towers housing the Philadelphia Art Alliance and the Philadelphia Orchestra and opera. Other parts of the three-block project were to contain a motel, shops, and an elevated pedestrian plaza.[5] In October 1946, the City Planning Commission hired a design team called Associated City Planners—including Oskar Stonorov and Louis Kahn—to create a redevelopment plan for the "Triangle Area," including a large tract of land along the eastern shore of the Schuylkill River adjacent to the Benjamin Franklin Parkway. The planned area extended to the south, so as to include the Chinese Wall site. The plan's concept design for the Chinese Wall area included three new buildings and a sunken, pedestrian esplanade resembling New York's Rockefeller Center.[6]

In the Better Philadelphia Exhibition, Stonorov included the designs from the forthcoming Associated City Planners study in the downtown model. This plan was no more than a vision, as the future of the property hinged on its private owner—the Pennsylvania Railroad—deciding to adopt and finance it. In January 1948, the City Planning Commission certified the Triangle Area as a redevelopment area, allowing federal funds to support development in the areas around the Chinese Wall site. About a week later, Associated City Planners released their "Report on the Redevelopment of the Triangle."[7]

Meanwhile, the Pennsylvania Railroad engaged in its own conceptual planning, hiring Raymond Loewy, the famous industrial designer of its streamlined train cars, as a consultant to create a model demonstrating the future potential of the Chinese Wall site. Loewy produced a tabletop-sized model encased in a wooden box—somewhat resembling a coffin—showing a new office tower, department store, and other buildings.[8] The surface layer was similar in concept to the Associated City Planners design.[9] Beneath this layer, however, Loewy showed a series of overlaid glass sections highlighting a complicated web of below-ground infrastructure, including waiting rooms, parking, underground roadways for buses and taxis, and underground freight and passenger tracks. This was an enormously complex model of how the railroad could maximize its real estate through a groundbreaking concept of a multimodal transportation network.

Thus, when Bacon became planning director in 1949, there had already been several design concepts produced for replacing the Chinese Wall site, including one paid for by the railroad. Bacon believed that, amid all the planning, there was the threat that the railroad would sell off its property in pieces. Bacon believed that the railroad's land held tremendous value but that the low-quality development to the south made it difficult for the railroad's board and business community to see the potential. Bacon had his own vision for the site but most of all wanted to ensure that the railroad developed the site as a single entity, creating a grand civic space in the heart of the city. His challenge was how to influence the executives of the Pennsylvania Railroad and gain buy-in for his vision.

Bacon's first step toward advancing his concept came in fall 1949, when he helped create the "Triangle Committee," under the umbrella of the local chapter of the American Institute of Architects (AIA).[10] Bacon did not have the jurisdiction to envision the future of the railroad's private property under the auspices of the Planning Commission, but he perhaps felt that the AIA presented an outside voice with the credence to influence the railroad and other powerful stakeholders. The committee brought together several prominent designers who had previously focused on the future of the Chinese Wall site, including W. Pope Barney, Roy Larson, Edmund Krimmel, and Louis Kahn as chairman. Bacon often attended meetings of the committee.[11]

In spring 1950, Kahn produced a model that synthesized the committee's ideas, showing the Chinese Wall replaced with a series of eleven identical slab buildings, stretching west all the way to the Schuylkill River. Passing under the eleven buildings was a continuous pedestrian concourse.[12] Bacon considered the model a positive first step toward introducing a compelling vision for the railroad and the public to embrace.[13] Soon, however, he started to lose confidence that the Triangle Committee was the right venue through which to have an impact on the railroad. He also realized that Kahn was not the right partner in this pursuit.

By now, Bacon and Kahn knew each other well. In October 1939, their mutual friend Fritz Gutheim had suggested to Bacon, "Look up Louis Kahn," and by December 1940 Bacon and Kahn had definitely met, as they both chaired organizing committees for a citywide demonstration for federal affordable housing legislation.[14] Bacon and Kahn clearly had mutual interests. Kahn was of the school of designers who merged affordable housing and modernist architecture and at one point had worked with Catherine Bauer at the U.S. Housing Authority as a technical advisor.[15] Kahn and Stonorov had been architectural partners, and Kahn would be a frequent guest at Stonorov's farm for Sunday lunches. Ideologically, Kahn and Bacon were very similar. However, in their philosophy of the role of a designer trying to turn ideas into reality, they were worlds apart.

Bacon tried to get Kahn to build a model that showed a clear design concept, but Kahn was stuck on the minor architectural details. Bacon recalled, "I would say, 'Let's make a model so we really show the earth transparent and show the concept,' [Kahn] would say, 'Oh, that's lovely, but I would like to put a tower over here and a curving staircase over here and a little grove of trees over here'."[16] There was another philosophical difference: Bacon was trying to influence decision makers, thinking politically about what it would take to get a project built, whereas Kahn was focused solely on the aesthetics of design. Bacon explained, "because of [Kahn's] very brilliant and individual creativity, Lou was unaware of the difficulties of the process and of the discipline that it imposed."[17]

Bacon praised Kahn as a "gifted designer" and the "greatest architect in the world."[18] But Kahn's theory was that "If your ideas are right, they—the businessmen and the politicians—will come to you."[19] Bacon, in contrast, believed that it is the planner's role to implement plans—to promote and market the vision. In late 1950, Bacon decided to terminate his working relationship with Kahn, and, in December, Kahn left the country to study at the American Academy in Rome. Their relationship seems to have remained cordial, however, and Kahn wrote to another member of the Triangle Committee encouraging the committee to continue its work with Bacon.[20] Over the coming years, the Planning Commission continued to give Kahn consulting jobs to design redevelopment projects, and Bacon would heap praise on Kahn's work.[21] Yet, on the matter of the Chinese Wall, they would not work together again.

The difference in philosophy between the two men provides insight into Bacon's view of the planner as implementer. Bacon believed that, to get things built, designers needed to ensure that people could see new ideas as a tangible extension of the world around them. In contrast, Kahn sought to introduce a new paradigm for the American city that was visionary but produced in isolation. For example, in 1941, Kahn created several drawings, published in the *Bulletin*, showing Philadelphia completely erased and rebuilt from the ground up, with superblocks and high-rise towers.[22] The two men simply had different goals and worldviews, so they parted ways.

Bacon needed to find a partner with the right connections and the ability to work with corporate clients. He passed over Stonorov and other colleagues and soon encountered the work of an architect named Vincent G. Kling, who appeared to be a strong prospect for the job. Bacon and Kling met at a dinner function hosted by the local chapter of the American Institute of Architects, where a model of Kling's design for Lankenau Hospital was on display. Bacon was impressed with Kling's design sense and his skill as a model maker.[23] However, Kling also had other, perhaps more important, qualities, namely, that he was close with several members of the Pennsylvania Railroad's board of directors and was already doing some architectural work for the railroad.

Kling was attractive and charming, with an intense smile. He was well spoken and connected within Philadelphia's corporate culture. If the challenge was to sell an idea to the Pennsylvania Railroad, Kling was a clearly superior choice over Kahn. But, in the process, Bacon had created another problem: the members of the AIA Triangle Committee resented the fact that Bacon had essentially circumvented the committee to work with Kling independently.[24] They saw this move as an "expression of lack of confidence in the committee," which, of course, it was. This move essentially marked the end of Bacon's dealings with the AIA committee, as he transitioned the visioning around the future of the Chinese Wall site to his own office—for

Figure 12. Vincent G. Kling and Bacon, taken February 20, 1959, in a
sunken garden area, part of the Penn Center development. Open-air,
below-grade areas were a primary component of the Bacon-Kling plan for
Penn Center. Photo by Lawrence Williams. Courtesy of the Edmund N.
Bacon Collection, The Architectural Archives, University of Pennsylvania.

the time being, straddling a hazy position as to whether he was promoting
the vision through the Planning Commission or simply working independently with Kling, on the side.

Kling and Bacon worked for months designing several models showing
three office buildings replacing the eastern blocks of the Chinese Wall. The
office buildings were thin rectangles, aligned north-south, with an open-
air, sunken concourse running below them, passing under the buildings
and streets. The concourse was to be a pedestrian-only esplanade, lined
with shops and direct connections to the below-grade Suburban Station
train concourse. It was similar to the model Kahn created, except a more
manageable three blocks long (instead of Kahn's eleven blocks). Bacon later
claimed that the concept of the north-south-oriented towers with the

concourse passing underneath was inspired by forms and system of movement he had seen at Forbidden City in Beijing during his time in China.[25]

In the Bacon-Kling scheme, pedestrians would walk along the concourse to the east. After passing under the last of the three buildings, they
would emerge into the final sunken concourse, faced with a stunning view
of City Hall rising up ahead. Surely, it was a dramatic architectural concept.
Whether the railroad's executives would buy into it was another matter.
With their models prepared, Kling and Bacon started aggressively to seek
out their contacts in positions of power with the railroad, to try to get
their concept in front of James Symes, the executive vice president and
heir apparent to aging President Walter S. Franklin. It was an unorthodox
situation: a planning director and architect voluntarily designing a concept
to develop a corporation's private real estate—and lobbying that corporation to adopt their view. However, this was the process that Bacon believed
was needed to implement complex plans designed for private property.

Bacon and Kling were successful in getting an audience with Symes,
and, to their relief, Symes was impressed with the plan.[26] At this point, with
the railroad's initial buy-in, Bacon began involving Planning Commission
staff in fleshing out the design concepts. It was still unorthodox for the
Planning Commission to be planning for private property, but with the
railroad's buy-in it became more legitimate, and Bacon felt comfortable
dedicating city resources to the project. He also presented the models to
the local chapter of the AIA, and, despite any lingering hard feelings from
Bacon's prior break with the Triangle Committee, the AIA issued a citation
in October 1951 calling the Bacon-Kling design an "inspiring plan."[27]

Soon Bacon learned that there was another important player at the
table. Apparently, Symes had been quietly working with New York real-
estate broker Robert Dowling, the prominent promoter of Pittsburgh's
Golden Triangle and New York City's Stuyvesant Town and Peter Cooper
Village.[28] Bacon and Kling recognized that they would need Dowling's support as well as Symes's. They secured a meeting with Dowling, and, in a
January 1952 memo, Bacon noted, "Mr. Dowling stated that his office is
proceeding with plans for the development of the Pennsylvania Railroad
property. . . . He is enthusiastic about the possibilities and has adopted the
basic elements of our proposal, including the pedestrian esplanade."[29]

Bacon and Kling could not have approached Symes and Dowling at a
better time. On February 6, 1952, the railroad applied to the Public Utilities
Commission to demolish Broad Street Station and the Chinese Wall, and,

by mid-February it was ready for a major announcement. Here Bacon scored another victory. He was able to convince Symes to announce the news at a grand luncheon to be hosted by the Citizens' Council on City Planning. Even more significantly, Symes agreed to allow Bacon to follow up his announcement with a presentation of the Bacon-Kling plan as a vision for what could replace the Chinese Wall. This was Bacon's chance to unveil his vision to a large crowd of prominent Philadelphians.

Bacon worked with the Citizens' Council and the railroad to send out 5,000 invitations. The luncheon was held on February 21, 1952, in the Grand Ballroom of the Bellevue Stratford hotel. It was attended by 950 people, and many more were turned away at the door. Walter Phillips welcomed the crowd. Then came the news everyone had spent a quarter of a century waiting for: James Symes took the podium and announced, "effective Sunday, April 27th this year, and I repeat (in case you did not hear it), effective Sunday, April 27th this year, all passenger train service, as well as Pennsylvania Greyhound bus service, will be removed from old Broad Street Station. It will then be possible to begin razing that famous old landmark."[30]

Symes continued, "What is the next step? No one really knows the answer—but we do know it will make available for downtown city development—twenty-two acres of property. . . . The City Planning Commission has been giving a lot of thought to this very important subject, and they are here to tell you about it."[31] With that, Symes turned the dais over to Bacon. Before presenting any images, Bacon explained, "[These plans] represent a conception of a way of rebuilding . . . the city core expressive of the dignity of Philadelphia as the center of a growing metropolitan region."[32] Images of the Bacon-Kling models shone on a screen, and Bacon carefully described each component of the design. He proposed that "a great shopping concourse be built, one level below the streets and passing under them, open to the sky, with shaded walks adjacent, with gardens, trees, and fountains, penetrating through the center of the entire tract, connecting with the subway concourse and flowing directly into the Suburban Station waiting room under Pennsylvania Boulevard."[33]

As Bacon concluded his speech, the lights went on and a large model was brought into the center room for the audience to inspect.[34] After the luncheon, the model was put on display in Wanamaker's department store, and Bacon released an official City Planning Commission document describing the project. Bacon also realized that, to have a tangible identity, the project needed a name. He gave it one: Penn Center. The response to the luncheon announcement was generally positive, and it looked as if Bacon was becoming effective at shaping the discussion about the future of the railroad's land. Following the announcement, Bacon received a letter from Louis Kahn praising the Penn Center plans. Kahn wrote to Bacon, "you have earned the distinction of being the Architect Planner. Few of us can really claim that title."[35]

Competing Plans

Broad Street Station closed on April 27, 1952, and the Philadelphia Orchestra played as the last train slowly pulled out of the station shed.[36] Despite the imposing nature of the Chinese Wall from the street, the ornate station was emblematic of the powerful Pennsylvania Railroad's heyday and held a nostalgic place in the heart of Philadelphians. The railroad soon began demolition, despite the fact that the future of its property was still unclear. At the same time that excitement was building about the Chinese Wall coming down, Symes and the railroad executives were under pressure to redevelop the site quickly. To Bacon's dismay, the railroad's chairman, Martin W. Clement, strongly favored piecemeal sale of the Chinese Wall site, to make an easy profit.[37] Symes, however, was more visionary, seeing the benefits of Bacon's idea of having the railroad put its brand on a landmark civic space, akin to Rockefeller Center, in New York (which would continually be the major precedent for Penn Center).

It appeared that the most likely developer of this new complex was Mutual Assurance Company of New York, a firm that had worked with Robert Dowling on past projects.[38] However, Philadelphia's prominent real estate broker Frank Binswanger was skeptical of the site's value and advised Mutual against investing. Mutual soon announced that it was passing on the opportunity.[39] Despite sitting in the center of America's third largest city, the Chinese Wall site was viewed as such an eyesore and the area around it as so low-grade that only a handful of investors could see any real prospects for the site.

By June 1952, with Mutual out of the running, three developers appeared interested in the project. The first was John Galbreath, the real estate giant who built Fairless Hills for U.S. Steel and the Mellon-U.S. Steel Building in Pittsburgh.[40] Another interested developer was Philadelphia's Albert M. Greenfield, known as "Philadelphia's biggest and richest real estate man."[41] Greenfield put together a team of investors to make an offer to buy the site for $50 million.[42] The third potential developer was Philadel-phian Matthew McCloskey in a partnership with local banker Maurice Massey. Dowling had approached McCloskey with an innovative idea of having the developers lease (rather than buy) the site from the railroad, to reduce everyone's risk.[43]

The railroad did not make a decision immediately, and Bacon and oth-ers remained concerned that it would sell off the parcels piecemeal after all. Mayor Clark told the media that "if there were any probability of [the Chinese Wall site] not being developed on an acceptable plan, I would recommend exercise of the Redevelopment Authority's power of condem-nation."[44] However, it was unclear whether the city could actually afford the railroad's land, thus making eminent domain practically infeasible. Meanwhile, the mayor asked Bacon to prepare a formal redevelopment plan for the Chinese Wall land and surrounding area.[45]

Following the public release of the Planning Commission's designs, a stream of letters from concerned citizens and civic groups flowed into Bacon's office. Most contentious was the proposed concept of removing City Hall, leaving just its tower.[46] Bacon was far from the first to call for doing this. In 1924, prominent architect Paul Cret believed City Hall was ugly and imposing, and proposed demolishing the building, inspiring a group of influential Philadelphians to form an organization dedicated to getting City Hall torn down.[47] Throughout the following decades, others would criticize City Hall for its architecture and the way it consumed the city's prime public square. The idea of tearing down City Hall also was suggested by an independent 1948 consultant study, reporting that "The City Hall is obsolete as an office building and has nothing, esthetically or otherwise to recommend it for perpetuation as a monument."[48] City Hall was a grand Second Empire-style building that could not have been more different from the modernist architecture popular in the 1950s.

Another controversial element of the plan was a proposed new munici-pal building on Reyburn Plaza, a downtown park to the north of City Hall. Bacon soon realized that these secondary concepts could overshadow his greater purpose of convincing the railroad to develop the area as a cohesive project. In order to do damage control, the Planning Commission sent out a press release stating, "the demolition of parts of City Hall and the erection of a new municipal building on Reyburn Plaza are not integral parts of the plan."[49] Bacon also stressed the conceptual nature of this preliminary plan, intended as the first step toward producing a more detailed plan, based on public feedback. In June, Bacon called a public hearing to discuss the Penn Center plan and was glad to see that the City Hall issue was barely mentioned.[50] Other issues came up, however, regarding road widening, parking, and various other components.

Based on all this feedback, in August 1952, the City Planning Commission released the Penn Center Redevelopment Area Plan—the official document needed for the city to engage in a redevelopment project.[51] Although the Chinese Wall site was private property, the areas surrounding it were within the jurisdiction of the city to redevelop itself. In a letter conveying the plan to Mayor Clark, Edward Hopkinson, Jr., said, "We believe that the plan, developed to encourage private enterprise to construct the projects, provides sufficient flexibility for a variety of possible developments."[52] In other words, Hopkinson highlighted the fact that this was the city making recommendations to a private corporation for what to do with its property—something that was not customary and that demonstrated Bacon's desire to experiment with the relationship of the public-private partnership.

The plan still showed City Hall removed, but included politically sensitive language stressing that the city should engage a study weighing the costs and benefits of demolishing versus restoring City Hall.[53] The plan showed a grand pedestrian concourse, a sunken Vine Street expressway, and four new surface transit lines. It also included changes in zoning and land use, roads added and removed, commercial floor area ratios, and a maximum height of 340 feet for new buildings.[54] This was perhaps the first reference made in a Planning Commission document to the notion of a height limit, maintaining City Hall tower as the tallest feature in the skyline. This concept of a height limit would become one that Bacon embraced and promoted throughout the rest of his career.

By the end of 1952, Bacon felt that he was really making progress in pushing the idea of Penn Center and in convincing the railroad to develop the site as a single, cohesive project. However, the railroad was now paying taxes on the property after the demolition of the Chinese Wall started, and the financial clock was ticking. Dowling must have had some serious doubts as to whether he could assemble enough investors and tenants to develop the site and probably also as to whether Bacon's scheme was actually a roadblock to his efforts to stimulate interest in the project. What Bacon did not realize was that Dowling was simultaneously developing his own

Figure 13. Photo from a March 6, 1953, article in the *Philadelphia Bulletin* about a new design for Penn Center. Clockwise from bottom left are James Symes, Pennsylvania Railroad executive vice president; Bacon; and real estate broker Robert Dowling. Courtesy of the Edmund N. Bacon Collection, The Architectural Archives, University of Pennsylvania.

complete scheme. On January 29, 1953, Dowling announced his preliminary plans, taking Bacon completely by surprise.[55] The Dowling plan proposed a public plaza, but it was at ground level rather than sunken. There were six office buildings rather than three (to maximize rent revenues), and instead of straddling the plaza, letting in light, as in Bacon's plan, they were shown as enclosing the plaza on all sides, a wall of office towers blocking the view of even City Hall to the east.

It was a functional and money-making concept, but certainly not the grand and iconic civic project Bacon had hoped for. *Architectural Forum* called the plan "much more novel financially than architecturally."[56] However, from Dowling's perspective, this was progress. He soon secured three separate institutions to finance the project, tenants to fill 70 percent of the proposed office space, and some interest from major hotel chains.[57] He touted the fact that he could rent the new development at an impressive $5 per square foot. Disheartened, Bacon held a special meeting of his senior staff on a Sunday afternoon to decide what they could do about the situation.[58] The conclusion was that there was no way to beat Dowling at his own game. He was one of the top men in his field, he was the consultant to the railroad, and it was the railroad's private property. The one positive aspect was that the Dowling plan did think of the project as a cohesive whole, rather than dividing it up into individual, piecemeal parcels. This was a starting point for Bacon to begin trying to pull the Dowling plan back in the direction he wanted to see.

Over the next two months, Bacon reached out to Dowling and Symes to try to convince them to alter the plans. After some back and forth, Dowling agreed to reinsert the below-ground pedestrian concourse but insisted that it needed to be covered with a roof and climate controlled. Bacon felt that the open-air concourse was a critical element, as the intent of the plan was to create a grand, public civic space like Rockefeller Center, which Bacon felt needed an outdoor space, rather than an enclosed shopping area. In order to give some of the feeling of the open-air concourse Bacon envisioned, Dowling agreed to build in a few sunken, open-air garden areas. He also agreed to reduce the density of the project, to provide more open space in the courtyard, and to offset the buildings, so there would be some gaps between them. Many people would have either given up or fought Dowling in an impossible struggle, pitting one ego against another. Bacon, however, chose to compromise, letting Dowling feel that his plan had prevailed.

In March 1953, Dowling presented his new plan at another luncheon of the Citizens' Council on City Planning—showing off a model that was in many ways a merging of his ideas and Bacon's. The new plan proposed five structures, four office buildings and one hotel, with a potential transportation terminal. The design included a public esplanade, one level belowground, and a public concourse aboveground, with garden openings leading down to the esplanade level. Bacon wrote to Mayor Clark about the circumstances, explaining, "In our opinion, this represents remarkable accomplishment by persuasion, rather than by legal controls."[59]

By May 1953, the Chinese Wall was almost gone, leaving a tremendous tract of barren land in its place. To date, there had been very little interest in the railroad's land from Philadelphia developers. The one exception was an offer by Albert M. Greenfield that the railroad turned down out of concern that Greenfield was primarily interested in protecting the interests of his other real estate holdings in the area.[60] However, on May 19, 1953, the Pennsylvania Railroad suddenly announced that it had signed a lease was on two blocks of Penn Center—one with Uris Brothers of New York and a second with Philadelphia media tycoon Walter H. Annenberg. Uris Brothers had a reputation as smart businessmen who did not develop great buildings but who knew how to make a profit.[61] While Uris Brothers was interested in office buildings, Annenberg planned to construct a community center, bus terminal, and parking structures.[62]

For Bacon, the situation looked pretty dim. After all his lobbying the railroad to develop the land as a single project, it looked as if it would be sold off in pieces after all. It was not just Bacon who feared for the fate of Penn Center. The Citizens' Council on City Planning formed a committee to review all development proposals for the site.[63] Together with the local chapter of the AIA, the Citizens' Council called on the railroad to hire a supervising architect.[64] This degree of skepticism from the design community was worrisome for Dowling, who had taken some slack for not including architects or planners in the process of developing Pittsburgh's Golden Triangle.[65] To avoid a repeat public relations issue, in June 1953, the railroad named a three-member Advisory Board of Design, comprised of Bacon, Dowling, and, as chairman, George Howe, one of Philadelphia's most renowned architects and codesigner of the celebrated Philadelphia Savings Fund Society (PSFS) building.[66]

In August, based on urgings from business leader Harry Batten and the Citizens' Council, the mayor appointed a Citizens' Advisory Committee as a public review board for the railroad's plans. The new committee comprised two city councilmen, businessmen, and designers who had some connection to the Penn Center site, including Arthur Kaufmann, Howard C. Petersen, Louis Kahn, Robert B. Mitchell, Councilman Thomas I. Guerin, Councilman-at-large Lewis M. Stevens, and architect C. Clark Zantzinger, Jr.[67] According to Mayor Clark, the committee was to work with all the parties involved in the development of Penn Center, "in their efforts to construct a development of which all citizens can justly be proud."[68]

It was unclear how much influence any of these bodies would have with the railroad and its developers. On September 15, Uris Brothers announced that it would break ground in a matter of months on its first building. The plan would not have a below-ground concourse and was situated over what was supposed to be an open-air area. Bacon and Howe were furious about this turn of events and voted over Dowling to reject the plan. Within days, the railroad announced that the site had been shifted to the west, leaving the eastern side as an open plaza; however, the issue of the below-ground concourse was still unresolved for the time being.[69]

On October 10, 1953, Uris Brothers released the first drawing of its new building, designed by New York architect Emory Roth & Sons. "Three Penn Center" was to be an unremarkable twenty-story slab structure. The architects had cut every corner, saved every cent, and clearly had no interest in developing a great civic project for Philadelphia. The response from the committees was sharply critical. Louis Kahn famously responded in critique, "An architectural student presenting such a plan could expect to be marked 'zero'."[70] Arthur Kaufmann called it "A glass showcase; I don't want to be connected with it."[71] An article in *Architectural Forum* called it "third-rate architecture."[72] However, despite this unanimous criticism, Uris Brothers did not make any changes to the plans.

George Howe was particularly livid about the state of affairs, explaining in a prominent keynote address in New York, "On the shape of this project, I was assured, the Board was to exercise a decisive influence. Needless to say the Board found everything of importance had been decided before its appointment. Its actual function was to make a fait accompli acceptable."[73] Mayor Clark voiced his opinion: "If this building fails to conform to the Penn Center Plan, then I fail to see how we can prevent a continuous and disastrous whittling away of Penn Center."[74] The mayor insisted that Uris Brothers voluntarily present its building to the city Art Commission—the public body with the authority to review buildings in certain geographic areas (the first Penn Center building was not in one of these areas). In what was becoming a power struggle between the mayor and the New York developers, Uris Brothers stalled on sending its plans to the Art Commission before telling the commission that the steel had already been ordered and there was realistically not a single change that could take place.[75]

The potential pitfalls of a public-private partnership where the public-sector's role was mostly advisory were quickly becoming apparent. For all the good will that Symes and Dowling tried to foster, when it came down to actually building the project, the bottom line trumped design or the public good. For his part, Bacon stayed behind the scenes, quietly trying to influence Dowling and the railroad to push for a better design. He was most concerned with the potential loss of the below-ground pedestrian concourse. Bacon believed the concourse was critical for creating an iconic civic space with retail, connected to transit. However, Bacon recalled that Dowling told him, "If we're going to make Uris go two levels underground, we're going to lose them."[76] So far, Bacon had been able to influence the project through a subtle interaction where he would continually massage positive elements back into the plan. However, he seemed to be coming to the end of his ability to affect changes in the designs.

All the while, the Citizens' Advisory Committee was publicly opposed to the plans and was not shy about making its opinions known. Bacon, who believed that subtle negotiations were a better way to influence business-men, became frustrated with the way this committee was functioning and criticized its lack of political savvy. He wrote to Mayor Clark, "The extremely negative reaction of the Committee certainly tended to tear down a great deal of this work and, so far as I can see, will serve no constructive purpose."[77] The committee continued angrily to oppose the project, while the railroad's developers and architects refused to budge, creating a starkly divisive situation.

Breaking Ground

On November 24, 1953, construction began on the first Penn Center build-ing—Three Penn Center. An assemblage of city officials, railroad execu-tives, prominent guests, and the media gathered for a groundbreaking ceremony. In a bizarre symbol of history meeting modernity, five-year-old Miriam Penn-Gaskel Hall, the youngest descendant of William Penn, waved a Geiger counter like a magic wand "setting off" an "atomic blast," signifying the dramatic groundbreaking of the future.[78] It was a big day for Philadelphia, and the eyes of the nation were on this experimental project. Penn Center would be one of the largest redevelopment projects in any urban downtown and an example of public-private partnership on a scale practically unparalleled in America.

Even after the groundbreaking had taken place, however, the struggles around the development plan had not been resolved. Mayor Clark called a meeting of the railroad, Uris Brothers, the Board of Design, and the Citizens' Advisory Committee, where the mayor admonished Uris Brothers and Dow-ling and demanded that they adhere to the city's basic plan for Penn Center that included the below-ground pedestrian concourse. However, Uris Broth-ers gave no indication that the next building would be any different.[79] It was unclear whether there was much even the mayor could do. Even if he favored taking the land through eminent domain, it might not have been financially feasible for the city—a fact that Uris Brothers surely knew.

Mayor Clark suggested that Bacon and Robert B. Mitchell—the Planning Commission's former director, now serving as chairman of the Urban Traffic and Transportation Board—meet with the railroad to make sure everyone was in agreement about the key elements of the Penn Center plan. Through these discussions, the railroad's representatives agreed to reintroduce one of the major components of the Bacon plan: the below-ground pedestrian concourse.[80] While Uris Brothers might not have been willing to build the concourse, the railroad could do so itself, with its own resources. In late 1953, the railroad contracted with Los Angeles-based retail design firm Welton Becket and Associates to create a plan for developing the below-ground concourse with over a hundred retail shops.[81] The railroad had saved one of the core elements of Bacon's Penn Center plan—providing the opportunity to build an innovative shopping complex, connected to mass transit.[82] However, more challenges were to come for the concourse.

The next structure to rise in Penn Center was to be the transportation building, Six Penn Center. By now the project's original developer, Walter Annenberg, had pulled out, and Philadelphian Matthew McCloskey's Tower Development Corporation took over the project, assisted by a $500,000 investment by the city to cover the expenses of moving underground utilities.[83] This building led Bacon into a power struggle with other city officials over the design of underground streets for freight deliveries. As designed, they would have interfered with the below-ground pedestrian concourse.[84] Bacon was drawn into a heated back-and-forth discussion with Streets Commissioner Henry Harral and Fred Thorpe of the Board of Surveyors, neither of whom thought much of Bacon's concourse.[85] Livid about the state of affairs, Bacon wrote to Mayor Clark, "It would be unfortunate that the City itself would be the major influence in destroying this important concept [the pedestrian concourse]."[86] Ultimately, the final ruling relied on the city's Law Department. Bacon called upon City Solicitor Abraham Freedman, who was a friend from their City Policy Committee days, and the Law Department ruled in favor of Bacon's position. Bacon cheered to the mayor, "Penn Center will not be destroyed after all."[87]

This episode was another example of the way that Walter Phillips's City Policy Committee, years earlier, had set the groundwork for a new generation of urban leaders to work together. Bacon might not have prevailed without help from Freedman—who was also instrumental in shaping the role of the Planning Commission in the Home Rule Charter, based on input from Bacon. This special relationship between Bacon and a number of key individuals in government and business was helpful in Bacon's ability to work effectively within the city bureaucracy. Bacon later acknowledged, "that all goes back to Walter Phillips, and the extraordinary quality of friendship."[88]

Next Bacon turned his attention to the above-ground esplanade. It was imperative for Bacon to develop a consistent theme and treatment, rather than letting each building's esplanade be designed independently. Bacon felt he had made real progress when the railroad's Paul Shantz agreed to go to New York with him and Vincent Kling to look at buildings and plazas— what Bacon called a "purely esthetic mission."[89] After this trip, Kling designed a curving promenade that George Howe praised.[90] However, Robert Dowling came out with a design for a traditional, linear plaza, in order to maximize building floor space. Bacon criticized this plan as "cold and inhuman."[91] The whole nature of Penn Center's development was becoming haphazard and piecemeal.

Bacon promoted the idea raised by several citizens and eventually embraced by the railroad, of building an outdoor ice-skating rink (continuing the trend of emulating aspects of Rockefeller Center).[92] He also made contact with the prominent sculptor Alexander Calder, and the railroad began negotiations with Calder to commission some pieces of artwork for Penn Center.[93] In April 1955, George Howe died, a giant in his field and a major voice in the design of Penn Center. The Board of Design remained dormant for almost a year without a chairman until the railroad finally appointed Vincent Kling to take Howe's place.[94]

Meanwhile, construction continued on the Uris building, the McCloskey transportation building, and a Sheraton hotel. In fall 1956, Uris Brothers released plans for their second building, Two Penn Center. It was just as unsightly as the first building that was now rising. By now, Bacon, Kling, and Dowling understood that Uris Brothers was stubbornly refusing to adopt different architecture unless forced to do it. The Board of Design approved the Uris plans but with a list of recommended changes to make the structure slightly more attractive.[95] This second building fell within the geographic purview of the Art Commission—close enough to the Benjamin Franklin Parkway, over which the Art Commission had legislated oversight.

The Planning Commission sent Uris Brothers a formal letter informing them of this required layer of review.[96]

The Art Commission was critical of the design and "questioned the desirability of repeating the architecture of Three Penn Center."[97] However, despite the requirement of gaining Art Commission approval before construction could commence, Uris Brothers tried the same tactic as before, arguing that the steel had already been ordered and there was nothing that could be changed. The Art Commission members were enraged, reminding those present of a past meeting where Uris Brothers and the railroad agreed that the Art Commission would have access to the designs before the steel was ordered. The Art Commission voted to defer the project for the time being.[98] Ultimately, however, the commission's members decided that their opposition was futile, eventually signing off on the project.

By the end of 1956, the hotel and the transportation center were almost finished.[99] The railroad agreed to develop a sunken, garden subway entrance at Fifteenth Street, right at the front of Penn Center. To complement this feature, the Department of Public Property requested money from the city's capital budget to remodel the Fifteenth Street subway station area.[100] Looking at ways to landscape the above-ground esplanade, Bacon reached out to the presidents of the major museums and found support for lending works of sculpture to adorn the area.[101] At the same time, the railroad was dedicating space for the sunken, open-air ice-skating rink nearby.

The heart of Philadelphia was abuzz with development activity, and Penn Center became known nationally as a major effort of a city working to revive its core. Penn Center was emerging entirely differently from the way Bacon had hoped; however, it was emerging nonetheless, and other cities were taking notice. According to one news story on Penn Center, "Philadelphia, for the first time since William Penn . . . finds itself a leader of urban planning in America."[102]

Half-Finished Dreams

Into the 1960s, conflicts continued among the stakeholders in Penn Center. Due to outstanding legal negotiations, Bacon learned that the contractors building Penn Center were "working at only about 35 percent efficiency on this job."[103] Bacon was not the only one who felt that the city and the railroad had gotten the run around by Uris Brothers. One of the main railroad executives dealing with Penn Center called their partnership with Uris Brothers a "phony deal."[104] More people began to take note of the unsightly architecture and the empty plazas that were emerging. One news article referred to Penn Center as "an uninspired compromise with real estate interests."[105] Bacon shared concerns about the public spaces, which he called "pretty miserable" in one letter.[106] He worked with a landscape architect to spruce up the plazas, and the Philadelphia Museum of Art installed some public art in the lower-level garden areas at Penn Center.[107] However, it would take more than some sculpture to shift public opinion, and by the end of 1959, many believed that Penn Center was a dismal failure.

Attempting to soothe those who protested, Bacon wrote, "Judging Penn Center now is like judging a room without its furniture or a park without its trees."[108] He also made excuses for the railroad. Comparing Penn Center to Rockefeller Center and Mellon Square in Pittsburgh, he wrote, "Each of these projects was made to glorify a great family name; each was done by a developer of unlimited resources. The Pennsylvania Railroad is not a family. It is a group of stockholders expecting dividends. And it certainly does not possess unlimited means."

It may seem curious that Bacon so vehemently defended Penn Center. It would have been simple to blame its owner, the Pennsylvania Railroad, its developer, and their architects. He could have easily disabused himself of the project. But this was not Bacon's style. Bacon was deeply committed to defending Philadelphia's redevelopment program until enough time had passed to assess it properly. Bacon saw Penn Center not as a stand-alone project, but rather as a crucial component to an overall vision for the rejuvenation of downtown Philadelphia.[109] To convince his planning colleagues and the national media of Philadelphia's bright future, Bacon could not afford a single failure. His reputation and the city's ability to compete for funding relied on every piece of the puzzle being a victory.

When Mayor Richardson Dilworth came into office, he replaced Edward Hopkinson, Jr., with Albert M. Greenfield as chairman of the City Planning Commission. Greenfield was a powerful and politically connected individual. However, he was seen by some as a poor choice, due to Greenfield's potentially conflicting interests as one of the city's largest real estate owners. An article in *Architectural Forum* said of Greenfield, "What Mayor Dilworth had in mind when he appointed Greenfield, other than paying a debt of political loyalty, is obscure."[110] However, Greenfield exceeded everyone's expectations, according to the *Architectural Forum* article, "playing the unpaid job perfectly straight."[111] In 1958, Greenfield resigned as chairman, and Mayor Dilworth promoted Dean G. Holmes Perkins of the University of Pennsylvania, who was currently vice chairman of the Commission.

Perkins was a prominent figure during this period, famous for remaking the University of Pennsylvania's design program as the renowned "Philadelphia School," hiring some of the most progressive practitioners in the fields of architecture, landscape architecture, and planning. Bacon taught two courses at Penn, one under Perkins's School of Fine Arts and one in the Wharton School of Business.[112]

With Perkins—an academic with an eye for design, rather than a real estate man—at the helm, Bacon sought to resolve a number of other issues facing the area around Penn Center and City Hall. Foremost was the fate of the site formerly occupied by Broad Street Station—a stand-alone block to the east of Penn Center, surrounded by city streets. By the time Dilworth became mayor, it was still unclear whether the railroad would develop the site, the city would buy it, or the railroad would sell it to a private developer who would probably construct an office building. In February 1958, the Planning Commission voted to support the city's purchasing the site, and Bacon set his staff to create plans for transforming the parcel into a new city park.[113] In July 1959, Bacon and the Planning Commission inserted an allocation of $2.5 million for the purchase of the station site into the capital program.[114]

However it was not at all a done deal, needing the support of City Council and the mayor. Bacon appealed to Mayor Dilworth to back the city's purchase, despite the high price tag. Here was an example of Bacon's changing his tune on an issue. In 1953, he wrote to Mayor Clark, "I feel very strongly that it would be a mistake to leave the Old Broad Street Station site an open park."[115] However, by 1959, he had reversed his position. In one report to Dilworth, Bacon wrote, arguing for a public park, "The construction of an office building here would . . . be a blow to the whole City Renewal Program."[116] In 1961, Dilworth publicly made a commitment to support the city's purchase of the site, a decision that Bacon remarked to Dilworth "established the idea that this City is going to be developed on a noble scale."[117] The land was planned to be a major public park, dubbed West Plaza and later renamed Dilworth Plaza.

Another element of Penn Center that excited Bacon was the prospect of a new open-air subway entrance at Fifteenth and Market Streets. A remnant of his idea of an exposed concourse, the subway entrance was to be a sunken garden—open to the sky. Bacon exclaimed, "This will be a major step toward making mass transportation more attractive, since it will be the only subway in the world with a garden in it."[118] The theme of connecting subways integrally with outdoor garden spaces is one that Bacon would continue to promote in other projects.

In the early 1960s, Bacon was working with Vincent Kling on designing a plaza at the eastern terminus of the Benjamin Franklin Parkway—covering an underground parking garage. This was a particularly exciting project for Bacon since he had included a park at this location in his thesis at Cornell University. In an act that demonstrated the power of Philadelphia's old-fashioned establishment elite, Public Property Commissioner Fred Corleto announced that the plans for the plaza would be delayed until Jacques Gréber, the famous French landscape architect and planner hired to design the parkway in 1917, could review them. Gréber indeed came to Philadelphia on March 1, 1962.[119] With some minor alterations, Gréber approved the plans, just two months before his death.[120] This plaza would eventually be named John F. Kennedy Plaza and later dubbed "LOVE Park," after the Robert Indiana sculpture that was positioned on its southeastern corner in 1976.

Along with Penn Center, Bacon was also concerned with private developments nearby. Since early on, Penn Center had been associated with the so-called Triangle Area, along the western side of the Benjamin Franklin Parkway. Bacon believed the North Triangle area (the first parcel offered to developers) was critical for completing the composition of the Parkway.[121] In June 1954, the Redevelopment Authority awarded a contract for the north Triangle development to the newly formed partnership of Madway-Weinberg. Due to regulations by the Federal Housing Administration (FHA), this complex project needed some creative ideas for its design and financing.[122] By 1956, however, the financing issues were resolved and Park Towne Place was well underway. In 1960, Bacon encouraged the mayor to support additional development along the Schuylkill River as a "continuous band of apartment houses."[123]

Related to the new construction around Penn Center, Bacon began focusing on the new buildings' impact on the skyline. Bacon saw the dominance of City Hall tower in the skyline as a critical element to the city's historical continuity.[124] He believed that, with City Hall as the tallest building, Philadelphians would always be reminded that its location was planned by William Penn hundreds of years earlier as the physical center of the city. He believed this feature, that the skyline had a connection to the city's original plan, was important and should be respected through a height limit. Bacon created an unwritten "gentleman's agreement" that no building would rise above the statue of William Penn atop City Hall. Developers would periodically meet with Bacon and propose a building taller than City Hall tower. They would query whether the height limit was legally mandated, to which Bacon would respond, "It's only a gentleman's agreement. The question is, are you a gentleman?"[125]

Bacon knew that this tact would only last so long before a developer came along who was not a gentleman. In early 1963, a developer proposed a sixty-story building at Twenty-Third Street. Bacon wrote that this project "for the first time in the history of Philadelphia, would violate the gentlemen's agreement that William Penn will not be topped by private construction."[126] In response, the Planning Commission approved a height limit ordinance and sent it to Mayor James H. J. Tate, who submitted it to City Council for its deliberation.[127] After the proposal went to the council, the issue became much more contentious. Developers who previously did not pay much attention to the matter suddenly saw the threat and came out with strong opposition to the official height limit. Bacon related to the mayor, "The reactions to this have been very mixed, some for it and some violently opposed to it. The Council has not yet held a hearing on the bill, and I have no idea how it will work out."[128] In the end, the bill died in City Council, and Bacon continued trying to enforce the height limit through persuasion.

In late 1964, another developer proposed a tower at Fifteenth and Market Streets that would rise higher than City Hall, and Bacon again appealed to the mayor.[129] In this case, Bacon was at odds with his Planning Commission, which backed the proposed tower. The issue continued for over a year, until eventually the developers agreed to a shorter building. Bacon lauded the new plans, designed by Vincent Kling for two office towers.[130] However, similar struggles would continue in the coming years and decades.

As would frequently happen throughout his career, Bacon's participation in Penn Center declined as the project progressed. In 1961, Mayor Dilworth saw that there was a void in the city's relationship with major commercial developers and promoted William Rafsky from housing coordinator to a new post of development coordinator, to work with various city departments and be the go-between with the city and developers on all real-estate projects.[131] Dilworth hoped that this position could "provide for the private developer a clear-cut line of communication, whereby his questions and problems can be handled without being referred from office to office." The position of development coordinator made sense, but, for Bacon, it put a level of bureaucracy between himself and the mayor, further reducing his official ability to promote his agenda, and creating another individual whom he would need to persuade to implement his planning ideas.

Penn Center was a turning point for Bacon's career. Despite his limited impact on the project's form, his ability to connect himself to the railroad and become a recognized participant in the process of Penn Center's planning greatly elevated his local and national profile. Even if Penn Center did not turn out the way Bacon had hoped, it gave him newfound recognition and fame that would allow him to play a more prominent role in future downtown projects. It was one of the major projects that would lead to his emerging national fame in the 1960s, ultimately landing him on the cover of *Time* magazine in 1964.

However, Penn Center was not the great success Bacon had hoped for. It demonstrated the weak position of city government in dealing with private developers and the business community during the urban renewal era.[132] Mayor Clark commented at one point that Penn Center represented "the best efforts that the free enterprise system can make to combine the acquisitive instinct and the public good."[133] In the end, the city lacked any real tools for enforcing the public good. It was exactly this weakness of the public sector that led Bacon to believe that implementing planning required a subtle but powerful method for bringing disparate parties into agreement and for convincing the private sector to embrace goals that were in the public's best interest. Even then, however, the quality of the outcome relied on the degree to which private-sector actors bought into the vision and carried it forward.

Bacon emerged from the struggles of Penn Center more convinced than ever that the planner's role is not just to put ideas to paper but to promote them actively to the decision makers who would be responsible for their realization. With Penn Center, Bacon tested several strategies. He selected the well-connected Vincent Kling to gain entrée to the railroad. He was able to share the dais with the railroad at the announcement that the Chinese Wall was coming down. He put a model of his scheme in a prominent downtown location, where it would attract the attention of the media. He continued his involvement by having the Planning Commission certify the larger environs as a redevelopment area. All these techniques were targeted at enlisting support for his vision and positioning himself to have some ongoing influence over the project. It was an unorthodox role for a planning director, subtly steering the course of a private corporation's real estate development.

While, in Bacon's mind, many of his concepts had fallen by the wayside, Penn Center did lay the foundation for the new downtown business district along Market Street, west of City Hall, which would emerge over the next half century. Additionally, with its focus on integrating retail and office space with the underground train station, Penn Center was a progressive, transit-oriented concept for the 1950s. Most importantly, at a time when Philadelphia was trying to assert its prominence among U.S. cities, Penn Center seemed like a stunning example of a major American city coming into the modern age. The way that the city had interacted with the railroad and the private developers was arguably unprecedented at that scale and laid the groundwork for other cities to embark on similar public-private endeavors.

In the end, Bacon's approach led to a product that was necessarily a conglomeration of ideas. One article on Penn Center by James Reichley, published by *Harper's* in 1957, called Penn Center "a case history in healthy compromise."[134] Reichley explained, "You cannot put a label on the single genius who brought Penn Center to fruition; there is no such person. There is not even a group of men who knowingly worked together in dedication to the common cause."[135] Reichley noted that one might have come away believing "the buildings and the plaza have been created by chance, or by forces mysterious beyond the knowledge of men."[136] Of all the people involved in Penn Center, perhaps Bacon was the only one truly aware of the subtle nature of the situation and the forces that could influence it.

Bacon would have a similar role within the complex web of public-private partnerships in the planning of Society Hill—the restoration and reinvestment in one of Philadelphia's oldest neighborhoods on the eastern end of Center City—and in Market East, rebuilding a downtown shopping district. Both projects would perhaps be even more complex than Penn Center in terms of the numerous players, relationships, and components needed to be coordinated for the projects to come to fruition.

Chapter 5

REINVESTING DOWNTOWN

Penn Center was just one component of Philadelphia's downtown, and in Bacon's mind he saw projects not as separate entities but as pieces of the same puzzle of an overall approach to reviving Center City. Other important pieces included Society Hill and Market East. Society Hill was one of Philadelphia's oldest neighborhoods, fallen on hard times. Bacon believed this area could be revived, its historic houses restored, and middle-class residents lured back from the suburbs. Market East was the name given to a major redevelopment project conceived to help an important downtown commercial corridor compete with suburban shopping malls. These projects, though very different, were physically close to each other and viewed by the business community as inherently connected—focusing on competing with the suburbs for residents and shoppers—creating a new, strong downtown neighborhood with the nearby shopping amenities needed to make it thrive.

As with Penn Center, Society Hill and Market East would require significant public-private partnerships, but they would be more complex than Penn Center in terms of structuring ownership, financing, and the roles and responsibilities of public, quasi-public, and private stakeholders. Using experimental real estate structures, these projects would test the boundaries of federal funding and the viability of public involvement to attract private investment. A common thread in these projects was Bacon's role as promoter of risky ideas, before others thought they were feasible.

Without Bacon, it is unlikely that Society Hill and Market East would have come to fruition. They are powerful examples of his savvy as a planner-implementer, promoting ideas and seeing them through the proper venues to become realized. Both projects were controversial, but both also left an indelible mark on Center City Philadelphia and became signature pieces of the city's planning program and Bacon's legacy. Yet, in both projects, he lost control at a certain point, becoming increasingly powerless to alter the implementation process as it evolved, and the final results deviated from his initial vision.

Historic Preservation as Urban Renewal: Society Hill

Prior to becoming planning director, Bacon had particular interest in the oldest section of Philadelphia, a neighborhood on the southeastern edge of Center City that had fallen on hard times. The neighborhood was initially settled by the Free Society of Traders, a Quaker corporation that purchased land from William Penn in the seventeenth century. By the 1940s, the neighborhood was comprised mostly of eastern European immigrants, with a smaller population of African Americans. Many of the old homes still had their historic Flemish-bond brick, double-hung windows, and federal pediments. Many others, however, had been torn down or altered. Some had boarded-up windows, and historic walls were replaced with glass blocks or aluminum siding, covering the colonial brick. By the late 1940s, these two-hundred-year-old homes sold for just a few hundred dollars, and the area became known as the "Bloody Fifth Ward," because of its reputation as a violent slum.[1] Obviously, this name would not work if Bacon were to sell a new vision for the area, so, starting in 1950, he would refer to the neighborhood by its historic moniker: Society Hill (after the Free *Society* of Traders that settled it and the *hill* on which the neighborhood was built).

Before historic preservation became an accepted strategy for neighborhood stabilization, Bacon believed that Philadelphia needed to find a way to preserve Society Hill's colonial-period buildings. His interest in preserving the neighborhood goes back to at least 1946. In a conference on planning for the central waterfront where Bacon, Robert Mitchell, Raymond Leonard, and others were in attendance, he presented his early vision for Society Hill.[2] In 1947, he gave physical form to this concept in the Center City model at the Better Philadelphia Exhibition, where he installed a series of garden paths weaving through the Society Hill area and showed the preservation of the small-scale, historic homes. He also showed several contemporary slab apartment buildings, merging the old and the new.

As with all his concepts, Bacon needed to find ways to bring others on board with his vision. One important selling point would be Society Hill's proximity to the new Independence Mall and Independence National Historical Park, emerging just to the northwest. The genesis of Independence Mall came in the late 1920s and early 1930s, thanks to Judge Edwin O. Lewis and State Representative Isidor Ostroff, two powerful individuals who felt that Independence Hall—site of the signing of the Declaration of Independence and the U.S. Constitution—deserved a more respectful setting, one that would protect the historic structures from fire hazard. In 1937, architect Roy Larson drew a "Plan for Redevelopment of Historic Area," showing a three-block park-like mall on the north side of Independence Hall and a two-block mall to the east.[3]

In May 1942, Lewis and Ostroff formed a group called the Committee for the Conservation of Historic Sites in Old Philadelphia, soon to be renamed the Independence Hall Association, which would become the major lobbying organization for building these parks.[4] In response to this lobbying, the federal government in 1945 created the National Shrines Commission to make recommendations for the eastern, federal section of the park.[5] Albert M. Greenfield was named the Commission chairman, and Judge Lewis was a member. Lewis also interested Pennsylvania governor Edward Martin in the northern mall, who assigned the state secretary of highways to start negotiations with city officials to work out a plan for land acquisition, pledging $4 million in state money.[6] In June 1948, Congress approved the Shrines Commission recommendations to create Independence National Historical Park, signed into law by President Truman, allocating $4 million in federal funds for acquisition of the eastern mall.[7]

When Bacon became city planning director in 1949, both the north Independence Mall and the east Independence National Historical Park were largely planned and funded, with support of U.S. Congress, Pennsylvania's governor, and influential citizens like Judge Lewis who had been working toward this goal for about two decades. In 1951, the Philadelphia Board of Surveyors officially added the three-block north mall to the city plan, and work began.[8] The City Planning Commission was the local agency charted with working with the state agencies to plan the mall area. Thus, Bacon had some influence but was overall a minor participant in the mall's design and implementation. The Planning Commission engaged the architecture firm of Harbeson, Hough, Livingston and Larson and the landscape architecture firm Wheelwright, Stevenson, and Langran as consultants.[9]

George Howe, with whom Bacon was serving on the Penn Center committee, was also retained as a consultant.[10] Bacon and Howe worked together on concepts for shaping Independence Mall. Howe suggested a treatment for the first block, similar to that at the Place de la Carrière in Nancy, France, where the palace is framed by a double row of trees.[11] In July 1952, the architects released their study for the treatment of the mall. The first block would have a double row of trees framing Independence Hall. A paved plaza and fountain would be placed in the second block, and the third would include landscaping and a "plaza of flagpoles."[12] By April 1954, the first block of the mall was already complete.[13]

Bacon had several disagreements with the National Park Service and other public-sector players during the construction of Independence Mall and Independence National Historical Park. To build a grand setting for Independence Hall, the National Park Service demolished numerous blocks of old buildings, significantly disrupting the urban fabric. Among these was a row of buildings on the 200 block of Chestnut Street that included the Frank Furness-designed Jayne Building, which the Park Service turned into a parking lot.[14] Bacon called the Park Service's demolition of this block and the Jayne Building "the worst single act of architectural vandalism that I've ever experienced."[15]

One of the big ideas behind Independence Mall was as the setting of corporate headquarters surrounding the mall. Rohm and Haas—the chemicals manufacturing giant—was the first corporation that agreed to build its world headquarters on the mall, giving hope that other companies would follow suit. To continue this vision, Bacon lobbied hard to keep a planned federal courthouse away from the key corner of Sixth and Market Streets, where he wanted to see a major corporate headquarters and street-level activity, not a dull public building. However, Senator (former mayor) Joseph Clark wanted the courthouse located at this prime spot and got his way.[16] When Bacon saw that he was not going to win the fight for the location, he turned his focus to the project's proposed sub-par design. He bemoaned, "In every respect it [the federal courthouse] is about as bad as it possibly could be."[17] He lobbied Stewart L. Udall, U.S. secretary of the interior, and was able to get some architectural alterations.[18]

Bacon sought to use the momentum around Independence Mall and Independence National Historical Park to advance his Society Hill plans. In April 1947, he and Robert Mitchell came to a meeting of the Shrines Commission to present their concepts for the Better Philadelphia Exhibition. The minutes of that meeting refer to "Mr. Bacon's Plan," and an addendum includes a description of the Planning Commission's concept for a "historic pathway," stretching south from the historic area into the neighboring residential neighborhood.[19] This is the earliest recording of what came to be known as the Society Hill Greenways. The idea was that these mid-block garden walks would tie Society Hill together, leading pedestrians through a human-scale journey, with short, winding passages. Travelers could get from place to place without having to mingle with cars, all the while experiencing their neighborhood in a new and exciting way—turning the corner to the pleasure of seeing a garden, a church, or a playground.[20]

This greenway system would physically connect Independence Mall to the historic neighborhood to its south through meandering garden pathways. From a design standpoint, it was the same concept as the "greenways" that Louis Kahn planned for Mill Creek and were incorporated into many redevelopment plans of the early 1950s. Although Bacon's garden pathway plans for the Better Philadelphia Exhibition predate Kahn's Mill Creek plans, he often gave Kahn credit for developing the greenway concept, which would become a primary feature of Society Hill.[21] The greenways were also certainly inspired by the Radburn principles of separating vehicles and pedestrians. Another important quality of the Greenway system was its role in "giving significance and meaning to a series of projects by individual architects."[22] Bacon saw this as a way to build an underlying system of movement that would provide a foundation for relating the works of the past, present, and future.

In 1948, the City Planning Commission officially certified the Old City Redevelopment Area, giving the Commission the authority to start creating a formal plan for Society Hill. Bacon believed that the best way to restore Society Hill was to encourage people of means to move into the neighborhood and spend their own money to fix up the historic homes.[23] This model would shift the burden of rehabilitation costs to the private sector and would also seek to combat the flight of middle class and affluent residents to the suburbs. But why would anyone reverse course on the suburban, American dream to move into a slum neighborhood? Bacon believed that the allure of living in a historic home in a community that someday could be a colonial-era village was a strong enough selling point.

However, the vision was essentially different from Colonial Williamsburg—the Virginia town redeveloped as a historical museum with financial backing from John D. Rockefeller, Jr.—which was the major precedent at the time for large-scale historic preservation. Bacon wanted to see reinvestment in a historic area that could be reborn as a living neighborhood, rather than a showcase for the past. He asserted, "The whole area cannot and should not become one large museum. It must be a well cared for, alive city, as it originally was."[24] In the case of the other redevelopment areas like Poplar, the city took the lead in selecting properties for restoration or new construction. Bacon's was a radical and untested idea of relying on individual home renovations as the foundation for urban renewal.

The Planning Commission engaged Eugene H. Klaber, a former architect for the U.S. Housing Authority, to carry out a feasibility study on financing Society Hill's redevelopment. Klaber's report was encouraging as to the potential for attracting middle-class residents. However, he cautioned that gentrifying Society Hill could displace existing residents who would no longer be able to afford to live in the neighborhood. Klaber estimated "a net displacement of 414 of the present families or about 34% [of the current population]."[25] Still, Bacon saw few government resources available for fixing up these historic homes and believed that a strategy of redevelopment through individual private investment was the most viable concept.

The federal Title I urban renewal dollars were specifically intended to pay for the costs of acquiring blighted land and bulldozing it so that a redeveloper could build on it anew. These funds could not easily be used for historic preservation. One 1950 letter from the director of the U.S. Housing and Home Finance Agency to a staff member at the Philadelphia Redevelopment Authority reflected this policy, stating, "Mr. Bacon's letter indicates that the redevelopment area plan will be concerned to a large extent with detailed plans for the restoration of historic old structures and sites. Such work probably would not be eligible for Title I assistance."[26] What Bacon was doing was outside the accepted concept of urban renewal, and he would have to be innovative in figuring out how to finance the idea and garner support from local, state, and federal actors to make it tenable.

The federal urban renewal dollars were tied to the concept of a redevelopment authority taking ownership of land through eminent domain and turning it over to a private redeveloper who would build on the land. There was no private redeveloper who would take over all of Society Hill and either restore the houses or sell them off to private owners. This would be both risky and unprofitable. To address this issue, Klaber proposed an innovative framework for financing the Society Hill project, by creating a "limited dividend corporation" that would act as the private redeveloper.[27] In other words, the public sector would help create an organization with a civic mission to link up interested and able individuals with historic homes in need of renovation, serving as the official "redeveloper," while simultaneously acting as the conduit between the Redevelopment Authority and private homebuyers.

With the Klaber report in hand providing data that showed Society Hill was a feasible proposal, Bacon began taking the idea to various civic groups. On June 8, 1950, at the annual meeting of the City Parks Association, he presented his vision for Society Hill, joined by Frank Lammer of the Redevelopment Authority, hoping to demonstrate that the concept was more than a pie-in-the-sky dream. Bacon announced that Society Hill would be "an entirely new approach to historical restoration."[28] Tying the concept to Independence Mall and the National Historical Park, he explained, "I believe that, when the whole system is completed, the experience of visiting Philadelphia will be unmatched in any other American City."[29]

Moving ahead, Bacon's immediate challenge was to make sure that Society Hill was not destroyed before it could be preserved. He wrote to Mayor Clark, stressing the urgency of the situation: "One of the finest very early Eighteenth Century houses, which could have been bought for $360.00, is now being torn down."[30] Bacon proposed that the mayor introduce to City Council the idea of a commission to review development proposals that affect historic buildings.[31] In 1952, a group of concerned citizens formed an organization called The Citizens' Council on Historic Restoration.[32] In 1955, Philadelphia's City Council created the Philadelphia Historical Commission as an official public body to protect the city's historic structures.

During this period, Bacon first encountered Charles Peterson, the National Park Service's architect for Independence National Historical Park and an outspoken preservationist. Seeing a potential ally, Peterson began reaching out to Bacon when issues emerged regarding the historic integrity of Society Hill. For example, Peterson was alarmed about the Redevelopment Authority's proposed demolition of several structures around "what appears to be the oldest market house in the country."[33] Bacon was responsive to his concern and pressured the Redevelopment Authority to reevaluate its demolition strategy, while asking Mayor Clark to consider investing city money to preserve the market shed.[34] Peterson continued to correspond with Bacon, sharing ideas, and inviting him to events and lectures.[35] The two men often worked together, though their relationship would not always be as cordial as in these initial interactions.

During his administration, Mayor Clark was never willing to dedicate true political capital to Society Hill, and no private developers came forward to invest.[36] In contrast, at Bacon's urging, Mayor Dilworth made Society Hill a centerpiece of his agenda. Dilworth bought into the idea developed in the Klaber report of using a "limited dividend corporation" as the redeveloper. He believed that the Greater Philadelphia Movement (GPM)—the group established in 1948 as the civic voice of the business community—was the perfect organization to enlist for the role. Recently, the organization had been working to build a modern food distribution center to replace the obsolete Dock Street Market on the eastern end of Society Hill and had a vested interest in the neighborhood's revitalization.[37]

The only problem was that GPM was in an ongoing conflict with Albert M. Greenfield, whom Dilworth had recently appointed chairman of the City Planning Commission. Soon after taking office, Dilworth used the weight of his office to encourage the creation of a new nonprofit organization that merged GPM's leadership with Greenfield. In June, Dilworth sat down with Harry Batten—one of the founders of GPM—and Greenfield at the Bellevue Stratford hotel and convinced them to cooperate for the good of making Society Hill a reality.[38] These civic leaders formed a committee in July 1956 that was formalized as the Old Philadelphia Development Corporation (OPDC) by the end of the year, chaired by bank president William L. Day, and with John P. Robin, who previously led the Pittsburgh Regional Industrial Development Corporation and served as Pennsylvania's secretary of commerce, as its paid executive vice president.[39] OPDC's mission was to promote the redevelopment of central Philadelphia, focusing initially on Society Hill and the Dock Street Market area. The organization's primary goal was not to raise money, rather "to create an environment in which private investment would come in on its own motivation."[40]

Meanwhile, the City Planning Commission hired a consultant team to create a physical redevelopment plan for Society Hill—technically called the Washington Square Redevelopment Area. The consultant team comprised three firms: Harbeson, Hough, Livingston and Larson; Oskar Stonorov and J. Frank Haws; and Vincent Kling and Associates.[41] The first version of the Washington Square Redevelopment Area Plan was finished and released in 1957, including both Society Hill and westward extension to Broad Street.[42]

The Planning Commission's role was focused on design and advising the process; the work of facilitating the rehabilitation of the historic homes in Society Hill would fall to the Redevelopment Authority, working with the OPDC. In 1960, City Council designated the OPDC as the exclusive redeveloper of individual properties within Society Hill.[43] The Redevelopment Authority would condemn any houses that were vacant or in poor condition and convey them to the OPDC, which would establish a committee for marketing the houses to prospective buyers. The OPDC would interview all interested homebuyers. Safeguards would be put in place to ensure that buyers had the means to restore the homes and would occupy them as primary dwellings.

Existing homeowners in Society Hill were given the option to keep their properties if they showed the means to restore them. In that case, the Redevelopment Authority still took ownership of the home but deeded it back to the original owner with a restrictive restoration agreement.[44] The Authority put several measures into place to help existing homeowners afford to stay in their homes, and restoration standards for existing homeowners were less stringent. In other cases, when properties were derelict or vacant, the Redevelopment Authority condemned the property, conveyed it to the OPDC, and left it to the OPDC to identify a potential buyer. Churches and schools were afforded the opportunity to gain new land around their buildings through the Redevelopment Authority condemning and demolishing nearby derelict structures.[45]

However, members of the community, as well as individuals like Charles Peterson, Judge Edwin Lewis, and Dorothy Montgomery (of the Philadelphia Housing Association), were not convinced that this procedure would protect the integrity of the historic houses.[46] Several ideas were proposed to protect all the houses in the district, including giving the Philadelphia Art Commission purview over private structures in Society Hill. Bacon favored this view and tried to convince Mayor Dilworth to support it.[47] However, apparently the Redevelopment Authority saw the Art Commission and the Historical Commission as potential roadblocks. Ultimately the Authority simply gave the responsibility for approving building alterations to its Advisory Board of Design, which comprised Bacon, architect Robert Geddes, and the Authority's Sydney Martin.[48]

The Advisory Board of Design created a set of standards for rehabilitation and new construction. The board desired to restore the area to its colonial feeling and did not value the late nineteenth-century structures. In addition, the restoration did away with the retail establishments peppering residential blocks, to restore the historical integrity of residential buildings. The board had a rule that new houses must be built in a modern style so they would not be confused with authentic, historic homes.[49] These rules created the type of community Bacon and others wanted to see, but ultimately changed the neighborhood's character substantially. Not everyone agreed this was a positive change, and these types of decisions would lay the groundwork for conflict with preservation advocates like Charles Peterson.

The requirement that new construction could not emulate historic architecture created something of a problem when Bacon received a request from Mayor Dilworth, who wanted to build a faux Colonial home on Washington Square. The board made an exception for the mayor, whose Colonial-Revival-style house, designed by G. Edwin Brumbaugh, was built in 1959. Mayor Dilworth, his wife, six children, and twelve miniature poodles moved onto the fringes of Society Hill.[50] This was a significant action—the mayor moving to the edge of an area that just recently had been considered by many to be a slum. However, Mayor Dilworth was not the first prominent individual to move into Society Hill. One of the earliest purchasers through the OPDC was C. Jared Ingersoll, a wealthy railroad executive, and his wife Agnes Ingersoll. Other affluent individuals followed, attracted by the growing social cachet and the neighborhood's connection to Philadelphia's colonial history. Henry M. Watts, chairman of the New York Stock Exchange, and his wife Anna Watts had a new house constructed for them in 1961. Other prominent families followed suit, showing that moving to Society Hill was not only possible but also socially desirable—a critical step to marketing the neighborhood to prospective homebuyers.[51]

As families from affluent areas like the Main Line and Chestnut Hill slowly began moving in and renovating homes, Bacon saw the opportunity to take an active role in persuading other elites to follow suit. On at least two occasions, he took groups of wealthy women for walks through the neighborhood, pointing out the architecture and talking about the plans for restoring this area to its former glory.[52] At the end of his walks, he took his guests up to a house at Fourth and Locust Streets, rang the doorbell, and entered a cheerful apartment. The residents of the apartment were Bacon's friends Constance Fraley—who formerly worked in Stonorov's office—and her husband Pierre. The Fraleys entertained the guests and served them tea at the conclusion of their tour.[53]

For its part, the OPDC also tried to tap into this newfound interest among the region's wealthy elites. In 1962, the OPDC set up a Historic Houses Committee to interview prospective homebuyers. Two of its members were Agnes Ingersoll and Anna Watts, thus placing high-society women on the committee who had already moved to Society Hill, giving the group instant cachet. There was a general feeling that if people like the Ingersolls and the Wattses (not to mention Mayor Dilworth) could move to Society Hill, so could others with means.[54]

From Open-Air Market to Modern Apartments

In the early days of Bacon's focus on Society Hill, the eastern end of the neighborhood was still occupied by the Dock Street Market, an open-air wholesale distribution facility for grocers, food vendors, and restaurateurs. However, by 1940, many outsiders and a good number of the merchants believed the market needed to be cleaned up or moved to another location. One author described the market this way: "Decaying refuse was piled along the curbs; incoming produce was heaped upon the bare sidewalk where rivulets of scum and urine wove their way around sprawling drunks."[55] In 1941, the Pennsylvania Railroad offered the market's merchants a site it owned in South Philadelphia for them to relocate the market, but the merchants balked at the offer.[56] In 1945, a local real estate broker also proposed developing a new market in South Philadelphia; again, the merchants were not ready to commit.[57]

The real pressure for the market to move came from the Greater Philadelphia Movement—the group that later morphed into the OPDC—which made the future of the wholesale market a top priority. The GPM viewed a modern market as critical for Philadelphia's commercial competitiveness, while portraying the current market as a noxious use occupying what could be a prime redevelopment site.[58] At the end of 1949, concerns about the market from the U.S. Department of Agriculture led to a federal investigation, and, in response, the GPM ramped up its pressure to get the market to move.[59]

For his part, Bacon felt that the market should move to free up the adjacent land in Society Hill for modern apartment buildings to complement the historic homes. Society Hill needed new construction to utilize the available federal funding, and the land adjacent to the market was clearly a prime site for new construction. Bacon had incorporated models of modern apartments at this location in the Better Philadelphia Exhibition model and made this element part of his concept for Society Hill.

Despite continued opposition from merchants and even from Greenfield, plans to relocate the Dock Street Market moved forward.[60] A new site for the market on 400 acres in South Philadelphia was certified by the City Planning Commission, and City Council granted more than $2.5 million for land acquisition. The city became the landowner, with the GPM assuming a long-term lease.[61] After the election of Mayor Dilworth and the formation of the OPDC, the city began working to obtain federal urban renewal funds for Society Hill—using the potential of new housing at the Dock Street site as a major selling point.

By the end of 1957, lobbying by the OPDC and the Redevelopment Authority proved successful, and the federal Urban Renewal Administration announced an allocation of $11.1 million in federal funds for Society Hill.[62] Bill Rafsky and the Redevelopment Authority's project manager, Walt D'Alessio, worked with the OPDC on the real estate end, while they coordinated with the U.S. Department of Housing and Urban Development (HUD) and its regional director, Jay Nathan. Although the federal government was willing to invest, Washington viewed Society Hill as a project that needed a lot of oversight due to its experimental nature. Nathan recalled, "I was told, come to Philadelphia and straighten the damn thing out, or else close the regional office down and get rid of the [redevelopment] program."[63] Through a collaboration among these three men, Philadelphia was able to bend the rules and jump through hoops to use federal dollars for elements like brick sidewalks and decorative Franklin lamps that federal money technically was not supposed to fund.[64] The federal funds also supported a program to clean up vacant lots by grading them, planting grass, and installing decorative fences to make the areas appear less derelict, while the Redevelopment Authority and the OPDC were trying to market them to prospective buyers.[65]

The next step was for the Redevelopment Authority to identify a developer to construct the new apartment buildings on the Dock Street site. This was done through a national competition. Instead of choosing the developer who made the lowest bid, the development team would be selected based on the quality of its design. This feature of the selection process made the competition the first of its kind for an urban renewal project.[66] Although the competition was the purview of the Redevelopment Authority rather than the Planning Commission, Bacon worked with community groups to incorporate their concerns. Most significant was the fear that high-rise buildings would be constructed in the heart of historic areas.

Indeed, the consultants' redevelopment plan called for "an extensive contemporary neighborhood of tall structures with a commanding view of the city and harbor."[67] Community opposition focused on one particular site—at the time occupied by a Yellow Cab parking lot—deemed too close to colonial-era homes. Bacon adjusted the plans to move this proposed structure to a location on Washington Square, relieving the "rather bitter opposition which the historic groups had been developing to the entire project."[68]

The competition program identified three sites for apartment construction: the Dock Street site and two locations to the west, near Washington Square. By October 1958, the competition had closed with four entries received. The teams were conglomerations of developers from across the East Coast, associated with various architecture teams.[69] Although not a member of the jury, Bacon weighed in on the selection of the developer.[70] Regarding the eastern Dock Street area, he championed a proposal by Webb and Knapp of New York with its architect I. M. Pei. The chief executive of Webb and Knapp was prominent developer William Zeckendorf, whom Jack Robin of the OPDC had been wooing for months. Zeckendorf's participation was a major reason the competition generated national attention.[71]

Decades later, I. M. Pei would go on to win the Pritzker Architecture Prize—the highest honor for an architect. In 1958, Pei was not yet famous, but he was qualified, having worked on similar urban renewal projects, first when employed by Zeckendorf and then with his new firm, I. M. Pei & Associates. The design of the structures for Society Hill resembled Pei's design for the Kip's Bay Towers in New York in terms of massing, materials, and distinctive windows; however, while Kip's Bay used slab structures, for Society Hill, Pei designed three narrow tower shafts. Bacon wrote of Pei's plan, "This plan is the only plan submitted which meets the objectives of the Illustrative Site Plan." He called the towers design "an admirable solution to the basic city planning problem."[72]

One of the most compelling features of the Pei designs was that the towers were offset from the streets, positioned to line up with the yet-unbuilt greenway system, and, because they were narrow, they let in light. In a later interview, he explained, "That greenway system was what led us to our design. . . . [W]e wanted a greenway to lead into our project—our development—and therefore the placement of the towers."[73] Another compelling element was that Pei called for the development of new townhouses wrapped around the base of the towers, creating a transition from the high-rise to the small-scale historic neighborhood.[74] While Bacon raved about the Pei design for the eastern site, he was less enthusiastic about any of the designs for the western sites. He gave a scathing review to the plan developed in part by Oskar Stonorov.[75] Since the Better Philadelphia Exhibition, Bacon and Stonorov had drifted apart in their design ideology, with Stonorov pioneering his own style of architectural modernism that differed from Bacon's aesthetic and focus on broader urban design.

By coincidence, Bacon also had the opportunity to influence Michael von Moschzisker, the Redevelopment Authority's chairman. Moschzisker had been Bacon's attorney in buying his house on Locust Street and had worked in Richardson Dilworth's District Attorney Office. Years later, Moschzisker recounted the story of how Bacon convinced him on the Society Hill competition:

> Models of the four proposals were displayed in the Mayor's reception room in City Hall, so that the public might see what we had to choose from. There, one rainy afternoon, I wandered from model to model, trying to make my mind up which to vote for, and having a hard time deciding—until I spied a single other visitor in the room. It was Ed Bacon. . . . [T]o the great good fortune of Philadelphia, something inspired me to consult Ed. "Which of these would you vote for and why?" I asked him, whereupon Bacon, with his characteristic clarity, explained the virtues of the Webb & Knapp-Pei proposal: the one with the three slender, graceful towers . . . so well spaced and carefully planned in their relationship to the historic area of Old Philadelphia. I left the reception room a convinced supporter of this proposal.[76]

When the Redevelopment Authority and Mayor Dilworth voted in December 1958, they selected the Zeckendorf/Pei concept for the easternmost section. In a later round, the Jefferson Square Corporation with Harrison & Abromovitz and Oskar Stonorov as architects was selected for the western section. Bacon was critical of the Jefferson Square proposal, as communicated in official Planning Commission documents, and to improve on the plan, Stonorov and Haws were demoted to "associate local architect," and I. M. Pei was brought on as "principal architect," with Harrison & Abromovitz as "supervisory" and "reviewing" architects.[77]

One of the advantages of the Jefferson Square proposal was that its developers proposed using conventional rather than FHA-insured financing.[78] This was important because the Pei towers were to use FHA financing; and because FHA-insured mortgages were at a premium and Philadelphia already had two other major buildings rising with FHA-securitization, it would have been difficult to try to build the I. M. Pei-designed towers and Washington Square projects at the same time. In addition, the Stonorov-designed Hopkinson House, slated for the south side of Washington Square, was already in FHA's pipeline, ready for construction by the end of 1959.[79]

The Redevelopment Authority's Advisory Board of Design (which included Bacon) worked with Pei's office to rework the original design and bring the cost down, while also adjusting parking and access issues.[80] Meanwhile, Zeckendorf also moved ahead in building the Pei-designed townhouses proposed in the original plan. However, these were met with opposition from several individuals, including Grant Simon, chairman of the City's Historical Commission; Harry Batten, one of the prominent founders of the Greater Philadelphia Movement; and local residents who felt the new townhouses should look colonial, rather than modernist.[81] Bacon and his colleagues on the Advisory Board of Design had long argued that new construction should be modern, so as to not be mistaken for the historical structures. The Redevelopment Authority ended up ignoring the opposition and moving ahead with the Pei townhouses as planned.[82] Throughout its renewal, Society Hill would continually present clashes of ideals about historic preservation and how to build a modern, thriving neighborhood, while saving and respecting the old.

Challenges and Successes

By 1962, when Mayor James H. J. Tate came into office, Bacon's role in Society Hill had greatly diminished, with the Redevelopment Authority and OPDC driving the project. Yet Bacon was called on to defend the project when the Redevelopment Authority's work came under attack from Charles Peterson. In January 1962, the *Bulletin* came out with the headline "Society Hill a Nightmare, Park Aide Says." Peterson accused the Redevelopment Authority of demolishing some historic properties and condemning others, only to let them fall into disrepair through neglect.[83] In addition, using his

Figure 14. Society Hill in 1959, looking east, showing the neighborhood before much of the redevelopment work had taken place. From Delaware Valley Regional Planning Commission, "A Report on Historic Preservation" (1969). Courtesy of the Edmund N. Bacon Collection, The Architectural Archives, University of Pennsylvania.

position as a federal employee, Peterson wrote to President John F. Kennedy, repeating his accusations of the city's negative actions in Society Hill. When Bacon heard about this turn of events, he was irate.[84] He countered Peterson's accusations by sending a packet of material to Washington demonstrating that historic preservation was a key objective in the redevelopment of Society Hill. This material satisfied the federal official assigned to investigate Peterson's claims, who wrote to Peterson,

I don't mean to defend Ed [Bacon] because he doesn't really need it, but I do think it is extremely unfortunate where we have such a monstrous job in the conservation and rehabilitation of cities to

Figure 15. Society Hill in 1969, after construction of the Society Hill
Towers and town homes designed by I. M. Pei. From Delaware Valley
Regional Planning Commission, "A Report on Historic Preservation"
(1969). Courtesy of the Edmund N. Bacon Collection, The Architectural
Archives, University of Pennsylvania.

have misunderstanding between the planners and/or architects
themselves. From what I have seen of your problem in Philadelphia,
I can only conclude that it is a misunderstanding that exists between
you and the Planning Commission.[85]

In some ways, Peterson surely was right, and he was not the only one to
accuse the Redevelopment Authority of abusing its powers. Bacon himself
recognized that the approach in Society Hill was not perfect. The *Bulletin*
reported "In Society Hill, he [Bacon] said, some old buildings have been
torn down, but others have been preserved and rehabilitated. He contrasted
this approach with that of the Philadelphia Housing Authority which, he

said, evicts people and tears down homes."[86] While Bacon saw the Society Hill approach as a balance of needs, Peterson was a preservation purist.

There were other difficulties in Society Hill. In 1963, William Zeckendorf ran into financial trouble and sold off his interest in seven major development projects, including the Society Hill Towers, to Alcoa Aluminum and Covent America Corporation.[87] I. M. Pei recalled that the project was very challenging to design, while attempting to keep costs down.[88] Despite the changeover in developers, however, the project remained on track. In June 1963, Pei wrote to Bacon, "Dear Ed: Isn't it nice to have a satisfied 'client'? Society Hill is not one of our easiest projects but I do share with you the same kind of satisfaction."[89]

Despite these struggles, by the 1960s it looked as if the dream of Society Hill becoming a desirable neighborhood—one where its historic homes could be restored through individual, private-market investment—might actually be possible. Residents moved into the neighborhood gradually, though the Society Hill Towers did not really start filling up until the 1970s.[90] As attitudes shifted, more people began buying into Society Hill—figuratively and literally. It was not just wealthy newcomers bringing Society Hill back to life. Many existing homeowners decided to stay, and the Redevelopment Authority convinced them it was worthwhile to invest in fixing up their homes.

These homeowners, who remained in their homes through the renewal period, were almost all white. The neighborhood's African American population, largely renters, were almost entirely displaced through the renewal of Society Hill.[91] As time went on, Society Hill became increasingly exclusively affluent. In many ways, it was the first true example of the kind of urban gentrification cities across the nation have since experienced. In a later interview, Bacon said of the residential displacement that occurred during the revitalization, "I knew it was cruel while I was doing it. But think of Philadelphia if Society Hill was still the way it was. It was more important to restore this area than to maintain the low-income residents."[92]

Two community groups came into being during this period. The Society Hill Civic Association represented newcomers, while the Society Hill Area Residents Association worked to fight urban renewal, maintain the area's character, and protect existing residents. Many people loved the changing face of Society Hill, but others did not like what it did to the existing community. Even Bacon's confederate Constance Fraley, who entertained and served tea to the wealthy socialites Bacon would bring by her Society Hill apartment, bemoaned in a later interview, "We were there before all the Society Hill renovation started. It was a fun little neighborhood. It had a lot of character. There was a Chinese laundry and there was an Italian grocer, and little businesses that disappeared during the cleanup, unfortunately."[93] Unlike most other urban renewal efforts in the U.S., Society Hill was a remarkable success in restoring the neighborhood physically. However, it was only slightly less destructive than other cities' renewal projects in preserving the social fabric of the community.

Society Hill was arguably Bacon's most successful project, in terms of realizing a complete "design idea." In contrast to Penn Center or the Far Northeast, no major compromises disrupted his vision of what Society Hill should become. Bacon's emerging national profile and his popularity with Mayor Dilworth certainly helped him convince the right influential individuals of his plan. Still, he had to persuade others to accept a concept that few imagined was possible at the start and that had never been attempted on a similar scale. In order for Society Hill to be successful, an array of public- and private-sector actors had to buy into a shared vision and collectively work toward its realization. Society Hill was as much the work of Mayor Dilworth, the OPDC and the Redevelopment Authority, and individuals like Walt D'Alessio, Jay Nathan, Jack Robin, and Jared Ingersoll as it was Bacon's. Perhaps for the first time in his career, Bacon had successfully carried through an idea—a complete idea—and watched as others worked together to bring it to fruition.

Meanwhile, to the east of Society Hill, plans were progressing for Penn's Landing—a new development along the Delaware River—which Bacon viewed as an extension of Society Hill.[94] The City Planning Commission's 1961 Annual Report stated, "Penn's Landing will include a Port Tower at the foot of Market Street, a restaurant, a boat basin, a historic ship basin . . . an embarcadero for overseas cruise ships, and the future home of the Academy of Natural Sciences."[95] The Planning Commission contracted with Robert Geddes as design consultant for Penn's Landing. A year later, community leaders in the neighborhood south of Society Hill formed a corporation called Queen Village Inc. and approached Bacon regarding ideas for redevelopment. He agreed that the Planning Commission would help them to produce a physical plan and was enthusiastic for the potential of extending the redevelopment energy from Society Hill into the neighborhood just to the south.[96]

Figure 16. Bacon on a greenway in Society Hill, April 12, 1962. The greenway system would eventually include a pedestrian pathway to St. Peter's Church (shown in background). Photo by Jules Schick. Courtesy of the Edmund N. Bacon Collection, The Architectural Archives, University of Pennsylvania.

Bacon saw Society Hill as an example of how the public sector can invest in a project that will generate private-market interest that can develop on its own and turn into something much larger, organically evolving.
The result was that Society Hill could be held up as a great triumph for a
new paradigm of urban living, an attractive alternative to the draw of the
suburbs. Bacon believed that this example would be followed in other cities
for years to come.[97]

Competing with the Suburbs

After the success of Society Hill, the next project that OPDC would focus
on was the redevelopment of Market Street east of City Hall. This area was
Philadelphia's historic shopping hub, but it was starting to show signs of
decline due to the popularity of suburban shopping centers. Since the early
nineteenth century, this section of Market Street had been lined with outdoor market sheds. In 1859, the city transferred the merchants to two new
indoor markets, giving Market Street its modern name (it was formerly
called High Street). In the 1890s, the Reading Railroad established its terminal at Twelfth and Market Streets and relocated the two markets under its
train depot in a massive, modern new facility that became known as the
Reading Terminal Market.

Around the same time, several entrepreneurs, including John Wanamaker, Justus Clayton Strawbridge, and Isaac Hallowell Clothier, also set
up shop on Market Street, creating the city's first major department stores
in Wanamaker's and Strawbridge & Clothier. In 1911, Wanamaker commissioned Daniel Burnham, the famous architect of Chicago's Columbian
Exposition, to build him a European-style palace of commerce, with twelve
floors, including a monumental pipe organ. Strawbridge and Clothier
established a more modest dry goods store nearby, creating a second anchor
for Market Street as a shopping hub. In the 1930s, the Philadelphia Savings
Fund Society (PSFS) commissioned its new headquarters at Twelfth and
Market Streets, a stunning Art Deco masterpiece designed by George Howe
and William Lescaze.

By the 1950s, Market Street east of City Hall was a thriving center of
commerce with the Reading Terminal Market, Wanamaker's, Strawbridge
and Clothier, and three other department stores: Gimbels (where the Better
Philadelphia Exhibition was hosted), Lit Brothers, and Snellenburg's.
However, the department store owners were already seeing a troubled

future. The postwar exodus to the suburbs put many shoppers farther from the downtown department stores, and new suburban developments clearly threatened the traditional model of downtown shopping.

Even before World War II, developers had been experimenting with new forms of compact shopping centers. Country Club Plaza in Kansas City was arguably the first modern suburban shopping mall, with plenty of parking.[98] Others followed, such as Highland Park in Dallas, Shoppers World outside Boston, and Mondawmin, developed by James Rouse in Baltimore. These new developments had innovative features such as multiple levels of shopping, connected with outdoor pedestrian concourses and ample parking lots.[99] In 1956, architect Victor Gruen designed a first-of-its-kind project called Southdale in a suburb of Minneapolis that had a department store anchoring both ends and was completely enclosed and climate controlled.[100] This new model for the suburban shopping mall presented a formidable threat for old-style urban department stores.

The result was clear for Philadelphia's downtown department store owners: they had to find a way to compete with the comfort, parking, and convenience of the suburbs if they were to survive. Gimbels owner Arthur Kaufmann had already toyed with moving his store to Penn Center but ultimately decided against it. Another department store, Frank and Seder, closed its doors in 1952, and that year Snellenburg's was sold to Bankers Security Corporation—sending warning signals to the rest of the downtown store owners. Many of the smaller shops were struggling, and there was an overall view that the Market Street corridor was on the decline.

Bacon had hoped that Penn Center could become a shopping hub connected with transit. While the vision did not truly pan out in Penn Center, he saw the opportunity to use some components from his prior vision to transform Market Street into a regional shopping hub that could compete with the suburban malls. As with the Far Northeast, he did not want to bring the suburbs into the city. Instead, he envisioned a project that was distinctly urban but could capture some of the qualities that made the suburbs attractive. Initially, he called his concept for the area east of City Hall "Penn Center East." He pictured a massive transportation hub and shopping and office complex that would be convenient by car, bus, or train but ultimately would be designed to maximize the pedestrian experience with open-air promenades. It would take almost twenty years to make this vision a reality.

Bacon and his urban design staff, led by its chief Willo von Moltke, began working on schemes for this new development. In March 1958,

Bacon brought his new concept to the City Planning Commission for the first time. He quickly learned that calling the project "Penn Center East" and associating it with the controversial project to the west might not be the best idea. One of the most vocal opponents of the new project was Harry Kalish, an attorney who sat on the Planning Commission.[101] Kalish was, in fact, skeptical of the entire premise that Market Street could be revived, calling the historic shopping district "a row of empty warehouses."[102] He was willing to support building just a bus terminal and parking garage—two components of the Penn Center East scheme.[103] He also suggested closing Market Street to through traffic and turning it into a massive parking lot, like those being built to accommodate suburban shopping malls. It was clear to Bacon that Kalish simply did not get the vision. In the end, with the support of chairman G. Holmes Perkins, the Commission gave preliminary approval for the whole project to move ahead, with the stipulation that it would need expert cost analysis.

Fortunately, as with Society Hill, Mayor Dilworth supported Bacon and his big vision for Market Street. After Bacon's initial plan was criticized, in May 1958, the Planning Commission released a new plan that sought to address some of the criticism and marketing missteps. Realizing the error of associating the concept with Penn Center, the plan gave the project its own name and identity: "Market East Plaza: A New Center for Transportation and Commerce."[104] The report showed a model of Market Street with four shimmering towers along two blocks on the north side, connected by lower buildings. The plan included an open-air garden subway station, special ramps for buses to a new terminal, and a six-level parking garage wrapped by the retail complex, with three levels of open-air shopping. Elevated and sunken walkways separated pedestrians from the streets, and a direct connection was made between this new lower-level concourse and the concourse at Penn Center. The plan competed with the scale of the suburbs, calling for 275,000 square feet of floor space, with an additional 1,320,900 square feet of office space in towers above the retail levels.[105]

One important feature of the Market East Plaza plan was that it did not just describe a single building, or even a complex of buildings; it proposed a whole structural diagram of how people would arrive and move around Center City. After arriving by train, bus, or car, Bacon envisioned a pedestrian's paradise. The report stated, "The transition from wheels to feet should be accomplished in an agreeable setting. . . . Distribution of

Figure 17. City Planning Commission drawing of the proposed Market East project, from the Commission's 1960 report "Center City Philadelphia: Major Elements of the Physical Development Plan for Center City." According to the report, Market East is "a project which can ultimately develop into one of the nation's great shopping centers." The drawing shows a multimodal development with an open-air, pedestrian shopping concourse, accessible from the street level, subway, and a new bus terminal and parking garage. Courtesy of the Edmund N. Bacon Collection, The Architectural Archives, University of Pennsylvania.

pedestrians along the core should be on pleasant walkways, separated from wheeled traffic where possible."[106] The plan's drawings by Willo von Moltke illustrated this complex web of interlocking systems for different modes of transportation. One drawing showed the subways running below the cars on the street, people emerging from the subway into the plaza, then proceeding upstairs to reach additional outdoor shopping levels, lined with sculptures and benches.

The drawings showed trees dramatically perched four levels in the air, cars parked on the fourth through eighth levels, buses arriving on the third level, and people flowing out of the buses into the retail concourse.[107] These were the kinds of visuals Bacon loved. Like Vincent Kling's models for Penn Center, these drawings attempted to illustrate a complex concept, while inspiring viewers with the wonderful possibilities of a new vision that would transform the present city.

The Planning Commission hired Larry Smith, one of the nation's top market analysts, to make recommendations on the bus depot location.[108] This component was seen as an immediate need for the city. While the bus terminal idea moved ahead, the rest of Market East Plaza remained dormant, as the business community remained skeptical of the notion that this mega-project could actually compete with the suburbs. However, at the same time Bacon proposed another big idea. The Pennsylvania Railroad and Reading Railroad maintained two separate rail systems that arrived in different terminals. The Pennsylvania terminal was at Suburban Station, connected to Penn Center, just west of City Hall. The Reading terminal was at Twelfth and Market Streets. Anyone who needed to go from a Pennsylvania to a Reading train, or vice versa, had to walk several blocks to make the connection. Bacon asked, why not build an underground tunnel joining the two rail systems? He credited Damon Childs, a planner on his staff, with the genesis of the concept.[109]

The idea meshed well with Bacon's overall vision. It would provide for the construction of a new regional train station at Market East Plaza, increasing the transit accessibility of the project. It would connect below ground with Penn Center and the new Municipal Services Building. Bacon proposed the idea to Jack Robin of the OPDC, who liked the notion. Robin, in turn, pitched it to James Symes, now president of the Pennsylvania Railroad, who thought it was "the most practical plan he had seen for this problem."[110] It looked as if this part of the plan, as bold, ambitious, and expensive as it would be, might actually gain the support it needed to become reality.

Support from the Business Community

Up to this point, Bacon had been lobbying the OPDC leadership to take an interest and an active role in advancing the concept of Market East. In July 1960, a small group of business leaders associated with the OPDC, including Bill Day, Gustave Amsterdam, Harry Batten, and Jack Robin, met to decide how to proceed.[111] They recommended that the OPDC, which so far had been focused on Society Hill, should create a committee to promote the Market East project. Indeed, the OPDC would become a powerful force in selling the concept of Market East in the coming years.

The first thing that the OPDC and the city had to do was to show that Market East was really viable from a business standpoint. The Planning Commission contracted again with Larry Smith to study the Market East proposals.[112] Market East needed all the institutional support it could get, as it would encounter significant local opposition along the way. For example, the United Business Men's Association sent postcards to all the shop owners around Market East stating, "Most of the buildings will be torn down to make way for a PENN CENTER EAST."[113]

In March 1961, the Planning Commission also engaged Louis I. Kahn on a small contract to develop "an aesthetic architectural expression" for Market East.[114] By this point, Kahn had gained significant national prominence. Despite their failure to work together on Penn Center, Bacon continued to have great admiration of Kahn as a big-picture thinker. In one article in 1958, he explained, "Lou [Kahn] has a very important function as a producer of ideas—and the equally important function of challenging other ideas. . . . There is a great need for men like Lou, disassociated from government and throwing ideas into the pot."[115] As to Kahn's role as consultant to the Planning Commission, however, records show that the meetings were tense and frustrating.[116] By spring 1962, only a fraction of his consulting time had been used, and he lost interest in the project. As one scholar put it, "Kahn and Bacon were like two skew lines that never crossed," and their meetings were plagued by "mutual frustration."[117]

In late 1961, the Planning Commission contracted again with Larry Smith to carry out a feasibility study for Market East, and Smith presented a preliminary analysis in January 1962.[118] However, the preliminary findings cast doubt on the project's economic feasibility.[119] Soon thereafter, Snellenburg's, the least prestigious of the five Market Street department stores, announced that it was merging with the neighboring Lit Brothers store and abandoning its Market Street building. This situation could potentially have jeopardized the Market East plans by giving the impression that the whole area was going downhill.[120] Bacon wrote to the mayor stressing that, with the OPDC supporting the project—showing private-sector buy-in—Market East could move forward, but the mayor would have to be prepared to make "a major announcement about Market East which would finally affirm the serious intent of the City to bring it about."[121]

The challenge for the OPDC was to bring the department store owners together and get them to agree to the plans and direction of the redevelopment. This was no easy task, as the store owners—most notably Arthur

Kaufmann of Gimbels and Stockton Strawbridge of Strawbridge & Clothier—saw themselves as in tight competition and were notoriously distrustful of one another. So it was no small feat when the OPDC was able to get the five department store heads together for a meeting at the City Planning Commission on June 25, 1962, leading to what Bacon called "An unprecedented act of cooperation" among the businessmen.[122] At this meeting, Larry Smith, the market analyst, admitted that he was rethinking his initial assessment and was "beginning to question his own conclusions."[123] The department store owners commissioned a new report from Smith, which came out in September 1962. It was a complete turnaround from his previous gloomy projections—now extremely enthusiastic about Market East's potential.[124]

With the OPDC on board and a market study in hand that supported the Market East project, Bacon, Jack Robin, and Bill Rafsky met with the department store owners to discuss next steps. They decided to bring in a dream team of consultants to move the project forward, consisting of Larry Smith, James Rouse, and Victor Gruen.[125] Smith was one of the nation's most respected market analysts, Rouse was a powerhouse shopping mall developer, and Gruen was the architect famous for originating the concept of the enclosed shopping mall. Around the same time, Bacon hired Romaldo Giurgola—an Italian-born designer whom G. Holmes Perkins had brought to Philadelphia to teach at the University of Pennsylvania—as a consultant for the Planning Commission to work on Market East.[126]

In February 1963, the Planning Commission released the next version of its Market East plans, adorned with images by Giurgola. The document was intended by Bacon to be a marketing tool, bringing the project back into the public limelight and giving the media something to write about.[127] The biggest shift in the design from prior iterations was the fact that the main shopping promenade was now enclosed and climate controlled. The other element that developed in this plan was the connection with transit. Connecting Market East with the subway, commuter railroads, bus station, and highways was always a major goal; however, with the new commuter rail tunnel concept, Market East became even more attractive as the hub of an entire regional transportation system. The *Bulletin* called the commuter rail tunnel "the key to the $218 million Market Street East renewal" and cited Bacon, explaining, "the project aims to 'truly coordinate' shopping and transit facilities."[128] In an age when suburban shopping malls focused exclusively on automobile travel, this was an innovative concept.

In spring 1963, after the Planning Commission document was released, Victor Gruen produced his own design study for Market East. It was his personal concept as an independent consultant for the OPDC and did not reflect the City Planning Commission's work. Gruen proposed an entirely different vision of turning Market Street into a double-decker roadway, closing the lower level to cars, and ramping vehicles up to an elevated street. The Gruen plan was rejected by the OPDC's Market East Task Force, and while notable because of its designer, it seems to have had no further impact in the evolution of Market East.[129]

In May 1963, Bill Rafsky left his post as the city's development coordinator to become the new executive vice president of the OPDC. Since the mid-1950s, Rafsky had directed the city's redevelopment program, bringing in funding from Washington and generally outranking Bacon on decisions that affected urban development. With Rafsky gone, Mayor Tate rotated in a series of weak development coordinators, over whom Bacon could exert more influence. Bacon would have a smoother relationship with Rafsky as head of the OPDC than he did when they were both working for the city. Rafsky was a strong supporter of Bacon's vision for Market East in his new role.[130] Together, they traveled to Baltimore and met with James Rouse to discuss the potential of the famed developer taking on Market East. However, at the time, Rouse was busy developing one of the most significant projects of his career in Columbia, Maryland, and did not have time to dedicate to Philadelphia.[131] In light of this setback, Bacon and Rafsky continued to search for a way to implement the ambitious Market East vision, a task that would surely require significant private capital.

In January 1964, the Planning Commission released a new version of the Market East Plan—evolving the concept and keeping it relevant and in the news.[132] That same year, the Redevelopment Authority obtained a planning grant from the federal government, and a commitment of major construction funding through the U.S. Department of Housing and Urban Development (HUD).[133] To this point, Bacon had been free to develop ambitious studies through the Planning Commission, but, now that real money was on the table and the Redevelopment Authority was more heavily involved, other actors stepped in and altered the concepts. Walt D'Alessio, the Authority's project manager for Society Hill and Market East, was unimpressed with the Planning Commission's designs and decided the Redevelopment Authority needed to bring in its own design team—a move sure to incite tension within the city departments and power structure.[134]

The Redevelopment Authority hired the Chicago-based design firm of Skidmore, Owings and Merrill as architectural consultants to produce a new set of plans.[135] The situation started to resemble Penn Center, when Robert Dowling introduced his own plan that ignored many of Bacon's design elements in the name of maximizing rent revenues. Bacon did not want to see Market East also reduced to sterile corporate architecture. In 1966, Skidmore, Owings and Merrill released its report on Market East. The plan retained some core components of Bacon's project, but the major difference was a shift from the linear concourse to a focus around four "urban plazas."[136] The Skidmore plan was also much more technical from a development standpoint. While Bacon was highly critical of some early drawings out of Skidmore's office, he was relatively satisfied with the final plan.[137]

When Market East was merely a vision in Bacon's head, few business leaders took the project seriously. By the mid-1960s, however, the same local leaders considered it a critical project that must get built. According to state Democratic majority leader George Schwartz, "if the [Market East] redevelopment isn't carried out, Center City would become a ghost town with its business going to the suburbs."[138] After a scare where it looked as if the federal government might recall its funding because progress was lagging, the city got a commitment from Washington that the money was still in place, allowing the Redevelopment Authority to move ahead with final design work.[139] In 1969, the Authority engaged Philadelphia-based architecture firm Bower and Fradley to design the project. Bacon knew John Bower, a principal at the firm, who had worked for Vincent Kling years earlier.

The commuter rail tunnel seemed to be stalled, however, because funding for that project was not forthcoming. In summer 1969, the federal government gave Philadelphia's allocated money for the tunnel to Boston because Philadelphia had not gotten the clearances it needed.[140] One of the major issues was the fact that new track area needed to be installed in part of the East Poplar neighborhood, and the residents there were adamantly opposed to running the line through their community—potentially creating an unsightly barrier and perhaps displacing residents.[141]

Here, Market East started to run into opposition for spending money that some groups and individuals felt should be going to neighborhood redevelopment and affordable housing, instead of a commercial center to compete with the suburbs. Cushing Dolbeare of the Philadelphia Housing

Association issued public statements arguing this point.[142] It was an argument that would continue to haunt the Market East project for years afterward, even once it was open for business.

Market East Becomes Reality

After dealing with some opposition from City Council president Paul D'Ortona, City Council ended up backing the Market East project, giving it the final green light in 1970.[143] By this point, Bacon had been transitioned out of the Market East development, to a large extent, and he retired from his service with the city in May 1970. However, by now, Market East had momentum of its own and came to fruition without Bacon's involvement, propelled by Francis J. Myers, Jr., the new director of the Redevelopment Authority, and Bill Rafsky, heading the OPDC. These participants encountered new challenges: the nation was in the midst of a recession, the project still lacked a private developer, and much of the financing was still not in place.[144]

In early 1972, the Market East effort was given a boost when a private development team constructed a new building between the Wanamaker's store and the PSFS building. Called 1234 Market Street and designed by Bower and Fradley, the simple glass structure included connections to the Market Street subway and a large, open atrium. Despite this private investment, it was still unclear whether Market Street east of City Hall could be revived from its economic decline. One *Bulletin* article asked, "Is East of Broad St. Really No-Man's Land?"[145] However, an editorial in the *Inquirer* asserted of 1234 Market, "It stands today not only as a vast improvement over the collection of eyesores it replaced but as a vote of confidence in the future of this historic area."[146]

After 1234 Market Street was built, Stockton Strawbridge, board president of the Strawbridge & Clothier department store, appealed to James Rouse to take another look at Market East. Finally, in 1974, the Philadelphia delegation convinced Rouse to have his company invest in Market East, and that year the Rouse Company signed a formal agreement with the Redevelopment Authority to enter into a public-private partnership to build the Market East project.[147] Rouse had already developed numerous suburban shopping malls, including the Cherry Hill Mall, just outside Philadelphia in New Jersey. Market East would prove perhaps his most challenging project, due to the fact that it was highly experimental. According to Rouse, "We were flatly turned down by many of the most intelligent, experienced and sophisticated real estate people in the U.S. as well as by local merchants."[148] His director of planning, Larry Wolf, said of Market East, "not one tenant came into the project with an ounce of enthusiasm. They were all frightened out of their minds."[149]

Assembling financing was difficult, and the Rouse Company could not secure all of it in time, forcing the company to take on some of the debt itself.[150] However, thanks in part to the civic leadership of PSFS president M. Todd Cooke, Rouse had the support of the local business community.[151] Rouse had to negotiate and collaborate with not just the Redevelopment Authority but also the transit agency—Southeastern Pennsylvania Transportation Authority (SEPTA). Gerald Maier, Redevelopment Authority director for Market East, was a major contributor in making this collaboration work. The final agreement involved the Redevelopment Authority retaining perpetual ownership of the building, with Rouse developing and leasing the interior spaces to retail tenants, and SEPTA developing and maintaining its Eighth Street subway station.[152]

The project, formally named The Gallery at Market East, broke ground on May 7, 1975. It opened on August 22, 1977, to a ceremony with 200,000 people present.[153] The Gallery was a four-level, 2.2 million square-foot, enclosed shopping mall, including 122 shops and restaurants. The project also included an 850-car parking garage and an underground truck street for deliveries. It was anchored by Strawbridge & Clothier and a new Gimbels store. In 1976, William Coleman, federal secretary of transportation (and conveniently also a former Philadelphian), approved funding for the commuter rail tunnel to connect the former Pennsylvania and Reading Railroad lines and link them to a new commuter station connected to the Gallery. City Council approved the project the following year.

The national press lavished attention on the Gallery and recognized the project as a unique element in the development of urban America. An article in the *Wall Street Journal* reported that the Gallery "represents a highly unusual $101 million gamble to pump life into the city's decaying retail district by applying successful suburban concepts."[154] An article in *Amusement Business* stated, "The Philadelphia venture is a completely new concept for the inner city and aims to prove that Americans are 'frustrated urbanites' who are eager to find exciting things to do in the city."[155] An article in the *Inquirer* magazine gushed, "The Gallery has triumphed over legions of skeptics. Its shops have reported astonishing sales figures for the year," and in the same piece, "James Rouse, the man whose malls created downtowns for the suburbs, may now have figured out how to save Downtown itself."[156] The stores in the Gallery found immediate success, averaging sales of $250 per square foot (other Rouse Company malls were earning $135 and the national average for retail was $77).[157] A later article in the *Philadelphia Business Journal*, reporting on these stunning sales figures, noted that, early on, the Gallery was "one of the most financially productive shopping malls in the country."[158]

The Gallery's success was not based on its ability to attract suburbanites. Instead, it thrived largely on an urban demographic, with 71 percent of its shoppers coming from the city, 35 percent them African American.[159] Nonetheless, the project saw major protests from August 1978 to February 1979, led by Pennsylvania state representative Milton Street, who criticized the city's lack of focus on minority inclusion in the construction and operation of the Gallery.[160] In 1980, the city approved moving ahead on a second phase of the Gallery, with much higher minority store ownership and minority contractors in its construction.[161] Gallery II opened in October 1983, featuring four stories with 105 additional shops.[162]

It took nearly two decades, but in 1977 "The Gallery at Market East" was a reality—an innovative development that merged mass transit and urban shopping. To the south, Society Hill was becoming one of the most affluent communities in the city. In both Society Hill and Market East, the projects were built through complex relationships between public and private actors, using experimental and ambitious approaches to urban investment. What they shared was Bacon promoting a visionary concept before the idea was widely accepted, then persevering to steer the project through the path of implementation until public and private actors—with the ability to carry out the project—bought into the idea and took over.

The success of the projects relied less on Bacon's original vision than on the actions and ideas of these other participants who transformed the vision into reality. The perpetual weakness of his position revealed itself once the business community and developers concluded that an idea was possible, took control, and reshaped it to their liking—in Penn Center, when Robert Dowling introduced his own plan, and in Market East, when the Redevelopment Authority brought in Skidmore, Owings and Merrill. Bacon's power was rooted in his ability to promote visionary ideas and understand the subtle implementation process, but that influence became limited as projects advanced to implementation and Bacon's role was less well defined.

The subtlety of Bacon's position became hazy when he attended public meetings and hearings to represent projects. Whether or not he had the power to alter results, as the public face of projects, he would take both credit and blame for efforts that were the work of a conglomeration of public- and private-sector individuals. This fact distorts Bacon's legacy because he became associated as the primary player in projects where he may have actually occupied a fairly minor role. This was the case in Independence Mall, when he served as the city's representative in public meetings with enraged business owners who would be displaced by the mall clearance.[163] Nowhere would this conflicting role be more prevalent than with the city's highways—contentious projects that came to overshadow much of Bacon's career as planning director.

Chapter 6

THE PLANNER VERSUS THE AUTOMOBILE

During Bacon's tenure as city planning director, much of Philadelphia's regional highway system was constructed, including the Schuylkill, Roosevelt Boulevard, Vine Street, and Delaware expressways. Another major planned highway, the Crosstown Expressway, was never built. Highway construction accelerated dramatically after the passage of the Federal-Aid Highway Act of 1956, under President Dwight Eisenhower. These highway projects were decades in the making, and planning for them began years or even decades before Bacon joined the City Planning Commission. Yet they were largely realized during Bacon's tenure as planning director. In highway development during the 1950s and 1960s, the Planning Commission's role was secondary to that of the Philadelphia Department of Streets, and both local departments took a backseat to the Pennsylvania Department of Highways—the main highway planning body, which was the conduit for federal funding and the agency in charge of proposing projects for the federally funded highway system.

Bacon's role in highway planning and development is somewhat ambiguous, and his views on highways appear to have evolved during his tenure as planning director. Some planners of the 1950s and 1960s were adamant highway lovers, but Bacon was never among them. His vision, as portrayed in documents like the Planning Commission's 1963 Center City plan, included equally elaborate networks for cars and mass transit, with a strong focus on the pedestrian experience. In a 1961 article, Bacon wrote, "It has been particularly difficult to maintain this balance [between cars and transit] in the face of the tremendous federal road building program with, until recently no federal aid to mass transportation."[1] In 1968, *Railway Age* magazine wrote, "Bacon doesn't preach 'balanced solutions'—he practices them, making room in his schemes for everything from high-speed main line trains to rapid transit to private automobiles."[2]

In many ways, the role of highways in Bacon's planning appears primarily to create access for bringing people downtown from the suburbs, via a Center City highway loop that terminated in a ring of parking garages on the outskirts of downtown.[3] This loop was a concept that dated back to the 1930s, heavily promoted by former planning director Robert Mitchell. *Time* magazine said of Bacon, "The inner city, he is convinced, as are most planners, must be restored to the pedestrian, and there are plans for parking garages at the center's edge."[4] Bacon was clear that the purpose of highways was to give pedestrians easy access to downtown, stating, "But a city is not for vehicles, it is for people."[5] Yet, in terms of getting vehicles easy access from the suburbs to downtown, he explained, "We think it better not to fight with the automobile, a losing battle at best, but rather to treat it as an honored guest and cater to its needs."[6]

As in cities across the nation, highway projects in Philadelphia created controversy when they were slated to cut through communities, displace residents, and create destructive barriers in the urban landscape. Bacon was indeed involved in highway planning—especially the downtown roadways: the Schuylkill Expressway, Delaware Expressway, and ill-fated Crosstown Expressway—and he represented the city at a number of community meetings related to these controversial roadways. His visible presence at these meetings led to his close association with these projects. Yet, evidence shows that his role in affecting highway projects was, in fact, fairly limited, and thus, contemporary writers seem to give him too much credit and blame for Philadelphia's highway planning. For example, an article shortly after his death in *Architectural Record* discussed "Bacon's very [Robert] Moses-ish idea for a crosstown expressway along South Street," this despite the fact that the advent of the Crosstown Expressway significantly predated him.[7]

What is interesting about Bacon's role in highway planning was how his personal views seemed to evolve from a supporter of highways as part of a balanced, urban transportation system to a radical critic of petroleum-based transportation, arguing quixotically in the 1970s for a world free of cars. This evolution of Bacon's personal beliefs creates a confusing and hypocritical situation in which he was representing the city at meetings, arguing for moving ahead with highway projects, while giving private interviews stating that "The car is losing its luster as something worth sacrificing for."[8] It is unclear why he did not more fully allow his beliefs to affect his public statements in the late 1960s when it was obvious that his anti-auto viewpoint was significantly evolved.

Bacon was involved in the development of Philadelphia's highway program, from the first major expressway constructed—the Schuylkill Expressway—through to the Delaware Expressway and Crosstown Expressway planning of the late 1960s. He was also involved in a project that closed Chestnut Street to automobile traffic, creating a downtown pedestrian-only mall. The result of the city's highway system dramatically changed Philadelphia's urban landscape and would become a significant piece of the legacy from the period of Bacon's tenure as planning director. It is also an example of cases where he appeared to have been less entrepreneurial and less driven to make known his personal beliefs.

Philadelphia's Highway Program

Philadelphia's boom in highway building was part of a national postwar trend. Congress enacted the Federal-Aid Highway Act of 1944, authorizing a roadway system up to 40,000 miles in length.[9] In response to the act, by 1947 the City of Philadelphia was negotiating agreements with the State of Pennsylvania for eight city-state highway projects, and the Planning Commission and Department of Public Works had agreed on preliminary designs for six of these highways.[10] Under President Eisenhower, the Federal-Aid Highway Act of 1956 provided generous new funding to state governments for the completion of segments that were approved as part of the Interstate Highway System. These projects were complex and often took years or decades to carry out.

In 1952, Mayor Joseph Clark appointed Henry D. Harral as commissioner of streets (Harral later became state secretary of highways) and created the Mayor's Master Traffic Committee to boost the city's ability to respond to new federal and state resources for highway construction. Around this same time, the Greater Philadelphia Chamber of Commerce formed the Greater Philadelphia-South Jersey Council, to begin a dialogue on interstate transportation issues. These actions added a number of players to a crowded playing field that would impact highway planning in the coming decades.

In 1953, the city's finance director, Lennox Moak, spearheaded the creation of the Urban Traffic and Transportation Board (UTTB), chaired by Robert B. Mitchell, former director of the Planning Commission. This was to be an eight-county regional transportation planning organization. In 1952, at the direction of the mayor and the Department of Streets, the Planning Commission undertook the largest origin-and-destination survey ever conducted in the U.S.[11] That same year, the Planning Commission began work with the Streets Department to develop a comprehensive expressway plan for the city.[12] In January 1955, the Streets Department jointly with the Planning Commission published a report on "Philadelphia's Program of Major Highways," laying out a concept of "an inner and outer ring" of highways to forge a vision for a comprehensive regional system.[13]

Several regional planning bodies came about during this period to foster collaboration on highway projects that spanned municipal boundaries. These included the Southeastern Pennsylvania Regional Planning Commission; PenJerDel (short for Pennsylvania, Jersey, Delaware), a regional plan created by the city's Urban Traffic and Transportation Board in 1957; and the Penn-Jersey Transportation Study commissioned by the Delaware River Port Authority.[14] Finally, in 1965, the Pennsylvania General Assembly passed a bill creating an official regional planning agency called the Delaware Valley Regional Planning Commission (DVRPC). New Jersey later enacted its own enabling legislation recognizing the DVRPC as the official regional planning body.[15] This agency became the funding conduit for federal transportation dollars, giving Bacon and the city an even farther removed role from having any real say on highway planning in the mid-to-late 1960s.

The City Planning Commission's role was curiously ambiguous when it came to highways. It would be part of the web of agencies, including the Pennsylvania Department of Highways and the Philadelphia Department of Streets, in charge of planning, engineering, and construction of highway projects. But its most meaningful role was as the agency responsible for working with the public. Bacon would often serve as the face of the city, explaining highway projects and communicating with communities that stood in their path.

Early in Philadelphia's highway program, Bacon was one of the individuals involved in the final stage planning of the Schuylkill Expressway.[16] Billed as "Philadelphia's first expressway," the Schuylkill was planned in concept in the mid-1930s but finally moved ahead in the late 1940s.[17] It would encounter opposition because it was slated to cut through part of Fairmount Park but, thanks to support from Mayor Clark and Governor John S. Fine in 1953, would eventually proceed with construction on the originally planned route.[18]

While the Schuylkill Expressway avoided residential areas, its Roosevelt Boulevard Extension was planned to cut through several dense communities, displacing over 1,500 residents, and Bacon would be in charge of representing the city to the communities along the proposed route.[19] While he publicly did his job of representing the administration's position, he quietly lobbied the Pennsylvania Department of Highways to find a way to reduce the number of people who would have to move from their homes. It appears that, based primarily on his perseverance, the roadway was reduced from six to four lanes, resulting in 500 fewer residents who would have to be relocated.[20]

By 1964 a number of key highway projects were completed or well underway. The new Walt Whitman Bridge was completed, the Roosevelt Boulevard and Vine Street Extensions of the Schuylkill Expressway were under construction, and in final engineering design were the Industrial Highway, Mid-County Expressway, and Delaware Expressway.[21] Major portions of the Schuylkill Expressway were not only finished but in fact already plagued by congestion.[22] In 1966, the Planning Commission released its "Comprehensive Plan for Expressways."[23]

Bacon recognized that the lack of community involvement in state highway planning was a serious problem, and, indeed, it would become the crux of several highway controversies in the 1960s.[24] He would be part of two primary highway controversies: the Delaware Expressway and the Crosstown Expressway.

The Delaware Expressway

The Delaware Expressway was among the first of Philadelphia's highways accepted into the federal highway program, with the federal government paying up to 90 percent of the $200 million price tag. This project was originally planned in the 1930s, long before Bacon came on the scene. The expressway would run along the eastern side of the city, connecting the southern port areas and the airport with the industrial waterfront in the city's northeast and roadways to the north, giving easy access to the cities of Princeton, Trenton, and New York. It was one of the four arms of Philadelphia's proposed downtown highway loop.

In 1956, the consultant engineering studies for the expressway were finished, and in 1958 the state Department of Highways made its plans for the roadway public. As designed, it would be an elevated roadway, running adjacent to the Delaware River. Even before the release of the plans, there was public opposition to the roadway.[25] One *Bulletin* editorial stated, "this eight-lane highway will be an imposing barrier between residential areas and the concentration of industry along the water front."[26] In a series of public hearings in 1958, Mayor Dilworth explained to residents that highway planning was done at the state level and that city influence was limited.[27]

By the 1960s, Bacon too had concerns about the expressway and its barrier effect along the waterfront.[28] One of the most sensitive areas in his mind was through Society Hill—still in the early stages of revitalization efforts. He and streets commissioner David Smallwood held a meeting in March 1960 with representatives of the state Department of Highways to discuss the treatment of the section running through downtown Philadelphia and Society Hill.[29] Bacon described the meeting as "extremely constructive," but it was unclear what concessions the state was ready to make.[30]

On December 1, 1960, some 200 Society Hill residents met with representatives of the city and state to discuss the Delaware Expressway. State secretary of highways Harral did not come, delegating the job to a lower-level staffer. Bacon, however, did attend to represent the city. The community was up in arms, and Jared Ingersoll, the distinguished and wealthy railroad executive who had recently moved his family to Society Hill, stood up and explained that the community was going to fight the highway.[31] For his part, Bacon was "convinced that this design is as good as can be worked out," creating a divisive situation.[32]

The charge to fight the Delaware Expressway was soon taken up by a new organization called the Philadelphia Architects Committee, comprised of a crew of progressive designers, headed by architect Frank Weise. Nonarchitect Society Hill residents formed another organization called the Committee to Preserve Philadelphia's Historic Gateway, led by Stanhope Browne, a young attorney and recent Society Hill transplant. The groups' collective aim was to promote a redesign for the expressway with a below-grade, covered roadway, as it passed through Center City.[33]

Browne soon learned that he had some strong allies. Senator Joseph Clark was sympathetic to the cause of redesigning the highway, and so was Bill Rafsky.[34] The citizens' groups filed petitions and collected support for fighting the highway. Rafsky helped lobby behind the scenes, bringing pressure from within the business community. Because a covered roadway would require significantly more labor than an uncovered one, the trade unions sided with the community groups. Eventually, these groups also secured the support of the Chamber of Commerce. However, there was significant opposition. The biggest obstacle was the stubborn Henry Harral, the state secretary of highways.[35] Other opposition came from trucking companies, the auto industry, and downtown firms that lobbied for the existing plans to proceed as soon as possible. These groups saw the expressway as a critical element for the city's economic competitiveness—one that should not be delayed.

Bacon may have made a political misstep, aligning himself with one of two sides that were inherently at odds. Once he recognized this fact, it appears that he became less adamant and worked to broker a compromise solution. While some considered Bacon the main target for affecting the highway plans, Browne soon recognized that the real decision makers were in the state Department of Highways. Browne later explained, "At that point, it was really out of Ed Bacon's hands."[36] With the state unwilling to budge, the committees and their allies were successful in going over Harral's head and pressuring the U.S. Bureau of Roads to study the feasibility of a new design. Browne credited Bacon with devising the concept for the new plan. Instead of an elevated highway, on stilts over the existing Delaware Avenue, the new design placed the highway adjacent to Delaware Avenue, sunken but uncovered.

This new design would require costly land acquisition at a sum of about $30 million. After the U.S. Bureau of Roads study showed the concept was feasible and created a model of the new design, the state Department of Highways endorsed it.[37] The concept was praised by important leaders like Bill Day, Senator Clark, and Mayor James Tate.[38] However, to Bacon's frustration, the Society Hill committees did not see this as a viable alternative. Although the highway was sunken, it could still be seen from Society Hill and would remain a barrier between the community and the river.[39] Frank Weise and the Philadelphia Architects Committee set to work on another plan, to serve as a counter-proposal.

The architects' plan, released in December 1965, proposed a six-block cover over the expressway from Arch to Pine Streets.[40] The cover would have been a tremendous added expense, but Bacon did not feel strongly about opposing it. His concern appears to have been getting the project built in a noncontroversial, politically popular, and financially feasible form. With the state unwilling to consider covering a sunken highway, the

Old Philadelphia Development Corporation (OPDC) and the Planning Commission independently identified funds to hire an engineering firm to perform analysis on the new design. The Planning Commission also officially supported studying the covered expressway design, both from Vine Street to Pine Street and a less-expensive alternative from Chestnut Street to Delancey Street, avoiding potential conflicts with the underground Market-Frankford subway.[41] The plans evolved to extend the highway cover over the adjacent Delaware Avenue as well as the ten-lane expressway. The Planning Commission engaged Robert Geddes and landscape architect John Collins to conceive designs for the expressway cover.[42]

Some additional issues occurred in the coming years that complicated the proposal. It was not clear whether state and federal funding could actually be used for a roadway cover. The state raised new opposition that the covered expressway would qualify as a tunnel and therefore could not be used by trucks carrying flammable materials.[43] For a time, Mayor Tate opposed the cover, preferring to use the same money for affordable housing in North Philadelphia.[44] However, in the end the covered expressway concept moved ahead, and by 1969 the concept received most of its needed funding dedicated by Governor Raymond P. Shafer.[45]

While Society Hill's residents were ultimately happy with the turn of events, Society Hill was not the only community opposed to the Delaware Expressway plans. Other vehement opposition came from the Southwark neighborhood, a blue-collar community to the south. Southwark was the earliest part of Philadelphia to be settled, prior to William Penn's land charter, and contained numerous homes certified by the Philadelphia Historical Commission. The state Department of Highways plans proposed condemning several blocks of homes for the expressway, including 131 historically designated properties. The plans also proposed passing on the west side of historic Gloria Dei (Old Swedes') Church, cutting it off from the rest of the city.[46]

Southwark residents had seen their community under siege for a few years already. It was part of the area targeted for redevelopment by the Planning Commission, working with the nonprofit Queen Village Inc., using a revolving fund for attracting the middle class, based on the success of Society Hill.[47] In the same year that Queen Village Inc. was to release its neighborhood revitalization plan, residents along the Southwark neighborhood's eastern edge found out that their homes might be taken for the Delaware Expressway. The local residents, many of whom were longshoremen at the nearby city port, were outraged.

A group led by Gloria Dei's rector, Dr. John C. Roak, proposed an alternate plan—inspired by the Society Hill committees—that would realign the highway to the east, depress it, and cover it as it passed by the historic church. The Southwark group argued that the realignment would require condemnation only of warehouses, not people's homes. The controversy came to a head in 1967, prior to the resolution of the Society Hill redesign plans. By this time, Governor-elect Raymond Shafer had announced his intent to install Robert G. Bartlett to replace Henry Harral as secretary of highways. With little to lose, Harral said he would ask for a restudy of the Southwark area if the Society Hill effort proved successful—laying the burden on his successor to follow through on the promise.[48] However, it appears Bartlett did not follow through.

As in Society Hill, Bacon attended community meetings, representing the city, while Harral remained in Harrisburg. John Roak did not have the political savvy of Stanhope Browne to know that he needed to reach the state level. To him and others in Southwark, Bacon was the culprit and the target for their rage.[49] Because the proposed highway would remove so many historic homes, Charles Peterson got involved, spearheading the largest Southwark protest, leading a crew of longshoremen to stage a mock funeral procession for the doomed homes of Southwark, interrupting a luncheon of the National Trust for Historic Preservation.[50]

In contrast to the more successful advocacy of the Society Hill groups, the protests of the Southwark community would be for naught. In late November 1967, the demolition crews came to start clearing the way for the expressway. Southwark lacked the wealthy residents with connections that now existed in Society Hill, and ultimately its battle to fend off the expressway was unsuccessful. Bacon did not seem to take any real action to redesign the highway or mitigate its impact through Southwark. The construction of the Delaware Expressway, designated Interstate 95, led to the demolition of historic homes and became a wall between Southwark and its industrial waterfront, the place where so many of the longshoremen in the community made their livelihood.

The Crosstown Expressway

The second controversial highway project of the 1960s was the Crosstown Expressway, the southern leg of the Center City loop, paralleling the Vine

Street Expressway to the north. Known at the time as the Lombard Expressway, it would have required the demolition of half the houses along this
east-west city roadway. The project was devised in the 1930s, shown in the
Better Philadelphia Exhibition, and promoted by Robert B. Mitchell when
he was planning director.[51] The project slogged along slowly in the 1950s
and was rejected for addition to the Federal Interstate System in 1957,
pushing it farther down the list of projects on the drawing board.[52] In 1959,
the Philadelphia Department of Streets worked with the Planning Commission to propose a new route for the expressway, moving it from Lombard
Street a block south to South Street and gaining it a new name: the Crosstown Expressway.[53] It was included in many Planning Commission plans,
including the 1963 Center City plan, shown feeding into a large parking
garage at the intersection of Broad and South Streets, so that drivers could
arrive downtown, easily park, and walk into Center City.[54]

All the while, there was some community opposition, but it had not yet
gotten heated since the project seemed far off and possibly a pipe dream.
Then, suddenly, in spring 1966, the first residents in the Grays Ferry neighborhood, at the western end of the proposed route, received notices from
the Pennsylvania Department of Highways that officials would be entering
their homes to appraise properties in the path of the expressway.[55] This first
sign of impending condemnation set off a wave of uncertainty and panic.
Community leaders tried to act early, inviting representatives from the
Department of Highways to meet with residents in Grays Ferry, but the
highwaymen never came.

The controversy spread quickly to the other communities along the
highway's path. The $60 million, 2.6 mile highway would cut through sev-
eral poor and working-class areas of the city, just south of the downtown
core. There seemed to be no sign that the city and state were prepared to
address the issue of more than 6,000 residents who would be displaced and
need to be rehoused.[56] Some noted that the roadway would create a barrier
separating neighborhoods racially and socioeconomically.[57]

A group of community leaders came together to oppose the highway as
planned, and insisted that it be sunken and covered. Community opposition
was led by George T. Dukes, executive director of the South Philadelphia
Fellowship Committee, who formed an organization called Independent
Citizens Committee to Preserve and Develop the Crosstown Community.
Other key voices were Robert J. Sugarman, a young attorney who lived a

Figure 18. Protest of the proposed Crosstown Expressway outside Philadelphia City Hall, *Bulletin*, March 22, 1968. Courtesy of Temple University Libraries, Urban Archives.

block from the proposed path of the expressway, and local resident Alice Lipscomb.[58]

Publicly, it seemed Bacon would continue to support the Crosstown Expressway, so long as that was the mayor's position.[59] His official role in the project was to plan for rehousing displaced residents and building new housing and businesses over the lid that would potentially cap the expressway.[60] However, it appears that Bacon privately was less supportive than he may have shown in public meetings, and sought to reduce the project's negative impacts. Bacon recalled, "what I did do on the Crosstown Expressway, when I finally saw how wrong it was, I saw to it that the neighbors got access to the State Department of Highways, and that they were able to express their disapproval directly."[61] In a July 1967 memo, he wrote that, after talking to the project engineer for the expressway, he had discovered, "the design of the roadway had certain flexibility and was not as 'sacred' as the Streets Department led us to believe."[62]

Soon thereafter, Mayor Tate hinted that he might end up opposing the highway altogether, due to the massive displacement of residents it would cause.[63] State highway secretary Robert Bartlett coldheartedly told the media, in response to inquiries about the project's potential residential displacement, "We're not in the housing business."[64] With the mayor starting to cast a pall of doubt on the project, the Pennsylvania Department of Highways decided to ignore Mayor Tate and move ahead on steps to condemn properties in the Crosstown's path, without the city's cooperation.[65] By the end of the month, Mayor Tate decided he was no longer going to support a Crosstown Expressway at South Street and gave Bacon the authority to start creating a community plan for the neighborhoods that, until recently, were in the highway's path.[66] The members of the Crosstown community hired the design firm of Venturi and Rauch to represent its interest in negotiations with the Planning Commission.[67] The need for this design work was evident because, since the expressway's planning began in earnest, merchants had been moving out and property values plummeted.[68]

Mayor Tate had thrown down the gauntlet, but new state highway secretary Bartlett took up the challenge. Bartlett came out with his own public announcement that, if the city was set on eliminating the Crosstown, then he would also remove the proposed Cobbs Creek Parkway from the state highway plan—a road many saw as necessary for access to the city's new airport.[69] Bartlett thought his threat would make the city waver, but, without flinching, Bacon recommended to the Planning Commission that it remove the Crosstown and a portion of the Cobbs Creek Expressway from the city's comprehensive plan.[70]

Bacon then focused his energies on replanning the "Crosstown Corridor" with the assumption that the highway was dead. The mayor announced his intention to create a $2 million community development fund to support the neighborhood project. Bacon also proposed having the city announce that it would be purchasing properties for public housing—thus discouraging private speculators and the threat of gentrification.[71] In December 1968, City Council approved ordinances authorizing the community planning for the South Street area, allowing applications to be sent to Washington for federal funding to support community investment.[72]

However, the proponents of the Crosstown had not yet given up, and the Greater Philadelphia Chamber of Commerce continued to push the mayor to revive the roadway.[73] The Chamber recruited other powerful voices in favor of the Crosstown, including David Wallace, former planning director at the Redevelopment Authority, who had continued his career in Baltimore.[74] However, it appears that these voices were not enough to sway Mayor Tate.

In March 1969, Bacon informed the mayor that he had heard from a reliable source that the federal Department of Housing and Urban Development (HUD) was going to withhold approvals needed to gain major redevelopment funding for the Crosstown communities—now called Southwest Central—until the city and state finally resolved the expressway issue.[75] The mayor indeed soon received a letter from HUD with an ultimatum to resolve the highway issue or lose federal funding.[76] Bacon jumped to action, asking the city's Law Department to write a memo to Washington, "outlining the City's legal authority and power to prevent the construction of the Crosstown Expressway . . . now that the proposed highway has been stricken from the City's Comprehensive Plan."[77]

While Bacon continued to fight for killing the highway, Mayor Tate caved in to the pressure and decided to reconsider the Crosstown, asking his officials to develop a new alternative.[78] The first alternative plan was conceived by streets commissioner David Smallwood and managing director Fred Corleto, calling for a split highway with one-way traffic on two separate streets.[79] Bacon suggested other approaches to the mayor in a confidential report, including "an elevated expressway on Washington Avenue," a wider, more industrial roadway to the south.[80] Overall, however, he made clear that his priority was regaining the HUD money, not building a highway.[81] The city passed on its alternatives to Washington, but soon learned that the federal government would continue to withhold the funds until the community agreed to one of these alternative approaches.[82]

Bacon took on the job of meeting with the community groups, trying to come to consensus on an acceptable course of action. However, it appears that he fumbled this undertaking. The residents responded with rage, seemingly believing the city was using the HUD money as a ploy to get them to discuss reviving the highway. In response, residents threatened "a pre-Christmas boycott of 'major' center city stores unless Mayor Tate states the road will not run along South St."[83] Bacon pushed on and met with Robert Sugarman, the attorney representing the community group, along with other community members. Resulting from these meetings, he reported to the mayor that the community leaders "said that they would favor a corridor on Washington Avenue."[84]

The participants agreed to engage third-party consultants to work with the state, city, and community to develop a set of alternatives everyone could agree to.[85] In June, however, the whole issue was laid to rest when the U.S. Department of Transportation alerted Secretary Bartlett that no federal aid funding would be provided for the study of the Crosstown alternatives, because it seemed that the communities did not support the process. Bartlett wrote back, arguing that there was indeed community support for the study.[86] However, the feds remained unconvinced, and the state effort to keep the highway alive fell by the wayside.

The Crosstown Expressway stayed on some plans for a few more years, at times looking as if it could possibly be revived before it was finally killed once the Delaware Valley Regional Planning Commission struck it from the region's official long-range transportation plan in October 1973.[87] Meanwhile, Bacon's effort to save the federal funding for community redevelopment was successful, and he happily moved ahead in working with the South Central communities to plan for a highway-free future.

A Car-Free Zone on Chestnut Street

For much of his career, Bacon endorsed plans with highways moving people in and out of Center City Philadelphia, but once people were downtown, it was long Bacon's view that they should walk. As he wrote in 1964, "Center City really belongs to the person on foot and he should be given every reasonable consideration."[88] To that end, Bacon put forward the notion of closing Chestnut Street, an existing city thoroughfare, to automobile traffic for twenty-two blocks, with a two-way trolley up the center. In this way, he believed, the congested downtown could be reclaimed for pedestrians. Bacon was not the first to propose the idea of closing Chestnut Street to cars. In November 1955, Louis Kahn publicly presented a series of concepts for improving systems of movement in Philadelphia, where he recommended closing Chestnut and Market Streets to all vehicular traffic except buses.[89]

In the early 1960s, the OPDC formed a task force to investigate the feasibility of outfitting a pedestrian-only Chestnut Street with a two-way trolley system. Victor Gruen was hired to study the Planning Commission's design concepts and make recommendations.[90] During this period, Bacon began actively meeting with merchants along Chestnut Street to develop

support and talk through concerns. At the time, Chestnut Street was Philadelphia's premier shopping street, called by *The Times* of London the
"equivalent of Fifth Avenue in New York."[91] Bacon hoped to make Chestnut Street even more of a landmark by creating this pedestrian-friendly
environment—away from the hazards and noise of vehicular traffic. He
took a trip to a conference in Ottawa, a city with a pedestrian-only shopping street, and on returning, used the Canadian success to argue his
point.[92]

However, by 1963, there was a small but vocal group of merchants
opposed to the plan. Their opposition was mainly about how traffic could
be rerouted to prevent congestion and how loading would take place for
businesses lacking alternate entrances. Some businesses were concerned
that removing the opportunity for curbside parking or the chance for
patrons to drive by the businesses, would mean they would lose their cus-
tomers. One business owner told the media that he feared the street closing
would "strike the death knell for Chestnut Street."[93] Bacon engaged in
meetings and public discourse with a representative of the opposition,
including several debates broadcast on the radio.[94] In October 1963 Mayor
Tate had formally backed the concept for the "Chestnut Street Transitway,"
and in November 1964 City Council approved $90,000 in public dollars to
start its planning.[95]

The Planning Commission engaged Arthur Kaufmann, formerly chief
executive of Gimbels department store, as a consultant to develop a feasibility study for the mall, and the firm of Simpson & Curtin to carry out a
traffic study. Despite Kaufmann's strong support, other major business
leaders were less enthusiastic, and the OPDC was divided on the matter.
The Simpson & Curtin traffic report came out in November 1966, showing
that the Chestnut Street plan was feasible, but only after the construction
of the Crosstown Expressway.[96] The Crosstown was, of course, very controversial at that point and, due to the divisiveness of the situation, Bacon
recommended to Mayor Tate "that we should not pursue the matter further."[97] For the time being, the Chestnut Street plan would go back on the
shelf.

The project remained dormant until it gained new attention on April
23, 1970, when Mayor Tate ordered Chestnut Street closed to traffic for two
hours as part of Earth Week. The *Bulletin* reported, "The response among
the shoppers and strollers—not to mention the stream of young people
who headed down to hear Ralph Nader and other Earth Week notables at

VIEW AT BROAD STREET

Figure 19. City Planning Commission drawing of proposed concept to close Chestnut Street to vehicular traffic and create a pedestrian street with a two-way trolley in the center. From the commission's 1960 report "Center City Philadelphia: Major Elements of the Physical Development Plan for Center City." Courtesy of the Edmund N. Bacon Collection, The Architectural Archives, University of Pennsylvania.

Independence Hall—appeared highly enthusiastic."[98] The street closure idea was revived (Bacon was now in retirement), and the Chestnut Street Association approved plans for the concept in 1974, despite some remaining opposition. From Eighth to Eighteenth Street, Chestnut Street was closed to automobile traffic, the sidewalks were expanded, and new midblock crosswalks were installed. Buses were still permitted down the street—hence the "transitway." The corridor was lined with brass and aluminum light poles, decorated with banners, and the sidewalks were equipped with benches, flower planters, and decorative bus shelters. It was funded through a combination of federal, state, and local dollars, with the federal Urban Mass Transportation Administration providing a grant covering 80 percent of the $7.4 million price tag.[99] The federal support for the transitway was surely aided by the national fuel crisis.

The transitway was celebrated almost universally in 1976, and an editorial in the *Inquirer* called the project "a milestone in the renaissance of Center City Philadelphia."[100] A 1985 public survey showed 71 percent of respondents believing Chestnut Street was better without automobile traffic.[101] However, as the years went on, the initial vision of a pedestrian-only street with electric trolleys started to fall apart. SEPTA—Philadelphia's transit authority—decided to run conventional, full-sized buses on the transitway, rather than building a trolley system or using smaller shuttle buses.[102] The city failed to keep up the streetscape; the bricks and lamps broke and the trees started to die.[103] Eventually, the city decided to allow automobiles on Chestnut Street between 6:30 p.m. and 6 a.m., and delivery trucks were allowed to unload on the transitway at all times.

After merchants protested for fully restoring automobile traffic, the city redesigned the street to have one lane of traffic and one bus and bicycle-only lane. However, the city allowed right turns from the bus/bicycle lane, leading the federal government to withhold millions in funding to the city for negating the effective use of the bus-only lane. In the end, Bacon's transitway concept was never truly realized in Philadelphia, and the project eroded rapidly after the initial investment was made. Meanwhile, other cities, like Denver, built true transitways and created successful and vibrant pedestrian streets.

Toward a Post-Petroleum Future

In the mid- to late 1960s, Bacon seems to have had a dual persona regarding highway planning. At home in Philadelphia, he was representing the mayor's position, but, behind the scenes, he was taking steps to attack the status quo of top-down highway planning, advocating an approach that gave citizens a greater voice. Bacon was nominated to serve on President Lyndon B. Johnson's Citizens' Advisory Committee on Recreation and Natural Beauty, where he was chosen to chair the Subcommittee on the Highway and the Environment. This was an important time for Bacon's topic since the new Department of Transportation Act had recently passed through the House and Senate, signed into law by President Johnson on September 13, 1966.

Bacon used his position to fight the destructive nature of highway building, surely informed by the lessons of the Delaware Expressway and the Crosstown Expressway. His report recommended that the federal government establish a set of safeguards to ensure public participation and a stronger role for citizens in appealing decisions about highway routes.[104] In June 1968, he made a presentation to Vice President Hubert Humphrey and First Lady Ladybird Johnson, where he asserted that the government should not be spending more money on building new highways.[105]

On December 16, 1968, Bacon represented the committee at a Department of Transportation hearing, where he made a powerful statement against the tactics of the highway planners:

> Our recommendations stressed the need for a formalized procedure which would give the interested citizen a right to express his ideas on where the road should go before that decision was irreversibly made. . . . It is true that, up until four or five years ago, the highway engineers had things pretty much their own way, and they successfully bulldozed through all obstacles on routes determined by the single value consideration of the cost-benefit analysis. . . . In case after case, in city after city, vast systems of highway construction have ground to a standstill because of citizen resistance. . . . It has already been recognized by Congress in legislative requirements for greater citizen voice in the formation of governmental policy which directly and drastically affects citizens' lives, notably in the field of housing and urban development. The establishment of similar provisions related to highway design is both timely and appropriate.[106]

By the mid-1960s, Bacon had in fact begun to voice skepticism of America's car-based society—though never in public venues. In an interview in 1966, he said, "there is a 'revulsion' against the automobile and the destruction it does to cities and the countryside. The car is losing its luster as something worth sacrificing for."[107] After his retirement in 1970, free of his public duty, Bacon was much more outspoken on this point. The gasoline price surge in the early 1970s heightened national awareness about the world's reliance on oil, and he saw the opportunity to promote a vision for a "Post Petroleum" future. He argued, "We've got to quit using petroleum for our basic way of getting around."[108]

For Bacon, the oil crisis was inherently connected to the wasteful nature of the suburbs and the possibility for a truly urban future. In 1973 he argued in an official committee report for the Urban Land Institute, "The most important issue affecting the building of cities is the shortage of oil and gasoline."[109] In a journal article, he argued, "Those who think the lack of availability of cheap gasoline will have little effect on the form of cities are probably as far wrong as were those early in the century who thought that its original application to the powering of motor vehicles also would have little effect."[110] Bacon was quick to note that this extreme reliance on oil was a relatively recent phenomenon: "With no aid from gasoline this country embraced the Industrial Revolution, developed the skyscraper, built cities of millions of population."[111] He continued, "Thus, habituated as we are to the idea that gasoline is essential to our national life, we have already proved to ourselves we can get along without it. We may even come to accept the idea that its use for mobility was a fleeting phenomenon on the American scene."

In passionate speech after speech, article after article, Bacon described a vision of a future without cars or petroleum-based transportation, where electric-powered mass transit and bicycles were the predominant means of everyday trips.[112] He was among a small group of advocates across the globe who envisioned a world without oil. However, he pushed the envelope farther, imagining a world also devoid of suburbs and automobiles. It was this leap that put him far beyond the mainstream. For Bacon, the direction America and the world needed to go in required a significant change in accepted lifestyles, rather than simply a new source of fuel for private cars.

Bacon suggested shortening the workday and creating three-day weekends to lower energy consumption. He proposed placing growth limits on suburban development, with new homes clustered around transit lines and in existing urbanized areas.[113] He wrote an article for the *Philadelphia Daily News* in April 1975, titled, "Clean Air, No Gangs, No Private Cars." In the piece, he described the year 2025 when the city would have no cars and streets would alternate between trolley and bicycle routes. Some neighborhood streets would be gated off, creating safe spaces for children to play. For Bacon the utopian city of the future merged his beliefs in racial integration and sustainable transportation. He mused, "Jose and Pearl and Mohammed and Ching See" would harmoniously take part in a game of hopscotch. The city would be quiet and clean because "there is no more gasoline for automobiles, buses and trucks."[114]

In his future world, Bacon imagined, "The great areas formerly occupied by the sprawling suburbs, wasteful of space and energy, are now turned back into agriculture and forestry; some few examples are preserved to show the younger generation the ways their ancestors once lived."[115] He argued that this future world would lead to a much better life for Americans. He explained, "it will mean a rediscovery of values that we have lost sight of. . . . We [will] have rediscovered the smell of honeysuckle and cow dung, the feeling of wind in our faces, the joy of being hot and cold, dry and wet, joys we had lost in the sealed insulation of the automobiles which encapsulated us."

Naturally, Bacon's notions were met with considerable skepticism. A columnist in the *Bulletin* commented, "Probably the Bacon view is somewhat extreme."[116] At a forum convened by *Scientific American*, another panelist challenged Bacon: "Ed Bacon has suggested that people act irrationally in making transportation decisions. It seems better, however, to consider ways in which their desires can be reasonably accommodated rather than to approach the issue only from the standpoint of changing their behavior."[117] Bacon wanted to hear none of this. He was looking for nothing short of immediate action, starting a wholesale revolution in the way Americans lived, that would lead to the quick demise of the suburbs, the end of the car, and a new heyday for America's cities. He argued, "we can be quite sure that by 2076 there will be no suburbs, or suburban way of life. And from my own point of view, that will be quite a benefit."[118]

Bacon traveled to gas-guzzling Houston, Texas, and stunned his audience with his vision of a car-free America. An article in the *Houston Chronicle* reported, "If the term post-modernism has thrown architectural design into a stylistic free for all, Edmund N. Bacon . . . tossed a hair-raising new term into the scene here last week. He hailed the arrival soon of the 'post petroleum era'."[119] Using this term, Bacon pitched a book concept, and in November 1973 he signed a publishing agreement with Viking Press for

"The Post Petroleum City."[120] However, after a string of postponements, distractions, changes in editors, and several assistants, he never did write the book.

He later tried to launch a "World Congress on the Post Petroleum City," where representatives of various cities would convene and present a vision for how they would adapt to a post-petroleum future.[121] He hoped this conference would act as a seed that would start to grow in cities across the globe, slowly infiltrating meeting rooms, city halls, and parliament buildings, starting to shift public policy.[122]

Bacon worked tirelessly, though unsuccessfully, at getting this conference off the ground between 1987 and 1991.[123] The project seemed to have steam for awhile, with the University of Pennsylvania's prominent design school dean Martin Meyerson as chairman and ten cities in nine nations agreeing to participate.[124] In one iteration of the conference, the United Nations Centre for Regional Development agreed to be a convener, while later the venue was to be Metropolis '93, the annual conference of the World Association of Major Metropolises.[125] Ultimately, however, the conference never happened. One of Bacon's colleagues on the project, Peter Newman, recalled, "There were very few people, planners in particular, who understood the [oil] crisis. . . . Ed was too early."[126]

Bacon's lasting contribution to imagining an energy-efficient world was to challenge others to think about it before there was broader public awareness of the crisis of "peak oil." He worked with a number of individuals who would go on to keep pushing for sustainable solutions to addressing a post-petroleum future. For example, Mark Bernstein, involved in Bacon's early conference planning, later worked in the administration of President Bill Clinton and then became a professor at the University of Southern California, where, in 2009, he was appointed managing director of the USC Energy Institute. Jeffrey Kenworthy and Peter Newman, professors at Curtin University in Perth, Australia, continued to stay at the forefront of scholarship on planning for a world without oil, together publishing *Sustainability and Cities: Overcoming Automobile Dependence* in 1999.

In 2009, Newman was the lead author of *Resilient Cities: Responding to Peak Oil and Climate Change*. In 2008, the University of Pennsylvania held an international conference called "Cities After the Age of Oil," in which world experts convened to discuss a sustainable future for cities—a concept very similar to Bacon's vision for the World Congress. However, Bacon would not get to experience this conference, having passed away in 2005.

While at one point in his career Bacon certainly favored highways as part of a comprehensive transportation system for getting people downtown, by the mid- to late 1960s it appears his view on this issue had changed significantly to one that was critical of top-down highway planning and radically doubting the sustainability of a car-based culture for America's future.

While he was outspoken in Washington, at home Bacon remained silent on what he really thought about the Delaware and Crosstown Expressways, continuing obediently to represent the position of the mayor. He explained, "I had a personal policy that I would always support the policies of the administration I was working for."[127] At times he seems to have made compromises to see the city's public works agenda move ahead without a snag. Sometimes it seems that he even pushed for highway projects to retain funding for community development.

It appears that part of Bacon's entrepreneurial approach was to take a stance of not rocking the boat at home, while advocating for changing the equation of highway planning via his Washington appointments. This behind-the-scenes advocacy was invisible to community groups in Philadelphia, whose only exposure to Bacon was as the forceful public official who came to meetings arguing for the need to build these massive road projects. As he stood at the height of his public visibility, the battles over highways would negatively affect his image in Philadelphia and ultimately create a confusing element in assessing his legacy.

Chapter 7

_____

ARTICULATING A VISION IN A SHIFTING WORLD

By the 1960s, the changes to Philadelphia's urban landscape already had gained considerable attention in the media. An article in the *Saturday Evening Post*, for example, recounted the civic projects from Penn Center to Society Hill, stating, "Today a visitor to Philadelphia would hardly know the place."[1] *Progressive Architecture* bestowed two national awards on Philadelphia projects in 1962 for Vincent Kling's Municipal Services Building and Robert Geddes's Penn's Landing Plan.[2] In November that year, the *New York Times* called Philadelphia "the city with the best urban redevelopment record to date."[3] In March 1963, Colin D. Buchanan, of the British Ministry of Transport, said at a conference in Philadelphia, "I have no doubt that what is happening in the heart of Philadelphia is something of enduring significance to human culture, from which the rest of the world has a great deal to learn."[4]

As Philadelphia's fame increased, so did Bacon's, leading to his cameo on the cover of *Time* magazine in 1964. Bacon was just one of a number of important players in Philadelphia, but he was consistently the city's public face. He leveraged his ever-growing fame to promote his own agenda—to move Philadelphia closer to becoming the first American city to prove that it could revive itself, against all odds, restore its neighborhoods and downtown, compete with the suburbs, and become known on the international stage. His long-term vision was to make Philadelphia into the first American city that could undergo a wholesale renaissance, ending up with a downtown to rival the great cities of Europe, with neighborhoods that were livable, diverse, and equitable.

A 1963 book called *Man and the Modern City* included a chapter by Bacon titled "The City Image." Here he wrote, "If American cities are to change into something worth having, there must be a clear image clearly conceived of what the city should be, and this image must be injected into and mature within the processes which actually dictate the form the city will take."[5] He questioned, "What image is there which will supplant the image of the suburban ideal?" If Philadelphia were to succeed, it would be by establishing a firm conceptualization for the future of the city— something to characterize it among an international audience. Bacon wrote, "While it may lack the single spectacular element of a New York or a New Orleans, the new image of Philadelphia is rising slowly but surely, and it is a complete image."[6] He would spend significant time attempting to articulate and promote this image of Philadelphia.

However, in the 1960s, Philadelphia and cities across the nation would see racial tension exploding in the latter half of the decade into urban violence and unrest. In addition, a landmark book, *The Death and Life of Great American Cities*, written by Jane Jacobs, symbolized the beginning of a major shift in the planning community that would significantly change how planners and government officials interacted with communities. Bacon's greatest moment of fame came as these societal shifts challenged both his approach and the immediacy of his dream for an impending renaissance for Philadelphia.

A Complete Vision

Since his days working in Flint, Bacon had had a concept of urban revitalization that relied on investing in downtown and rebuilding neighborhoods. In Philadelphia, his vision came to focus on restoring the city's international prestige, while rivaling the suburbs as a desirable place to live, leading to a future with racially and economically integrated urban neighborhoods. Bacon relied on a number of tools to articulate and promote this vision. One of these was through the Planning Commission's official documents.

In 1954 Bill Rafsky invited Bacon's colleague Walter Blucher to carry out an assessment of the Planning Commission and its professional staff.[7] Blucher's greatest criticism was that the Commission was spending too much time on individual projects and not enough on comprehensive planning.[8] In response, in 1955 Bacon hired Arthur T. Row, who previously had served as assistant director of the Detroit Metropolitan Area Traffic Study, as a second assistant executive director to head up a citywide master planning effort.

In May 1960, the Planning Commission released its Comprehensive Plan for the City of Philadelphia, a 375-page oversized document laying out a future course for the city.[9] The plan contained very little in the way of physical design, using a number of charts and diagrams to demonstrate statistical analysis. It appears that Bacon was neither excited about the plan nor very involved in its creation.[10] His lack of enthusiasm had to do with the fact that the plan was technical in nature, citywide in scale, and thus unable to provide a succinct, compelling image that could be promoted to excite the public and the media.

However, while Art Row was developing the citywide plan, Bacon was spearheading his own planning effort. Following the release of the Comprehensive Plan, the City Planning Commission presented to the mayor a report called "Center City, Philadelphia: Major Elements of the Physical Development Plan for Center City."[11] This plan would be repackaged in 1963 into a large-scale document for mass distribution, with an iconic blue cover.[12] Unlike the Comprehensive Plan, it did not have analysis, numbers, and charts. Instead, it contained stunning, colorful spreads with elaborate images by Willo von Moltke and others on the Planning Commission design staff. It had transparent overlays illustrating the complex interrelationship between land use and transportation in the heart of town. This document, for the first time, showed a complete image of the future downtown Bacon had been imagining in his head to this point, with all these Center City projects fitting together—Penn Center, Market East, Society Hill, Independence Mall, mass transit, expressways, and a number of brand new ideas.

This 1963 Center City plan showed these numerous projects seamlessly flowing into each other. Penn Center's concourse tied into the promenades of Market East, running into the greensward of Independence Mall, stretching down and connecting to the Society Hill Greenway System, with these garden paths meandering to the river and connecting with a new set of waterfront recreational amenities at Penn's Landing. The plan gave the impression that these spaces were truly interconnected and that any one project would leave a gaping void in the continuous chain of this mostly imaginary city landscape. It became Bacon's showroom model.

A final illustration called "The Site Plan" wove all these projects into a single, crisp drawing, spanning river to river. The accompanying text states, "The site plan on the facing page presents the full realization of the Center City Plan. . . . It disrupts the smallest amount possible in order to conserve

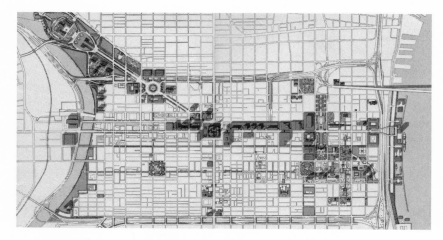

Figure 20. "The Site Plan," illustration from the Philadelphia City Planning Commission, 1963, "The Plan for Center City Philadelphia." Personal collection of the author.

what is already here. . . . All of the new buildings are related to each other and to the larger area in a clear and organized way. . . . It is built upon the original plan of William Penn, and attempts to carry forward into our present day the clarity and simplicity of his idea for Philadelphia."[13]

However, Bacon's interest in Center City was not the end of his vision by any means—it was merely the apparatus for achieving a grander set of goals. Bacon saw the revival of Center City as the basis for a larger citywide transformation that was long term and abstract. He imagined Philadelphia's future as a city with racially and economically integrated neighborhoods that could be achieved only after half a century of effort and would need national and international attention to provide the political impetus to make it possible. In a 1959 article, Bacon laid out his long-term vision, imagining what Philadelphia could look like in the year 2009. Bacon stated that "roughly the first half of our fifty-year period will be spent on economic and technical advances making downtown the symbol of our region, a symbol that commands world respect."[14] After envisioning Philadelphia as a great world-class city, he continued, "I think, the second half of this period will be a great, concentrated social and human effort . . . [in which] we will finally turn our full energies to the job of housing our people."

Imagining the year 2009, Bacon saw a future in which the middle class was again interested in urban living, renovating and reoccupying Philadelphia's existing housing stock. He argued, "The suburban idea as the only healthy American way of life has been challenged by a significant minority who find greater values for family living in the cultural and social advantages of the city."[15] Meanwhile, he prognosticated, "the newer but less well built suburbs just over the city line are deteriorating." In Bacon's vision of the future, a renewed interest in urban living would create market forces leading to economic integration. He argued, "by the process of the natural operation of the market . . . there is automatically occurring a breaking up of large accumulations of a single income group."

It is important to recognize that this was Bacon's vision alone. The overall vision of the Center City plan, the long-term renaissance—these were not part of the city's formal agenda, or necessarily the will of the mayor. In fact, these arguments did not jibe entirely with the beliefs of other powerful city officials like Bill Rafsky. At the same time that Bacon was pushing his ideas, others were focusing on regaining Philadelphia's industrial job base, improving the city's schools, or building high-rise public housing projects. Bacon's long-term vision was difficult if not impossible to sell, since it did not immediately address short-term problems like public education. Instead, it took a broader view, looking at solving problems more comprehensively, decades down the road through an approach that looked to market Philadelphia on an international level.

In the 1960s, Bacon had an increasing number of venues for selling his vision, as the major professional organizations were excited to come to Philadelphia and see the urban renewal work, as well as be exposed to the hotbed of ideas at the University of Pennsylvania Fine Arts School, under the leadership of G. Holmes Perkins. With each presentation, Bacon honed his message and marketing approach, so as to make the greatest impact on his audience.

One of Bacon's most influential productions came on Thursday, April 27, 1961, when he made a presentation to the national conference of the American Institute of Architects (AIA), which was meeting in Philadelphia. He took the audience through a virtual journal of nearly three hundred years of Philadelphia architecture and planning. On stage was a twenty-four-by-fourteen-foot white panel. Key members of his staff joined Bacon onstage, explaining the projects they had headed up and drawing the plans

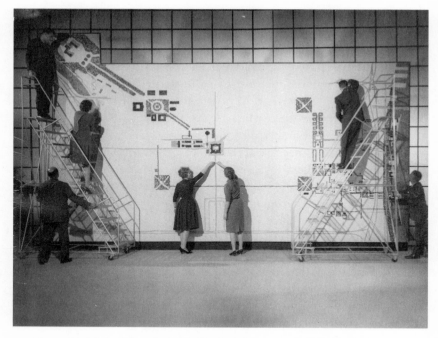

Figure 21. Photo from the 1961 filming of *Form, Design and the City*, reenacting a presentation from the American Institute of Architects 1961 conference in Philadelphia, in which Bacon, his staff, and prominent designers drew on a giant wall to illustrate Philadelphia's evolving physical development. Courtesy of the Edmund N. Bacon Collection, The Architectural Archives, University of Pennsylvania.

for these projects in colored chalk on the panel, sometimes climbing on ladders to reach parts of the enormous canvas. Before the audience's eyes, piece by piece, the modern and future city took shape. As the audience was struck with the completed composition, Bacon explained, "This is not the work of one man. This is the cumulative effect of the individual efforts of a great many people over an extended period of time."[16] He announced, "Here we have a three-dimensional system of space organization. . . . It is not planning as it is generally done. It is not architecture, but the form that should precede architecture awaiting the designer's touch to bring it into life."

If Bacon had explained the concepts in words, the projects might have seemed abstract and disconnected. Drawn together on the giant canvas, running into each other, with connecting systems of movement, it seemed obvious that these were not stand-alone projects; they were the interlocking elements of a complete vision—a singular plan. He explained, "Without a central design idea as an organizing force, the individual efforts under urban renewal will lead to chaos. With a central design idea to relate to, the creative energies of the individual architects will be stimulated to new heights, and the result will truly be architecture."[17]

Just as the Better Philadelphia Exhibition had captured the minds of the public, so did Bacon's 1961 presentation capture the minds of the architectural profession. Within a week of the event, he received a telegram from Philip Will, Jr., president of the AIA, informing him that the AIA wanted to make a film based on the presentation and had gotten an agreement from Reynolds Metals to finance the production.[18] Bacon agreed, and the performance was repeated, this time with a script, resulting in the film *Form, Design, and the City.*[19] It premiered on March 27, 1962, at the Philadelphia Museum of Art to an invitation-only audience of more than 200 members of Philadelphia's business and civic elite. Within a year it was shown 167 times in 23 states, as well as Austria and Canada.[20] Over the coming years, *Form, Design, and the City* became well known in the architecture and planning world, today available on DVD from the AIA Bookstore in Philadelphia.

"Things do get built": *Design of Cities*

Another major venue for Bacon to promote his ideas on an international stage would be his 1967 book *Design of Cities.* The book capped a period of intense research, travel, and writing that Bacon packaged into the volume with writings and images. Perhaps the most influential trip was to Italy in 1955 hosted by the National Town Planning Institute of Italy, involving ten scholars from America and ten from Italy, hosted by renowned Italian architect Bruno Zevi.[21]

Bacon produced a highly visual book that he hoped would appeal to both practitioners and students of urban design. He started it in the early 1960s, and in fall 1965 took a month off of work, without pay, to finish it.[22] He asked his staff members to help him and paid them for the extra work—with his designers often putting in time on weekends to finish the project.[23] Some of the most significant staff support came from his chief cartographer, Alois Strobl, who designed many of the images and diagrams.

Design of Cities was a fluid book, without chapters, capturing concepts through stand-alone two-page spreads. Bacon was enamored with the work of the late Swiss artist Paul Klee and included a number of Klee's sketches and watercolors in his book. He designed the book around the images and laid the text in the empty spaces and adjacent pages. Many of the images were in full color and bled to the edge of the page. Bacon insisted on complete control over the layout.[24] Surely, it was a complex book to edit and an expensive book to produce. A note from his editor, years later, indicates that there was some tension at Viking regarding Bacon's micromanagement of the layout process.[25]

Design of Cities starts with an overview of key principles and concepts in urban design. Then the book explains these concepts in the context of numerous world cities, from ancient Greece to the present. It concludes, showing the realization of the lessons throughout the book applied to Philadelphia's development. It was a not-so-subtle intimation that Philadelphia's contemporary planning reflected the lessons of hundreds of years of best practices from cities around the globe, making it a model for modern urban planning and design.

One of the historical precedents Bacon included in *Design of Cities* was the work of Pope Sixtus V in Rome, who reigned as pontiff from 1585 to 1590 and whom one prominent scholar praised for merging disparate planning ideas "together into a unified scheme—his master plan."[26] Bacon often used Sixtus to demonstrate the notion that great cities in Europe were not built by a single designer; rather, they were developed over time by individuals who were cognizant and respectful of the work of past designers. This case study would become one of the most prominent historical examples in his speeches and presentations throughout the 1960s and the rest of his career.

Design of Cities provides insight into the way Bacon viewed the world. The first lesson of the book is the idea of "The City as an Act of Will," arguing that cities are shaped by human ideas, not accidental forces. Bacon provided his own definition of architecture: "the articulation of space so as to produce in the participator a definite space experience in relation to previous and anticipated space experiences."[27] His concept of successful design was architecture that created and was part of a journey, rather than a static building. Perhaps more clearly than ever before, Bacon acknowledged the importance of the planner as promoter of ideas. He argued, "So it is the function of the designer to conceive an idea, implant it, and nurture its growth in the collective minds of the community in such a way that the final product has a reasonable chance of coming close to his original concept."[28] Using Philadelphia as a case study, Bacon demonstrated how, by building on the work of others over the course of the city's history and nurturing these ideas, he and others had birthed modern-day Philadelphia, demonstrating that "things do get built," but they take patience.[29] He explained in the Foreword, "My qualifications for writing this book are those not of the scholar or historian but of a participator in the recent history of the rebirth of Philadelphia."[30]

Another important element of *Design of Cities* is Bacon's discussion of "democratic feedback," the relationship of designers with community stakeholders. In other places, he admitted that he based his view of feedback on a concept developed by Norbert Wiener, the prominent mathematician, for manufacturing.[31] Bacon argued that Philadelphia's redevelopment "proves the value of setting up a procedure whereby the process itself involves the citizen in the planning, enriching the plan thereby and building up public acceptance of the plan once it is made."[32] It is the planner's job to respond, retool the plan, and learn from the naturally occurring feedback process. This was a topic he would write and speak about prolifically in the coming years.

Design of Cities gained almost instant acclaim, and was soon reprinted in a half dozen languages. Reviews of the book ran in publications such as the *London Observer*, *Progressive Architecture*, and *Architectural Forum*.[33] In a review in *Progressive Architecture*, Ervin Galantay wrote, "due to Bacon's impact on the city of Philadelphia and the influence of Philadelphia's renewal on other cities, the book may rank as an historical document."[34] In *Architectural Forum*, Douglas Haskell called the book "more fascinating than most dramas."[35] However, the reviews also demonstrated the changing face of planning in America. Galantay noted that "the social and economic determinants of urban design are hardly considered."[36] Indeed, while other urban reformers focused on issues such as education and economic development, Bacon remained obsessed with a physical vision.

Another area of criticism was Bacon's view that the plan starts with a concept by a designer, then cycles through review by the community and by society at-large. During this period, planners in America were increasingly turning to communities to spearhead their own grassroots planning efforts. One local reporter wrote, "Bacon's point of view is quite straightforward. He believes the designer's image starts the planning process, which is a premise most planners consider antiquated, if not downright invalid."[37]

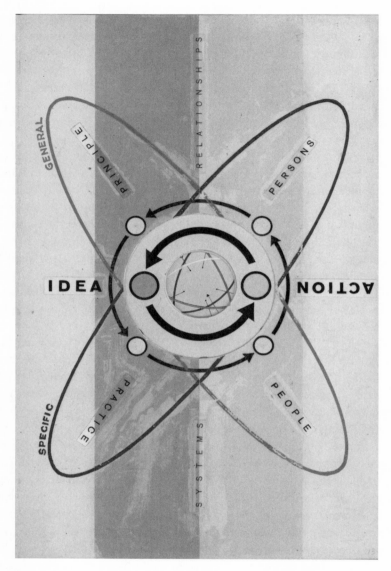

Figure 22. Diagram of the "process of interaction and feedback," from a short, unpublished 1967 book by Bacon titled *Cyclical Feedback*. Bacon produced numerous writings, images, and diagrams illustrating the planning and decision-making process, focusing on the role of feedback in shaping an evolving idea. Courtesy of the Edmund N. Bacon Collection, The Architectural Archives, University of Pennsylvania.

While Bacon was at the height of his fame, he was increasingly running into shifting terrain within his profession. Perhaps the most troubling comment in a review of *Design of Cities* came from his old friend and colleague Fritz Gutheim, who questioned, "Perhaps we must ask in what way Philadelphia is different or better than it was 18 years ago."[38] The urban decline and racial tension of the mid- to late 1960s would certainly provide grounds to question whether Philadelphia was on a positive trajectory as Bacon argued. *Design of Cities* came at a point of rapidly shifting planning ideology that would challenge some of the book's core notions and lead Bacon to have to defend his views continually, struggling to stay relevant in the final years of his career as planning director.

Challenging the Status Quo

While Bacon was gaining recognition for Philadelphia and an international reputation for himself, another individual was staging an all-out affront on the planning profession. Jane Jacobs was a journalist, married to an architect, who had been involved in community protests to protect her adopted community of Greenwich Village in New York City from the urban renewal bulldozers. Jacobs received a grant from the Rockefeller Foundation to record her ideas on the failings of urban renewal, and in 1961 produced her groundbreaking book, *The Death and Life of Great American Cities*.

Jacobs began *Death and Life* stating, "This book is an attack on current city planning and rebuilding." The book was unrelenting, accusing planners and city builders of squandering enormous sums of money, using the funds to destroy vibrant neighborhoods and erect highways and soul-less, large-scale projects.[39] Jacobs argued that the planners blindly ignored the human elements that make cities work—front stoops, crowded streets, mix of uses, small blocks. In response, she promoted a hands-off approach, letting residents plan for themselves. Her statements quickly sparked both support and controversy. Her ideas about what makes strong urban areas resonated, and the voice of a community organizer, rather than a trained expert, was refreshing. However, she was highly criticized as well, especially from within the planning and development professions.[40] The book would endure, continuing to be a major text read by design professionals and students of all fields of urbanism for generations to come.

Jacobs received some criticism even from those who generally lauded the book. For example, sociologist Herbert Gans criticized her for focusing too heavily on physical planning as a solution to urban ills, leading her "to ignore the social, cultural, and economic factors that contribute to vitality or dullness."[41] Gans wrote of *Death and Life*, "Her book is a path-breaking achievement, and because it is so often right, I am all the more disappointed by the fact that it is also so often wrong."[42] Still, Jacobs's book helped launch a generation of scholars and social commentators— including Gans and Paul Davidoff, who argued that the role of the planner was as "advocate" for the public—rejecting many notions of urban renewal era planning and promoting citizen participation as the core of the planning process.[43]

Following the publication of her book, Jacobs went on a tour of major U.S. cities, giving speeches and producing writings, verbally tearing apart the city officials who had worked on their urban renewal programs. One journalist wrote, "She has made a career of chopping city planners and urban renewal experts . . . into small pieces, which she feeds to cats."[44] In one visit to Pittsburgh, for example, Jacobs concluded, "Pittsburgh is being rebuilt by city-haters."[45] When Jacobs came to Philadelphia in June 1962, however, her response was nowhere near as hostile: "I like Philadelphia," she began.[46] She certainly had her criticisms. She called Penn Center "an island instead of part of the continuing fabric." She disliked the new buildings rising in Society Hill. As she had done in her book, she attacked Philadelphia's City Beautiful period and the Benjamin Franklin Parkway. Yet she admired the modernist "flying-saucer" hospitality center near City Hall. She loved some of the older parts of the city, as well as the redevelopment going on in the Morton section of Germantown, because "intermingled with the new, were old buildings, which were being restored, and corner stores." It was a rare example of Jacobs admiring urban renewal projects.

Bacon was no fan of Jacobs's book, and he resented the fact that he felt she criticized while hardly proposing any substantive solutions.[47] In a February 1962 talk to the Architectural League of New York and the Museum of Modern Art, he remarked, "[Jacobs's] notion that the delightful set of circumstances which happen to converge on one block of Hudson Street will, by some mysterious means, extend their benign influence to solve the problems of the slums of America; I can assure you that this will not work."[48] In another talk, where Bacon and Ed Logue, Boston's redevelopment czar, were panelists, Jacobs criticized both men from the audience, leading Bacon to question, with "almost a sigh . . . what Mrs. Jacobs was for."[49] He did meet with Jacobs when she was in Philadelphia in 1962, but there does not seem to be any firsthand record from that meeting.[50]

A few years earlier, Jacobs had encountered Bacon while writing for *Architectural Forum*. In a much later interview, she discussed how this exposure to his work exhibited the planners' preference for soul-less order as opposed to the messy urban chaos she felt should be cherished and preserved.[51] However, she did not express this view in *Death and Life*. Most of the vitriol in her book was saved for Robert Moses and his plans for New York City. Jacobs only mentioned Bacon by name in a footnote, and her relatively mild criticism of Philadelphia in *Death and Life* is split between attacks on the urban renewal projects of the 1950s and the City Beautiful period of the early twentieth century.[52]

Jacobs never acknowledged Bacon as any different from other powerful city officials. However, her admiration of Philadelphia's historic preservation indicates that her assessment was perhaps too simplistic. Indeed, though neither Bacon nor Jacobs would ever admit it, the two had many similar beliefs. Bacon was adamantly against wholesale bulldozing and rebuilding. He was a strong proponent of historic preservation. He was an outspoken advocate for the pedestrian. He explained in one article that, through community-based efforts at restoring neighborhoods, "there has been achieved a warmth and richness that no government agency, by direct action can produce."[53]

While he publicly panned Jacobs's work, Bacon seems to have appreciated and adjusted his views as a response to her criticisms of urban renewal. For example, in the year after *Death and Life* came out, Bacon wrote to Mayor Tate arguing that the city's new Community Renewal Program, focusing on North Philadelphia and intended as a "reappraisal of redevelopment," was "particularly important because of the popularity of the Jane Jacobs book which attacks the methods used in cities so far."[54] It is too easy to simplify the Bacon-Jacobs relationship, and it appears that Jacobs simply never saw the shades of gray in what Philadelphia's chief planner was attempting to do.

While Jacobs was espousing the values of diverse urban neighborhoods, so was Bacon, though in his own way: he was going on the speaking circuit proclaiming the evils of suburbia. In a speech at Berkeley, he said of life in the suburbs, "Scarcely ever do the children see a real painting . . . and scarcely ever do they see a Chinese or a Negro except in some lurid picture in the respectable tabloids."[55] For Bacon, the type of exposure to culture and diversity the city embodied was not to be taken lightly. In fact, he claimed that it was critical to have "childhood conditioning toward recognizing the world is made up of a great many kinds of people." He saw hope that urban neighborhoods could attract back suburbanites and the middle class, to build vibrant and diverse communities—places only possible in the city. In the Berkeley speech, he explained, "And so, return to city living begins, just as a trickle at first, but a trickle that is growing. . . . At one swoop it smashes the image of the core surrounded by a ring of the lowest income group. . . . It smashes the picture of the city abandoned by the whites to become a ghetto of only one race."

Across the nation, Jacobs's work helped spark a backlash against planners and urban developers. As a result, many planners recoiled, giving way to a new philosophy of community-generated plans, with planners playing a more withdrawn role. Bacon respected the importance of empowering communities; in an interview with the *Philadelphia Inquirer*, he explained, "The planner of the future will have to earn the right to work in the community by demonstrating his own usefulness. The days of the autocratic approach are over."[56] However, Bacon disputed the idea that plans could be developed by consensus.[57] He argued planners had to "think big and act small."[58] He explained, "The planner must create the image of the vital, viable, cultural-residential core in terms that stir the passions of people and motivate politicians."[59] While he saw the future as a diverse, urban landscape, Bacon believed planners had to be the ones to exert the leadership to get there—not just creating plans but working through the policy and political process of figuring out how to implement them. In this regard, he and Jacobs were worlds apart.

The Fair of the Future

Bacon used his public presentations, articles, and *Design of Cities* to promote a vision of a vibrant future for Philadelphia. He hoped that the actual projects coupled with the buzz and attention would lead the city to experience an unprecedented renaissance, with nothing short of the world taking notice. However, he knew that it would take more than books and films really to market this concept on a large scale. Around this time, he got an idea for how to achieve this grandiose goal. First, of course, the city had to realize these projects, attracting federal money, mobilizing the business community, and gaining buy-in. However, if Philadelphia could achieve substantive results in the coming decades, Bacon believed the city could show off its new face to the world at a fair—a really big fair.

This idea can be traced back to a December 1947 suggestion by Oskar Stonorov for "a 'Philadelphia Fair' . . . to show the world Philadelphia's and Pennsylvania's importance."[60] Bacon believed that such a fair would have to be timed to celebrate a major milestone if it was to get any kind of broad financial support and audience. He looked ahead and imagined Philadelphia hosting a world's fair in 1976, celebrating the nation's bicentennial. The timing was perfect for the estimated completion of a number of big Center City projects. There was precedent for Philadelphia hosting major national celebrations. The city hosted the successful Centennial Exhibition in 1876—arguably America's first world's fair. However, the city failed in effectively pulling off the 1926 Sesquicentennial, and the memory lingered of the under-attended and debt-ridden celebration, considered by many an embarrassment for the city.[61] Bacon had to hope that enough people would have the confidence to believe that the city's contemporary leadership could do better.

Bacon was surely influenced by the success of the Better Philadelphia Exhibition, although this Bicentennial celebration would have to be much larger to be successful. He was also highly influenced by the 1893 World's Columbian Exposition in Chicago as an example of how a fair could lay the groundwork for long-term urban redevelopment ideas and projects. He particularly admired how its chief designer, Daniel Burnham, parlayed the event into his *Plan of Chicago* in 1909.[62] Another major influence for Bacon was surely New York's 1939 world's fair, which transformed Flushing, Queens, and attracted significant private-sector interest and investment.[63]

In 1957, Bacon began meeting with a committee of the Junior Chamber of Commerce to flesh out the idea of a major Bicentennial celebration in Philadelphia. Mayor Richardson Dilworth was supportive and officially designated the Junior Chamber as the entity responsible for creating a preliminary plan for the celebration.[64] In spring 1959, Bacon pitched the idea to senator Joseph Clark, who loved the notion of Philadelphia hosting such a celebration. Clark said he would gladly introduce a resolution in Congress establishing Philadelphia as the celebration site of the nation's two-hundredth birthday.[65]

With this buy-in from Mayor Dilworth and Senator Clark, in October 1959, Bacon publicly launched the concept in an article called "A Fair Can

Pace It," published in *Greater Philadelphia Magazine*. The subtitle read, "What Will Philadelphia Be Like in 50 Years? A World's Fair in 1976 Could Set the Stage."[66] Bacon envisioned Independence Mall as a major focus area of the Bicentennial celebration, with visitors able to venture just south and see the transformation of Society Hill. They could go to the Delaware River and see the marina and embarcadero he envisioned being finished by 1976. The area just north of Independence Mall, around Franklin Square and known as the "skid row" area, would be revived as "the center of commercial and industrial renewal." Some of the projects Bacon imagined would be built for the fair but retained long after, including Schuylkill River Park and the rebirth of Chestnut Street as a pedestrian and trolley thoroughfare.

Bacon envisioned this celebration as a world's fair, which meant it would need approval by the U.S. government and recognition from the Bureau of International Expositions in Paris, which permitted only one official world's fair per year.[67] The plan that evolved was for the main fairgrounds to be in Fairmount Park at the site of the 1876 Centennial Exhibition—creating a clear historical parallel. In Bacon's usual style of visually showing a historical continuum, a Planning Commission promotional document contained a map with the area where William Penn landed (marked "1682"), Independence Hall (marked "1776"), City Hall (marked "1871"), and Fairmount Park (marked "1876" and "1976"). A transportation system of trolleys, trams, and ferry boats were proposed to take visitors between the fair grounds and downtown.[68]

When he came into office, Mayor James H. J. Tate bought into the Bicentennial idea, creating an organizing committee in 1964, hosting a promotional dinner at Memorial Hall in 1965, and forming an 18-member Bicentennial Planning Committee with Henderson Supplee, Jr., retired president of Atlantic Richfield Company, as chairman.[69] With the mayor's support, the Planning Commission created a report for a Bicentennial celebration and world's fair in Philadelphia that the mayor sent to President Lyndon Johnson, for the first time elevating the effort to the national level.[70]

With these local efforts, Bacon started lobbying for federal support for his proposal.[71] As a starting point, in 1962, Bacon and Bill Rafsky had already met with Ewen Dingwall, manager of Seattle's world's fair and an expert on obtaining federal funding for world's fair financing.[72] In July 1966, President Johnson, by now convinced there should be some national celebration in 1976, established the American Revolution Bicentennial Commission to "develop the ground rules for the Bicentennial" and ultimately select a host city.[73] Boston was also vying to be the host city by this point, and Chicago would explore the idea as well.[74]

In response to President Johnson's establishment of the federal commission, Mayor Tate helped create a nonprofit organization called the Philadelphia 1976 Bicentennial Corporation, to prepare Philadelphia's bid to host the fair, combining the Bicentennial Planning Committee with members of an existing committee established to organize an Olympic bid for Philadelphia.[75] The mayor appointed himself, Bacon, and other city officials to serve as its executive committee. In May 1968, Bacon and others met with grassroots groups in the low-income largely African American community of Mantua, closest to the proposed Fairmount Park site, including Mantua Planners and the Young Great Society, to begin a course of community involvement.[76] He also discussed inviting the Mantua Planners to develop their own community plan to present to the Planning Commission.[77]

Pulling off this event for Philadelphia was not a sure thing. After New York's abysmal performance with the 1964 world's fair, many were becoming increasingly skeptical of the ongoing viability of the world's fair model.[78] In a report to Mayor Tate, Bacon explained that a report done as part of Chicago's fact finding concluded, "Worlds Fairs of the traditional type are apparently obsolete."[79]

While the official bicentennial corporation was working, another group of young planners and civically involved individuals formed a counterproposal for the Bicentennial. This group, known as the Young Professionals, included John Gallery, one of Bacon's staff members, and Stanhope Browne, who had led the charge to bury and cover the Delaware Expressway. Another influential member of the group was architect Richard Saul Wurman, who had already irked Bacon by writing a letter to President Johnson, arguing for a more broad-based celebration rather than a fair based in Philadelphia.[80] The Young Professionals began promoting a rival proposal for the Bicentennial, with a "megastructure" built over the train tracks behind Philadelphia's Thirtieth Street Station.[81]

In February 1968, Mayor Tate acknowledged that he liked the Young Professionals' ambitious plan and folded the rival group into the Bicentennial Corporation.[82] Subsequently, the group hired architect/planner David A. Crane to assist in the physical design of the megastructure. The megastructure idea was controversial, and while it was born from a group of young progressives, it stung of the large-scale physical projects that were rapidly going out of style as social planning became more prevalent.

Catherine Drinker Bowen, a member of the federal American Revolution Bicentennial Commission, wrote Bacon a letter voicing concerns about the megastructure: "Isn't there something inappropriate, even offensive, in such a gigantic plan of city advancement along lines which do not take into account the urgent and dangerous problems with which the city is now involved?"[83]

Finally, and with great fanfare, Bacon and the Bicentennial Corporation traveled to Washington, D.C., to give a presentation to the American Revolution Bicentennial Commission and the U.S. Department of Commerce in late September 1969.[84] They worked feverishly to prepare their materials, including a full-color presentation book with vibrant images, to sell the concept, called "Toward a Meaningful Bicentennial." One of Bacon's staff members recalled significant tension and frustration in preparation for this presentation.[85] The delegation to Washington included Bacon and other members of the committee, as well as at least two delegates from the Mantua community.[86]

Following the presentation, Bacon and his colleagues met with representatives in Washington to talk specifically about the prime issue regarding Philadelphia's proposal—the cost and feasibility of covering over the railroad yard.[87] The cost was significant—potentially prohibitive.[88] In addition, the Bicentennial Corporation offered $6 million for the land it needed, but the Penn Central Railroad that owned the land balked, asking for much more.[89] Soon thereafter, in June 1970, the Penn Central filed for bankruptcy protection, adding an additional level of uncertainty. At this point, Bacon again tried to push for focusing the celebration around the western area of Fairmount Park.

The debate over the bicentennial site was one that the media portrayed as ideological and generational. Bacon represented one view, while the young planners represented the other. An article in the *Bulletin* explained, "Bacon, formerly considered a liberal city planner, now finds himself opposed by younger members of the City Planning Commission who consider his advocacy of the Fairmount Park site to be contrary to all that's liberal, new and progressive in redesigning cities."[90] In July, he visited EXPO '70, the world's fair in Osaka, Japan, to see the design by architect Kenzo Tange.[91] He made recommendations based on the Osaka fair to Mayor Tate, but the Philadelphia project was at a very different place, still stuck in the debate over choosing a site. In August 1970, word came that the federal commission was indeed favoring a national celebration focusing on Philadelphia.[92]

In 1970, the Philadelphia Bicentennial Corporation created a new proposal, a three-part plan called the "Agenda for Action." This was a plan to
share the limelight of the bicentennial with Camden, New Jersey, Philadelphia's poorer neighbor to the east, and allocating $277 million for
"community development."[93] The Bicentennial Corporation hired an experienced community organizer named Catherine Leslie to spearhead citizen
involvement.[94] However, despite efforts to involve low-income and minority communities in the planning, there was a significant racial dimension
to the whole discussion, as some African American leaders argued that the
Bicentennial was a boondoggle, wasting money that should be spent directly on the city's disinvested neighborhoods and on public housing. The
black members on the Bicentennial Corporation board decided to support
Bacon's Fairmount Park plan, believing it would funnel more money into
African American neighborhoods.[95]

The staff consultants recommended a plan to hold the Bicentennial predominantly over the Thirtieth Street Station railyard, with a total cost of a
whopping $658,790,000.[96] After the board voted narrowly to continue to
promote the Thirtieth Street site, in October 1970, black members of the
board dramatically walked out of a meeting and staged a sit-in at the corporation's office.[97] However, in November, the whole issue became moot as
the federal commission rejected the new plan, and, soon thereafter, the
Penn Central Railroad publicly stated it would not sell its air rights for the
area at Thirtieth Street Station.[98] Meanwhile, the District Attorney's Office
was investigating the Bicentennial Corporation, characterized in the press
as a black hole for money.[99]

At this point, the planning process fell apart. Several members of the
Corporation resigned, and in the face of this uncertainty the Commission
voted to disband and adopt a new board comprised of thirty members,
with an additional thirteen government representatives. The new board was
much broader in scope, more diverse, and included a number of people
with views that differed significantly from Bacon's.[100] Bacon, in retirement
by this point, was not appointed to this new board, and he effectively with-
drew from the planning process.

The new board would continue to run into political and racial problems, jumping from one failed site to the next—Byberry, Petty's Island,
Port Richmond, Camden, and Eastwick. Louis Kahn was selected as the
lead designer for the exposition in Eastwick, and, as late as March 1972, it
still looked like Philadelphia might host a major national celebration.[101]

However, in May 1972, the administration of President Richard M. Nixon decided not to select a single site for the Bicentennial celebration, after all.[102] The Bicentennial Corporation disbanded and was replaced in May 1973 by a new corporation called Philadelphia '76 Inc. appointed by mayor Frank Rizzo. After over a decade of planning, the idea of grand bicentennial celebration was dead.[103]

Still, Philadelphia did celebrate in 1976. In an ambitious effort, the city hosted a test run in September 1974, almost two years prior to the Bicentennial, attracting a robust crowd to a day of dance, music, theater, outdoor markets, and tours in the areas around Independence Hall. The *Inquirer* reported, "The Bicentennial arrived in Philadelphia Sunday and, to the amazement of many, it worked."[104] In 1976, the city hosted a year-long celebration, with a stream of local events that were relatively successful. The Bicentennial celebration also gave the opportunity for the city to invest in a host of civic projects, including a Living History Center, the African American Museum, the Mummers Museum, and the installation of flags of the nations of the world on the Benjamin Franklin Parkway—creating an effect that has become a permanent hallmark of Philadelphia's downtown.[105]

For Bacon's part, the Bicentennial started as a grand vision for putting Philadelphia on the world stage. After over fifteen years of frustrating planning, the fair of his imagination was not to be. In addition, the planning represented a changing of the guard, with a new generation of planners challenging Bacon and ultimately winning out. According to one scholar, "The deviation from Bacon's '2009' vision shows two quite specific urban historical processes working in conjunction: the decline of the 'master planner' and by extension New Deal/Great Society urban liberalism, and the rise of a consensus-seeking planning model driven by the maturation of urban community-based protest movements."[106] The bicentennial planning was a sobering experience for Bacon, who so recently was at the top of his game, but whom new voices in the planning and development world viewed as increasingly out of touch.

New Approaches

In some aspects, Philadelphia's image was improving in the 1960s, but on the ground the city was experiencing profound problems. Foremost was the growing unrest in the African American community. By the early 1960s about 30 percent of Philadelphia residents were black, and that number was climbing. One in five African Americans in Philadelphia were unemployed; many lived in substandard housing and in poverty.[107] The so-called "jungles" of North Philadelphia were rapidly deteriorating, transforming formerly vital communities into bastions of gang activity, crime, and desperation.

In his 1964 State of the Union address, President Johnson declared a "war on poverty," a major component of his Great Society Policy agenda. In the beginning of January 1964 the federal government designated the entire city of Philadelphia a "redevelopment area" because of the city's "continuous high level of unemployment."[108] A few months later, Malcolm X would deliver his famous speech "The Ballot or the Bullet." In July, Johnson signed the Civil Rights Act into law, just before race riots exploded in Harlem later that month. Cities across the U.S. would see serious race riots in the coming years, with perhaps the most infamous being the Watts Riots in Los Angeles. In August 1964, Philadelphia erupted in three days of race riots, leading to the arrest of 308 people, and more riots would follow.[109] While the problems of urban racial tension and poverty were not unique to Philadelphia, the city was clearly a major focus for Washington, D.C., containing the nation's third highest African American population.[110]

By the late 1960s, Bacon was a prominent national and international figure, with constant opportunities for speaking and promoting his ideas. He certainly grasped the crisis of the times and started speaking prolifically about the need for leadership to combat the problems of urban decline, poverty, and racial segregation that were isolating communities. In a talk in Australia in 1966, he said, "we must not let our great cities fall apart into isolated, self-sufficient suburbs and isolated, totally dependent slums."[111] In another speech, he announced, "The time has come for a new concern for the underprivileged, for a fresh approach to the problems which surround them."[112] He warned, "Unless we can solve the problem of the underprivileged and the deprived which cluster in our great cities better than would be indicated by the recent riots in Watts, California, the penalty will be paid not only in the great cities themselves, but in the towns and rural areas as well." In another instance, he was reported in the *Inquirer* as stating, "The achievement of a fine Center City will be a hollow victory unless, at the same time, we are able to provide every Philadelphia family with a good home in a decent neighborhood."[113]

Starting in 1962, Philadelphia had been trying to refocus on its poverty-stricken communities through an effort called the Community Renewal

Program (CRP), supported by the 1961 federal Area Redevelopment Act, under President John F. Kennedy, providing new funds for inner-city redevelopment through public-private partnerships.[114] The Ford Foundation put up additional dollars to fund the new approach in Philadelphia.[115] The CRP was to compile a narrative of the city's various strategies for dealing with urban renewal over the past ten years, examining the roots of urban blight and determining ways to stave off its spread. Next, the CRP would develop a real estate inventory of the city's distressed areas and, working with the Health and Welfare Council of Philadelphia, come up with solutions for both physical and social problems.[116]

The CRP staff would be housed under the Planning Commission, and Bacon hired a new assistant executive director named Graham Finney to assist in running the CRP. Finney had worked in Boston with Ed Logue and replaced Bacon's former deputy Art Row, who had recently taken a teaching position at Yale.[117] However, Bill Rafsky—still serving as development coordinator—muscled his way to establish himself as the head of the program, colocating the CRP staff partly in his Office of the Development Coordinator.[118] Bacon soon abandoned his hopes of having a real impact on the CRP, letting Finney work with Rafsky and carry the program forward, while he took a more withdrawn role.

One part of the CRP strategy that Bacon did get to focus on was changing the methodology for community planning. In late 1963, the Planning Commission adopted a strategy of district planning, complete with a new staff division, headed up by Irving Wasserman. The city was divided into ten districts, each to receive a closer look than was done on the citywide level, determining which communities should receive even more detailed planning work.[119] The Planning Commission also attempted an approach where the planners helped organize house parties in various neighborhoods to allow community members to discuss their problems with city representatives who would direct them to public-sector resources.[120]

During this period, Bacon also worked to push for a new strategy he devised for restoring abandoned housing and providing a new type of public housing, through an initiative he called the "Used House Program."[121] His idea was to have the city take ownership of abandoned and tax-delinquent homes scattered across the city, identify developers to rehabilitate them affordably, and transfer them to the Redevelopment Authority or Housing Authority to use as "scattered-site" public housing. The city created the nonprofit Philadelphia Housing Development Corporation

(PHDC) to serve as a development intermediary for transferring these homes. This solution created an alternative from high-rise public housing, put abandoned homes—scattered throughout the city—back into active use, and encouraged mixed-income communities. However, the program ran into a number of difficulties, including pushback from white neighbors, as well as and legal and financial issues.[122] Still, by 1969, 3,500 dilapidated and abandoned houses had been taken by the city and converted into public housing units in neighborhoods like Haddington in West Philadelphia and Ludlow in North Philadelphia.[123] Despite this early success, the Housing Authority would ultimately fail in maintaining the units, allowing many to fall into disrepair, as the program disintegrated.

In October 1965, President Johnson appointed a national Task Force on Urban Problems that included Bill Rafsky, following on the heels of the landmark report by Daniel L. Moynihan, citing the problems of the black ghetto as rooted in the breakdown of family values and a lack of educational equality between blacks and whites.[124] Based on the recommendations of the task force, on November 3, 1966, Congress passed the Demonstration Cities (a.k.a. Model Cities) Act, by which the government would issue planning and development grants for "model" neighborhoods.[125] Thanks to the involvement of Rafsky and Oskar Stonorov (one of the originators of the act), Philadelphia had a good chance of receiving funding.[126]

In December 1967, Philadelphia received a federal grant for $278,000 (of the national total $900,000 allocated for planning grants) to focus on the North Philadelphia district, a large area between Vine Street and Lehigh Avenue, stretching river to river and encompassing the "jungles" of North Philadelphia.[127] In Model Cities, the city government would work closely with the black community, via the new "Area Wide Council" to develop plans and programs.[128] While Bacon was supportive of Model Cities and presented several key speeches about its impacts, he ended up playing a fairly minor role in its implementation.[129]

On August 28, 1968, Mayor Tate appointed Bacon as the new development coordinator, while also keeping him as director of the City Planning Commission. Several individuals had cycled through the development coordinator position after Bill Rafsky left, but none had left a strong mark on the office. Suddenly, however, Bacon was a part of the mayor's cabinet and, for the first time in his career, held the power to guide the Redevelopment Authority. However, as he set off to pursue his dual role as planning director and development coordinator, he quickly ran into conflicts between the roles, leading him to spend more time focusing on real estate issues and drawing him away from supervising the Planning Commission.[130]

With the new focus on social planning through Model Cities, Bacon tried to steer the Planning Commission to interface better with this agenda. In spring 1968, the Planning Commission started a Social Research Division "to design and perform the necessary research and analysis of the social problems of the City in order to strengthen the capabilities of the Commission for long-range comprehensive planning."[131] But the new division director, George R. Beetle, became quickly frustrated and resigned after about a year and a half, allowing the new division to stagnate.[132] In late 1968 and early 1969, Bacon created a program for "involving black planners in the planning process" and hired a number of African Americans to his staff.[133] Still, it was unclear whether any of these efforts would make any meaningful impact.

Much of the final years of the Tate administration would be spent fending off crises and, ultimately, a grand jury investigation of City Hall corruption. During this period, one prominent area where Bacon contributed as development coordinator was in mediating racial conflicts that broke out around Temple University in North Philadelphia. Following protests of the city's redevelopment around the University of Pennsylvania and Drexel University in West Philadelphia, a similar and highly explosive situation of racial tension and community unrest was evolving in North Philadelphia.[134] The Temple area conflict was rooted in the erection of a housing project in 1954, which abutted Temple's campus and, according to Bacon, "Temple in all its delicate feelings, erected a chain link fence all along the edge of the campus. The human beings in the project were infuriated, and they announced that they were going to tear down Temple."[135]

Early in 1969, Temple had plans to build a multimillion-dollar health and sciences complex on twenty-seven acres of North Philadelphia land. The university owned much of the land but would have to rezone it and take additional land, some of which was occupied by people's homes. This was the straw that broke the camel's back for the communities, whose leaders threatened violence, protested, went to City Council, and escalated the tense situation, essentially forcing a public response from the city. That response came in March 1969 when City Council president Paul D'Ortona halted a rezoning bill and ordered the university to involve the community in its planning before he would consider putting his stamp on the rezoning.[136] At the same time, groups of black students were protesting on

Temple's campus. In response to both pressures, Temple put a moratorium on its campus expansion.[137]

In May, Temple and the residents reached a preliminary agreement, indefinitely halting almost all Temple's expansion plans.[138] However, this was a stopgap measure until more negotiating could take place. In November, Temple and the community groups agreed to sit down together for a five-day conference to work out their differences.[139] After the initial session ended in a deadlock, Mayor Tate appointed Bacon to act as mediator.[140] New negotiations opened on January 21, 1970, at the neutral setting of the Bureau of Employment Services on Arch Street.[141] The parties refused to meet in the same room. Bacon recalled, "The neighborhood community group was in one room at one end of the hall and the trustees of Temple were in the other, and I would shuttle back and forth and bring different kinds of peace proposals."[142]

After three contentious sessions, both sides agreed to a sixteen-page "Community Temple Agreement of 1970." Bacon exuberantly wrote to Mayor Tate, "I think this is an historic achievement."[143] Temple would give the community more than nine acres of land, agreed not to engage in any attempts at rezoning or redevelopment without making a good-faith effort at gaining community buy-in, and also agreed to provide the community with local healthcare, education, employment, and community development resources.[144] The document was approved by both groups at a public ceremony with governor Raymond P. Shafer on March 24, 1970.[145] In a speech earlier in the month, Bacon remarked of the Temple agreement, "It would be an odd quirk of fate if my part in this jointly produced non-physical edifice would prove to be my most enduring contribution to the city of my birth."[146]

Since early in his career, in Flint, Bacon had been a liberal, pushing for affordable housing and community planning, over a decade before these issues came to the fore of the federal agenda for cities. Community investment was again a priority in the 1960s but in a social and racial landscape that was much more foreign to him. Bacon's ideology on government's role in shaping the future of urban renewal was, arguably, progressive for its time, as concepts like the Used House Program were quite innovative. According to one scholar, writing about Bacon's 1959 article "A Fair Can Pace It," "Bacon is asserting that localized urban renewal would emerge as part and parcel of broader trends in progressive governance, anticipating policies like Lyndon Johnson's 'Model Cities' program."[147]

   Still, the degree of racial tension was something Bacon was entirely
unprepared to address; in addition, a new generation of planners was focusing primarily on social rather than physical aspects of city planning. While
earlier practitioners of social issues, like Catherine Bauer, argued for physical solutions, the new generation pushed back against the physical redevelopment mentality that shaped the urban renewal era, seeking new
nonphysical solutions for which Bacon had no training and had trouble
adapting.
   For nearly two decades, Bacon had written and given talks about the
promise of Philadelphia's bright future—a renaissance of urban living. He
continued to believe that Philadelphia would see a return of suburbanites
who became disillusioned with the suburbs and rediscovered the benefits
of urban living, creating the impetus for mixed-income, mixed-race neighborhoods.[148] However, while Center City provided a glimmer of hope,
throughout the city, neighborhoods were sinking into decline, disinvestment, and poverty. Bacon was unprepared for the massive level of racially
motivated violence across the U.S. These dark years of rioting and urban
destruction were truly a wake-up call to Bacon and others who thought the
problems of urban decline could be dealt with gradually.
   Bacon did not view the problem of America's cities as one of money or
public will. To him, it was much more profound. He was invited as a panelist at the White House Conference on International Cooperation in 1965,
at which he told the audience, "The failure of cities is an intellectual failure.
It is a failure of the human mind to grasp the complex organism as a
functioning whole, and to conceive methods of interlocking the fragile
human need of the individual with the pulsating, massive fact of the
metropolis."[149] It is unclear, however, whether Bacon himself had the solutions to these problems, the energy to take them on, or the political ability
to position himself to be effective.
   In the late 1960s, Bacon should have been celebrating his achievements
and the publication of his book. Instead, he was increasingly called on to
defend his work. He must have realized that the basic problem of city planning in Philadelphia had changed dramatically from the early days of his
directorship. In the optimistic glow following the Better Philadelphia Exhibition, Bacon's job was to promote compelling images of Philadelphia's
bright future. Philadelphia's post-World War II planning had indeed succeeded in reversing the city's long-held image as a sleepy city. However, by
the end of the 1960s, the basic equation had changed. Massive amounts of

federal money had been spent on America's cities, while the problems of those cities had simultaneously increased. Bacon made a career talking about the promise of the future, but by 1969 the conversation was not about the future; it was about the present, and the present did not look promising.

Chapter 8

NEW VISIONS OF PHILADELPHIA

By the end of the 1960s, Bacon was tired and increasingly finding that he was out of touch with shifting trends both in Philadelphia and in his profession. When he retired from the Philadelphia City Planning Commission in May 1970, cities across the U.S. were entering a period of financial hardship, with a scarcity of federal funding to support any large-scale work. At the same time, the planning profession shifted to a more consensus-based approach, to counter what was seen as top-down planning of the urban renewal era. A series of political corruption scandals erupted in the administration of Mayor James Tate, stimulating Bacon to take his exit from city government earlier than planned.

During this period Bacon was enjoying international fame, speaking prolifically across the globe, and serving on committees in Washington, while, in Philadelphia, he was increasingly stymied about how to be effective in his public-sector role. In different contexts, Bacon was concurrently a renowned intellectual and a frustrated public official. Thus, Bacon escaped from city government as soon as he could collect his full pension, making a formal statement: "I have found public service to be arduous and want to withdraw to private life."[1] However, surely he also saw the promise of trying to affect influence from outside city government.

In his retirement Bacon took on a new role working for a private-sector real estate company, trying his hand at impacting large-scale urban projects from the other side of the negotiating table. He continued to teach his course at the University of Pennsylvania, working with the next generation of urban planners. He continued to speak and serve on boards and committees, promoting topics like the "Post-Petroleum City" and discussing the dangers of suburban development. He also refused to step away quietly from the civic scene in Philadelphia, instead throwing himself into major planning and development debates over the coming decades that created a new image of Bacon as an unrelenting voice for what he saw as the right direction for Philadelphia. However, not everyone agreed with Bacon, and the battles that he fought in Philadelphia after his retirement would be contentious and often ideological.

After his retirement, Bacon utilized the tools of policy entrepreneurship to affect change but, for the first time in decades, outside of the public-sector structure. In his role as developer, intellectual, educator, and advocate, Bacon continued to rely on salesmanship and marketing of ideas, continued to have his ideas effectively reported in the media, lobbied powerful decision makers, used physical designs and models to get his point across, and sought to influence other groups and individuals to take up causes he promoted. Thus, Bacon's work after retirement presents an important contrast to his strategies of policy entrepreneurship within city government. In some ways, it was helpful to have the power of public office behind his efforts, but, in other ways, Bacon was much freer as a private citizen to express himself and work on his own schedule to advance ideas.

It is difficult to gauge how influential Bacon was within the academy and in influencing ideas in an international context. However, locally, he lost all the battles he fought in Philadelphia after his retirement. Still, in a final (unsuccessful) crusade at age ninety-two. For legalizing skateboarding in a downtown park, Bacon proved that he was able to remain relevant and influential—to capture the imagination of the public and inspire the next generation—even into his ninth decade.

A Changing Tide

In November 1969, Bacon's deputy development coordinator, Paul S. Weinberg, went to the press accusing Bacon of "not doing enough for housing and development in the city's low and moderate income areas."[2] Weinberg also called for Bacon's resignation, a statement about which the *Philadelphia Inquirer* reported "carried all the weight of a small dog barking at its master."[3] Bill Rafsky went to bat in Bacon's defense, calling Weinberg "completely off base, both in his facts and in his evaluation of the city's programs."[4] Still, Weinberg's accusations struck deep with Bacon, who later said in an interview of Weinberg's remarks, "It was one of the most painful things of my career."[5]

Many in Philadelphia started to feel that the city was failing to respond to the changing times, and Bacon was caught up in this backlash against an old, out-of-touch generation. In July 1968, *Philadelphia* magazine had run a particularly scathing story about Bacon, featuring an image of a crumpled copy of the 1964 *Time* cover that with Bacon's face, accompanied by the caption "Ed Bacon's dream of the City Beautiful has turned out to be a nightmare."[6] The author was not just critical of Bacon but of Mayor Tate, the Redevelopment Authority, and many elements of the city's planning and development program. The critique of Bacon was essentially that he was "ill-equipped to change with the times."[7] The writer argued that the city's agenda was not in line with communities' best interests and that Bacon was too much of a physical planner, attempting too late to "get on the social planning bandwagon."[8] The author argued that Bacon was supporting the wrong priorities. For example, he should not have been wasting his time to encourage downtown shopping at Market East because "everyone in the world realizes that the trend is toward suburban shopping."[9]

Bacon sat through a brutal public hearing in January 1970 where thirty-six people testified for nearly four hours about the faults of the Planning Commission. According to the *Bulletin* coverage, "the most frequently heard complaint was the alleged failure of the planning commission and other city agencies to involve the communities and the residents in the planning process."[10] How much the world had changed: the age of urban renewal had come and gone, and the greatest issue facing many cities was poverty and racial tension. Planning was aided by computers. The suburbs were thriving, sucking the life out of many American cities. Bacon's planning commission had become known as the best in the nation but could not find a way to solve the growing problems of the disintegrating ghettos in North and West Philadelphia. Bacon was increasingly out of touch with the trends and ideas of the young planners in his office.

Bacon's job required a grueling schedule—one that he had a harder and harder time keeping up with. He had toyed with the idea of leaving Philadelphia, and, in 1967, the *San Francisco Chronicle* reported that Bacon "gave a tentative acceptance" to that city's Mayor John F. Shelley's offer to hire him as planning director, but Mayor Tate convinced Bacon to stay in Philadelphia and gave him a $6,000 pay raise.[11] Still, this and other signs hinted at Bacon's dissatisfaction and increasing fatigue with his job in Philadelphia in the late 1960s. After two decades heading the Planning Commission, under four different mayors, Bacon decided it was time to think about retiring. In 1969 he finally announced that in December 1971, when Mayor Tate's final term expired, he would resign his post.

End of an Era

In early 1969, lame-duck Mayor Tate started to lose his political support, and his administration came under attack for corruption. District Attorney Arlen Specter called a grand jury investigation into suspicion of political graft related to a downtown office project called 1500 Market Street. Across from Penn Center, Vincent Kling designed this pair of office towers with an atrium space connecting to the lower-level Penn Center concourse, developed at the cost of $80 million by National Land and Investment Co.

There were several facets of the district attorney's investigation; however, the element that involved Bacon was an investigation of the city's payment of $600,000 to National Land to reimburse the company for the costs of widening Sixteenth Street. Bacon had apparently encouraged National Land President Jack Wolgin to build a ramp from the underground parking garage in his project to Market Street, to ease traffic. The ramp was built on right-of-way that National Land owned. The city could have widened the roadway for the ramp by taking land through eminent domain but chose instead to reimburse National Land for its cost of widening Sixteenth Street.[12]

District Attorney Specter thought that there was favoritism, due to Wolgin's close connections with the mayor, calling the payment a "giveaway."[13] Meanwhile, Bacon contended that the payment was "legitimate compensation for land-taking."[14] Bill Rafsky supported Bacon's position, explaining, "government usually pays for the cost of boundary streets in development projects."[15] In an official statement in July 1969, Bacon said "every step of its [1500 Market Street's] development has been carried out in accordance with the highest principles of government operations and public-private cooperation."[16]

The whole situation was heavily enmeshed in politics. In 1965, Specter changed his political party affiliation from Democrat to Republican to run for district attorney, beating the incumbent Democrat James C. Crumlish. In his new position, Specter "went on the offensive against the Democratic organization."[17] In 1967, Specter ran for mayor as the Republican candidate, against Mayor Tate. Tate had lost much of his popularity, but thanks

to his support from the Catholic and Italian-American community (attributed in large part to his appointment of Police Commissioner Frank L.
Rizzo), Tate won by a razor-thin margin of 11,000 votes.[18] In the 1969
election, Specter was reelected as district attorney, and Republicans won
other key victories to municipal posts. It was under this contentious and
politically charged atmosphere that Specter led the grand jury investigation,
scrutinizing everyone and everything in the Tate administration. The grand
jury traced a complicated money train, leading to key financial supporters
of the mayor, including Albert M. Greenfield, banker and City Planning
Commission member Sander Field, and Redevelopment Authority chairman Gustave Amsterdam.[19]

It appears from Bacon's confidential reports to the mayor that he did
not believe there was any wrongdoing related to his role in 1500 Market
Street and that the city's conduct was ethical.[20] When Bacon was called as
a witness to testify, he was outraged. His colleagues often viewed him as
someone who was honest to the extreme. Architect Henry Magaziner, for
example, lauded Bacon's honesty and called Bacon "straight as an arrow,"
in one interview.[21] Bacon's son Michael recalled that every year Vincent
Kling would send Bacon a turkey around the holidays. However, Bacon was
not allowed to receive gifts from consultants employed by the Planning
Commission, and each year he would send the turkey back. The past year
he had been too busy to send back the turkey and was ashamed to have to
admit the gift during the grand jury investigation.[22]

Bacon appeared for questioning before the grand jury over a two-day
period on May 19 and 20, 1969, and turned over plans of the development
project. Presiding over the grand jury investigation was Judge Joseph
Sloane, and Specter was aided by his assistant district attorney, Gilbert
Stein. The whole affair was seen by some as a face-off between the young,
conservative district attorney's office and the aging liberal establishment
represented by Bacon, Mayor Tate, Bill Rafsky, and others. In its third presentment, in September 1969, the grand jury reported "strong suggestion
of fraud."[23]

In February 1970, still embroiled in the grand jury investigation, Bacon
announced that he was planning to start his retirement sooner than he
had previously planned—retiring on his sixtieth birthday, May 2, 1970 (the
earliest date Bacon could collect his full pension). In a letter to Mayor Tate
and Planning Commission chairman William B. Walker, Bacon wrote, "I
have found public service to be arduous and want to withdraw to private

life."[24] The *Inquirer* also surmised that Bacon's early retirement had to do with "the double duties [of planning director and development coordinator] or the continuing tension with community groups."[25] Mayor Tate was caught off guard by this announcement. With his administration embroiled in the controversy at Temple University, the grand jury investigation, striking sanitation workers, and a fight for federal funding, this was the worst possible time for Tate to lose his internationally renowned planning director and development coordinator.

It was especially inopportune since Tate had already lost some high-ranking officials in the melee, including Commissioner of Streets David Smallwood, Finance Director Edward Martin, and City Representative S. Harry Galfand, who was indicted by a federal grand jury for tax fraud. It also looked as if Managing Director Fred Corleto was on the way out, after being rebuked and stripped of most of his duties by the mayor.[26] It is common for lame-duck administrations to start losing appointees, but with the scandal and legal proceedings, the Tate administration seemed to be unraveling especially rapidly. Tate appealed to Bacon to reconsider, but his appeals were not effective.[27] Bacon had made up his mind.

In private meetings, Bacon was famous for his fiery demeanor, but in public venues, he was generally diplomatic and even-tempered. However, at a March 11, 1970, speech to the Rotary Club, Bacon let his anger escape. He began the speech, meant to be on the topic of "Planning for Philadelphia's Future," by stating, "I will try to make a few observations about things I have learned [as planning director]. . . . Before I do so, I must treat with one piece of unfinished business."[28] In a later interview, Bacon recalled what happened next: "I said, I am now going to perjure myself. . . . They [the audience] looked at each other in horror. . . . There was silence in the room. Then some naughty person in the back of the room laughed. Then everybody laughed."[29] Bacon went on to talk candidly about the grand-jury investigation, revealing what went on in the witness chamber, mercilessly attacking Arlen Specter, his deputy Gilbert Stein, and Judge Sloane.

Bacon recounted, "What Mr. Stein did was to confront me with the accusation that a nefarious deed had been committed and that I had a major responsibility for it. What Mr. Stein mistook for nervousness was anger, pure, unvarnished anger, and the only evasiveness involved was my evasion of punching him in the nose."[30] Bacon continued, "it is a very serious accusation, more serious in my opinion than, for example, stock manipulation, for it concerns not money but principle, and were it true that I failed responsibly to exercise my obligations of citizenship, I should be severely punished." Of the grand-jury presentment, he told the crowd, "I do wish somebody would read this incredible document. . . . I don't know exactly what the 'Big Lie' is, but I nominate this document as eligible for consideration." After accusing Specter, Sloane, and Stein of "having wrecked one of the finest civic projects ever to be conceived in Philadelphia," he finally shifted gears and explained, "So now we turn to a more cheerful subject which is the future, which is not yet messed up."

The *Inquirer* reported, "The 300 Rotarians packed into the Burgundy Room of the Bellevue Stratford sometimes cheered at Bacon's tirade, sometimes laughed at his quips."[31] As one would expect, the speech was also a big hit with the media. The next morning's paper ran a story on Bacon's speech on the front page above the fold, with a screamer headline: "Bacon Rips D.A.'s Office for Grand Jury 'Big Lie'."[32] After quoting the juiciest parts of Bacon's speech, the article ran responses from Specter and Stein. Specter called Bacon's remarks "way out of line." Stein told the paper, " 'better men have tried' to punch his nose and that he believed Bacon was 'emotionally upset'." In a much later interview, Stein recalled, "We had to ask some tough things of a lot of people. . . . When you served under Arlen Specter you kept your eyes focused on the job ahead and didn't worry what people said about you."[33]

The next day, Bacon sought to further explain himself. An *Inquirer* article stated, quoting Bacon, " 'What I did . . . was extremely painful,' he [Bacon] said, pacing his book-lined office. 'It violated my whole family conditioning and background of privacy and modesty. . . . I don't think that I have ever before in 24 years with the city done anything like this,' he continued. 'I did it because I felt it had to be done'."[34] Bacon's speech received an outpouring of public support. Mayor Tate applauded Bacon for his remarks, and some of Bacon's colleagues wrote supportive letters.[35] With one month before his retirement, it was clear that Bacon would go out with a bang.

In the coming weeks, the media interviewed Bacon constantly, and he used the publicity to try to shape his own legacy. Indeed, the way that many viewed him by 1970 differed dramatically from the way he viewed himself. An editorial in *The Bulletin*, for example, stated,

> Mr. Bacon was in the vanguard of the imaginative army of citizens
> that blueprinted the renewal of center city and the real estate tax

base in the early 1950s. He is still in the vanguard now, 20 years later . . . [but] Mr. Bacon would like to be associated with more than Penn Center. He would like, too, to be identified with other victories of perhaps grittier, less exciting legend. These include renewal projects in North Philadelphia, Germantown and West Philadelphia. No victory there has ever been a rout. The fighting has been hard, often inconclusive. A review of Mr. Bacon's record shows he fought there. His generalship was effective, too. He has, for all of Philadelphia, been a good and faithful servant.[36]

This review was fairly glowing, but it pointed out that many perceived Bacon as a planner focused on Center City, while he saw himself more as an advocate for housing and underserved communities. In another interview, a few days before his retirement, Bacon explained, "Center City has really been a sideline. . . . It is not the significant part of my work. . . . My principal preoccupation has been with housing. . . . I think the housing program in Philadelphia has been a success simply because it is 'invisible'."[37] The reality, of course, was that Bacon had focused on both, but he now began to realize that he had failed at selling himself in the way he wanted to be remembered and sought to use the publicity to redefine his legacy.

As his retirement date approached, Bacon asked specifically for "no recognition whatsoever of this event, no resolution, no engrossed scroll, no present, no social event of any kind."[38] May 2, 1970, was a Saturday, so his staff threw him a small party on Friday May 1, including a cake with a miniature model of City Hall on it. After Mayor Tate accepted the fact that Bacon was really leaving, he invited Bacon to stay on his cabinet as a special advisor and also to continue to serve as a member of the Bicentennial Committee.[39] In a send-off letter, Bacon explained, "I shall devote the major part of my energies to the problems of pollution and environmental quality."[40] Finally, after twenty-one years and four mayors, Bacon's tenure with the city had ended, leaving an uncertain future for planning in Philadelphia.

Changing of the Guard

The tumultuous 1960s left a nation scarred by Vietnam and race riots. Philadelphia was losing population and jobs, with white flight to the suburbs continuing to leave a poorer city behind. The city lost 13 percent of its population between 1970 and 1980.[41] Adding to the tension of these decades, Mayor Tate's police commissioner, Frank Rizzo, was elected mayor in 1971. Rizzo was a divisive figure in Philadelphia. According to one scholar, Rizzo was "antipathetic to young radicals, white as well as black, homosexuals, and other nonconformists," creating sociopolitical divisiveness.[42] He dramatically cut city services, focused on police protection as a main function of city government, and spouted "sentiments previously unthinkable among responsible government officials, couched in imagery of physical intimidation."[43] Bacon recalled, "I had no connection with Rizzo at all. He was a racist."[44]

With far fewer federal resources and a declining local tax base, the Planning Commission's work in the 1970s became more routine.[45] The Commission was involved in advancing some major projects of the 1960s, like Schuylkill River Park and Market East, but the its role was much reduced.[46] In addition to Bacon's departure, the spirit of the times had changed drastically in the final years of Bacon's tenure, and the civic landscape was entirely different. As Richard Huffman, then a member of the Planning Commission staff, explained, "[Bacon] was coming to the end of a period of strong central planning. . . . It was going to change no matter what."[47]

Damon Childs, Bacon's deputy, took over as planning director, and was replaced by John Mitkus in 1973. Both Childs and Mitkus were ineffective at establishing the Planning Commission's continuing prominence. An article in the *Bulletin* about Mitkus started inevitably by recalling the golden Bacon era.[48] Then the paper reported Mitkus explaining, "I'm not a big-dream man, I'm an implementer." Later G. Craig Schelter, another former Bacon staffer, took over the directorship for several years.[49]

Lacking a strong director, Bernard Meltzer, Commission chairman and a developer with the Albert M. Greenfield Company, did not help things. One article reported on a Planning Commission meeting where Meltzer was almost half an hour late, none of the ex officio city officials on the Commission bothered to attend, and Meltzer took anything controversial off the agenda, finishing up in less than an hour.[50] Meltzer made headlines when he proposed an audacious $750 million "megacity" proposal for reviving the controversial Crosstown Expressway, which was quickly dismissed.[51] It was clear that, in a few short years, the Planning Commission's role in Philadelphia's power structure had shifted dramatically.

For cities across the U.S. during the 1970s and 1980s, there was much less federal money available, and there were similarly severe problems in many urban areas, with distressed neighborhoods, poor fiscal conditions, and deteriorating infrastructure. New York City was on the brink of bankruptcy in the 1970s, and after President Gerald Ford and the federal government refused to offer a "bail out," a famous headline in the *New York Daily News* read "Ford to City: Drop Dead."[52] It was a bleak time for urban America.

Promoting Ideas Outside Government

Bacon's early retirement was surely influenced by the tumult in city government and the changing times. However, it can also likely be attributed to his frustration with the public sector and desire for the freedom to speak and teach his own ideas as an intellectual unfettered by the yolk of public office. In his retirement, Bacon would be entrepreneurial in ways that he was unable to do in city government, via his teaching, a new position in the private sector, extracurricular activities, commission appointments, and international speaking engagements.

In his retirement, Bacon continued teaching his course at the University of Pennsylvania, "History and Theories of Civic Design," until 1988. He had strong views on the way planning was taught in the academy. In one lecture, he said, "I have been horrified to find students who say it is our job as urban designers to evaluate, not to produce an urban design. . . . Who the hell are you to evaluate? Your job is to stand up [before] the community and let them evaluate you. And they will have no difficulty in doing it. But in order for you to do that you have to see something, you have to stand for something and you have to believe in something and defend it."[53]

His course was a dynamic seminar that involved hikes through the city and physical experiences of urban spaces (like walking through fountains blindfolded) and concluded in a final project where students had to present a three-dimensional simulation of some city in the world in the most creative and kinesthetic way possible. Using sets, costumes, lights, and sound, students transformed their classrooms into foreign places. To show the hilliness of San Francisco, the presenters made the spectators walk up several flights of stairs, arriving at the top floor to find one of the presenters dressed like a "Flower Child" playing a guitar and distributing R-rated fortune cookies.[54] For a presentation on Mont Saint-Michel, the lights were turned off, and the classroom was dominated by "the smell of incense and the surging rhythms of Gregorian chants."[55] Of Bacon's unorthodox course, one former student recalled, "It was different from the rest [of my courses]. It gave you a new way of thinking about things."[56]

In 1991, Bacon accepted the position of Plym Distinguished Professor at the University of Illinois at Urbana-Champaign.[57] In this role, he led his students to create visionary design concepts for the area around Philadelphia's Thirtieth Street Station, based on its key location along AMTRAK's Northeast Corridor.[58] At the center of this train corridor between Boston and Washington, Bacon envisioned Thirtieth Street Station as becoming "the economic center of northeastern United States."[59] The student designs were displayed in an exhibition entitled "New Visions for Philadelphia," in 1993 and became the seed for a planning study carried out by the city in 2008 to develop this area as "Station Square."[60]

Bacon's course at Illinois was also considered unorthodox, merging design disciplines in a dynamic way. According to Urbana-Champaign professor Robert I. Selby, "the idea of [having students] setting an agenda rather than reacting to one set by others was difficult and upsetting for many students on the Philadelphia project." Selby continued, "We teach design backwards. Our pedagogical approach should be from . . . the design of cities to the design of individual component buildings."[61] He also explained, "We teach environmental design in studios segregated by professions—architecture, landscape architecture, and urban planning." He reflected, "This policy of academic isolationism teaches students specific fragments but not the broad scope of environmental design." Invited by Bacon, prominent Philadelphia-based landscape architect Laurie Olin came to Illinois as a guest lecturer and called Bacon's course "remarkable and stimulating."[62]

Bacon participated in a number of professional activities, such as the annual Delos Symposion, hosted by Greek planner Constantine Doxiadis, which convened a group of fewer than three dozen international experts in a variety of disciplines (including architect R. Buckminster Fuller and cultural anthropologist Margaret Mead) and put them together on an Aegean cruise to philosophize and create ideas for the future of urban civilization.[63]

Through the 1970s, Bacon continued to serve on boards and commissions, including the board of the American Academy in Rome, the board of the American Society of Planning Officials, several prominent leadership positions with the Urban Land Institute, and two federal commissions.[64] He maintained an active speaking schedule at venues across the country

Figure 23. Bacon making a presentation at Delos Symposion II in 1964. This annual event was hosted by architect/planner Constantine Doxiadis, convening international experts in a variety of disciplines, who went on an Aegean cruise to philosophize and create ideas for the future of urban civilization. Courtesy of the Edmund N. Bacon Collection, The Architectural Archives, University of Pennsylvania.

and wrote articles for an array of publications. He also served on several organizations focusing on environmental issues. He was appointed by President Richard Nixon to serve on the Pennsylvania Avenue Commission, chaired by Bacon's colleague architect Nathaniel Owings.[65] Bacon also served on a federal Urban Transportation Advisory Council, chaired by secretary of transportation John A. Volpe.[66]

During his retirement, Bacon spoke prolifically across the globe on topics such as the "Post-Petroleum City," the dangers of suburban development, and the need for a new priority on urban reinvestment. In his mind,
these themes were inherently connected. Bacon saw the deterioration of
urban neighborhoods coupled with rapid suburban development as an
issue of epic proportions and the continued development of new suburbs
as a short-sighted, unsustainable growth pattern. He told one audience in
Washington, "The National Growth Policy discussions to date seem to have
used for their intellectual model the Mad Hatter's Tea Party. Now we have
come to the end of the table, so we'll either have to go back and clear up
the mess at the other end of the table or we will go hungry."[67] He told a
committee of the U.S. House of Representatives focusing on the renewal of
Washington, "Here, I think, we turn our eyes away from the monumental
malls and architectural vistas to the neighborhoods where the people
live."[68] "In my opinion," he argued in one article, "there must be a total
national commitment to restore or rebuild every vacant, abandoned house,
to put to constructive use every vacant lot in the nation."[69]

In the late 1970s and early 1980s, Bacon developed a series of five films
on the development of cities, focusing on the theme of reinvesting in urban
areas to plan for a post-petroleum future. He created the films with his son
Michael, his assistant David Clow, and filmmaker Art Ciocco. The Urban
Land Institute produced the films, funded in large part through a grant
from the U.S. Department of Energy.[70] The films focus on the planning of
Rome, London, Paris, "The American Urban Experience," and "The City
of the Future." In each film, Bacon narrates, starting with the challenge,
"As our use of energy changes, our civilization will change as well. Our
cities will become testing grounds for new ways of living, but will our cities
be ready for us?"[71] The films earned some acclaim, winning a handful of
awards and gaining air time on the Learning Channel.[72]

In 1972, Bacon was approached by developer I. Rocke Ransen, who
offered him a job as vice president at Mondev, a Montreal-based real estate
development company.[73] Ransen created a subsidiary, Mondev U.S.A., with
an office in Boston. It would not be a full-time job, and to a large degree,
Ransen brought Bacon on for his name and prestige. It was Bacon's job to
travel around the country and represent the real estate development company to key decision makers and civic leaders. Ransen's hope of Bacon
gaining company credibility seems to have paid off. An article in *Architectural Record* five years later lauded "the creative alliance [Ransen] has forged

with [Bacon] the architect-planner whose philosophy and public career have illuminated the humane possibilities of 'the city as an act of will'."[74]

After decades of representing the public sector while working with private developers, Bacon was excited to sit on the other side of the table. The private sector presented him with new venues for being entrepreneurial, helping shape innovative development projects and figuring out creative ways of selling city government officials, business leaders, and the public on those ideas, but from the vantage of a company that would benefit financially from their realization. Market East demonstrated how critical private-sector investment was to the future of urban development projects. It was a logical next career move for Bacon, who never really seemed to have believed in comprehensive planning and, throughout his tenure at the Planning Commission, preferred to work with the private sector to realize individual, transformative projects like Penn Center and Market East.

Few federal funds were available in the 1970s to support urban investments. In light of the lack of federal resources and the subdued role of planning departments across the country, Bacon explained, "the true planners of the city today are in private enterprise."[75] In one report, he wrote, "The most important need is for the developer to see himself as a part of a unified effort involving the city government, all of the various citizen groups, the architect and the development team, in one seamless process of revitalizing a city."[76]

The kinds of projects Bacon worked on at Mondev held similarities to those he had promoted in Philadelphia—complex projects, focused on urban downtown reinvestment, often involving public-private partnerships, and design features that harkened to Penn Center, Market East, and Society Hill. With Mondev, Bacon worked on projects like a forty-acre downtown project in Salem, Massachusetts, that involved historic preservation and the creation of a pedestrian greenway system; a $25 million project in Colorado Springs to rebuild two cleared city blocks as a new city hall, galleria, and civic plaza, with architect Richard Meier; a new civic center in Burlington, Vermont, with architect Ludwig Mies van der Rohe; and a $60 million mixed-use shopping center with a monorail in Seattle.[77]

Overall, Bacon's work with Mondev seems to have been positive, and several of these big civic projects were built. *Architectural Record* said of the Mondev approach, "They [Mondev's projects] certainly demonstrate that there is no truth in the commonly held notion that quality in architecture and profit-making in the marketplace are incompatible goals."[78] Mondev took up only a fraction of Bacon's time, but it gave him a professional title and an ongoing credential that perhaps allowed him to stay at the forefront of national issues in a way a retired expert could not as easily do. Ransen was totally enamored with Bacon's businesslike approach yet quirky, progressive demeanor. Ransen recalled, "We had one meeting with a city councilman, and Ed went and did tai chi in the corner for twenty minutes."[79]

While Bacon worked on projects across the country and spoke at international venues, he stayed committed to Philadelphia and became a visible figure in debates over large-scale development projects during the coming decades. His role in local debates best demonstrates his attempts as a policy entrepreneur outside government. While he was free to speak his mind and develop arguments the way he pleased, he lacked the backing of public office and the resources of city government. He employed creative marketing techniques and strategies of salesmanship, but, in this role of entrepreneurial private citizen he would often find his efforts falling short of the mark. Bacon gained a reputation in Philadelphia as a stalwart defender of the city's urban environment but also an argumentative and sometimes cantankerous figure, who stubbornly refused to retire quietly and withdraw from the public scene.

The Battle of Billy Penn

The first time Bacon reintroduced himself into a local debate in Philadelphia was over the issue of a developer wanting to break the city's unofficial height limit in the early 1980s. Philadelphia was one of the last U.S. cities without a modern skyscraper office district. In the early 1980s, a number of national developers viewed the area around Penn Center, along Market Street, west of City Hall, as prime office real estate and began jockeying to purchase sites, secure big-name tenants, and be first to break ground on a shiny new building. One of these developers was Willard (Bill) Rouse, III, nephew of James Rouse, who had developed The Gallery at Market East. Bill Rouse already could take credit for several suburban shopping center developments and the award-winning Philadelphia Stock Exchange building at Nineteenth and Market Streets.[80]

By 1983, Rouse and Pittsburgh developer Oliver Tyrone (who had built 1234 Market Street) were vying for a set of Market Street properties between Sixteenth and Seventeenth Streets. At the time, this location was the site of dingy low-rise buildings housing "fast food . . . pinball . . . and dirty movies."[81] Through a complicated set of events, they both ended up with pieces of the same block. After a legal battle and a private, high-stakes auction, Rouse paid a small fortune and came out with the property.[82] Rouse engaged the local design firm of Wallace, Roberts and Todd as his architect and charged the firm with figuring out what he could build on his new land to make a profit. Bacon's former staff member Richard Huffman was a member of the design team.[83] After much designing and redesigning, the architects presented Rouse with the best scheme the designers could come up with, including three blocky 38-story buildings that practically filled the site. Neither Rouse nor the architects were happy.[84]

One problem was that Rouse had paid so much for the site that it was difficult to design a building that could net a profit. The other problem was the unwritten rule that buildings in Philadelphia could not be taller than the statue of William Penn on top of City Hall tower. There was no law on the books that Philadelphia had a formal height limit; it was simply a "gentleman's agreement" that Bacon famously enforced during his tenure and that amazingly was still in place in the 1980s. The gentleman's agreement was considered so unchallengeable that Rouse's architects never considered breaking it. However, Rouse was not a Philadelphian; for him, it did not have the same untouchable stature that it held for local developers. He directed his architects to design a building that would rise above Billy Penn.[85] They went back and developed a new plan with two tall, narrow towers, both considerably higher than the bronze figure of Philadelphia's founder.[86]

Rouse & Associates released the plans for the two skyscrapers on April 5, 1984, estimated to cost $500 million and billed as "the largest commercial development ever undertaken in the City of Philadelphia."[87] One of the towers was planned to reach 60 to 65 floors, the other 50 to 55 floors, with a 300–350-room hotel and 100 condo units, restaurants, stores, a health club, a 700-seat movie theater, and an underground parking garage. Despite commissioning Wallace, Roberts and Todd for the conceptual design, Rouse held a competition to select an architect for the final design. The winner was the Chicago firm Murphy/Jahn, with its celebrated principal Helmut Jahn. Rouse's announcement of the project and architect launched a period of uncertainty and controversy—creating a topic that hit at the heart of Philadelphia's struggle between staid traditionalism and progressivism.[88]

Even before Rouse had announced the plans for his project, some surmised that breaking the height limit was not such a bad thing. Thomas

Hine, *Inquirer* architecture critic, called the reluctance to build tall sky-scrapers akin to those in New York "the reason that Philadelphia has become America's most forgotten city."[89] Bacon disagreed vehemently and wrote a response, published in the next Sunday's paper. Speaking of the height limit, he wrote, "Here is a characteristic that sets Philadelphia apart from all others in the United States. It has been maintained through the years by a delicate threat, a gentleman's agreement."[90] He continued, "Once smashed it is gone forever and Philadelphia will join the rest of the Ameri-can cities with their continuous chaotic struggle to see which commercial interest can dominate the skyline."

Bacon felt that City Hall's dominance in the skyline was a physical reminder of the city's original plan of a town designed around a central square at the intersection of its two major roadways.[91] He also felt, as indi-cated by his previous quote, that it was both uncharacteristic and positive to have the tallest element be a symbol of the public interest, rather than a corporate skyscraper, "that the interests of all the people shall forever rise above the interests of any individual or corporation."[92] A soon-to-ensue public debate showed that many Philadelphians agreed with Bacon but largely due to their desire to maintain Philadelphia's trademark tradition as a human-scale city of Quaker modesty.[93]

This challenge to what Bacon saw as one of the core elements of Phila-delphia's connection to its historical development came to dominate his life for the next year, to the point of obsession. He wrote a stream of op-ed articles, some published in the *Inquirer*, opposing the project. The Founda-tion for Architecture, a local nonprofit organization of which Rouse was on the board, became a major platform airing the issues surrounding the height limit debate. On April 25, 1984, the foundation held a memorable public forum, with five people invited to speak, including Rouse, Bacon, and John Bower, in which Bacon had two assistants come up on stage and unroll a long sheet of brown butcher paper, held upright, so that the other panelists, including Rouse were blocked from the audience's view.[94] Bacon had an image of the city skyline drawn on the paper, over which he pasted red cutout forms, to demonstrate the impacts of the towers. Bacon argued, "Downtown Philadelphia has flourished while the downtowns of other cities with much higher towers, notably Detroit, have fallen apart." He con-tended, "The integrity of this city is not for sale." He mused, "Maybe Ath-ens will build a sixty story office building next to the Acropolis."[95]

There were a host of other panel discussions, television interviews, articles, and presentations. WHYY, Philadelphia's public broadcasting affiliate, held an all-day forum on the topic, featuring Mayor W. Wilson Goode. However, as time went on, it seemed that political momentum was swinging in Rouse's favor. There were nine major development projects in the works for the area west of City Hall, and Rouse was under pressure to be the first to break ground.[96] With time of the essence and inflation pushing construction costs ever higher, he projected a sense of urgency to Mayor Goode and City Council. Additionally, the Planning Commission reviewed the matter, and, according to its chairman, Graham Finney, "there were no legal reasons why it [the Rouse project] couldn't be built."[97]

At this point, Bacon wrote to Mayor Goode urging him not to support the Rouse plan: "History has placed you in a pivotal position as Philadelphia contemplates two routes from which there is no return."[98] He continued, "The decision will set the form of Philadelphia for all time to come." On May 15, 1984, Mayor Goode presented his testimony to City Council, for the first time publicly putting his cards on the table: "While I oppose a wholesale exemption from the traditional height limit, I do feel that, on a case-by-case basis, and within certain geographic areas, we should be flexible."[99] However, Goode requested that the Council table the matter until the Planning Commission finished drafting a new development plan for Center City—the first since Bacon's 1963 plan.

Planning Commission director Barbara Kaplan set the staff on a rapid schedule to get the plan finished. Bacon was enraged and accused Goode of making "deals in secret," in which "Rouse seduced Mayor Goode by promising that he would do some housing in North Philadelphia if the Mayor went along with breaking the height limit."[100] It is unclear whether there was truth to the accusation. In a letter to the editor in the *Inquirer*, Bacon decided to resign publicly from a board position appointed by the mayor, using the letter as a bully pulpit to attack every imaginable aspect of the issue related to the Rouse towers and the height limit debate.[101]

The Rouse building was but one of several major development projects slated during this period, but its progress set off a battle to see who could break ground first. In June 1984, developer Richard I. Rubin announced his plan to develop a new high-rise office complex east of City Hall. In March 1985, developer Robert F. Maguire announced that he had secured

IBM as the lead tenant for a proposed office complex, farther west than the Rouse site. Maguire explained that he was not trying to break the height limit, and this major tenant would allow him to start construction immediately on the project, to be designed by I. M. Pei's firm.[102]

As the office building race turned into a sprint, Rouse quickly secured financing for the first tower and set a date for the groundbreaking: May 13, 1985. Rouse sent Bacon a personal letter—an olive branch of sorts—inviting him to the groundbreaking, noting "even in our disagreement I have never tried to insult you."[103] Bacon did not write back until the day of the groundbreaking, and his note was not as polite: "By breaking this ground today you have destroyed one of the most remarkable artifacts of all time. . . . This is a day of infamy."[104] That last line of Bacon's note turned out to be prophetic. The very day of the groundbreaking, the Philadelphia police dropped plastic explosives from a helicopter on a West Philadelphia rowhouse occupied by members of MOVE, the activist black liberation organization. The explosion from the bomb burned down almost an entire city block, killing eleven people and making international headlines.[105] This singular event would come to overshadow the administration and legacy of Mayor Goode.

With no hope of halting the Rouse development, Bacon turned his attention to preventing a proliferation of tall buildings from crowding City Hall. He first suggested that the city adopt a zone without height controls on both sides of City Hall to "eliminate any unfair advantage to West Market Street . . . [and] help to restore the balance of development."[106] Later, he changed his mind and proposed a formal height limit of 491 feet in Center City, arguing "Better one sore thumb than total chaos."[107] In 1987, he came to favor the idea of a "zone of respect" around City Hall, with building heights limited in a four-block radius. In contrast, the City Planning Commission recommended establishing two view corridors that would be maintained by limiting building heights and placement.[108]

When the first Rouse tower was finished in 1987, Paul Goldberger, the *New York Times* architecture critic, wrote about the structure, now called One Liberty Place: "The way people talked about One Liberty Place" Goldberger wrote, "you would have thought that this was not a new building but some sort of nuclear weapon." However, with the controversy over and the building complete, he asserted, "it is not only far and away the best tall building Mr. [Helmut] Jahn has ever designed, it is the best tall building that has been built in Philadelphia in more than 50 years." He continued, "this building is far too good to be dismissed in Philadelphia as the violator of the urban order. It transcends the old order, and establishes a new one, at a level of quality good enough to justify throwing away the old."[109]

The Battle of Billy Penn was over, and Rouse had won. A host of modern skyscrapers followed suit, turning Market Street into the city's new signature office district and creating a dramatic new skyline. Ironically, it was Penn Center that first established Market Street as the city's emerging commercial district and created a context for future office developments in the vicinity. Bacon's work in the 1950s had, arguably, laid the foundation for the height limit battles that ensued.

Through the height limit issue, Bacon had attempted to use some of his customary techniques as a policy entrepreneur but outside the realm of government. He turned to the media to shape public opinion, made appeals to powerful policy makers, and sought to establish and consistently sell a cogent argument, often using strong language to accentuate the significance of the issue. However, his demeanor and rhetoric was less restrained than when he was a public official, and his ties to policy makers were much less direct as a private citizen.

In the end, the strategy failed, and this episode gave Bacon's legacy a new twist. The famous planning director, while admired by some for sticking to his guns during the height limit debate, was seen by others as an aging crank. He would continue to jump angrily into confrontations, using and expanding his entrepreneurial tactics to promote his ideas for Philadelphia's future. However, these attempts generally yielded little success. Another contentious example was around the redesign of Independence Mall in the 1990s.

Independence Mall Revisited: Bacon Versus the National Park Service

Bacon's role in the design of Independence Mall during the 1950s was relatively minor, though he viewed the mall as an important element in the overall revitalization of Philadelphia's downtown. By the 1980s, Bacon could see as well as anyone that the mall's northern two blocks were vastly underused, but he continued to believe future generations would realize the mall's untapped potential. He was concerned about what he saw as a series of affronts to the integrity of the mall by the National Park Service, including the construction of a modernist Liberty Bell pavilion and new visitors' center for the Bicentennial, both of which Bacon found architecturally distasteful.[110]

In 1988, the mall's Edwin O. Lewis Fountain stopped working, and the Park Service proposed replacing it with a new Constitution Memorial and reflecting pool, designed by Philadelphia architecture firm MGA Partners. The Park Service used the Constitution Heritage Act of 1988, authorizing a memorial to the Constitution in Philadelphia's historical park, as the impetus for fundraising to replace the broken fountain.[111] Bacon immediately went on the offensive, criticizing the design in the press and enlisting support of national public figures.[112] He was not the only person who disliked the design, just the most adamant and vocal.[113] Soon he heard from someone close to the project that he could call off the proverbial hounds, as the lack of funding had become too severe and the project would not move ahead.[114]

In 1991, Edward G. Rendell, a former Philadelphia district attorney, was elected mayor. After spending his early years bringing the city back from the brink of bankruptcy, Rendell set his sights on attracting major development projects and institutions to the struggling city. One of his keynote projects was to be a National Constitution Center—a much larger and grander iteration of the former Constitution Memorial—envisioned as a museum that could attract tourists, school groups, and major events and celebrations. The Pew Charitable Trusts announced it would also in part finance a new visitors' center on the mall.[115] Coupled with these efforts, the Park Service engaged in an effort to redesign Independence Mall entirely, including a new Liberty Bell Center.[116] To start the planning process, the Park Service held a series of public forums and developed a "General Management Plan," containing value statements regarding the future of the mall, based on public input.[117]

The Park Service was attempting to carry out a new type of planning methodology that focused on involving the public in a two-part process of generating ideas and goals, then focusing on physical design, working with professional planners and architects. According to planner Barbara Faga, "the trend line of public involvement in planning and design has been rising steadily for decades, following parallel developments in activism in other areas of public life."[118] In planning circles, there was clearly pressure by the late 1990s for large-scale projects to use this type of approach. Whether it would work or whether the National Park Service had the skill to lead a successful public planning process was another question altogether.

Bacon did not understand the Park Service approach, nor did he think much of it once it was explained to him. Bacon believed that, for the public to be engaged, people had to see physical concepts in plans and models so they could imagine them as part of their urban landscape. Then the plan would evolve through the feedback cycle that had shifted the form of projects like Market East over the course of decades. He criticized the Park Service planning process as undemocratic. To Bacon, soliciting public feedback without a plan represented the illusion of involvement, ending up with a plan designed by committee, which nobody could alter. The media were sympathetic, noting that it was true that the Park Service had "only talked about its plans in conceptual terms."[119]

Enraged that the Park Service would hold citizen hearings without having a plan, Bacon took it upon himself to correct what he saw as a reversal of the sequence of the planning process. He hired a team of ten architects, model makers, and artists to create a full-scale model and plans for redesigning Independence Mall. His plan proposed installing the Visitors Center at the northern end, farthest away from Independence Hall. On the second block would be a below-ground Constitution Center, with a glass roof, connecting to a glass and bronze domed Liberty Bell pavilion. Bacon did not alter the first block, leaving it as open space, lined with trees. He reprogrammed the existing parallel rows of brick archways on the second block into a "Promenade of States" and created more of a family atmosphere with a carousel and festival marketplace.[120] He proposed redeveloping the barren third block of the mall as a hotel. He also reimagined his Promenade of States as a "Children's World," with "doors children can open to find surprises within."[121]

Bacon was quoted in the media explaining, "My role is getting people to think, to move the debate from numbers and words to the physical reality of what we're trying to accomplish."[122] He put his plan on exhibition in a space just adjacent to Independence Mall. It made all the major newspapers. An *Inquirer* editorial said, "What a terrible mistake it would be to dismiss veteran city planner Edmund Bacon as a lovable old cuss who just doesn't know when to let go." The editorial called Bacon's plan "breathtaking," creating "a showpiece for *the nation*."[123] Robert Butera, director of the Pennsylvania Convention Center, wrote in a letter to the editor, "[Bacon's] plan would provide much of the excitement currently lacking in the Park Service's approach to the restoration."[124]

At this point, Martha Aikens, Park Service superintendent, pushed back, responding with a letter in the *Inquirer*. The Park Service plan, Aikens explained, "does not include physical design, but instead provides the foundation on which subsequent design can be based. . . . The paper's comparisons of the management plan to physical-design proposals (such as Edmund Bacon's) is a comparison of apples and oranges."[125] Aikens was surely well intentioned in her approach, but she was losing the publicity battle. In a private letter to Bacon, Janet Haas, vice chair of the William Penn Foundation, wrote, "I have written to Mayor Rendell to request that he . . . cut Martha Aiken [*sic*] out of the loop."[126] Nobody was going to quiet Bacon this time. W. Russell G. Byers, a columnist in the *Daily News*, wrote, "someone wants this guy to cool it? Forget it."[127] Bacon had used a tool he employed throughout his career—the power of a physical plan or image to excite the public.

At this point, a third party stepped into the fray. The Pew Charitable Trusts put in its own money to hire celebrated designers Robert Venturi and Denise Scott Brown to create a physical design for the Park Service to call its own. In essence, it was an effort to take Bacon on his own terms, but with bigger-name designers and much more money. It was an unexpected move, treated by the *Inquirer* with skepticism, calling Pew "a new, rich and (so far) secretive player . . . which gained power by dangling the cash the Park Service lacked."[128] The Venturi, Scott Brown plan left the Liberty Bell on the first block but in a new pavilion. It called for the Visitors Center stretching across the second block, east to west. Behind the Visitors Center would be a bus turnaround in front of the new Constitution Center. The *Inquirer* reported that, in June 1996, the Venturi, Scott Brown plan had "received the tentative blessing of the National Park Service."[129]

Mayor Rendell, who was vying to get the Constitution Center built, was not thrilled with the new plan, but he gave it his approval.[130] For his part, Bacon was glad there was finally another plan to discuss; however, he did not like the design—calling it "very bad," in an op-ed in the *Inquirer*, taking issue with the notion of running the Visitors Center east to west, plugging off the mall at the second block.[131] Others seemed to agree with Bacon, and a new Park Service design concept in September 1996 shifted the buildings to keep a view-shed down the center of the mall.[132] This new design, however, moved the Liberty Bell pavilion to the eastern edge of the first block, replacing the rows of trees that were currently standing. Seeing the destruction of the trees as an unconscionable offense, Bacon staged a protest in which he chained himself to one of the trees, gaining him a write-up in the *New York Times*.[133]

With the Venturi, Scott Brown plan continuing to be controversial, the Park Service switched designers, bringing in the Olin Partnership, with its principal, landscape architect Laurie Olin. On October 1, 1997, the Park Service held a public forum to unveil its final plans for Independence Mall. Bacon was appalled by the new plan that, in his words, "destroyed every blade of grass, every tree, every brick and marble wall, every living thing. It reduced the entire first block to scorched earth."[134] However, the Olin plan had received "sustained applause" at the forum, and it looked like it was going to be the final word.[135] Bacon was furious, arguing that "The entire pretense of citizen participation . . . has been a sham from the beginning."[136] Of course, in Bacon's process of planning, he was right. By unveiling the Olin plan and then aggressively moving ahead in building it, the Park Service never gave the public the months, years, or decades necessary to develop feedback and revise the physical plan, as per Bacon's view of how the planning process should function.

Bacon kept up the fight for awhile, and some people agreed with him. TV personality Liz Matt wrote, "Why isn't anybody listening to Ed Bacon before it's too late?"[137] Bacon continued to write letters to the papers, but his protesting did little. As with Liberty Place, he had to concede defeat. The *Inquirer* reported, "Pioneering city planner loses battle over mall."[138]

In retrospect, it is interesting to note that for a time Bacon appeared to have the upper hand. This moment came when he introduced a physical design concept. It was perhaps the Better Philadelphia Exhibition that first demonstrated to Bacon the power of images and models, and he continued to use the introduction of compelling visuals as a core strategy of his policy entrepreneurship. Though he was not ultimately successful, the battles of Independence Mall also showed that Bacon still had the respect of some influential individuals and policy makers, and that compelling physical design models continued to have a public impact.

Yet, these episodes further accentuated Bacon's bitterness and the public's view of him as an outdated old man. His actual influence had likely declined significantly as a result of his angry tirades in some of the Park Service's public meetings. *Inquirer* writer Tom Ferrick proclaimed of Bacon, "This was his last battle over an important public space."[139] Perhaps this was wishful thinking on Ferrick's part, hoping Bacon would now depart the scene gracefully. However, Bacon had no such intention.

A Labor of LOVE: Bacon's Last Battle

Bacon's true final battle would be over a tiny, one-block-square park in the center of town, the plaza that had come to be known as LOVE Park. Bacon had included a plaza at this location in his 1932 thesis at Cornell.[140] It was constructed in 1965 with a design by Vincent Kling and was officially dedicated as John F. Kennedy Plaza, though it became better known as LOVE Park after the iconic Robert Indiana sculpture at its southeast corner. The park had a massive fountain, encircled by a gradual, spiral of stairs in the central space, large granite tiles on the ground, and an upper level lined by granite walls and planters.

By the 1980s, the park was underutilized, mostly serving as a respite for city employees on their walk to work and a good place for homeless people to take a rest. However, during the coming decades, the park would find a popular new use by skateboarders; the curving stairs, long, flat walls, and straight granite surfaces were perfect for the sport, not to mention that the park was located right by a major rail station, in the center of town. Originating in the 1940s and '50s, skateboarding was first a suburban, West-coast sport, but by the 1980s it was making inroads in urban areas like New York, Washington, San Francisco, and Philadelphia.[141] Rather than utilizing custom skate parks, however, the new urban "street skating" form of the sport used "natural" elements found around the city—benches, walls, railings. The core of street skating became high-precision moves on low surfaces, making long, flat walls and benches the perfect obstacles.

By the 1990s, a vibrant skateboarding community had formed around LOVE Park, and some of these skateboarders were well-paid professionals, making six-figure incomes as skateboarding gained legitimacy and air time on sports networks. Some of the biggest international names in the sport based their reputations on their association with LOVE Park.[142] In 2000, California-based DC Shoes released a footwear model named for professional skateboarder Stevie Williams, with a picture of the LOVE sculpture on the box.[143] Hundreds of skateboarders converged on the park daily.[144] The plaza was featured in skateboarding videos, magazines, and video games, gaining an international reputation as an icon of a multibillion-dollar sport.

Skateboarders brought new life to an abandoned urban space; however, city officials did not share the enthusiasm. In fall 2000, Philadelphia City Council passed and Mayor John F. Street signed into law a bill "prohibiting skateboarding on all public property unless otherwise authorized."[145] In

2001, Philadelphia signed a two-year contract with ESPN's X-Games—the Olympiad of extreme sports, which featured skateboarding as one of its major events. The games were broadcast to 150 million viewers in 18 countries, and many of the promotional events, featuring skateboarding, were filmed in LOVE Park.[146]

The next year, in spring 2002, Mayor Street announced that he was closing LOVE Park for an $800,000 overhaul, with part of his intent to make LOVE Park unusable for skateboarding.[147] Ironically, that same year DC Shoes filmed a commercial at LOVE Park to advertise its shoe label.[148] The park reopened just before Independence Day, with pink stucco planters and wooden benches replacing the old granite ones. Planters now stood in the way of some of the ledges and walls. Most significant, there was now a twenty-four-hour police watch to keep skateboarders out. If people dared skateboard, they faced confiscation of their board and a $300 fine. For many skateboarders and sports enthusiasts, the second year of the X-Games was overshadowed with disgust at the mayor and disappointment that one of the world's most famous "skate spots" was ruined.[149]

Some of the city's professional skateboarders started to leave town, bemoaning the end of an era.[150] In September 2002, Richard Florida, author of *Rise of the Creative Class*, lectured in Philadelphia and commented on the LOVE Park situation. He said, "Skate parks are very important to young people, an intrinsic part of their creative culture, part of their identity. We should be expanding skate parks. . . . To take the park away is to tell them that they are not valid. Big mistake."[151] David Thornburgh, executive director of the Pennsylvania Economy League—a local think tank—seconded Florida's statement, commenting on the decision to kick out the skateboarders, "I think that was an unfortunate turn of events. This was an attraction that was world-renowned, that was sending signals about Philadelphia as a hip, creative and diverse place."[152]

Bacon could not have agreed more. He loved physical activities taking place as part of the urban landscape: open-air theater, break dancing, street performance. In his *Understanding Cities: Paris* film, Bacon made sure to highlight the athletic feats of roller bladers jumping up a flight of stairs.[153] Obviously, neither he nor Vincent Kling had skateboarding in mind when they planned and designed LOVE Park. But that was exactly the point: people had organically found a new and exciting use for an underutilized public space and transformed that space into a world-famous icon, energizing it with their presence, and turning it into an attraction (as the X Games proved).

Bacon was livid about the policy against skateboarding in LOVE Park and began to stage a public attack on the mayor and City Council, writing and speaking out on the issue. In one letter to the editor, Bacon wrote, "I am deeply disturbed by the hypocrisy of City Council. After decrying the drugs and crime of our young people, it then adopted legislation forbidding the one harmless thing that young people had developed strictly on their own, the wonderful national network of skateboarding focusing on LOVE Park."[154] However, Bacon did not feel that writing letters was enough. He had to take action.

By this point, the author was working as Bacon's assistant. One day as I arrived at Bacon's home to begin our projects for the day, Bacon called me over and said, "I want to skateboard in LOVE Park." He described a protest with the media present to drum up attention for the issue. I was concerned for his safety, but Bacon was set on his idea, so I helped him make it happen. At my suggestion, we met with Howard Altman, the tenacious editor-in-chief of the free weekly publication *Philadelphia City Paper*—a journalist known for taking controversial stances and favoring Philadelphia's hip, young, and edgy personality.

As Bacon passionately explained his plan and his desire for *City Paper* to cover it, I saw a smile start to crawl across Altman's face. In Altman's own words, "This is a fascinating offer, too good to pass up. I imagine the news ticker: '92-year-old father of Kevin Bacon arrested in Philly for skateboarding'."[155] Before committing, Altman took Bacon into the hall, and, with him and me holding onto Bacon's shoulders, we tested Bacon's balance on a half-sized skateboard that Altman had sitting around the office, skating a few feet on the carpeted newsroom floor. "I feel so alive again," Bacon proclaimed after finishing his trial run. Bacon felt confident that he could do it, and Altman agreed to organize the logistics and cover the story.

The day finally came, October 28, 2002. I arrived at Bacon's home early in the morning and found him ready and anxious to go, decked out in a dark gray Brooks Brothers suit. We took a taxi to LOVE Park. It was a cool, overcast, autumn day. At the park were a gathering of news film crews, and Howard Altman with two members of his staff, a skateboard and blue bicycle helmet in hand. Some prominent members of the local skateboarding community were there. Vincent Kling soon arrived and strode toward the group, with a grimace on his face and a brass-tipped cane in hand. The news crews interviewed Bacon and Kling as they waited to begin. The elderly Kling boomed into the microphones, "I built this place so that people could enjoy it," he said, "And that includes skateboarders."[156]

A police officer standing guard soon realized that something involving skateboarding (and, therefore, illegal) was going to happen. She went up to the group and told the news crews to stop filming. Next, she turned to Bacon and said, "Don't do this." When it became clear that Bacon was not going to listen, she called on her radio for reinforcements. Altman reported that a police sergeant later explained they did not arrest Bacon "because we use our discretion. . . . we didn't want to cause more trouble than it was worth."[157]

Just after 10 a.m., Bacon put on the blue helmet and took out a statement he had prepared. A handful of passersby, seeing the news crews, moved closer to find out what was happening. With the helmet on his head and a determined look on his face, Bacon read a brief statement in which he declared, "I conceived Love Park. . . . I make no claim to be a leader, but, by God I am a person and I stand up to Mayor Street and tell him to go to Hell and stay there until he sees the light and changes his ways by going to Love Park each day with a smile on his face and a warm welcoming handshake, to greet the skateboarders of the world."[158] Bacon proclaimed, "And now, in total defiance of Mayor Street, I will skateboard in LOVE Park!"

Howard Altman and one of Altman's staff stationed themselves on each side of Bacon, holding onto his arms. Bacon slowly crept forward on the skateboard, gingerly trying to keep his balance. It was a wild sight, with his suit still buttoned, a microphone clipped to his tie, the blue helmet on his head, and two men holding onto his arms with all their might. The photographers walked a few steps in front of Bacon as he skateboarded forward about twenty-five feet, toward the LOVE sculpture. After finishing, Bacon stepped off and, according to Altman, "howl[ed] in delight, once again blasting the mayor."[159]

With the main event finished, I helped the exhausted Bacon into a taxi, so I could stay around to observe the aftermath. The skateboarders began to roll around the plaza as the news crews dispersed. Suddenly, a police van pulled up, a handful of officers jumped out, roughed up the skateboarders, confiscated their boards, and ejected them from the plaza.

After his protest, Bacon received a stream of phone calls and letters from skateboarders, parents, and other supporters. One skateboarder wrote a letter to *Skate* magazine stating, "Today I discovered my own personal

Figure 24. Bacon skateboarding on October 28, 2002, in protest of the city ban on skateboarding in LOVE Park. On Bacon's left is Howard Altman, former editor of *Philadelphia City Paper*. Courtesy of the Edmund N. Bacon Collection, The Architectural Archives, University of Pennsylvania.

Rosa Parks. His name is Edmund Bacon."[160] Bacon's action sparked a major campaign in the city to return skateboarding to LOVE Park. Leading the charge were three nonprofit groups: the Independence Hall Association, Young Involved Philadelphia, and the newly formed Skateboard Advocacy Network.

The venerable Independence Hall Association, founded in 1942 to establish Independence National Historical Park, launched a website (www.ushistory.org/lovepark) about the issue, including a petition, which a year later closed with 10,000 signatures from forty countries. Young Involved Philadelphia, a group that represented the interests of a new generation of Philadelphians, hosted a well-attended forum on the topic, with Bacon as one of the panelists. Carla Anderson, *Daily News* "Urban Warrior" columnist, produced a series of articles covering the LOVE Park saga as it unfolded. Bacon's movie-star son Kevin supported the effort, saying: "I know that the perception of Philadelphia is often that it is a straight-laced city, steeped in history but with little to offer a hip young crowd. Of course anyone who has visited the city knows this couldn't be farther from the truth. LOVE Park was starting to change that perception."[161]

By summer 2003, a mayoral campaign was in full swing with incumbent Mayor Street challenged by Republican businessman Sam Katz. Despite the fact that Philadelphia had been a Democratic stronghold since Joseph Clark's election in 1951, early polls showed it was going to be a tight race. Skateboarding became a campaign issue when the *Daily News* ran an online poll reporting 69 percent public support for returning skateboarding to LOVE Park.[162] Soon thereafter, Katz announced that he was going to support returning skateboarding to LOVE Park if elected. He held a press conference in the plaza where he, too, mounted a skateboard.[163]

In July, the three nonprofit groups, now named the Coalition to Free LOVE Park, engaged in negotiations with the city and developed a "Compromise Solution," that included allowing skateboarding only after 3 p.m. on weekdays and all day on weekends and creating no-skate pedestrian zones. Both the *Inquirer* and *Daily News* supported the compromise in editorials.[164] A majority of City Council members went on record supporting it as well.[165] On October 5, the Coalition held a rally attended by about five hundred people, where members of City Council and the city controller came to the microphone to voice their support. To exuberant cheers, Bacon took the microphone, delivering a passionate speech. At ninety-three, Bacon proved that he was eminently relevant to the young crowd.

California-based DC Shoes—which saw skateboarding in LOVE Park as a critical part of its marketing—agreed to donate $1 million to the city over ten years if it would reopen LOVE Park to skateboarding.[166] In June 2004, the Coalition to Free LOVE Park publicly unveiled the million-dollar commitment. The president of DC Shoes flew in from California, and skateboarders, parents, city officials, and members of the public assembled in LOVE Park for the announcement. Bacon was on hand, signing autographs for a line of avid young fans. However, when the media asked the city for a statement, managing director Phil Goldsmith responded, "There's never going to be any skateboarding in LOVE Park, period." The *Daily News* ran a cover story the next day with a photograph of LOVE Park and the banner headline, "Take that $1M and . . ." Chris Satullo, then editorial board editor of the *Inquirer*, wrote a passionate piece, blasting the city for its stubbornness and inability to think outside the box: "LOVE Park is a test case of whether this city can do the things that cities must do to thrive. . . . The mayor and his top aides . . . just don't get it. They don't get how cities save themselves. It's enough to make you cry."[167]

Bacon again had to concede defeat, despite all the media coverage, public support, and advocacy around the effort to return skateboarding to LOVE Park. In this issue, he used a tool of policy entrepreneurship that was paramount to his career—creating an advocacy platform and inspiring others to take up the cause on their own. Projects like Society Hill and Market East were built largely thanks to the work of other stakeholders who bought into an idea that Bacon originally promoted. Bacon knew that, on the LOVE Park issue, he needed to inspire a large-scale advocacy effort, and he took the steps he felt he could to spark that effort, allowing him to step away letting others move the issue ahead. As in other projects throughout his career, the ultimate success of the LOVE Park effort relied on the work of others. The momentum and buy-in show Bacon's skill in this realm of policy entrepreneurship, but the disappointing end result also shows the vulnerability of Bacon's approach.

Bacon had been privy to plenty of disappointment in his life, opportunities where he felt city leaders were not enlightened enough to grasp visionary ideas or where other stakeholders failed in realizing ideas he promoted. But this defeat at LOVE Park was particularly difficult. At ninety-four, Bacon knew this was his final battle. He had lost. And so, he believed, had Philadelphia.

In 1984, *The Philadelphia Inquirer* sent its architecture critic, Thomas Hine, to interview Bacon for his obituary.[168] It was reasonable to believe that, at seventy-four, retired from the City Planning Commission, Bacon would recede quietly into private life. However, Bacon lived and stayed active for another twenty-one years, continuing to promote ideas, rile critics, and remain in the limelight on various civic issues.

After leaving the public sector, Bacon took on several goals in the next stage of his career. He sought to promote high-level ideas on an international stage through his speaking and teaching engagements and his film projects. He attempted to influence large-scale urban developments by representing Mondev in its real estate deals—working with big-city planners and development departments. Concurrently, he spent a tremendous amount of time fighting battles for his beliefs about the future of Philadelphia. It was this final role that most significantly shaped his image and legacy in Philadelphia.

It is interesting to consider Bacon's dual persona—the renowned intellectual speaking to audiences across the globe about a post-petroleum future or about the dangers of the suburbs contrasted with the cantankerous old man writing angry articles to stop a local skyscraper project. Bacon surely developed a distinctly different image in each of these roles. What these roles share, however, is evidence of his attempts to use his policy entrepreneurship to shape issues on differing scales in ways he was not able to as a public official. One of Bacon's core strategies was to influence the dialogue on an issue so that other stakeholders adopt ideas that Bacon promoted and advocate for them more broadly. This was Bacon's approach in attempting to inject ideas about the post petroleum future through speeches and films, just as it was in trying to inspire groups to take on his campaign for LOVE Park.

When advocating for local issues, Bacon stuck to many of the same strategies he had employed through his tenure as planning director, but with rhetoric and actions that were (for better or worse) liberated from the restraint he felt as a public official. Bacon relied heavily on the media to promote his ideas, and he continued to show is acumen for getting reporters to tell the story his way. Bacon focused on the power of physical images and models to promote his ideas. He also continued to reach out to policy makers behind the scenes, to align advocates to his cause. Although, in the case of Liberty Place, Independence Mall, and LOVE Park, Bacon failed in his pursuit, in all three cases it seemed viable at some point along the way that he could succeed.

The ongoing influence of Bacon's policy entrepreneurship on the international stage is difficult to gauge—though it seems plausible that his speeches, teaching, and films had some impact on stakeholders and contemporary dialogue regarding policy on issues such as peak oil, urban reinvestment policy, and suburban growth. On the local scene, Bacon's impact late in life, though not significant in shaping Philadelphia's physical landscape, was meaningful in influencing the realm of ideas and in defending his hometown legacy. The final decades of Bacon's life are significant for this discussion, however, as they provide examples of policy entrepreneurship outside government. While there were significant advantages for Bacon to holding a public office, he demonstrated that policy entrepreneurship is decidedly not limited to the role of government actors.

CONCLUSION

The Planner in the Twenty-First Century

Edmund N. Bacon passed away on October 14, 2005, at age ninety-five. Obituaries in national publications like the *New York Times, Architectural Record,* and *Metropolis* hailed him as one of the most influential planners of the twentieth century. The *New York Times* called him "a leading postwar urban planner who remade much of Philadelphia."[1] Several obituaries included comparisons to Robert Moses, and Bacon was frequently characterized as a "visionary."[2] However, when writers tried to pin down exactly what Bacon actually *did*, it became more challenging. In *Metropolis,* Philadelphia journalist Inga Saffron noted that "some Philadelphians may have been a little fuzzy on the scope of his [Bacon's] accomplishments."[3] In another piece, Saffron wrote of Bacon that it was "infuriatingly hard to evaluate his historic legacy."[4]

Indeed, even to those who were part of Philadelphia's development program—who worked with Bacon—his functions were often undefined and difficult to characterize. His actual role was, indeed, often overstated and distorted, and his ability to become the face of Philadelphia's urban renewal era had more to do with his skill as an effective marketer of ideas and policy entrepreneur than as evidence of his mythical position as a power broker who exerted primary influence over Philadelphia's urban renewal program.

Throughout his career, Bacon worked to promote and implement important ideas, though as a player on a team and often with a declining role as other more powerful actors became involved and guided projects to their realization. This fact both led Bacon to have a high degree of influence and left him frustrated, often forced into compromises he did not necessarily want to make. Bacon's vision was largely physical, and he left the broader spectrum of policy planning to others, while opening him to criticism for not being holistic enough in his approach.

The evolution of Bacon's work was shaped by the once progressive philosophy of solving social ills through better planned communities—popular among Bacon's colleagues such as Louis Kahn, Catherine Bauer, Lewis Mumford, and Oskar Stonorov. Bacon was a Roosevelt liberal, focused early in his career on housing for workers and the poor. However, he spent much of his career in Philadelphia working on downtown projects. This was so partly due to the fact that federal legislation in the 1950s refocused urban renewal nationally toward investments downtown, in industrial areas, and around universities, thus reframing Philadelphia's redevelopment program until the Great Society legislation of the late 1960s moved the spotlight back to underserved communities.

Throughout his career Bacon wrote and spoke prolifically about the need for community involvement and "democratic feedback" in the planning process. In his words, he sought a "process [that] itself involves the citizen in the planning, enriching the plan thereby and building up public acceptance of the plan once it is made."[5] However, Bacon often failed in his own efforts to work with community groups, in part perhaps due to his confrontational personality. He ended his career at the Planning Commission in 1970 as a frustrated public official—criticized for not keeping up with the trends in his profession. In the final thirty-five years of his life, Bacon applied his entrepreneurial approach to the private sector and to civic campaigns to influence the dialogue around remaking important spaces in Philadelphia, though often with unsuccessful outcomes.

Bacon was involved in envisioning, promoting, and implementing a number of important development projects in Philadelphia. His was a multifaceted and dynamic role that inherently intertwined planning and implementation. Thus, his work should not necessarily be assessed on the physical outcomes of projects built during the 1950s and 1960s, rather as a case study of policy entrepreneurship practiced by a city planner. By studying Bacon and other effective policy entrepreneurs, planners can perhaps reinvent their troubled profession for the twenty-first century in a way that is sensitive to their shifted role, while maintaining a focus on vision and a grasp of implementation strategies that will allow ideas at any scale to become effectuated.

The Legacy of Philadelphia's Urban Renewal

During his long life, Bacon witnessed two periods of major federal investment in cities, followed by a profound era of urban decline and disinvestment. Near the end of his life, he was encouraged by an emerging trend of a new national interest in urban living. He said in one interview, "If you look at the rate at which neighborhood after neighborhood after neighborhood has been transformed after decades of decay to become a hot real estate market, then you've got a trend that promises a bright future for Philadelphia."[6]

Philadelphia saw a 26.6 percent increase in its downtown population between 1990 and 2010, and the 2010 U.S. Census would show the first citywide population increase for Philadelphia in decades.[7] The city also saw an increase in Hispanic and Asian populations.[8] However, Philadelphia maintained a high poverty rate and continues to be largely a racially divided city, with little evidence of the kind of strong, racially and socioeconomically integrated neighborhoods Bacon hoped for.[9]

The legacy of the physical 1950s and 1960s urban renewal-era projects continue to affect Philadelphia's urban landscape in significant ways. Society Hill became one of Philadelphia's most affluent neighborhoods—sought after for its restored colonial homes and key geographic position downtown. The average home sale price in 2010 for the city of Philadelphia was $140,520, whereas in the city's downtown it was $295,956, and in the zipcode that includes Society Hill and Old City it was $683,084.[10]

Penn Center continues to sit across from City Hall with its unremarkable architecture and underutilized plazas. However, Suburban Station, below ground, serves as the city's major commuter rail hub. Furthermore, the original Penn Center buildings indeed reinvented the city's downtown commercial district, followed by dozens of new construction buildings stretching westward that now form the backbone of the city's central business district. In 2007, Liberty Property Trust completed the Comcast Center (1701 John F. Kennedy Boulevard), designed by Robert A. M. Stern, adjacent to the original Penn Center buildings. It is the tallest structure in Philadelphia, with 58 stories and 1,253,876 total square feet of space. Its below-ground market and shops link directly with Suburban Station, creating the type of transit-oriented connectivity that Bacon envisioned for the whole of Penn Center.[11]

The Gallery at Market East largely failed at reviving Market Street east of City Hall as a shopping district that could compete with suburban malls. Its brutalist architecture lines the street with blank walls, and its dark, below-ground halls and outdated décor create unappealing spaces. An article in the *Philadelphia Business Journal* in 2010 characterized the area around the Gallery as "a worn-down section of Center City."[12]

Figure 25. Philadelphia skyline, taken from City Hall tower, March 11, 2008, looking west. Photo by R. Bradley Maule.

However, the Gallery succeeds as a transit-oriented destination accessible to people of all races and incomes, in every neighborhood of Philadelphia. It is a key example of an urban shopping mall connected with a robust mass transit network. Nearby developments, including the Pennsylvania Convention Center, the renovation of the historic PSFS building as a hotel, and Reading Terminal Market, laid the groundwork for a revitalization of Market Street east of City Hall. In 2010 the Gallery's owner, Pennsylvania Real Estate Investment Trust (PREIT), announced "$100 million in a phased project transforming the Gallery into a modern, upscale urban mall."[13] According to Joseph Coradino, president of PREIT Services, about the Gallery at Market East, "We want to open it to the street, with cafes and retail that will capture the customers in that area."[14] Perhaps this kind of investment can create a more integrated and open, urban shopping complex, more in line with Bacon's original vision.

The Far Northeast persists as a mix of urban-style rowhouse neighborhoods and tracts of suburban-style, single-family and semidetached homes, in the midst of a suburban context of auto dependence and strip malls. One resident, writing in *Philadelphia* magazine, characterized the Northeast this way: "It's a huge swath of amorphous terrain that for the last half of the 20th century existed in a kind of suspended state of contented blandness, a big lumbering caboose of workaday white people tacked onto the train that was the city."[15]

However, the Northeast's racial homogeneity is rapidly shifting. A report by the Pew Charitable Trusts Philadelphia Research Initiative cites a significant increase in black, Asian, and Hispanic populations in the Northeast, with substantial population growth in some neighborhoods. The report says, "In no part of the city have the changes over the last 20 years been more pronounced than Northeast Philadelphia."[16] Pockets of immigrant communities have vastly changed the landscape of the Northeast, such as its vibrant Brazilian community, bringing with it a host of restaurants and bakeries.[17] Bacon pushed to have rowhouse communities affordable to blue-collar and middle-class residents, and it is this expanse of affordable homes, in part, that makes the area so attractive for Philadelphia's rapidly growing immigrant communities.

Some urban redevelopment sites have been rebuilt as part of federally funded Hope VI projects (a program administered by Bacon's daughter, Elinor Bacon, at the U.S. Department of Housing and Urban Development) or have blended into the urban landscape. Eastwick retained much of its

planned street network, homes, and parks from its urban renewal development; however, today the southwest part of the city that includes Eastwick
is one of Philadelphia's poorest and most distressed. Ludlow, a major site
of the "Used House" program, has huge tracts of vacant lots where public
housing units were demolished because the city could not adequately maintain them. An active community development corporation, Asociación
Puertorriqueños en Marcha Inc. (APM), is working to revive this area
through new home construction. One of the most successful redevelopment
projects of the 1950s and 1960s is Yorktown, which remains today a stable,
well-maintained, low-vacancy, middle-class African American community.[18]

Some of the transportation infrastructure built during the 1950s and
1960s is nearing the end of its functional life, requiring rebuilding or
replacement. Nowhere is this fact more apparent than with I-95 (the Delaware Expressway), running along the eastern edge of the city. Currently,
the Pennsylvania Department of Transportation is carrying out a "long-
term, multi-phase infrastructure initiative to improve and rebuild I-95 in
Philadelphia."[19] Meanwhile, some people (the author included) have questioned the decision to rebuild the expressway, which was controversial
when it was built and remains controversial today for cutting off Center
City from the Delaware River waterfront. Some have called for burying
I-95 or removing the roadway entirely, akin to initiatives in cities like New
York, San Francisco, and Milwaukee that replaced expressways with urban
boulevards. For example, when he visited Philadelphia in 2008, John Nor-
quist, former mayor of Milwaukee and current president of the Congress
for the New Urbanism, called for the removal of I-95 and said, "I-95 should
never have been built through the city."[20]

Philadelphia today is different from the city Bacon imagined for the
future, in places like his 1959 article where he envisioned the year 2009.
There are encouraging trends for the urban future but also profound challenges that will require vision and leadership from those whose job today
is to shape the physical, economic, and social landscape.

The Shifting Planning Profession

The twentieth century saw a significant shift in the roles and expectations
of the planning profession. During Bacon's days in Flint, the profession
was still struggling to establish itself within the framework of urban

government. By the early 1960s, city planners were solidly under attack for the failings of urban renewal policies and the way they were applied on the ground to urban neighborhoods. In the late 1960s and 1970s, a new generation of social planners took center stage, refocusing on issues like workforce development, poverty, education, public health, and social services. The even more substantial shift was redefining the planner as a facilitator of community-based planning efforts. The combination of these shifts left the profession struggling in the twenty-first century to determine its ongoing role, place in government, and responsibility to the public—accentuated by a lack of financial resources for urban investment.

After Philadelphia saw its real estate boom in the 1980s that bred Liberty Place, its Planning Commission was weak, largely trying to provide some planning framework, reactively, behind the new private investment. However, the ongoing efficacy of its efforts was unclear. In the 1990s and early twenty-first century, Philadelphia saw continued growth and reinvestment, but it was mostly market based, supported by private capital. The type of public interventions that came into being were local (rather than federal) in nature and focused on attracting private investment, with the City Planning Commission minimally involved. For example, City Council passed a ten-year tax abatement on new and rehabilitated residential construction that stimulated builders (some of whom had focused primarily on the suburbs prior) to develop a rash of urban projects. One scholar characterized this type of policy incentive for private development as "financing without cash."[21]

The first decade of the twenty-first century saw an increase in local government intervention in planning and development but a continued weak role for city planning. In 2002, Philadelphia Mayor John F. Street launched the $300 million Neighborhood Transformation Initiative (NTI) but created a new office to administer the program, rather than housing it with the City Planning Commission. Most of the city's ongoing capital investments (for example, community development block grants) were funneled through its Department of Commerce, rather than the Planning Commission. Mayor Michael A. Nutter created a deputy mayor for planning and economic development—effectively restoring the position of development coordinator—but continuing the tension seen during the 1960s of this position favoring the goals of the Department of Commerce over those of the Planning Commission. Active nonprofit community development corporations (CDCs), aided by a city enabled tax-credit program, became the primary entities engaged in neighborhood-based planning in many communities.

The Planning Commission recently led a wholesale rewrite of Philadelphia's zoning code, a new comprehensive planning process, and district planning. Still many of the most successful planning and development efforts of the 1990s and 2000s continued to come from the private or non-profit sectors (albeit sometimes using public dollars). Central Philadelphia Development Corporation—the latest incarnation of Old Philadelphia Development Corporation—and its Center City District, invested in sidewalk cleaning, signage, street lighting, and other positive elements that would make downtown more attractive.[22] In the late 1990s, under President Judith Rodin, the University of Pennsylvania launched its West Philadelphia Initiative—investing in a public school, commercial development, and a homeowner mortgage program around its campus. Penn's approach has been acclaimed as an outstanding model of a major institution investing in an urban area.[23] Under President John Fry, Drexel University is now working to emulate Penn's success through a similar initiative.

Starting in 2003 The *Philadelphia Inquirer* and Penn Praxis—the clinical arm of the university's School of Design—held a large-scale public process to help the city plan for the future of Penn's Landing along the Delaware riverfront. The city became involved in this effort and, through funding by the William Penn Foundation, hired outside planning firms to create a master plan for the riverfront. The process leading up to the plan was large scale, involving the public in a series of educational and planning workshops, to collect input, and allowing citizens to sit with designers in a "charrette" setting to put their ideas on paper in real time.[24]

This latter project reflected the current trend for a process of involving the public in urban planning, and a specific type of charrette process that had became increasingly expected for large-scale projects. Still, the impact of such a process and even its necessity in getting large-scale projects built remains unclear. Philadelphia recently saw some large-scale public processes that brought people together for design workshops but yielded few tangible results. At the same time, some of the city's largest projects—often supported with public dollars and tax breaks—had no charrette process. Examples of the latter include projects like the city's Convention Center expansion, the Comcast Center, and the redesign of City Hall's Dilworth Plaza.

Looking to the Future

Events in Philadelphia's recent planning history point to the larger question: what is the role of the planner in the twenty-first century? Has the planner's job become entirely that of the facilitator of public discourse around public-sector investments? To a large degree, it seems to be the case in America that planners have recoiled from the attacks on top-down planning and are settling into a new role as passive mediators of public consensus. Indeed, it is critical for communities to be involved in determining the course of their neighborhoods' and cities' future. However, the author believes this cannot be the extent of the planner's role. Especially in an age when public dollars are scarce and the trends of urban investment are not well understood, it is more important than ever to have individuals who possess the skills to envision the future and the savvy of policy entrepreneurship to spend years or decades promoting and advancing these ideas within a particular political framework.

As the planning profession struggles to define its ongoing role and relevance, the case study of Edmund N. Bacon provides an important example of a planning director who functioned as an integral part of the political implementation process—a planner-implementer and policy entrepreneur. For sure, policy entrepreneurs exist outside the planning profession. However, Bacon demonstrated the efficacy of a *planner* filling this position—building a link between envisioning the future and realizing policy goals in the present. The fact is that society does not make important decisions in charrettes or controlled public meetings. For planners to be effective, they must realize this and come to understand how to influence the true, complex process of societal decision-making in the political and policy context. This cannot be done by considering a printed plan document as the end of the planner's role or decisions written on a white board at a community meeting as the final word.

Bacon said in one talk in 1987, "The architect, the landscape architect, the urban designer, the city planner of the future will not be the passive professional. He or she will be the activist."[25] In his 1959 essay, Bacon wrote, "The future of Philadelphia will be determined, not by technological advances, but by the character of its leadership and by the strength and quality of the ideas it supports."[26] Today's planners will decide whether their profession becomes increasingly passive, allowing decisions to shape the future of our cities based on political and financial motivation, or whether they can become savvy enough to influence the decision-making process in significant ways. If the next generation of urban leaders can master the skills of the planner-implementer, then Bacon's legacy will live on in a positive way.

Abbreviations and Sources

AAUP—Architectural Archives, University of Pennsylvania
ENB—Edmund N. Bacon
CCCP—Citizens' Council on City Planning
GLH—Gregory L. Heller (author)
Mayor Reports—ENB, Confidential Reports to the Mayor, AAUP 292.II.C.1–6.
PCA—Philadelphia City Archives
PCPC—Philadelphia City Planning Commission
TUA—The Urban Archives, Temple University
WMP—Walter M. Phillips
WMP Papers—Papers of WMP, TUA Collection #527

Edmund Bacon's papers are housed at The University of Pennsylvania Architectural Archives in two separate collections (Coll. 095 and 292). Madeline L. Cohen, who researched and wrote about Bacon, has research papers housed at the Architectural Archives (Coll. 278). The author's research papers and original documents used in this book will be donated to the Architectural Archives after publication. Papers from Bacon's tenure at the Philadelphia City Planning Commission are in the Philadelphia City Archives (Group 145).

Notes

Foreword

1. Edmund N. Bacon [ENB], *Design of Cities* (New York: Viking, 1967).
2. Ibid., 13.
3. ENB, Conversation with Alexander Garvin, August 11, 2002.
4. Conv. w. AG, November, 22, 1998.
5. Conv. w. AG, July 11, 2001.

Preface

1. ENB, *Design of Cities*, rev. ed. (New York: Penguin, 1974).
2. ENB et al., *Imagination Builds a City* (King of Prussia, Pa.: Creative Concepts Holding, 2005).

Introduction

1. "The City—Under the Knife, or All for Their Own Good," *Time*, November 6, 1964, 19.
2. Ibid., 60.
3. Ibid., 69.
4. Ibid., 70.
5. A. T. Baker, letter to ENB, April 19, 1965, AAUP, 095.68.
6. ENB, "Response to *Time* Magazine Article—Mr. Bacon," AAUP, 095.67.
7. "City's Rebirth: A Billion in New Projects," reprinted in C. Allen Keith, *Problems and Progress: A Series of Articles from the Philadelphia Inquirer* (Philadelphia: Philadelphia Inquirer, 1955).
8. For example, see "Recent Work of Edmund N. Bacon," *Kenchiku Bunka* 304, AAUP, 292.II.E.78.
9. Beth Dunlop, "Post-Renaissance Philadelphia," *AIA Journal*, March 1976, 31.
10. See, for example, "The Philadelphia Cure: Clearing Slums with Penicillin, Not Surgery," *Architectural Forum* 96, 4 (April 1952): 113; William Bunch, "Truly, a Man with a Plan," *Philadelphia Daily News*, October 15, 2005.
11. Adrian I. Lee, "Bacon's Battle Against the Bulldozer," *Bulletin*, February 27, 1970.

12. Nathaniel Burt, "Race and Renaissance in Philadelphia," *Harper's*, September 1964, 66.

13. Thomas Hine, "Savoring the Cities' Vitality," *Philadelphia Inquirer*, February 26, 1984.

14. Stephan Salisbury et al., "City Visionary Edmund Bacon, 95, Dies," *Philadelphia Inquirer*, October 14, 2005.

15. Inga Saffron, "Flaws and All, Edmund N. Bacon Molded a Modern Philadelphia," *Philadelphia Inquirer*, October 16, 2005.

16. Suzanne Stephens, "A Look Back: Planner Ed Bacon," *Architectural Record*, November 22, 2005.

17. Notes from interview with Ralph Hirsch by GLH, Philadelphia, October 10, 2008, GLH Papers.

18. Taped interview with Richard Huffman by GLH, October 10, 2008, GLH Papers.

19. Videotaped interview with G. Craig Schelter, by Charles Cook, copy in GLH Papers.

20. Charles Marcus, "Looking into an Urban Crystal Ball," *Wharton Account*, Winter 1980, 8.

21. ENB, quoted in "Bacon on the State of Planning and the Role of Participation," *Colloqui* 1, 1 (Fall 1986): 16.

22. ENB, letter to Mark Hughes, October 4, 1989, AAUP, 292.II.A.3.48.

23. ENB, "The New Paradigm for Design Education," talk at University of Michigan, February 19, 1987, AAUP.

24. ENB, *Design of Cities*, rev. ed. (New York: Penguin, 1974), 13.

25. ENB, "Westward Ho!" *Philadelphia*, September 1988, 127.

26. Paul Goldberger, "Robert Moses, Master Builder, Is Dead at 92," *New York Times*, July 30, 1981.

27. David W. Dunlap, "Edward Logue, Visionary City Planner, Is Remembered," *New York Times*, April 23, 2000.

28. Ibid.

29. David A. Wallace, "Renaissancemanship," *Journal of the America Society of Planners* 26, 3 (1960): 171.

30. Jay Nathan, full interview for the making of *Mr. Philadelphia: The Story of Albert M. Greenfield*, documentary film, Albert M. Greenfield Foundation, 2011 (7:44–8:06), http://www.mrphiladelphiathefilm.com/jay-nathan/.

31. John W. Kingdon, *Agendas, Alternatives, and Public Policies*, 2nd ed. (New York: Addison-Wesley, 1995), 204–5.

32. Ibid., 116–17.

33. Ibid., 124.

34. ENB, *Design of Cities*, rev. ed., 254–62.

35. Kingdon, *Agendas, Alternatives, and Public Policies*, 31.

36. Ibid., 127–29.

37. Ibid., 129.

38. Ibid., 140–41.

39. Ibid., 1.

40. Salisbury, "City Visionary."

41. ENB, "The View from Billy Penn's Feet," undated ms., AAUP, 292.II.D.357.

42. Gwen Wells, "The Face of the City," *The Player*, May 1988, 80.

43. James Reichley, "Philadelphia Does It: The Battle for Penn Center," *Harper's*, January 31, 1957, 51.

44. Ibid.

45. ENB, unpublished ms., March 17, 1991, GLH papers.

46. Walt D'Alessio, notes from interview with GLH, March 19, 2009, GLH Papers.

47. ENB, quoted in *Colloqui*, 15.

Chapter 1. Planning for a New Deal

1. For Bacon's family history, see John B. Atkinson, *The Atkinsons of New Jersey from the Records of Friends Meetings and from Offices of Record in the State* (Earlington, Ky.: Earlington Bee Print, 1890), Historical Society of Pennsylvania, Gen At1:2; George Norwood Comly, *Comly Family in America* (Philadelphia: Lippincott, 1939), Historical Society of Pennsylvania, Fa 929.2 C734c 1939; John Comly, *John Comly's Journal*, AAUP, 292.57.

2. ENB, "Bacon—On Being a Quaker," unpublished ms., GLH Papers.

3. ENB, transcribed interview with GLH, "Childhood," January 13, 1988, GLH Papers.

4. ENB, quoted in David Clow, "Edmund Bacon: A Biographical Sketch of His Life from 1910 to 1939," unpublished ms., 2000, GLH Papers.

5. ENB, interview with Madeline Cohen, tape recorded, January 13, 1988, AAUP, 278.III.A.21.

6. ENB, "The Little Kid 3—The Outsider," unpublished ms., GLH Papers.

7. *Friends' Central School System: Seventy Eighth Year*, 1922–1923, Friends Central School.

8. Philip S. Benjamin, *The Philadelphia Quakers in the Industrial Age, 1865–1920* (Philadelphia: Temple University Press, 1976), 72.

9. For information on Rose Valley, see George E. Thomas, *William L. Price: Arts and Crafts to Modern Design* (Princeton, N.J.: Princeton Architectural Press, 2000).

10. ENB, interview with Madeline Cohen.

11. "The Art of Building," Cornell University Library, http://rmc.library.cornell.edu/aap-exhibit/aap8.html.

12. Announcement of the College of Architecture, 1930–1931, Cornell University Archives, College of Architecture.

13. "Inspiring Consensus," *Cornell University College of Architecture, Art, and Planning Newsletter,* Summer/Fall 2002, 5: 2.

14. Madeline L. Cohen, "Postwar City Planning in Philadelphia: Edmund N. Bacon and the Design of Washington Square East," Ph.D. dissertation, University of Pennsylvania, 1991, 66.

15. ENB, "A Civic Center for Philadelphia," June 23, 1932, senior thesis plan, elevations, Class A plan study, Cornell University College of Architecture, Art, and Planning Records, 1905–1997, Coll. 15-1-512, Division of Rare and Manuscript Collections, Cornell University Library.

16. Information from Bacon's post-college travels is based on letters to his parents and other relatives, Personal Collection of Elinor Bacon (hereafter Travel Letters).

17. ENB, letter to "Mother and Dad," Pera, January 15, 1933, Travel Letters.

18. ENB, untitled ms., 1945, GLH Papers.

19. ENB, letter to "Mother and Dad," Ryde, August 18, 1932, Travel Letters.

20. ENB, letter to "Mother and Dad," Athens, December 30, 1932, Travel Letters.

21. Untitled ms., 1945, GLH Papers.

22. ENB, letter to "Mother and Dad," "On Train to El Cantana," March 15, 1933, Travel Letters. For information on Adamson, see Jeffrey W. Cody, *Building in China: Henry K. Murphy's "Adaptive Architecture," 1914–1935* (Hong Kong: Chinese University Press, 2001), 91.

23. ENB, letter to "Mother and Dad," Cairo, March 10, 1933, Travel Letters.

24. Peter Hibbard, *The Bund: Shanghai Faces West* (New York: Norton, 2007), 79–83.

25. Eleanor M. Hinder, *Life and Labour in Shanghai: A Decade of Labour and Social Administration in the International Settlement* (New York: International Secretariat Institute of Pacific Relations, 1944), 82; Harriet Sergeant, *Shanghai: Collision Point of Cultures: 1918–1939* (New York: Crown, 1990).

26. Hibbard, *The Bund*, 70.

27. Ibid., 10.

28. Cody, *Building in China*, 109.

29. Cohen, "Postwar," 74.

30. ENB, letter to "Mother and Dad," "Shanghai," July 10, 1933, Travel Letters.

31. Cody, *Building in China*, 5.

32. ENB, *Design of Cities*, rev. ed. (New York: Penguin, 1974), 244.

33. ENB, letter to "Mother and Dad," "Shanghai," May 2, 1910 [*sic*, actually 1933], Travel Letters.

34. ENB, letter to "Mother and Dad," "Shanghai," May 14, 1933, Travel Letters.

35. "Plans Completed for Construction of Big Airport in Shanghai," *China Press*, September 24, 1933, in Travel Letters; ENB, letter to "Mother and Dad," "Shanghai," September 26, 1933, Travel Letters.

36. ENB, letter to "Mother and Dad," "Shanghai," June 25, May 25, 1933, Travel Letters.

37. ENB, letter to "Mother and Dad," "Shanghai," April 13, 1934, Travel Letters.

38. Cohen, "Postwar," n78.

39. "W. Pope Barney," *American Architects and Buildings* database, http://www.philadelphiabuildings.org.

40. Richard Pommer, "The Architecture of Urban Housing in the United States during the Early 1930s," *Journal of the Society of Architectural Historians* 37, 4 (December 1978): 235–64.

41. For discussion of early American suburbs, see David Gosling, *The Evolution of American Urban Design* (Chichester: Wiley, 2003). For a specific discussion of the Radburn design concept, see Alexander Garvin, *The American City: What Works, What Doesn't* (New York: McGraw Hill, 2002), 325–31.

42. Gail Radford, *Modern Housing for America: Policy Struggles in the New Deal Era* (Chicago: University of Chicago Press, 1996), 69.

43. Catherine Bauer, *Modern Housing* (Boston: Houghton Mifflin, 1934), xvii.

44. George Young, Jr., letter to ENB, September 16, 1935, Cranbrook Archives, Alumni Records, "Bacon, Edmund, 1990–19."

45. Robert J. Clark et al., *Design in America: The Cranbrook Vision, 1925–1950* (New York: Harry Abrams with Detroit Institute of Arts and Metropolitan Museum of Art, 1983); Albert Christ-Janer, *Eliel Saarinen: Finnish-American Architect and Educator* (Chicago: University of Chicago Press, 1979); Mark Treib, "Urban Fabric by the Bolt: Eliel Saarinen at Munkkiniemi-Haaga," *Architectural Association Quarterly* 13 (January–June 1982): 43–58; Marja Riitta Norri, Elina Standertskjold, and Wilfried Wang, eds., *Twentieth Century Architecture: Finland* (New York: Prestel, 200).

46. Richard P. Raseman, Cranbrook Academy of Art Annual Report, June 1936, Cranbrook Archives, "1981–05—CAA Annual Reports, Jun 1936."

47. Ibid.

48. ENB, untitled reflections, Cranbrook Archives, "1:2 correspondence. Edmund Bacon, Apr 1995–99– 2001–14."

49. ENB, interview with Mary Riordan and Cranbrook students, March 9, 1979, Cranbrook Archives, "Excerpts and Miscellany, Bacon, Edmund."

50. Eliel Saarinen, *The City* (New York: Reinhold, 1945), 2, 4.

51. ENB, "Account of the Past Three Years," undated, GLH Papers.

52. Raseman, Annual Report, June 1936.

53. Cohen, "Postwar," 115–16.

54. Robert Averill Walker, *The Planning Function in Urban Government* (Chicago: University of Chicago Press, 1941), 38.

55. ENB, letter to parents, May 30, 1936, AAUP, 292.I.A.2.

56. ENB, letter to parents, July 24, 1936, AAUP, 292.I.A.2.

57. ENB, letter to parents, September 3, 1936, AAUP, 292.I.A.2.

58. Ewald Pfeiffer, "Hundreds See Model Exhibit: Model City of Future Put on Display for Public; Project Is Praised," *Flint Journal*, March 26, 1936.

59. ENB, letter to parents, September 3, 1936, AAUP, 292.I.A.2.

60. "Carl W. Bonbright," Genessee County Biography Series, B: 378, 381, 386, 394, Flint Public Library.

61. ENB, letter to parents, March 16, 1937, AAUP, 292.I.A.3.

62. Ibid.

63. ENB, letter to parents, April 28, 1937, AAUP, 292.I.A.3.

64. Ibid.

65. Ibid.

66. Flint Institute of Research and Planning, "A Comprehensive City Plan for Flint, Michigan: Part I—Traffic Survey and Thoroughfare Plan," 1937, AAUP, 292.II.D.55.

67. ENB, letter to parents, September 25, 1936, AAUP, 292.I.A.2.

68. "Traffic Survey," 63.

69. Ibid., 23.

70. Ibid., 8.

71. Walker, *The Planning Function in Urban Government*, 24.

72. Eliel Saarinen, *The City: Its Growth, Its Decay, Its Future* (New York: Reinhold, 1945), 204.

73. Walker, *The Planning Function in Urban Government*, 25.

74. ENB, "Transportation and Land," *Shelter*, February 1939.

75. ENB, letter to parents, January 16, 1938, AAUP, 292.I.A.3.

76. ENB, letter to parents, March 31, 1938, AAUP, 292.I.A.3.

77. "Unified Traffic System Plan Offered to City Commission," *Flint Journal*, January 18, 1938, 13.

78. "Young Leaders Paid Tribute," *Detroit Times*, February 2, 1938.

79. ENB, letter to parents, May 12, 1938, AAUP, 292.I.A.3.

80. ENB, letter to parents, February 4, 1937, AAUP, 292.I.A.3.

81. ENB, letter to parents, April 21, 1938, AAUP, 292.I.A.3.

82. Radford, *Modern Housing for America*, 188–89.

83. A. C. Findlay, "The Housing Situation in Flint, Michigan," Reports of the Flint Institute of Research and Planning, February, 1938, Flint Public Library.

84. Walker, *The Planning Function in Urban Government*, 38–39.

85. Meeting record, Citizen's Housing Commission, October 13, 1937, AAUP, 278.I.16.

86. "Robert P. Gerholz," Genesee County Biography Series, G:81, 191,192, 197, 198, Flint Public Library.

87. Proceedings of Flint City Commission, October 18, 1937, Flint Public Library, 352 Fl; "History of the Housing Movement in Flint," November 14, 1948, copy in GLH Papers.

88. Flint City Commission, September 26, 1938.

89. Nathan Straus, letter to Flint Housing Council, December 9, 1938, copy in GLH papers.

90. "Business Group Opposes Housing," *Flint Journal*, February 22, 1939.

91. Flint City Commission, October 31, 1938.

92. Bacon's wife Ruth Holmes Bacon took photographs that were part of this exhibition; see AAUP, 292.VII.26.

93. ENB (?), "Housing in Flint From 1934," undated, copy in GLH Papers.

94. Ruth Bacon, letter to Elmore Jackson, March 1939, "Excerpts from Ruth Bacon's Letter to Elmore Jackson," copy in AAUP, 278.I.17.

95. "City Refuses to Grant $6,500 Asked for Housing Plan," *Flint Journal*, January 4, 1939.

96. "Recall Action Union Threat," *Flint Journal*, January 22, 1939.

97. "City Refuses to Grant $6,500."

98. "Will Discontinue Institute of Planning," *Flint Journal*, January 29, 1939.

99. Eliel Saarinen, "Confidential Report on Candidate for Fellowship," John Simon Guggenheim Memorial Foundation, Cranbrook Archives.

100. Flint City Commission, October 7, 1938.

101. "Will Discontinue Institute of Planning."

102. ENB, letter to Board of Directors of the Flint Community Association, February 2, 1939, copy in AAUP, 278.I.17.

103. G. Frank Cordner, letter to ENB, February 3, 1939, AAUP, 292.II.A.16.

104. Flint Institute of Research and Planning, "Report of City Planning Division," February 8, 1939, AAUP, 292.II.A.21.

105. "Housing Project Loss Threatened," *Flint Journal*, January 19, 1939.

106. Flint City Commission, January 25, 1939.

107. "Research Leader of USHA Coming," *Flint Journal*, February 11, 1939.

108. "Business Group Opposes Housing," *Flint Journal*, February 22, 1939.

109. ENB, letter to Catherine Bauer, March 7, 1939, AAUP, 292.

110. Edmund H. Hoben, letter to ENB, March 11, 1939, AAUP, 292.II.A.5.

111. Untitled article, *Flint Journal*, 1939, Scrapbook #3, AAUP, 292.IV.A.1.

112. "Housing Commissioners Resignations Stand Unretracted," *Flint Journal*, March 8, 1939.

113. Elmore Jackson, memorandum to Advisory Committee of Flint Work Camp, summer 1938, AAUP, 292.1.A.10.

114. ENB, quoted in Gerald McKelvey, "Philadelphia Urban Planning: Looking Back, Forward," *Philadelphia Inquirer*, May 3, 1970.

115. ENB, interview with GLH, tape recorded, September 24, 2002, GLH Papers.

116. Walker, *The Planning Function in Urban Government*, 47.

Chapter 2. Toward a Better Philadelphia

1. Coleman Woodbury, letter to ENB, September 22, 1939, AAUP, 292.II.A.48; Robert Paige, letter to ENB, September 9, 1939, AAUP, 292.II.A.48.

2. Eliel Saarinen, "Confidential Report on Candidate for Fellowship," John Simon Guggenheim Memorial Foundation, Cranbrook Archives.

3. U.S. Social Security Administration, "Security, Work, and Relief Policies: A Report by the National Resources Planning Board," 1942, http://www.ssa.gov/history/reports/NRPB/NRPBreport.html, accessed June 5, 2012.

4. ENB, "A Diagnosis and Suggested Treatment of an Urban Community's Land Problems (Flint, Michigan)," *Journal of Land and Public Utility Economics* 16, 1 (February 1940): 71–88.

5. ENB, "Tax-Delinquent Subdivisions: A Liability That Might Become a Municipal Asset," *American City* 55, 4 (April 1940): 87, 89.

6. ENB, "A Diagnosis," 79.

7. ENB, "Tax-Delinquent, 89.

8. "Bacon Heads Housing Assn.," *Bulletin*, October 15, 1940.

9. Philadelphia Housing Association, "How's Your House?" November 1941, copy in AAUP, 278.I.23.

10. David B. Brownlee, *Building the City Beautiful: The Benjamin Franklin Parkway and the Philadelphia Museum of Art* (Philadelphia: Philadelphia Museum of Art, 1989), 13.

11. John Andrew Gallery, *The Planning of Center City Philadelphia* (Philadelphia: Center for Architecture, Inc., 2007), 26.

12. "Report of the Meeting of the City Policy Committee on February 21st, 1940," WMP Papers, 15, "City Policy Committee, Meetings and Minutes, 1940–1944, 53–55, 1961, 72–73."

13. Gallery, *Planning of Center City Philadelphia*, 27.

14. "Report of the Meeting."

15. Gallery, *Planning of Center City Philadelphia*, 27; "Report of the Planning Commission," 1930, Philadelphia City Planning Commission Library.

16. Gallery, *Planning of Center City Philadelphia*, 29–30.

17. Ibid., 31.

18. "Philadelphia's Hole," *Time*, January 8, 1940, 17.

19. Margaret B. Tinkcom, "Depression and War: 1929–1956," in *Philadelphia: A 300-Year History*, ed. Russell F. Weigley (New York: Norton, 1982), 602.

20. "State and Local Organizations Which Have Taken Favorable Action in Regard to the New City Charter," April 17, 1939, WMP Papers, 11, "City Planning: Charter Committee Organization & Articles, 1939."

21. F. L. Allen, letter to ENB, February 9, 1940, AAUP, 292.II.A.57.

22. "A Plan for a 'City Policy Association," draft, WMP Papers, 15, "City Policy Committee: Reports, 1940."

23. WMP, letter to ENB, January 13, 1940, AAUP, 292.II.A.53.

24. "City Policy Committee Membership List," May 15, 1940, WMP Papers, 15, "WMP City Policy Committee: Membership Lists, 1940–41."

25. Paul M. Lunkenheimer, City Policy Committee, October 16, 1940, WMP Papers, 15, "City Policy Committee, Meetings and Minutes, 1940–1944, 53–55, 1961, 72–73."

26. "Proper City Planning Would Save Philadelphia Money, Says Expert," *Bulletin*, May 17, 1941, City Planning Supplement, 1.

27. WMP, letter to ENB, February 13, 1940, coll. 292.

28. WMP, letter to Frederick C. Fiechter, Jr., Esq, March 11, 1940, WMP Papers, 15, "City Policy Committee, letter 1940–1942."

29. William C. Beyer, letter to WMP, April 10, 1941, WMP Papers, 6, "Bureau of Municipal Research, letter 1938–1941."

30. "What Is the Bureau of Municipal Research?" undated brochure, 1943 or 1944, WMP Papers, 6, "Bureau of Municipal Research: Pamphlets, 1932, 1941–54."

31. ENB, interview with GLH, tape recorded, September 24, 2002, GLH Papers; "The National Conference on Planning," Conference Program, May 12–14, 1941, WMP Papers, 6, "Bureau of Municipal Research: Pamphlets 1932: 1941–1954."

32. "Proper City Planning Would Save Philadelphia Money, Says Expert," *Bulletin*, City Planning Supplement, May 17, 1941.

33. "Sketch of Mayor Lamberton's Life Traces Rise as Political Independent," *Philadelphia Inquirer*, August 23, 1941; "State and Local Organizations Which Have Taken Favorable Action in Regard to the New City Charter," April 17, 1939, WMP Papers, 11, "City Planning: Charter Committee Organization & Articles, 1939"; "Report: Joint Committee on City Planning for 1941 National Conference," Presented by the City Policy Committee, the Lawyers' Council on Civic Affairs, Junior Board of Commerce of Philadelphia, Reprinted by the City Parks Association of Philadelphia," WMP Papers, 12, "City Planning: CPC—documents 1941–42."

34. Hugh R. Pomeroy, "Philadelphia's Planning Problems," speech at National Conference on Planning, 1941, copy in AAUP, 278.I.26.

35. Roger Scattergood, "The City Policy Committee: A Philadelphia Story of a Civic Organization Which 'Made Good'," March 20, 1956, copy in AAUP, 278.I.24, 5.

36. Ibid., 10–11.

37. Joint Committee on City Planning, "Report on the Suggested Organization of a Philadelphia City Planning Commission Prepared for Hon. Robert E. Lamberton, Mayor of Philadelphia," August 15, 1941, AAUP, 292.II.B.2.47.

38. Robert A. Walker, *The Planning Function in Urban Government* (Chicago: University of Chicago Press, 1950), 166–84.

39. "Mayor Lamberton of Philadelphia," *New York Times*, August 23, 1941.

40. ENB, interview with GLH, tape recorded, September 24, 2002, GLH Papers.

41. "Fund for Planning Commission Asked," *Bulletin*, November 20, 1941.

42. "Milner, Winnet Named As Judges," *Evening Public Ledger*, February 9, 1940.

43. ENB, "How City Planning Came to Philadelphia," *American City*, 1943, TUA, Pamphlet collection, part 18, 62; ENB, transcript of interview with WMP, November 13, 1974, and January 9, 1975, WMP Oral History Project, TUA, transcripts box 1, "Bacon, Edmund."

44. "History of the Joint Committee on City Planning," April 25, 1942, copy in GLH Papers.

45. ENB, transcript of interview with WMP.

46. "Organizations Endorsing Ordinance to Create a City Planning Commission for Philadelphia," September 15, 1942, WMP Papers, 13, "City Planning: Joint Committee on City Planning, 1941–42."

47. Madeline L. Cohen, "Postwar City Planning in Philadelphia: Edmund N. Bacon and the Design of Washington Square East," Ph.D. dissertation, University of Pennsylvania, 1991, 270.

48. "Action Committee on City Planning. Progress Report #2," November 5, 1942, WMP Papers, 13, "City Planning: Joint Committee on City Planning, 1941–42."

49. ENB, transcript of interview with WMP.

50. *Journal of City Council*, December 10, 1942, PCA.

51. Action Committee on City Planning, "Progress Report 4," undated, WMP Papers, 13, "City Planning: Joint Committee on City Planning, 1941–42."

52. Action Committee on City Planning, "Memorandum: Suggested Organization of Citizens' Council on City Planning," March 12, 1943, WMP Papers, 13, "City Planning: Joint Committee on City Planning, 1941–42."

53. CCCP Newsletter, September 1943, WMP Papers, Box 11, Folder "City Planning: CCCP—Newsletter, 1943, 1945–49, 1960."

54. CCCP Newsletter, July 1943, WMP Papers, Box 11, Folder "City Planning: CCCP—Newsletter, 1943, 1945–49, 1960."

55. ENB, "How City Planning Came to Philadelphia," 62.

56. Raymond Leonard, letter to Judge L. Stauffer Oliver, March 30, 1948, PCPC Papers, A-2906, "United Nations—Site Selection November 1946-May 1952."

57. "Dwight D. Eisenhower National System of Interstate and Defense Highways," U.S. Department of Transportation, Federal Highway Administration, http://www.fhwa.dot.gov/programadmin/interstate.cfm, accessed June 5, 2012.

58. PCPC, "1946 Annual Report," 1947, PCPC Papers, A-1620.

59. PCPC, "1947 Annual Report," 1948, PCPC Papers, A-1620.

60. ENB, letter to Mr. and Mrs. Ellis W. Bacon, December 19, 1943, AAUP, 292.I.A.4.

61. For more on Bacon's service in the navy, see his collection of letters in the AAUP, 292.I.A.

62. Ruth H. Bacon, letter to Michael Bacon, March 11, 1987, copy in GLH Papers.

63. Hilda, Elinor, Kevin, and Michael Bacon, phone interview with GLH, tape recorded, February 23, 2008, GLH Papers.

64. ENB, letter to Ruth H. Bacon, March 7, 1945, AAUP, 292.I.A.15; ENB, letter to Ruth H. Bacon, July 10, 1945, AAUP, 292.I.A.16.

65. William H. Whyte, "The Philadelphia Story," unpublished ms., November 4, 1947, AAUP, 292.II.D.218.

66. PCPC, "Notice of Appointment," October 7, 1946, copy in GLH Papers.

67. "The Better Philadelphia Exhibition," exhibition brochure, September 1947, AAUP, 292.III.C.1.2.

68. Whyte, "The Philadelphia Story."

69. Robert B. Mitchell, letter to Leonard T. Beale, November 29, 1947, PCPC Papers, 145.2, A-2914, "Lombard 1947–1955."

70. Robert B. Mitchell, letter to Planning Committee of the Old Christ Church Businessmen's Association, December 12, 1947, PCPC Papers, 145.2, A-2914, "Old City 1946–1953."

71. ENB, Better Philadelphia Exhibition Notebook, AAUP, 292; Anne Griswold Tyng, *Louis Kahn to Anne Tyng: The Rome Letters 1953–1954*, ed. A. G. Tyng (New York: Rizzoli, 1997), 33.

72. ENB, notes from meeting, May 5–8, 1946, suggestions received at ASPO Conf, Better Philadelphia Exhibition Notebook, AAUP, 292, 16.

73. PCPC, "1946 Annual Report," 1947, PCPC Papers, A-1620.

74. "Philadelphia Plans Again," *Architectural Forum*, December 1947, 66–87.

75. ENB, "Oskar Stonorov and the City," undated, AAUP, 292.II.B.2.264.

76. ENB, notes from meeting, March 14, 1946, Engineers Club, Better Philadelphia Exhibition Notebook, AAUP, 292, 35.

77. ENB, notes from meeting, March 6, 1946, Racquet Club, Better Philadelphia Exhibition Notebook, AAUP, 292, 12.

78. "Philadelphia Plans Again."

79. The descriptions of the Better Philadelphia Exhibition are based largely on the set of photographs available in AAUP, 292.V.B.2.6.

80. ENB, "Are Exhibitions Useful? A Postscript to the Philadelphia Show," *Journal of the American Institute of Planners* (Spring 1948).

81. ENB, "Oskar Stonorov and the City."

82. Whyte, "The Philadelphia Story."

83. PCPC, "1947 Annual Report," 1948, PCPC Papers, A-1620.

84. Kathy Brennan, "'City of Future' a Model of (M)old," *Daily News*, January 8, 1993.

85. ENB, "Are Exhibitions Useful?" 23–28.

86. Whyte, "The Philadelphia Story."

87. "In Memoriam: Raymond Forbes Leonard," *Journal of the American Institute of Planners* (Summer 1948).

88. Cohen, "Postwar," 317–18.

89. PCPC, media release, December 31, 1948, AAUP, 292. II.B.22.

90. CCCP Newsletter, November 1949, PCPC Papers, A-2917.

91. ENB, Mayor Reports, May 29, 1953.

92. Joseph S. Clark, Jr., and Dennis J. Clark, "Rally and Relapse: 1946–1968," in Weigley, ed., *Philadelphia: A 300-Year History*, 652.

93. WMP, "City Policy Committee—Its Major Theme," September 19, 1943, copy in GLH Papers.

94. WMP, letter to Arthur C. Kaufmann, December 10, 1948, AAUP, 278.I.31; WMP, letter to Richardson Dilworth, December 13, 1948, AAUP, 278.I.31.

95. Jeanne R. Lowe, *Cities in a Race with Time* (New York: Vintage, 1968), 325; Joseph D. Crumlish, *A City Finds Itself: The Philadelphia Home Rule Charter Movement* (Detroit: Wayne State University Press, 1959), 39.

6. Clark, Jr., and Clark, "Rally and Relapse," 654.

97. Philadelphia Home Rule Charter, April 17, 1951, annotated edition, http://www.seventy.org/Files/Philadelphia_Home_Rule_Charter.pdf.

98. PCPC, "Comments on Specific Provisions of Draft III, Proposed Philadelphia Home Rule Charter prepared by Philadelphia City Planning Commission for Consideration by Philadelphia Charter Commission," November 15, 1950, PCPC Papers, A-2917, "City Charter 1950."

99. James Reichley, ed., *The Art of Government: Reform and Organization Politics in Philadelphia* (New York: Fund for the Republic, 1959), 17.

100. Joseph S. Clark, quoted in David Clow, "A Short Distance in the Right Direction: Penn Center and City Planning During the Clark Years in Philadelphia, 1952–1956," paper presented to Seventh National Conference on American Planning History, October 23–26, 1997, Seattle, AAUP, 292.II.E.153, 4.

101. Reichley, *Art of Government*, 36.

Chapter 3. Planning for People

1. Alexander Garvin, *The American City: What Works, What Doesn't* (New York: McGraw-Hill, 2002), 19.

2. Ibid., 396–99.

3. Jon C. Teaford, "Urban Renewal and Its Aftermath," *Housing Policy Debate* 11, 2 (2000): 443–63.

4. "The Philadelphia Cure: Clearing Slums with Penicillin, Not Surgery," *Architectural Forum* 96, 4 (April 1952): 112–19.

5. David A. Wallace, "Renaissancemanship," *Journal of the America Society of Planners* 26, 3 (1960): 160–63.

6. Garvin, *The American City*, 396–99.

7. John F. Bauman, *Public Housing, Race, and Renewal: Urban Planning in Philadelphia, 1920–1974* (Philadelphia: Temple University Press, 1987), 84.

8. Nathaniel Burt, "Race and Renaissance in Philadelphia," *Harper's*, September 1964, 65.

9. Guian McKee, "Edmund Bacon and the Complexity of the City," in *Imagining Philadelphia: Edmund Bacon and the Future of the City*, ed. Scott Gabriel Knowles (Philadelphia: University of Pennsylvania Press, 2009), 57.

10. Garvin, *The American City*, 19.

11. Teaford, "Urban Renewal and Its Aftermath," 446.

12. Ibid., 447.

13. Pittsburgh's Lower Hill project displaced 8,000 (Teaford, 449). Boston's West End project displaced 2,248 families; Thomas H. O'Connor, *Building a New Boston: Politics and Urban Renewal, 1950–1970* (Boston: Northeastern University Press, 1993), 126. Chicago's Hyde Park-Kenwood project displaced 4,987 families; Julia Abramson, *A Neighborhood Finds Itself* (New York: Harper, 1959), 210.

14. David M. Walker, letter to Frederic D. Garman, June 6, 1949, copy in GLH Papers.

15. Graham Finney, interview with GLH, Philadelphia, April 30, 2008, GLH Papers; David A. Wallace, "90 Words for Ed Bacon," AAUP, 292.IV.A.6.

16. Wallace, "Renaissancemanship," 171.

17. Bauman, *Public Housing*, 178.

18. McKee, "Complexity of the City," 55.

19. ENB, interview with GLH, tape recorded, Philadelphia, October 16, 2002, GLH Papers; ENB, interview with GLH, tape recorded, Philadelphia, September 24, 2002, GLH Papers.

20. ENB, "Urban Designs of Today: Philadelphia," *Urban Design*, condensed report of an invitation conference sponsored by Faculty and Alumni Association of Graduate School of Design, Harvard University, April 9–10, 1956, AAUP, 292.II.D.342.

21. ENB, reprinted from "Urban Redevelopment I: Urban Redevelopment—An Opportunity for City Rebuilding," *Planning 1949: Proceedings of the Annual National Planning Conference held in Cleveland, Ohio, 10–12 October 1949* (Chicago: ASPO, 1950).

22. Ibid., 18.

23. Ibid., 24.

24. Ibid., 20.

25. Ibid., 23.

26. PCPC, 1950 Annual Report, February 2, 1951, PCPC Papers, A-1620.

27. ENB, "Urban Redevelopment," 20.

28. Ibid., 21.

29. Ibid., 22.

30. Philadelphia Housing Association, "A Citizen's Guide to Housing and Urban Renewal in Philadelphia," 2nd ed., June 1960, 59.

31. Ibid, 56.

32. Ibid, 58–59.

33. PCPC, 1947 Annual Report, 1948, PCPC Papers, A-1620.

34. Housing and Home Finance Agency, media release, June 22, 1951, PCPC Papers, A-2914, "Redevelopment—Poplar 1950–1951"; PCPC, *East Poplar Redevelopment Area Plan*, 31 July 1948, PCPC Papers, A-1607, "City Planning Commission Reports, 1948–1949, Redevelopment."

35. W. A. Clarke, letter to Earle N. Barber, July 7, 1948, PCPC Papers, A-2914, "Redevelopment—Poplar 1945–1949."

36. "Specific Proposal for Cooperation of Friends Neighborhood Guild with Friends Service, Inc. in Executing the Above Plan," copy in GLH Papers.

37. ENB, letter to Raymond F. Leonard, January 23, 1948, PCPC Papers, A-2914, "Redevelopment—Poplar 1945–1949."

38. PCPC, media release, June 13, 1949, PCA, PCPC Papers, A-2914, "Redevelopment—Poplar 1945–1949."

39. Walter Blucher, letter to ENB, July 19, 1949, PCPC Papers, A-2914, "Redevelopment—Poplar 1945–1949."

40. ENB, letter to Raymond F. Leonard, January 23, 1948.

41. PCPC, East Poplar Redevelopment Area Plan, July 31, 1948, PCPC Papers, A-1607, "City Planning Commission Reports, 1948–1949, Redevelopment."

42. HHFA, media release, June 22, 1951.

43. "The Philadelphia Cure," 116.

44. PCPC, East Poplar Redevelopment Area Plan.

45. PCPC, 1952 Annual Report, March 1, 1953, PCPC Papers, A-1620.

46. Bauman, *Public Housing*, 110.

47. Anne Whiston Spirn, "Restoring Mill Creek: Landscape Literacy, Environmental Justice and City Planning and Design," *Landscape Research* 30, 3 (July 2005):
396.

48. Ibid., 399.

49. PCPC, Mill Creek Redevelopment Area Plan, September 1, 1954, PCPC
Papers, A-1611, "City Planning Commission Reports, 1954–1957."

50. Aaron Levine, memo, December 7, 1951, PCPC Papers, A-2914, "University
1951."

51. "The Philadelphia Cure," 113.

52. PCPC, Mill Creek Redevelopment Area Plan.

53. The term "greenway" seems to have first been used in PCPC, 1953 Annual
Report, March 1, 1954, PCPC Papers, A-1620.

54. "City May Raze 40 Houses in Collapse Area," *Philadelphia Inquirer*, July 19,
1961; "City Acts to Condemn 104 Homes Periled by Sewer," *Philadelphia Inquirer*,
July 21, 1961.

55. PCPC, 1953 Annual Report, March 1, 1954, PCPC Papers, A-1620.

56. PCPC, Eastwick Redevelopment Area Plan, November 5, 1954, PCPC Papers,
A-1611.

57. Paul H. Depman, memo to C. A. Howland, subject: "Eastwick Area; Drainage & Soil Condition, Racial Distribution, and Drainage Canals," April 11, 1950, PCPC
Papers, A-2913, "Redevelopment—Eastwick—General Letter 1948–September 1952."

58. ENB, letter to Mayor Clark, May 1, 1953, PCPC Papers, A-2913 "Eastwick
1952–1953."

59. Eastwick Planners, memo "Re meetings held 16 June, 1953," June 17, 1953,
PCPC Papers, A-2913, "Eastwick 1952–1953."

60. E. L. Tennyson, letter to Francis Lammer, January 14, 1957, PCPC Papers,
A-2913, "Eastwick 1956–1958."

61. ENB, Mayor Reports, July 2, 1954.

62. ENB, Mayor Reports, November 5, 1954.

63. Philadelphia Redevelopment Authority, "Answers to Philadelphia Redevelopment Authority Questions Regarding Reynolds-Berger Proposal for Eastwick," January
1, 1960, PCPC Papers, A-2924, "Eastwick—1960."

64. Marjorie E. Weissman, "Metal for Modernization: Facelifting Cities with Aluminum," reprinted from *Modern Metals*, March 1962.

65. ENB, "Philadelphia Yesterday, Philadelphia Today," *Today: The Philadelphia
Inquirer Magazine*, September 10, 1961; ENB, "Urban Redevelopment I: Urban Redevelopment—An Opportunity for City Rebuilding," *Planning 1949*.

66. ENB, letter to Albert M. Cole, September 14, 1961, PCPC Papers, A-2907,
"Mr. Bacon's Folder June-December 1961."

67. "The Philadelphia Cure," 113.

68. Burt, "Race and Renaissance in Philadelphia," 69.

69. Richard M. Flanagan, "The Housing Act of 1954: The Sea Change in National Urban Policy," *Urban Affairs Review* 33, 2 (November 1997): 271.

70. Burt, "Race and Renaissance in Philadelphia," 70.

71. David M. Walker, letter to ENB, August 5, 1949, subject: "Eastwick," PCPC Papers, A-2913, "Redevelopment—Eastwick Letter, 1948–September 1952."

72. Jeanne R. Lowe, *Cities in a Race with Time* (New York: Vintage, 1968), 355.

73. ENB, "Proceedings of the 1949 Public Works Congress," APWA, Chicago, 1949, UPAA, 095.75.

74. PCPC, media release, April 29, 1949, PCPC Papers, A-2906, "Schuylkill Expressway-Roosevelt Boulevard Extension 1950–1952."

75. Ibid.

76. PCPC, media release, January 24, 1950, PCA, PCPC Papers, A-2906.

77. Leonard Blumberg, "Urban Rehabilitation and Problems of Human Relations," *Phylon Quarterly* 19, 1 (1st quarter 1958): 100.

78. For example, ENB, letter to Aaron Levine, February 2, 1955, PCPC Papers, A-2913, "Eastwick 1955."

79. Advertisement, *Pittsburgh Courier*, September 28, 1958, PCPC Papers, A-2924, "Eastwick 1958–1959."

80. George Schermer, letter to Aaron Levine, May 29, 1958, PCPC Papers, A-2924, "Eastwick 1958–1959."

81. Philadelphia Housing Association, "A Citizen's Guide to Housing and Urban Renewal in Philadelphia," 59.

82. Burt, "Race and Renaissance in Philadelphia," 69.

83. ENB, Mayor Reports, March 31, 1960.

84. Burt, "Race and Renaissance in Philadelphia," 69.

85. Ibid., 66.

86. Ibid.

87. Ibid.

88. Arthur T. Row, Jr., "Summary of Eastwick Housing Market Analysis Reports," December 3, 1957, PCPC Papers, A-2913, "Eastwick 1956–1958."

89. Arnold M. Rose, Five Publications of the Commission on Race and Housing, *Commentary*, July 1961, https://www.commentarymagazine.com/article/five-publications-of-the-commission-on-race-and-housing/.

90. Chester Rapkin and William G. Grigsby, *The Demand for Housing in Racially Mixed Areas: A Study of the Nature of Neighborhood Change*, Publications of the Commission on Race and Housing (Berkeley: University of California Press, 1960), x.

91. Row, "Summary of Eastwick Housing Market Analysis Reports."

92. Burt, "Race and Renaissance in Philadelphia," 70.

93. *Time*, "Cities, Philadelphia's New Problem," February 24, 1958.

94. Philadelphia Neighborhood Recovery Tour, "Tour Stop #4: Yorktown," http://www.whitecarp.com/pnrt/html/04_home.htm, accessed June 5, 2012.

95. ENB, Mayor Reports, August 15, 1963.

96. ENB, Mayor Reports, September 12, 1963.

97. "Victory at Yorktown 40 Years Ago an Inner-city Community Was Born, and Today It's a Model for Urban Renewal," *Philadelphia Inquirer*, July 13, 1996, http://articles.philly.com/1996-07-13/news/25623075_1_empowerment-zones-neighborhoods-city-housing-officials.

98. Burt, "Race and Renaissance in Philadelphia," 69.

99. Ibid., 70.

100. Ibid.

101. PCPC, West Poplar Redevelopment Area Plan, July 1953, AAUP, 292. IV.B.106.

102. Burt, "Race and Renaissance in Philadelphia," 68.

103. PCPC, "1950 Annual Report," February 2, 1951, PCPC Papers, A-1620.

104. For example, PCPC, "1951 Annual Report," March 1, 1952, PCPC Papers, A-1620; also ENB, Mayor Reports, July 15, 1955.

105. Bacon discussed a pilot of this scattered-site public housing program in 1963: ENB, Mayor Reports, June 6, 1963.

106. Flanagan, "The Housing Act of 1954," 266, 274.

107. Ibid., 265.

108. Ibid.

109. Teaford, "Urban Renewal and Its Aftermath," 445.

110. Jacob Kobrick, "'Let the People Have a Victory': The Politics of Transportation in Philadelphia, 1946–1984," Ph.D. dissertation, University of Maryland, 2010, 32.

111. Flanagan, "The Housing Act of 1954," 279.

112. Ibid., 273.

113. Ibid., 275.

114. Wallace, "Renaissancemanship," 161.

115. McKee, "Complexity of the City," 62–63.

116. Ibid., 63.

117. For Dilworth's public housing program, see Bauman, *Public Housing*, 160–64.

118. PCPC, Preliminary Physical Development Plan for the Far Northeast, January 1955, PCPC Papers, Series 145.5.

119. ENB, interview with GLH, tape recorded, Philadelphia, September 9, 2002, GLH Papers.

120. Ibid.

121. S. B. Barnes, memo to ENB, subject: "Meeting with A. Moser in his office, City Plans Division, BESZ, re North Rhawnhurst Site Plan, Tuesday, September 21, 1948," September 22, 1948, PCPC Papers, A-2906, "Subdivisions 1946–1953"; Frederick T. Thorpe, Jr., letter to ENB, April 9, 1949, PCPC Papers, A-2906.

122. ENB, interview with GLH, tape recorded, Philadelphia, September 9, 2002, GLH Papers.

123. "Ideal Residence Area Is Planned for Northeast," *Bulletin*, May 5, 1949.

124. Ibid.

125. PCPC, 1951 Annual Report, March 1, 1952, PCPC Papers, A-1620.

126. ENB, Mayor Reports, August 7, 1953.

127. ENB, letter to M. P. Potamkin, June 2, 1953, PCPC Papers, A-2906, "Subdivisions."

128. PCPC Technical Advisory Committee on Zoning, minutes of meeting, August 11, 1952, PCPC Papers, A-2933, "Zoning—Revision of Text—C-1 Residential 1952–1955."

129. "Planners Seek $190,000 of City for Zoning Job," October 8, 1952, *Bulletin*.

130. ENB, interview with GLH, tape recorded, Philadelphia, January 9, 2003, GLH Papers.

131. John. S. Shultz, correspondence to Mayor Joseph S. Clark, October 10, 1952, PCPC Papers, A-2933, "Zoning—Revision of Text—C-1 Residential 1952–1955."

132. ENB, Mayor Reports, April 22, 1953.

133. ENB, Mayor Reports, July 24, 1953.

134. ENB, Mayor Reports, August 7, 1953.

135. ENB, Mayor Reports, December 17, 1953.

136. Philadelphia City Council, Bill No. 570–1952, March 4, 1954, PCPC Papers, A-2933, "Zoning—Revision of Text—C-1 Residential 1952–1955."

137. Philadelphia City Council, Philadelphia Subdivision Ordinance, June 4, 1954, *Journal of Council*, PCPC Papers, reference shelf.

138. Ibid.

139. ENB, Mayor Reports, May 6, 1954.

140. ENB, Mayor Reports, May 14, 1954.

141. Philadelphia City Council, Philadelphia Subdivision Ordinance.

142. PCPC, media release, "Explanation of Proposed Physical Development Plan—Far Northeast, For Release Following Planning Commission Action, May 5, 1954," May 3, 1954, PCPC Papers, A-2933, "Zoning—Revision of Text—C-1 Residential 1952–1955."

143. PCPC, "1950 Annual Report," February 2, 1951, PCPC Papers, A-1620.

144. PCPC, media release, "Explanation of Proposed Physical Development Plan."

145. ENB, notes from meeting, April 24, 1946, Better Philadelphia Exhibition Notebook, AAUP, 292, 73.

146. John Bodine, letter to WMP, September 24, 1952, PCPC Papers, A-2933, "Zoning—Revision of Text—C-1 Residential 1952–1955."

147. PCPC, Preliminary Physical Development Plan for the Far Northeast.

148. ENB, Mayor Reports, January 28, 1955.

149. "Planners Offer Development Project for Far Northeast," *Bulletin*, March 2, 1955.

150. Discussion with Irving Wasserman, ENB, and GLH, tape recorded and transcribed, Philadelphia, October 10, 2002, GLH Papers.

151. Discussion with ENB, Berton Korman, and GLH, tape recorded, Philadelphia, November 18, 2002, GLH Papers.

152. PCPC, Report on Commercial Redevelopment in the Far Northeast, March 1959, PCPC Office Library.

153. Joseph S. Clark, Jr., and Dennis J. Clark, "Rally and Relapse: 1946–1968," in *Philadelphia: A 300-Year History*, ed. Russell F. Weigley (New York: Norton, 1982), 699.

154. Discussion with Irving Wasserman, ENB, and GLH.

155. Discussion with ENB, Korman, and GLH.

156. Elliot M. Block, letter to ENB, September 8, 1965, PCPC Papers, A-2918, "Mr. Bacon's Letter July–October 1965."

157. William H. Whyte, Jr., "A Plan to Save Vanishing U.S. Countryside," *Life*, August 17, 1959, 89.

158. Urban Land Institute, *The Community Builders Handbook*, ed. J. Ross McKeever, Anniversary ed. (Washington, D.C.: ULI, 1968).

159. PCPC, 1962 Annual Report, January 19, 1963, PCPC Papers, A-1620.

160. William H. Whyte, *The Last Landscape*, rev. ed. (Philadelphia: University of Pennsylvania Press, 2002), 223.

161. ENB, quoted in McKee, "Complexity of the City," 65–66.

162. Walt D'Alessio, interview with GLH, Philadelphia, March 19, 2009, notes in GLH Papers.

163. ENB, "Urban Redevelopment," 24.

Chapter 4. The Architect Planner

1. For "design idea," see ENB, *Design of Cities*, rev. ed. (New York: Penguin, 1974), 13. He used the term "organizing concept" and sometimes "controlling concept" later in life. For example, ENB, interview with GLH, tape recorded, August 15, 2003, Philadelphia, GLH Papers.

2. ENB, interview with GLH, tape recorded, Philadelphia, August 15, 2003, GLH papers.

3. Cyril B. Roseman, "Public-Private Co-Operation and Negotiation in Downtown Redevelopment: A Study of Decision Process in Philadelphia," Ph.D. dissertation, Princeton University, 1963, 158.

4. PCPC, 1946 Annual Report, PCPC Papers, A-1620.

5. W. Pope Barney, "The Architecture of Business Streets," *T-Square Club Journal* 1, 7 (June 1931): 14–17.

6. Illustration in *The Louis I. Kahn Archive: Personal Drawings*, vol. 1 (New York: Garland, 1987), 18.

7. Associated City Planners, "Report on the Redevelopment of 'The Triangle'," January 19, 1948, PCPC Papers; PCPC, Certification of the Triangle Area for Redevelopment, January 8, 1948, PCPC Papers.

8. The model, without the surface layer, is in the possession of Myles Pettengill of Philadelphia; for a discussion of the Loewy plan and an image of the surface layer, see "Penn Center: Let's Face the Facts," *Delaware Valley Announcer* 32, 6 (June 1959): 18–22.

9. "Penn Center: Let's Face the Facts," 18–22.

10. Minutes of "A.I.A. Triangle Committee Meeting, January 5th, 1951," January 12, 1951, AAUP, 030.II.A.60.20.

11. Peter Shedd Reed, "Toward Form: Louis I. Kahn's Urban Designs for Philadelphia, 1939–1962," Ph.D. dissertation, University of Pennsylvania, 1989, 82.

12. Henry S. Churchill, "City Redevelopment," *Architectural Forum* 93 (December 1950); also discussed in Reed, "Toward Form," 85–86.

13. Robert Chantigan, letter to Louis I. Kahn, August 14, 1950, "AIA Triangle Committee," AAUP, Louis I. Kahn Collection, Box 60.

14. Letter from Fritz Gutheim to ENB, October 24, 1939, AAUP 292.II.A.46; David B. Brownlee and David G. De Long, *Louis I. Kahn: In the Realm of Architecture*, abr. ed. (New York: Universe, 1997), 25.

15. Reed, "Toward Form," 4.

16. ENB, interview with GLH, tape recorded, September 19, 2002, Philadelphia, GLH Papers.

17. ENB, untitled ms., undated, AAUP, 292.II.D.261.

18. ENB, interview with GLH, tape recorded, September 6, 2002, Philadelphia, GLH Papers.

19. James Reichley, "Philadelphia Does It: The Battle for Penn Center," *Harper's*, January 31, 1957, 51.

20. Louis I. Kahn, letter to Alfred Bendiner, November 28, 1950, AAUP, Louis I. Kahn Collection, Box 60, "PSA AIA—Director 1950, 48, 49."

21. For example, ENB, "Urban Designs of Today: Philadelphia," *Progressive Architecture* 37, 8 (August 1956): 108–9.

22. "This Plan Puts City Hall in Fairmount Park," *Bulletin*, City Planning Supplement, May 17, 1941.

23. Discussion with Vincent G. Kling, ENB, and GLH, tape recorded, November 2, 2002, Chester Heights (Pa.), GLH Papers.

24. Minutes of "A.I.A. Triangle Committee Meeting, January 5th, 1951."

25. ENB, "Architectural Lessons of the Forbidden City," unpublished ms., 2002 (?), GLH Papers.

26. Discussion with Vincent G. Kling, ENB, and GLH.

27. Philadelphia Chapter of the AIA, resolution, October 24, 1951, PCPC Papers, A-2913, "Penn Center 1951–1952."

28. Roseman, "Public-Private Co-Operation and Negotiation," 146–47.

29. ENB, memo to files, January 3, 1952, PCPC Papers, A-2913, "Penn Center 1951–1952."

30. James Symes, "Statement on Penn Center Plan," Address made at the luncheon of the CCCP, February 21, 1952, PCPC Papers, A-2913, "Penn Center, 1951–1952."

31. Ibid.

32. ENB, "Statement on Penn Center Plan," Address at luncheon of the CCCP, February 21, 1952, PCPC Papers, A-2913, "Penn Center, 1951–1952."

33. Ibid.

34. George W. Elliot, letter to ENB, February 8, 1952, PCPC Papers, A-2913, "Penn Center 1951–1952."

35. Louis I. Kahn, letter to ENB, July 3, 1952, PCPC Papers, A-2913, "Penn Center July-December 1952."

36. Joseph S. Clark, Jr., and Dennis J. Clark, "Rally and Relapse: 1946–1968," in *Philadelphia: A 300-Year History*, ed. Russell F. Weigley (New York: Norton, 1982), 658.

37. Roseman, "Public-Private Co-Operation and Negotiation,"146.

38. "Bob Dowling Climbs Philadelphia's Chinese Wall," *Architectural Forum* 98, 4 (April 1953): 150.

39. Ralph W. Olmstead, letter to ENB, April 9, 1952, PCPC Papers, A-2913, "Penn Center 1951–1952."

40. "Philadelphia's Hour of Decision," *Architectural Forum* 96, 6 (June 1952): 124.

41. Ibid.

42. "Bob Dowling Climbs," 149.

43. "Philadelphia's Hour of Decision," 124.

44. Ibid.

45. ENB, letter to Mayor Joseph S. Clark, April 3, 1952, PCPC Papers, A-2913, "Penn Center 1951–1952."

46. For example, Sidney E. Martin, letter to Edward Hopkinson, Jr., May 9, 1952, PCPC Papers, A-2913, "Penn Center 1951–1952"; Frederick D. Dagit, letter to ENB, April 27, 1952, PCPC Papers, A-2913, "Penn Center 1951–1952."

47. David B. Brownlee, *Building the City Beautiful: The Benjamin Franklin Parkway and the Philadelphia Museum of Art* (Philadelphia: Philadelphia Museum of Art, 1989), 86.

48. Clarke, Rapuano, Holleran, "Pennsylvania Boulevard," February 11, 1948, PCPC Papers, A-1607.

49. PCPC, media release, June 15, 1952, PCPC Papers, A-2913, "Penn Center 1951–1952."

50. See statements in PCPC Papers, A-2913, "Penn Center 1951–1952."

51. PCPC, Plan for Penn Center—Redevelopment Area Plan, August 1952, PCPC Papers, A-1610, "City Planning Commission Reports 1951–1954."

52. Edward Hopkinson, Jr., letter to Mayor Joseph S. Clark, October 29, 1952, PCPC Papers, A-2913, "Penn Center July–December 1952."

53. PCPC, "Plan for Penn Center."

54. Ibid.

55. Theodore D. Bower, memo to files, February 4, 1953, PCPC Papers, A-2913, "Penn Center 1953 memo to files."

56. "Bob Dowling Climbs," 150.

57. Ibid., 149.

58. ENB, interview with GLH, Philadelphia, tape recorded October 16, 2002, GLH Papers.

59. ENB, Mayor Reports, April 14, 1953.

60. Reed, "Toward Form," 163–64.

61. Reichley, "Philadelphia Does It," 49–56.

62. "Chronological Outline of Major Events in Connection with Penn Center," December 1, 1953, PCPC Papers, A-2913, "Redevelopment—Penn Center 1953."

63. John W. Bodine, letter to ENB, May 28, 1953, PCPC Papers, A-2913, "Penn Center 1953."

64. Roseman, "Public-Private Co-Operation and Negotiation," 150.

65. "Bob Dowling Climbs," 149.

66. "Three to Advise on Penn Center," *Bulletin*, June 5, 1953.

67. Memo, August 8, 1953, PCPC Papers, A-2913, "Penn Center 1953."

68. "Mayor Appoints Advisory Group on Penn Center," *Bulletin*, August 9, 1953.

69. Roseman, "Public-Private Co-Operation and Negotiation," 153.

70. "Citizen Advisors Criticize Slab Design for Penn Center," *Architectural Forum* 99, 4 (October 1953): 37.

71. Roseman, "Public-Private Co-Operation and Negotiation," 153.

72. Douglas Haskell, "Architecture: Stepchild or Fashioner of Cities?" *Architectural Forum* 99, 6 (December 1953): 117.

73. George Howe, Opening address, 1953 Regional Conference—Middle Atlantic District, AIA, October 23, 1953, Avery Architectural and Fine Arts Library, Columbia University, George Howe Collection, quoted in Reed, "Toward Form," 185.

74. Roseman, "Public-Private Co-Operation and Negotiation," 156.

75. Ibid., 154–55,

76. Discussion with Vincent G. Kling, ENB, and GLH.

77. ENB, Mayor Reports, October 15, 1953.

78. "The View From Billy Penn's Hat: The Changing Face of Center City," *Bulletin*, June 9, 1968.

79. Roseman, "Public-Private Co-Operation and Negotiation," 157.

80. ENB, Mayor Reports, September 17, 1954.

81. Pennsylvania Railroad, media release, May 23, 1954, copy in GLH Papers.

82. ENB, Mayor Reports, April 9, 1954.

83. Roseman, "Public-Private Co-Operation and Negotiation," 151.

84. ENB, letter to Murray L. Shusterman, August 4, 1955, PCPC Papers, A-2913, "Redevelopment—Penn Center 1955."

85. Frederick T. Thorpe, Jr., letter to John A. Bailey, September 12, 1955, PCPC Papers, A-2913, "Redevelopment—Penn Center 1955"; Henry D. Harral, letter to ENB, August 10, 1955, PCPC Papers, A-2913, "Redevelopment—Penn Center 1955."

86. ENB, Mayor Reports, September 9, 1955.

87. ENB, Mayor Reports, December 1, 1955.

88. ENB, interview with GLH, tape recorded, Philadelphia, December 5, 2002, GLH Papers.

89. ENB, Mayor Reports, January 28, 1955.

90. Job meeting memo, Penn Center, February 25, 1955, copy in GLH Papers.

91. ENB, letter to Vincent Kling, November 15, 1954, PCPC Papers, A-2913, "Penn Center 1954."

92. Robert W. Crawford, letter to ENB, March 30, 1954, PCPC Papers, A-2913, "Penn Center 1954."

93. ENB, Mayor Reports, July 16, 1954.

94. ENB, Mayor Reports, June 22, 1956.

95. ENB, Mayor Reports, July 27, 1956.

96. PCPC, memo, subject: "Meeting of the Art Commission on October 24, 1956," October 29, 1956, PCPC Papers, A-2901, "Art Commission Memorandum."

97. PCPC, memo, subject: "Meeting of the Art Commission on November 14, 1956," November 15, 1956, PCPC Papers, A-2901, "Art Commission Memorandum."

98. PCPC, memo, subject: "Meeting of the Art Commission on November 29, 1956," November 29,1956, PCPC Papers, A-2901, "Art Commission Memorandum."

99. PCPC, "1956 Annual Report,"May 1, 1957, PCPC Papers, A-1620.

100. ENB, Mayor Reports, April 6, 1956.

101. ENB, Mayor Reports, April 20, 1956.

102. Reichley, "Philadelphia Does It," 49.

103. ENB, Mayor Reports, December 10, 1959.

104. ENB, Mayor Reports, May 28, 1959.

105. Wolf von Eckardt, "The City," *Show*, December 1963, 142, AAUP, 292.II.E.37.

106. ENB, Mayor Reports, January 29, 1959.

107. For reference to work with the landscape architect, see ENB, Mayor Reports, April 30, 1959; for reference to the Art Museum donation, see ENB, Mayor Reports, June 10, 1960.

108. "Dream of Penn Center Being Realized, Planner Feels," *Bulletin*, August 25, 1959.

109. PCPC, "1958 Annual Report,"January 13, 1959, PCPC Papers, A-1620.

110. "Philadelphia's Redevelopment," *Architectural Forum* 105, 6 (December 1956): 130.

111. Ibid, 131.

112. *University of Pennsylvania Bulletin* 52; *University of Pennsylvania Bulletin* 57, Penn University Archives.

113. ENB, Mayor Reports, February 20, 1958.

114. ENB, Mayor Reports, July 9, 1959.

115. ENB, Mayor Reports, October 9, 1953.

116. ENB, Mayor Reports, April 2, 1959.

117. ENB, Mayor Reports, December 8, 1961.

118. ENB, Mayor Reports, February 6, 1962.

119. G. Holmes Perkins, letter to ENB, February 20, 1962, PCA, A-2911, "City Planning Commission Files, Mr. Bacon's Correspondence January-February 1962."

120. ENB, Mayor Reports, April 5, 1962.

121. ENB, Mayor Reports, April 22, 1953.

122. Roseman, "Public-Private Co-Operation and Negotiation," 186.

123. ENB, Mayor Reports, November 10, 1960.

124. For example, PCPC, Center City Philadelphia, January 8, 1963, PCPC Papers, A-1605, 32.

125. ENB, interview with GLH, tape recorded, September 24, 2002, Philadelphia, GLH Papers.

126. ENB, Mayor Reports, March 1, 1963.

127. "Top of Midcity Buildings Limited to 450 Feet by Planning Board," *Bulletin*, March 3, 1963.

128. ENB, letter to Donald C. Rosinski, May 31, 1963, PCPC Papers, A-2918, "Mr. Bacon's Letter May–June 1963."

129. "Bacon Predicts Business Hub at 30th-Market," *Bulletin*, September 24, 1965.

130. ENB, letter to David R. Albright, August 5, 1967, PCPC Papers, A-2928, "Mr. Bacon's Letter May–April [sic] 1967."

131. "Mayor's Administrative Order," November 27, 1961, copy in GLH Papers.

132. Guian A. McKee, "Blue Sky Boys, Professional Citizens, and Knights-in-Shining-Money: Philadelphia's Penn Center Project and the Constraints of Private Development," *Journal of Planning History* 6, 1 (February 2007): 48–80.

133. Quoted in McKee, "Blue Sky Boys, 60.

134. Reichley, "Philadelphia Does It," 49.

135. Ibid.

136. Ibid., 56.

Chapter 5. Reinvesting Downtown

1. Stanhope Browne et al., interview with Charles Cook and GLH, June 24, 2006, video recorded by Charles Cook, Philadelphia, copy in personal collection of GLH.

2. R. May, memo, subject: "Conference with R. B. Mitchell, R. F. Leonard, H. M. Mayer, E. Bacon, and H. Blumenfeld on Central Waterfront Study," September 19, 1946, PCPC Papers, A-2914, "Old City 1946–1953."

3. Constance M. Greiff, *Independence: The Creation of a National Park* (Philadelphia: University of Pennsylvania Press, 1987), 48.

4. Cyril B. Roseman, "Public-Private Co-Operation and Negotiation in Downtown Redevelopment: A Study of Decision Process in Philadelphia," Ph.D. dissertation, Princeton University, 1963, 46.

5. Ibid., 54.

6. Ibid.

7. Ibid., 60.

8. Ibid., 63.

9. PCPC, "1950 Annual Report," February 2, 1951, PCPC Papers, A-1620.

10. Ibid.

11. ENB, interview with GLH, tape recorded, December 4, 2002, Philadelphia, GLH Papers.

12. Harbeson, Hough, Livingston & Larson, Architects, et al., *Preliminary Studies for Independence Mall*, prepared for PCPC, July 18, 1952, PCPC Papers, A-1610.

13. ENB, Mayor Reports, April 22, 1954.

14. "Time, Turf, Architects and Planners," *Architectural Record*, March 1976, 102.

15. ENB, talk to National Trust for Historic Preservation, Philadelphia, October 28, 1976, AAUP, 292.II.D.26.

16. ENB, "The Liberty Bell and the Courthouse Ears," March 25, 1997, copy in GLH Papers.

17. ENB, Mayor Reports, February 11, 1965.

18. Stewart Udall, letter to ENB, October 6, 1965, AAUP, 295.II.B.1.4; Stewart Udall, letter to Lawson B. Knott, Jr., October 6, 1965, AAUP, 295.II.B.1.4.

19. Madeline L. Cohen, "Postwar City Planning in Philadelphia: Edmund N. Bacon and the Design of Washington Square East," Ph.D. dissertation, University of Pennsylvania, 1991, 341–42,

20. ENB, *Design of Cities*, rev. ed. (New York: Penguin, 1974), 264–67.

21. ENB, "Civic Design," talk at Invitation Conference on Urban Design, Harvard University, April 9–10, 1956, AAUP, 095.86.

22. Ibid.

23. ENB, letter to Mayor Joseph S. Clark, PCPC Papers, A-2914, "Old City 1954–1957."

24. PCPC, media release, subject: Society Hill, June 8, 1950, PCPC Papers, A-2914, "Redevelopment—Old City, 1946–1953."

25. Eugene H. Klaber, Report on Design for Redevelopment of Old City Area, prepared for PCPC, February 9, 1950, PCPC Papers, series 145.6, A-2914, "Redevelopment—Old City, 1946–1953."

26. N. S. Keith, letter to David M. Walker, September 22, 1950, attached to Francis J. Lammer, letter to ENB, April 30, 1970, AAUP, 292.II.A.3.2.

27. Klaber, Report on Design for Redevelopment of Old City Area.

28. ENB, Address to the Annual Meeting of the City Parks Association," June 14, 1950 [*sic*, actually June 8], AAUP, 095.78.

29. Ibid.

30. ENB, Mayor Reports, May 14, 1954.

31. Lawrence M. C. Smith, letter to ENB, May 14, 1954, PCPC Papers, A-2914, "Old City 1954–1957."

32. Edward T. R. Wood, Jr., "Tentative Plan for Organizing 'The Citizens' Council on Historic Preservation'," November 29, 1952, PCPC Papers, A-2914, "Old City 1946–1953."

33. Charles Peterson, letter to ENB, June 26, 1953, PCPC Papers, A-2914, "Old City 1946–1953."

34. ENB, Mayor Reports, May 20, 1955.

35. Charles Peterson, letter to ENB, June 26, 1953.

36. ENB, Mayor Reports, April 22, 1953; ENB, Mayor Reports, December 9, 1953.

37. Cohen, "Postwar," 400–419.

38. Roseman, "Public-Private Co-Operation and Negotiation," 110.

39. Cohen, "Postwar," 445–50.

40. Ibid., 451.

41. Ibid., 452.

42. PCPC, "Lombard Redevelopment," Kling, Larson, Stonorov, consultants, 1957, PCA.

43. Cohen, "Postwar," 546–47.

44. Ibid.

45. Ibid., 547–48.

46. Roseman, "Public-Private Co-Operation and Negotiation," 128.

47. ENB, Mayor Reports, April 24, 1958.

48. Roseman, "Public-Private Co-Operation and Negotiation," 129.

49. ENB, interview with GLH, tape recorded, August 15, 2003, Philadelphia, GLH Papers.

50. Pennsylvania Historical Society, "Preserving the Legacy of Richardson Dilworth," http://www.hsp.org/node/2797.

51. Cohen, "Postwar," 550.

52. Discussion with ENB, Constance Fraley and GLH, tape recorded, March 28 2003, Phoenixville (Pa.), GLH Papers.

53. Ibid.

54. Cohen, "Postwar," 550.

55. Roseman, "Public-Private Co-Operation and Negotiation," 77.

56. Ibid., 80.

57. Ibid., 80–81.

58. Ibid., 82.

59. Ibid., 83.

60. Ibid., 85–91; PCPC, "Report on Proceedings—Urban Land Institute—on Dock Street and Old City Area," January 12, 1951, PCPC Papers, A-1609, "City Planning Commission Reports, 1950–1951.

61. ENB, Mayor Reports, November 5, 1954; December 3, 1954; Roseman, "Public-Private Co-Operation and Negotiation," 91; Greater Philadelphia Movement,

"Summary Facts—Greater Philadelphia Food Distribution Center," undated, PCPC Papers, A-2914, "Redevelopment—Pattison Ave. East July 1954–December 1955."

62. Roseman, "Public-Private Co-Operation and Negotiation," 121.

63. Jay Nathan, full interview for the making of *Mr. Philadelphia: The Story of Albert M. Greenfield*, documentary film, Albert M. Greenfield Foundation, 2011 (0:43–0:53), http://www.mrphiladelphiathefilm.com/jay-nathan/.

64. Walt D'Alessio, interview with GLH, March 19, 2009, Philadelphia, notes in GLH Papers.

65. Jay Nathan (0:54–1:40).

66. Stephen G. Thompson, "Philadelphia's Design Sweepstakes," *Architectural Forum* 109, 12 (December 1958): 94–99.

67. PCPC, "Lombard Redevelopment."

68. ENB, Mayor Reports, July 23, 1958.

69. Thompson, "Design Sweepstakes," 94–99.

70. ENB, Mayor Reports, October 3, 1958.

71. Cohen, "Postwar," 488.

72. ENB, "Philadelphia City Planning Commission Report to Redevelopment Authority," November 18, 1958, in Mayor Reports, November 11, 1958.

73. I. M. Pei, interview with GLH, tape recorded, September 23, 2004, New York, GLH Papers.

74. I. M. Pei Associates, "Society Hill, Philadelphia: A Plan for Redevelopment/ Section A—Washington Square East Urban Renewal Area, Unit Number One," 1958, copy in AAUP 278.I.41.

75. ENB, "Philadelphia City Planning Commission Report to Redevelopment Authority."

76. Michael von Moschzisker, "Bacon's Foresight Led to Hill Towers," *Bulletin*, May 24, 1970.

77. Cohen, "Postwar," 508–9.

78. Ibid., 507.

79. Ibid., 514.

80. Ibid., 511–12.

81. ENB, Mayor Reports, December 1, 1960; February 23, 1961.

82. ENB, Mayor Reports, June 1, 1961.

83. "Society Hill a Nightmare, Park Aid Says," *Bulletin*, January 14, 1962.

84. ENB, letter to Robert C. Weinberg, April 23, 1962, PCPC Papers, A-2911, "Mr. Bacon's Letter March–April 1962."

85. Matthew L. Rockwell, letter to Charles E. Peterson, May 21, 1962, PCPC Papers, A-2911, "Mr. Bacon's Letter May-June 1962."

86. "City Planner Urges Renewal in the 'Spirit of Society Hill'," March 10, 1967, *Bulletin*.

87. Cohen, "Postwar," 515.

88. I. M. Pei, interview with GLH.

89. I. M. Pei, letter to ENB, June 7, 1963, PCPC Papers, A-2918, "Mr. Bacon's Letter May-June 1963."

90. Walt D'Alessio, interview with GLH.

91. Cohen, "Postwar," 530.

92. ENB, interview with GLH, tape recorded, August 15, 2003, Philadelphia, GLH Papers.

93. Discussion with ENB, Constance Fraley, and GLH.

94. ENB, Mayor Reports, February 6, 1962.

95. PCPC, "1961 Annual Report," January 19, 1962, PCPC Papers, A-1620.

96. ENB, Mayor Reports, June 13 1962.

97. ENB, "The Changing City," a talk presented to the National Association of Real Estate Boards, Detroit, November 15, 1962, AAUP, 095.220.

98. Joshua Olsen, *Better Places Better Lives: A Biography of James Rouse* (Washington, D.C.: Urban Land Institute, 2003), 78–79.

99. Ibid.

100. Ibid., 79.

101. "$100 Million Midcity Job Okd by Planning Board," *Inquirer*, April 2, 1958.

102. ENB, discussion with GLH, tape recorded, September 6, 2002, Philadelphia, GLH Papers.

103. "$100 Million."

104. PCPC, Market East Plaza, May 1958, PCPC Papers, A-1612.

105. Ibid.

106. Ibid.

107. Ibid.

108. ENB, Mayor Reports, June 5, 1958.

109. ENB, quoted in Alexander Garvin, "Philadelphia's Planner: A Conversation with Edmund Bacon," *Journal of Planning History* 1, 1 (February 2002): 77; discussion with ENB and GLH, September 6, 2002.

110. ENB, Mayor Reports, April 2, 1959.

111. ENB, Mayor Reports, July 8, 1960.

112. ENB, Mayor Reports, September 22, 1960.

113. ENB, Mayor Reports, May 25, 1961.

114. Peter Shedd Reed, "Toward Form: Louis I. Kahn's Urban Designs for Philadelphia, 1939–1962," Ph.D. dissertation, University of Pennsylvania, 1989, 248.

115. ENB, quoted in "Louis I. Kahn and the Living City," *Architectural Forum* 108, 3 (March 1958): 118–19.

116. Reed, "Toward Form," 253–54.

117. Ibid., 254.

118. PCPC, "1961 Annual Report," January 19, 1962, PCPC Papers, A-1620.

119. ENB, Mayor Reports, June 28, 1962.

120. ENB, Mayor Reports, February 6, 1962.

121. Ibid.

122. ENB, Mayor Reports, June 28, 1962.

123. Ibid.

124. Larry Smith & Company, "Study of Market Street East," September 4, 1962, PCPC Papers, A-1613.

125. ENB, Mayor Reports, November 14, 1962.

126. "Giurgola, Romaldo," Philadelphia Architects and Buildings, www.phila delphiabuildings.org.

127. PCPC, "Market East Study," February 1963, PCPC Papers, A-1613, "City Planning Commission Reports 1960–1963."

128. "$40 Million Underground Rail Loop Is Called Key to Market Street East," *Bulletin*, March 12, 1963.

129. ENB, Mayor Reports, May 9, 1963.

130. ENB, Mayor Reports, September 5, 1963.

131. ENB, Mayor Reports, October 10, 1963.

132. PCPC, "Market East Study."

133. "Philadelphia: The Gallery at Market East," AAUP, 292.II.E.184, 39.

134. Walt D'Alessio, interview with GLH.

135. Gladstone Associates, "Review Draft: Case Study #3, The Gallery—Philadelphia," produced for Urban Land Institute, April 1978, copy in GLH Papers.

136. Skidmore, Owings and Merrill, "Market St. East: Report on the General Neighborhood Renewal Plan," June 1966, AAUP, 292.IV.B.59.

137. ENB, Mayor Reports, December 16, 1965.

138. "Market East Seen Creating 80,000 Jobs," *Bulletin*, September 27, 1967.

139. ENB, Mayor Reports, June 22, 1967; ENB, Mayor Reports, September 19, 1968.

140. ENB, Mayor Reports, July 3, 1969.

141. ENB, Mayor Reports, July 11, 1969.

142. ENB, Mayor Reports, December 1, 1968.

143. ENB, Mayor Reports, December 4, 1969.

144. Lou Antosh, "Market Street East: An 'Orphan' Waits," *Bulletin*, January 20, 1974.

145. Raymond A. Berens, "Is East of Broad St. Really No-Man's Land?" *Bulletin*, January 27, 1974.

146. "Market Street East Gets a 'Go'," editorial, *Philadelphia Inquirer*, February 14, 1974.

147. "Philadelphia: The Gallery at Market East," in Urban Land Institute with Gladstone Associates, *Joint Development: Making the Real Estate Transit Connection* (Washington, D.C.: ULI, 1979), 33–56.

148. Mary Walton, "What Hath Rouse Wrought?" *Today, The Inquirer Magazine*, August 6, 1978, 11–16.

149. "Philadelphia: The Gallery at Market East," 47.

150. Ibid.

151. Richard L. Williams, "Our Older Cities Are showing Age But Also Showing Signs of Fight," *Smithsonian*, January 1979, 74.

152. "Philadelphia: The Gallery at Market East," 33–56.

153. Ibid.

154. Daniel Machalaba, "Municipal Mall: Philadelphia's 'Gallery' Tests a City's Ability to Lure Back Shoppers," *Wall Street Journal*, March 30, 1978, Eastern edition.

155. "Rouse's Gallery in Philadelphia Potpourri of Food & Merch Shops," *Amusement Business*, September 17, 1977, 18.

156. Walton, "What Hath Rouse Wrought?" 11.

157. Ibid.

158. John McCalla, "Sales of $230 per Square Foot," *Philadelphia Business Journal*, January 7, 2000.

159. Andrea Knox, "Who Shops the Gallery?" *Inquirer*, January 9, 1978.

160. William Storm, "Judge Limits Pickets at the Gallery," *Bulletin*, August 27, 1978; Elmer Smith, "Activist Faces Contempt in Gallery Boycott," *Bulletin*, October 13, 1978; "Milton Street Arrested," *Bulletin*, October 9, 1978; David Runkel, "Street Arrested Again at Gallery," *Bulletin*, February 23, 1979.

161. Linn Washington, "Gallery II's an Exhibition of Minority Participation," *Daily News*, October 10, 1983.

162. Jennifer Lin, "Opening Day: Despite Rain, a Festive Air Reigns at Gallery II," *Inquirer*, October 13, 1983.

163. Roseman, "Public-Private Co-Operation and Negotiation," 64.

Chapter 6. The Planner Versus the Automobile

1. ENB, "Philadelphia Yesterday, Philadelphia Today," *Today: The Philadelphia Inquirer Magazine*, September 10, 1961.

2. "Transit Has Key Role in Philadelphia Planning Process," *Railway Age*, March 4, 1968, 22.

3. PCPC, *Capital Program, 1948–1953*, PCPC Papers, box 145.3.

4. "The City—Under the Knife," *Time*, November 6, 1964, 84, 70.

5. ENB, "Resigning Downtown Philadelphia: A Presentation Given at the Annual Meeting of the American Institute of Architects," April 27, 1961, AAUP, 095.157.

6. Ibid.

7. Suzanne Stephens, "A Look Back: Planner Ed Bacon," *Architectural Record*, November 22, 2005, http://archrecord.construction.com/news/daily/archives/051122 bacon.asp; Robert B. Mitchell, letter to Leonard T. Beale, November 29, 1947, PCA, A-2914, "Lombard 1947–1955."

8. ENB, interview by Phil Willon and Ed Smith, 1966, PCPC Papers, box 2928, "Mr. Bacon's Letter, September–December 1966."

9. U.S. Department of Transportation, Federal Highway Administration, "Dwight D. Eisenhower National System of Interstate and Defense Highways," http://www .fhwa.dot.gov/programadmin/interstate.cfm.

10. PCPC, 1946 Annual Report, 1947, PCPC Papers, A-1620.

11. ENB, Mayor Reports, June 27, 1952.

12. Ibid.

13. PCPC, "Philadelphia's Program of Major Highways," January 1955, PCA, group 145.

14. Jacob Kobrick, "'Let the People Have a Victory': The Politics of Transportation in Philadelphia, 1946–1984," Ph.D. dissertation, University of Maryland, 2010, n199.

15. ENB, Mayor Reports, June 2, 1965.

16. Kobrick, "'Let the People Have a Victory'," 40–74.

17. PCPC, 1948 Annual Report, March 9, 1949, PCPC Papers, A-1620.

18. Joseph S. Clark, letter to Governor John S. Fine, November 25, 1953, PCPC Papers, A-2906, "Schuylkill Expressway-Roosevelt Boulevard Extension 1951–1953."

19. PCPC, media release, January 24, 1950, PCPC Papers, A-2906, "Schuylkill Expressway-Roosevelt Boulevard Extension 1950–1952."

20. Ibid.

21. PCPC, 1957 Annual Report, January 6, 1958, PCPC Papers, A-1620.

22. "Visit to a Big Highway," *Bulletin*, October 12, 1961.

23. PCPC, Philadelphia's Comprehensive Plan for Rapid Transit, January 7, 1966, PCPC Papers, A-1614, City Planning Commission Reports 1963–1966.

24. ENB, Mayor Reports," May 29, 1953.

25. "Expressway Plans Draw Fire of Northeast Residents," *Bulletin*, March 13, 1957.

26. "Expressways on Paper," Editorial, *Bulletin*, June 5, 1958.

27. "Expressway Plans Draw Fire."

28. ENB, Mayor Reports, December 14, 1967.

29. ENB, Mayor Reports, March 24, 1960.

30. Ibid.

31. ENB, Mayor Reports, December 3, 1964; Stanhope Browne et al., interview with Charles Cook and GLH, June 24, 2006, video recorded by Charles Cook, Philadelphia, copy in personal collection of GLH.

32. ENB, Mayor Reports, December 3, 1964.

33. Kobrick, "'Let the People Have a Victory',"169.

34. Interview with Browne et al.

35. Ibid.

36. Ibid.

37. The Philadelphia Architects Committee and the Committee to Preserve Philadelphia's Historic Gateway, "The Proposal for a Covered Below-Grade Expressway Through Philadelphia's Historic Waterfront," 1965, AAUP, 254.VII.2.

38. "U.S. Study Opposed 'Chinese Wall' in Society Hill," *Inquirer*, February 2, 1965.

39. Philadelphia Architects Committee, "The Proposal."

40. Ibid.

41. ENB, Mayor Reports, May 26, 1966.

42. ENB, Mayor Reports, October 19, 1967.

43. ENB, Mayor Reports, October 26, 1967.

44. "Tate Suggests Crosstown Expressway May Be Abandoned," *Bulletin*, November 10, 1967.

45. "City Assured of State Funds for Expressway Lid," *Bulletin*, February 5, 1969.

46. Bill Wingell, "A Neighborhood in Agony," *Sunday Bulletin Magazine*, January 8, 1967.

47. Lawrence M. Campbell, "Queen Village Plan Detailed by Consultant," *Bulletin*, June 19, 1964.

48. Wingell, "A Neighborhood in Agony."

49. "Gloria Dei's Rector Assails Bacon on Expressway Plan," *Bulletin*, August 18, 1966; Wingell, "A Neighborhood in Agony."

50. ENB, "Opening Session: Bicentennial Evaluation," presented to National Trust for Historic Preservation (Philadelphia), October 28, 1976, AAUP, 292.II.D.26.

51. Robert B. Mitchell to Leonard T. Beale, November 29, 1947, PCA, A-2914, "Lombard 1947–1955."

52. ENB, memo to files, January 30, 1957, PCPC Papers, A-2914, "Old City 1954–1957."

53. "Crosstown Expressway Route Picked," *Bulletin*, October 7, 1959.

54. PCPC, Center City Philadelphia, January 8, 1963, PCPC Papers, A-1605.

55. Ward Welsh, "Crosstown Highway Facing Stiff Protest from Grays Ferry," *Inquirer*, May 15, 1966.

56. Eugene L. Meyer, "Planners Assailed over Relocation for Expressway," *Bulletin*, May 4, 1967.

57. Christopher Klemek, *The Transatlantic Collapse of Urban Renewal Postwar Urbanism from New York to Berlin* (Chicago: University of Chicago Press, 2011), 135.

58. Ibid., 135–36.

59. Crosstown Expressway Task Force, "Memorandum of Meeting," November 9, 1967, PCA, A-2965, "Crosstown Expressway, 1958–1967."

60. ENB, letter to Richard J. McConnell, July 13, 1967, PCA, A-2965, "Crosstown Expressway, 1958–1967."

61. ENB, interview by GLH, tape recorded, September 24, 2002, Philadelphia, GLH Papers.

62. ENB and Richard Huffman, memo to files, subject: "Crosstown Expressway," July 28, 1967, PCA, A-2965, "Crosstown Expressway, 1958–1967."

63. "Tate Suggests Crosstown Expressway May Be Abandoned."

64. Michelle Osborn, "The Crosstown and City Planning," *Bulletin*, March 21, 1969.

65. Mayor James H. J. Tate, letter to George Dukes, November 6, 1967, PCA, A-2965, "Crosstown Expressway, 1958–1967"; "Tate Says Road Bureau Tries to Embarrass Him," *Bulletin*, November 6, 1967.

66. Mayor James H. J. Tate, letter to ENB, April 18, 1968, PCA, A-2965, "Crosstown Expressway, 1968"; Kos Semonski, "Crosstown Link Is 'Dead' Tate Declares,". *Bulletin*, March 25, 1968; "City to Foster Integration in Route of Expressway," *Bulletin*, May 7, 1968.

67. Alice Lipscomb, letter to ENB, June 24, 1968, PCA, A-2973, "Redevelopment—South Central (Including Crosstown Community), 1968–1969."

68. Peter H. Binzen, "Whites Despair for South St.; Blacks Rage over Conditions," *Bulletin*, June 3, 1969.

69. "Tate Tells Bartlett He's Still Against Crosstown Link," *Bulletin*, April 29, 1968.

70. ENB, Mayor Reports, June 13, 1968.

71. ENB, Mayor Reports, June 20, 1968.

72. Francis M. Lordan, "South Phila. Renewal Project Starts Next Spring," *Bulletin*, December 22, 1968.

73. George T. Dukes, letter to ENB, March 13, 1969, PCA, A-2965, "Crosstown Expressway, 1969."

74. David A. Wallace, letter to Mayor James H. J. Tate, March 24, 1969, PCA, A-2965, "Crosstown Expressway, 1969."

75. ENB, Mayor Reports, March 27, 1969.

76. "Dispute on Midcity Route Delays Renewal Funds," *Bulletin*, April 8, 1969.

77. Matthew W. Bullock, Jr., letter to Donald W. Kramer, subject: "Crosstown Expressway," December 30, 1968, PCA, A-2965, "Crosstown Expressway, 1968."

78. Constance Faulk, "City Studying New Route for Crosstown," *Bulletin*, April 9, 1969.

79. Ibid.

80. ENB, Mayor Reports, April 10, 1969.

81. Ibid.

82. ENB, Mayor Reports, June 27, 1969.

83. Eugene L. Meyer, "Expressway Foes Threaten Center City Store Boycott," *Bulletin*, December 9, 1969.

84. ENB, Mayor Reports, December 24, 1969.

85. Stephen C. Lockwood, Crosstown Transportation Study, June 18, 1969, PCA, A-2965, "Crosstown Expressway, 1969."

86. Robert C. Bartlett, letter to George F. Fenton, June 17, 1970, PCA, A-2965, "Crosstown Expressway, 1970–1972."

87. Gene Harris, "Crosstown Expressway Plan Dies," *Bulletin*, October 30, 1973.

88. ENB, Mayor Reports, September 24, 1964.

89. "Plan Bans Cars on Main Streets," *Inquirer*, November 18, 1955.

90. ENB, Mayor Reports, January 10, 1963.

91. "Philadelphia Street as Shoppers' Haven," *The Times* (London), November 12, 1963.

92. ENB, Mayor Reports, December 12, 1963.

93. "Philadelphia Street as Shoppers' Haven."

94. "Bacon Walks Out on Mall Debate—One Too Many," *Bulletin*, November 14, 1963.

95. "City Planners Reject Junket to View Malls," *Bulletin*, February 5, 1964.

96. Simpson & Curtin Transportation Engineers, "Traffic Feasibility Study of a Chestnut Street Mall in Center City Philadelphia," for PCPC, November 1, 1966, PCPC Papers.

97. ENB, Mayor Reports, November 16, 1967.

98. "Chestnut St. Pedestrians Love It Without the Autos," *Bulletin*, April 24, 1970.

99. Harvey M. Rubenstein, *Pedestrian Malls, Streetscapes, and Urban Spaces* (New York: Wiley, 1992), 205.

100. "Transitway Is a Giant Step," *Inquirer*, editorial, November 27, 1975.

101. Rubenstein, *Pedestrian Malls*, 206

102. Howard S. Shapiro, "Chestnut Is Open at Last," *Inquirer*, November 25, 1975.

103. Mark Davis, "Sparks Fly over Chestnut Street," *Inquirer*, June 16, 1998.

104. Citizens' Advisory Committee on Recreation and Natural Beauty, "Annual Report to the President and the President's Council on Recreation and Natural Beauty," preliminary draft, June 1967, AAUP, 95.B.1.10.

105. "Minutes—Joint Meeting—President's Council on Recreation and Natural Beauty and Citizens' Advisory Committee on Recreation and Natural Beauty," June 21, 1968, AAUP, 095.17.

106. ENB, "Statement before the Federal Highway Administration on Highway Hearing Procedures," December 16, 1968, AAUP, 095.18.

107. Interview with ENB by Phil Willon and Ed Smith.

108. ENB, untitled, *National Geographic*, 150, 1 (July 1976): 74.

109. ENB, "Report of the Urban Development Committee," Urban Land Institute Spring Meeting, Minneapolis, May 16, 1973, AAUP, 292.II.A.3.22.

110. ENB, "Energy: Shaper of Future Living Patterns," *AIA Journal* 60, 6 (December 1973): 39.

111. ENB, "Energy and the City," talk at International Conference on Energy Use Management, Tucson, Arizona, October 24–28, 1977, AAUP, 292.II.D.128.

112. Ibid.

113. Ibid.

114. ENB, "Clean Air, No Gangs, No Private Cars," *Daily News*, April 14, 1975, 24.

115. ENB, "Future of Cities," talk prepared for Cooper-Hewitt Museum, October 19, 1980, AAUP, 292.II.D.143.

116. John Betz, "Architect Decries Waste of Abandoned Houses," *Bulletin*, February 29, 1976, 4.

117. ENB, statement at the Conservation of Energy in Transportation Round Table, hosted by *Scientific American*, Washington, D.C., March 17–18, 1974, AAUP, 292.III.A.61.

118. ENB, talk to National Trust for Historic Preservation, October 28, 1976, AAUP, 292.II.D.26.

119. Ann Holms, "After Petroleum," *Houston Chronicle*, March 4, 1979, 15.

120. Agreement between ENB and Viking Press, November 26, 1973, AAUP, 292.II.D.250.

121. ENB, letter to Walter Annenberg, October 23, 1989, AAUP, 292.II.D.251.

122. ENB, letter to Bill Moyers, August 7, 1989, AAUP, 292.II.D.251.

123. It appears that Bacon first started recruiting support for this conference during a trip to Kyoto in 1987. See ENB, "International Seminar on Innovative Planning Strategies for Metropolitan Development and Conservation," keynote address, Kyoto (Japan), November 14, 1987, AAUP, 292.II.D.174. A letter from November 14, 1991, seems to indicate that the post-petroleum program was no longer happening; ENB, letter to John P. Keith, November 14, 1991, AAUP, 292.II.D.253.

124. Post Petroleum City—Planning Committee, meeting minutes, September 5, 1989, AAUP, 292.II.D.251; "1993 World Congress on the Post Petroleum City—Participating Cities," June 1, 1990, AAUP, 292.II.D.250.

125. Post Petroleum—Planning Committee, meeting minutes, November 21, 1989, AAUP, 292.II.D.251; André Gamache, letter to ENB, November 29, 1990, AAUP, 292.II.D.252.

126. Peter Newman, phone interview with GLH, March 28, 2009, notes in GLH Papers.

127. Thomas Hine, "Savoring the Cities' Vitality," *Inquirer*, February 26, 1984.

Chapter 7. Articulating a Vision in a Shifting World

1. Roul Tunley, "Comeback of a Shabby City," *Saturday Evening Post*, December 5, 1959, 35.

2. ENB, Mayor Reports, January 18, 1962.

3. "No Architect," Editorial, *New York Times*, November 6, 1962.

4. ENB, letter to PCPC, March 11, 1963, PCPC Papers, A-2918, "Mr. Bacon's Letter March–April 1963."

5. ENB, "The City Image," in *Man and the Modern City: Ten Essays*, ed. Elizabeth Geen, Jeanne R. Lowe, and Kenneth Walker (Pittsburgh: University of Pittsburgh Press, 1963).

6. ENB, statement on Samuel Grafton's article, September 6, 1963, PCPC Papers, A-2918, "Mr. Bacon's Letter September 1963."

7. David A. Wallace, "Renaissancemanship," *Journal of the America Society of Planners* 26, 3 (1960): 164.

8. Walter H. Blucher, "The PCPC, an Appraisal," August 1954, PCPC Papers, A-1611, "City Planning Commission Reports 1954–1957."

9. PCPC, *Comprehensive Plan for the City of Philadelphia*, 1960, AAUP, 292.44.

10. Wallace, "Renaissancemanship," 164.

11. PCPC, Center City Philadelphia: Major Elements of the Physical Development Plan for Center City, May 1960, AAUP, 292.IV.B.129.

12. PCPC, Center City Philadelphia, January 8, 1963, PCPC Papers, A-1605.

13. Ibid., 40.

14. ENB, "A Fair Can Pace It," *Greater Philadelphia Magazine*, October 1959, 242.

15. Ibid., 244.

16. "Redesigning Downtown Philadelphia: A Presentation Given at the Annual Meeting of The American Institute of Architects," April 27, 1961, AAUP, 095.157.

17. "Transcript of Bacon's Introduction," *AIA Journal* 35, 6 (June 1961): 90.

18. Philip Will, telegram to ENB, May 2, 1961, AAUP, 095.3.1A.3.

19. See letters and documents in AAUP, 095.2. relating to *Form, Design and the City*.

20. "Twelve-Month Report on Film 'Form, Design and the City'," March 18, 1963, AAUP, 095.5.

21. "List of Seminar Participants," April 26, 1955, AAUP, 095.71.

22. Philip Klein, memo to members of Planning Commission, August 23, 1965, PCPC Papers, A-2918, "Mr. Bacon's Letter July–October 1965."

23. Agnes Kelly, interview with Charles Cook, videotaped, September 13, 2006, Philadelphia, copy in GLH Papers.

24. James N. Kise, untitled essay, October 19, 2005, GLH Papers.

25. Barbara Burn, memo to "DLB," October 16, 1974, AAUP, 292.IV.A.28.

26. Siegfried Giedion, *Space, Time and Architecture: The Growth of a New Tradition* (Cambridge, Mass.: Harvard University Press, 1967), 92.

27. ENB, *Design of Cities*, rev. ed. (New York: Penguin, 1974), 21.

28. Ibid., 23.

29. Ibid., 297.

30. Ibid., 7.

31. ENB, "Man in the Urban Complex," presentation at First Centennial Symposium, Loyola University, October 1, 1969, AAUP, 095.453.

32. ENB, *Design of Cities*, 301.

33. R. Furneaux Jordan, "Making Sense of Cities," *The Observer* (London), June 11, 1967; Ervin Galantay, "The People's Art," *Progressive Architecture* 48, 8 (August 1967): 178, 182, 188, 196; Douglas Haskell, "Design of Cities," book review, *Architectural Forum* 127, 2 (September 1967): 80–81.

34. Galantay, "The People's Art,"178.

35. Haskell, "Design of Cities," 80.

36. Galantay, "The People's Art,"188.

37. Michelle Osborn, "The Obelisks of Philadelphia," *Bulletin*, date unknown, copy in AAUP, 292.IV.A.22.

38. Frederick Gutheim, "The Urban Condition Modified," *New Republic*, September 2, 1967, 34.

39. Jane Jacobs, *The Death and Life of Great American Cities* (1961; New York: Vintage, 1992), 3, 4.

40. See a discussion of the response to *Death and Life* in Anthony Flint, *Wrestling with Moses: How Jane Jacobs Took on New York's Master Builder and Transformed the American City* (New York: Random House, 2009), 121–31.

41. Herbert J. Gans, "Urban Vitality and the Fallacy of Physical Determinism," in *People and Plans* (1968), reprinted in H. J. Gans, *People, Plans, and Policies: Essays on Poverty, Racism, and Other National Urban Problems* (New York: Columbia University Press, 1991), 36.

42. Ibid., 41.

43. Paul Davidoff, "Advocacy and Pluralism in Planning," *Journal of the American Institute of Planners* 31, 4 (November 1965): 331–38.

44. Frederick Pillsbury, "I Like Philadelphia . . . with Some Big IFs and BUTs," *Sunday Bulletin Magazine*, June 24, 1962.

45. James V. Cunningham, "Jane Jacobs Visits Pittsburgh," *New City*, September 15, 1962, reprinted by Action Housing Inc (Pittsburgh).

46. Pillsbury, "I Like Philadelphia."

47. ENB, letter to Robert E. MacNeal, October 13, 1961, PCPC Papers, A-2907, "Mr. Bacon's Folder June–December 1961."

48. ENB, "Planning in Philadelphia," paper for Architectural League of New York and Museum of Modern Art, February 3, 1962, AAUP, 095.188.

49. Walter McQuade, "Architecture," *The Nation*, March 17, 1962.

50. William Rafsky, letter to ENB, April 12, 1962, PCA, A-2911, "City Planning Commission Files, Mr. Bacon's Letter March–April 1962."

51. Paul Goldberger, "Uncommon Sense," *American Scholar* 75, 4 (Autumn 2006): 122–26.

52. Mention of Bacon by name: Jacobs, *Death and Life*, n.358 (Jacobs also mentions Bacon regarding the planning of the Society Hill Greenways, 416–17); Criticism of Philadelphia City Beautiful design: 93, 192, 355.

53. ENB, "Philadelphia Yesterday, Philadelphia Today," *Today: The Philadelphia Inquirer Magazine*, September 10, 1961.

54. ENB, "Plans for 1962," memo to Mayor James H. J. Tate, Mayor Reports, February 6, 1962.

55. ENB, "The Future of Cities—Urbanity or Suburbanity," talk presented to conference on The Metropolitan Future, Berkeley, California, September 26, 1963, AAUP, 095.248.

56. ENB, quoted in Gerald McKelvey, "Phila. Urban Planning: Looking Back, Forward," *Inquirer*, May 3, 1970.

57. ENB, "Current Problems of the Planning Profession," talk to Annual Conference of the American Institute of Planners, Milwaukee, October 27–31, 1963, AAUP, 095.256.

58. ENB, remarks, in *The Land, the City, and the Human Spirit*, ed. Larry Paul Fuller (Austin: University of Texas Press, 1985), 66.

59. ENB, "The Future of Cities—Urbanity or Suburbanity."

60. Oskar Stonorov, letter to ENB, December 31, 1947, AAUP, 278.I.75.

61. Arthur P. Dudden, "The City Embraces 'Normalcy': 1919–1929," in *Philadelphia: A 300-Year History*, ed. Russell F. Weigley (New York: Norton, 1982), 573–75.

62. Scott Gabriel Knowles, "Staying Too Long at the Fair: Philadelphia Planning and the Debacle of 1976," in *Imagining Philadelphia: Edmund Bacon and the Future of the City*, ed. S. G. Knowles (Philadelphia: University of Pennsylvania Press, 2009), 83–85.

63. Ibid., 85–86.

64. "World's Fair Proposed Here for 1976," *Bulletin*, July 26, 1959.

65. ENB, Mayor Reports, May 21, 1959.

66. ENB, "A Fair Can Pace It," *Greater Philadelphia Magazine*, October 1959.

67. Daniel B. Crofter, "Philadelphia 1976: A World's Fair for the Nation's 200th Birthday," *Sunday Bulletin Magazine*, July 19, 1964.

68. PCPC, *United States of America Bicentennial*, 1963, copy in GLH Papers.

69. Knowles, "Staying Too Long at the Fair," 94.

70. Ibid., 92.

71. ENB, Mayor Reports, October 18, 1963, ENB, Mayor Reports, November 19, 1964.

72. Knowles, "Staying Too Long at the Fair," 92.

73. Mayor James H.J. Tate, statement, July 8, 1966, PCPC Papers, A-2928, "Mr. Bacon's Letter May–August 1966."

74. "World's Fair for Boston in 1975 Backed by Business," unknown publication, November18,1965, PCPC Papers, A-2918, "Mr. Bacon's Letter November–December 1965"; ENB, Mayor Reports, July 15, 1965.

75. Knowles, "Staying Too Long at the Fair," 94–95.

76. ENB, Mayor Reports, May 16, 1968.

77. ENB, Mayor Reports, May 24, 1968.

78. Knowles, "Staying Too Long at the Fair," 94.

79. ENB, Mayor Reports, July 15, 1965.

80. Knowles, "Staying Too Long at the Fair," 95–96.

81. ENB, Mayor Reports, November 16, 1967; for discussion of the Young Professionals, see Knowles, "Staying Too Long at the Fair," 97–101.

82. Knowles, "Staying Too Long at the Fair," 101.

83. Quoted in ibid., 100.

84. ENB, Mayor Reports, August 14, 1969.

85. G. Craig Schelter, interview with Charles Cook, videotaped, August 3, 2006, Philadelphia, copy in GLH Papers.

86. Knowles, "Staying Too Long at the Fair," 103.

87. ENB, Mayor Reports, October 16, 1969.

88. ENB, Mayor Reports, December 18, 1969.

89. ENB, Mayor Reports, April 9, 1970.

90. "City's Bicentennial Committee Split over Park, 30th Street Location," *Bulletin*, May 27, 1970.

91. Travel Center of Japan, "Japan Tour Itinerary," July 7, 1970, copy in GLH Papers.

92. "Commission Reverses Self in 18–14 Vote," *Bulletin*, July 1, 1970.

93. "U.S. Financial Help Is Essential for Expo 76, Bacon Says," *Bulletin*, October 16, 1970.

94. Knowles, "Staying Too Long at the Fair," 103.

95. Donald Cox, "Greed and Incompetence on the Bicentennial Corp," *Distant Drummer*, 1972 (?), copy in AAUP, 292.II.A.3.18.

96. ENB, "Report to Mayor Tate—Bicentennial Planning," September 21, 1970, AAUP, 292.II.A.3.4.

97. Knowles, "Staying Too Long at the Fair," 105.

98. ENB, letter to the Editor, *Philadelphia Inquirer*, not sent (?), December 15, 1970, AAUP, 292.II.A.3.6.

99. Robert E. Gabriel, letter to ENB, January 27, 1971, AAUP, 292.II.A.3.8; Stephanie G. Wolf, "The Bicentennial City 1968–1982," in Weigley, ed., *Philadelphia: A 300-Year History*, 727.

100. Telegram to ENB, February 25, 1971, AAUP, 292.II.A.3.8.

101. ENB, "Landscape Architecture and Land Design," March 2, 1972, 10–11, AAUP, 292.II.D.176.

102. Wolf, "The Bicentennial City 1968–1982," 726.

103. Mike Mallow, "How They Blew the Bicentennial," *Philadelphia* 66, 6 (June 1975): 116.

104. Chapin A. Day, "A Million People Jam Olde City," *Inquirer*, September 23, 1974.

105. Wolf, "The Bicentennial City 1968–1982," 730.

106. Knowles, "Staying Too Long at the Fair," 81.

107. Warren Eisenberg, "Enter the Age of Tate," *Greater Philadelphia Magazine*, January 1964.

108. James H.J. Tate, letter to ENB, January 2, 1964, PCPC Papers, A-2918, "Mr. Bacon's Letter January 1964."

109. John F. Bauman, *Public Housing, Race, and Renewal: Urban Planning in Philadelphia, 1920–1974* (Philadelphia: Temple University Press, 1987), 188.

110. Nathaniel Burt, "Race and Renaissance in Philadelphia," *Harper's*, September 1964, 65.

111. ENB, "The City as Systems of Order," presented at the Australian Planning Institute, April 21, 1966, PCPC Papers, A-2928, "Mr. Bacon's Letter May–August 1966."

112. ENB, remarks delivered at Shippensburg State College, February 16, 1966, AAUP, 095.320.

113. ENB, "Philadelphia Yesterday, Philadelphia Today."

114. U.S. Dept. of Commerce—Area Redevelopment Administration, "Planning for New Growth—New Jobs," January 1, 1962, PCPC Papers, A-2918, "Mr. Bacon's Letter January 1964."

115. ENB, Mayor Reports, February 6, 1962.

116. PCPC, 1962 Annual Report, January 19, 1963, PCPC Papers, A-1620.

117. ENB, Mayor Reports, June 1, 1961.

118. Graham Finney, interview with GLH, tape recorded, April 30, 2008, Philadelphia, GLH Papers.

119. PCPC, The West Philadelphia District Plan, January 1964, PCPC Papers, A-1614, "City Planning Commission Reports, 1963–1966."

120. Alexander L. Crosby, untitled (draft), April 13, 1963, PCPC Papers, A-2918, "Mr. Bacon's Letter March–April 1963."

121. For evidence of Bacon credited with conceiving the program, see Nancy Love, "Paradise Lost," *Philadelphia*, July 1968, 87.

122. ENB, Mayor Reports, March 16, 1967; Bauman, *Public Housing*, 196–97; Jeanne R. Lowe, *Cities in a Race with Time* (New York: Vintage, 1968), 359.

123. Joe J. Jordan, "The Potential for Housing Rehabilitation," prepared for PCPC, May 1, 1969, PCPC Papers, A-1615.

124. Paul Welch, "Grim Conclusions," *Life*, December 24, 1965, 119–21.

125. Bauman, *Public Housing*, 193.

126. For evidence of Stonorov's involvement, see H. Peter Oberlander and Eva Newbrun, *Houser: The Life and Work of Catherine Bauer* (Vancouver: UBC Press, 1999), 106.

127. Bauman, *Public Housing*, 193; Graham Finney, interview with GLH.

128. ENB, "Answers to Questions Pertaining to City Planning," undated, copy in GLH Papers.

129. For Bacon's enthusiasm, see ENB, Mayor Reports, January 27, 1966; ENB, "Pomeroy Memorial Lecture," Selected Papers from the ASPO National Planning Conference, San Francisco, 1968, reprinted from *Planning* (1968), AAUP, 095.418.

130. G. Craig Schelter, interview with Charles Cook.

131. PCPC, 1968–1969 Annual Report, December 1, 1969, PCPC Papers, A-1620.

132. "City Planning Aide Resigns, Charges Lack of Support," *Bulletin*, October 8, 1968.

133. ENB, Mayor Reports, September 12, 1968.

134. For more on the situation in West Philadelphia, see Philip Herrera, "Philadelphia: How Far Can Renewal Go?" *Architectural Forum* 121, 2 (August–September

1964): 186; ENB, Mayor Reports, September 17, 1969; "Drexel Tract to Be Picketed," *Inquirer*, December 2, 1969.

135. ENB, interview with GLH, tape recorded, June 6, 2003, Philadelphia, GLH Papers.

136. "Temple Ordered to Bring Residents into Planning," *Daily News*, March 20, 1969.

137. "Temple Freezes Expansion Without Community's OK," *Bulletin*, March 28, 1969.

138. "Temple Curtains Expansion as Joint Plan Is Approved," *Inquirer*, February 30, 1969.

139. "Temple Area Planning Talks Set Next Week," *Bulletin*, November 27, 1969.

140. ENB, interview with GLH, June 6, 2003.

141. "Hearings Open in Expansion Row at Temple," *Inquirer*, January 21, 1970.

142. ENB, interview with GLH, tape recorded, February 24, 2003, Philadelphia, GLH Papers.

143. ENB, Mayor Reports, February 11, 1970.

144. "Community Temple Agreement of 1970," AAUP, 095.468; "An 'Almost' Agreement," editorial, *Bulletin*, February 10, 1970.

145. ENB, Mayor Reports, March 26, 1970.

146. ENB, "Planning for Philadelphia's Future," presented to Philadelphia Rotary Club, March 11, 1970, AAUP, 095.461.

147. Knowles, "Staying Too Long at the Fair," 90.

148. "More Affluent Moving Back, Bacon Says," *Bulletin*, December 11, 1966.

149. ENB. "The Need for a World Conference on Cities," presented at White House Conference on International Cooperation, November 30, 1965, UPAA, 095.314.

Chapter 8. New Visions of Philadelphia

1. "Bacon Quits Both Jobs After 20 Years with City," *Bulletin*, February 20, 1970.

2. Gerald McKelvey, "The Tate Regime: How Crisis Piles on Crisis," *Inquirer*, March 1, 1970.

3. Ibid.

4. "Bacon Denies Aide's Charges on Housing Program," *Bulletin*,November 18, 1969.

5. Adrian I. Lee, "Bacon's Battle Against the Bulldozer," *Bulletin*, February 27, 1970.

6. Nancy Love, "Paradise Lost," *Philadelphia*, July 1968, 72–75, 87–88, 90, 95–96, 98–99.

7. Ibid.,99.

8. Ibid., 87–88.

9. Ibid., 90.

10. "Planning Chief Denies Insensitivity to Needs of Lower-Income Sections," *Bulletin*, January 28, 1970.

11. Mel Wax, "Planning Chief Just Eludes S.F," *San Francisco Chronicle*, January 10, 1967.

12. "$300 Million in Projects Outlined Before Council," *Bulletin*, April 22, 1969.

13. "Bacon Continues Testimony; Housing Payrolls Face Probe," *Bulletin*, May 21, 1969.

14. "$300 Million."

15. Ibid.

16. ENB, "Statement on 1500 Market Street," July 14, 1969, AAUP, 292.IV.A.25.

17. Joseph S. Clark, Jr., and Dennis J. Clark, "Rally and Relapse: 1946–1968," in *Philadelphia: A 300-Year History*, ed. Russell F. Weigley (New York: Norton, 1982), 662.

18. Ibid., 663.

19. McKelvey, "The Tate Regime."

20. ENB, Mayor Reports, July 11, 1969.

21. Henry Magaziner, interview with Charles Cook, July 19, 2005, Philadelphia, personal collection of Charles Cook.

22. Michael Bacon, interview with GLH, October 19, 2008, New York City, notes in GLH Papers.

23. Francis M. Lordan and Leonard J. McAdams, "Bacon Rips D.A.'s Office for Grand Jury 'Big Lie'," *Inquirer*, March 12, 1970.

24. "Bacon Quits Both Jobs."

25. McKelvey, "The Tate Regime."

26. Ibid.

27. "Bacon Rejects Tate's Plea to Remain in Post," *Bulletin*, February 26, 1970.

28. ENB, "Planning for Philadelphia's Future," presented to the Philadelphia Rotary Club, March 11, 1970, AAUP, 095.461.

29. ENB, interview with GLH, tape recorded, September 10, 2002, Philadelphia, GLH Papers.

30. ENB, "Planning for Philadelphia's Future."

31. Lordan and McAdams, "Bacon Rips D.A.'s Office."

32. Ibid.

33. Gilbert Stein, phone interview with GLH, August 2008, notes in GLH Papers.

34. "Bacon Says He Spoke Out Despite Disliking Politics," *Inquirer*, March 13, 1970.

35. Sylvan M. Cohen, letter to ENB, March 19, 1970, AAUP, 292.IV.A.25; Charles W. Nulf, letter to ENB, March 17, 1970, AAUP, 292.IV.A.25.

36. "Mr. Bacon's Legacy," editorial, *Bulletin*, February 27, 1970.

37. ENB, quoted in McKelvey, "The Tate Regime."

38. "Bacon Quits Both Jobs."

39. ENB, Mayor Reports, April 30, 1970.

40. "Bacon Quits Both Jobs."

41. Stephanie G. Wolf, "The Bicentennial City 1968–1982," in Weigley, ed., *Philadelphia: A 300-Year History*, 707.

42. Ibid., 722.

43. Ibid., 723.

44. ENB, interview with GLH, tape recorded, September 24, 2002, Philadelphia, GLH Papers.

45. PCPC, Annual Report, 1970–1971, PCA, A-1620.

46. PCPC, Annual Report, 1974, PCA, A-1620.

47. Richard Huffman, interview with GLH, tape recorded, September 10, 2008, Philadelphia, GLH Papers.

48. Harry Toland, "Mood and Methods Change for Phila. Planners," *Bulletin*, March 9, 1976.

49. See Jonathan Barnett and Nory Miller, "Edmund Bacon: A Retrospective," *Planning* 49, 11 (December 1983): 4–11.

50. Toland, "Mood and Methods."

51. Gene Harris, "Crosstown Expressway Plan Dies," *Bulletin*, October 30, 1973; Brian C. Feldman, "City Unveils $750 Million Crosstown Corridor," *Bulletin*, April 23, 1977; "Shapp Denies Giving OK for Crosstown," *Inquirer*, March 24, 1972; Bernard C. Meltzer (Albert M. Greenfield & Co.), letter to ENB, April 18, 1969, PCA, A-2965, "Crosstown Expressway, 1969."

52. "Ford to City: Drop Dead," *Daily News* (New York), October 30, 1975.

53. ENB, untitled lecture at Cornell University, undated, AAUP, 292.II.B.2.60.

54. Peter A. Angelides, interview with GLH, February 9, 2009, Philadelphia, notes in GLH Papers.

55. ENB, "Bringing Us Back to Our Senses: The New Paradigm for Teaching Design," *Ekistics* 55, 328/329/330 (January–June 1988): 118–19, AAUP, 292.II.D.29.

56. Angelides, interview with GLH.

57. "School of Architecture, Plym Professor Schedule," Fall 1991, AAUP, 292.II.B.2.119.

58. Ron Schmitt, memo to "Fall Arch 373 Faculty," July 2, 1991, AAUP, 292.II.B.2.119.

59. "Bacon Predicts Business Hub at 30th-Market," *Bulletin*, September 24, 1965.

60. Thomas Hine, "Bacon Is Back, Dangling a Glimpse at the Shape of Cityscapes to Come," *Inquirer*, October 15, 1993; Thomas J. Walsh, "'Station Square' Design Unveiled," Plan Philly, November 19, 2008, http://planphilly.com/node/4487.

61. Robert I. Selby, *Urban Synergy: Process, Projects, and Projections* (Champaign: Board of Trustees of the University of Illinois at Urbana-Champaign, 1993), 15, 22.

62. Laurie Olin, "Afterword," in Selby, *Urban Synergy: Process, Projects, and Projections*, 31.

63. "World Experts Hunt Way to End Threat of Chaos in Urban Living," *New York Times*, July 7, 1963; "West, Reds Foresee Serious Urban Plight," *Washington Post*, July 14, 1963.

64. Mary T. Williams, The American Academy in Rome: Special Meeting of the Board of Trustees, September 21, 1972, AAUP, 292.II.A.3.16; American Society of Planning Officials, resolution, AAUP, 292.IV.A.24; Roy P. Drachman, letter to ENB, April 18, 1972, AAUP, 292.II.A.3.14; Martha Peitzke Wilson, letter to ENB, January 10, 1973, AAUP, 292.II.A.3.20; "Minutes of the Transportation Task Force, Research Subcommittee," February 12, 1971, AAUP, 292.II.B.2.295.

65. ENB, untitled, November 21, 1970, AAUP, 292.II.B.2.236.

66. John A. Volpe, letter to ENB, May 8, 1969, AAUP, 292.II.B.2.306.

67. ENB, "Remarks Prepared for Informational Seminar on Regional Growth and Development, Washington D.C," October 30, 1975, AAUP, 292.II.D.267.

68. ENB, "Statement before Committee on the District of Columbia, House of Representatives, Washington D.C," May 24, 1977, AAUP, 292.II.D.290.

69. ENB, "Total National Commitment Needed to Restore Abandoned Property," *Urban Land* 35, 1 (January 1976): 4.

70. Michael Bacon, interview with GLH.

71. Urban Land Institute, *Understanding Cities: Rome,*1984, Distributed by Insight Media.

72. ENB, Ronald R. Rumbaugh, June 29, 1983, AAUP, 292.II.D.32; Claire Monaghan, letter to Urban Productions, June 1984, AAUP, 292.II.D.335; Urban Land Institute, "ULI Films Win Award in International Film and Television Festival," media release, undated, AAUP, 292.II.D.326; Bobbi L. Kamil, letter to Trish Bryan, July 13, 1984, AAUP, 292.II.D.335.

73. I. Rocke Ransen, phone interview with GLH, October 29, 2008, notes in GLH Papers.

74. Jeanne M. Davern, "The Case for Design Quality in Today's Marketplace," *Architectural Record*, December 1977, 96.

75. ENB, "Westward Ho!" *Philadelphia*, September 1988, 127.

76. ENB, "Downtown Revitalization and Redevelopment Handbook," Urban Land Institute, draft manuscript, September 22, 1997, AAUP, 292.II.D.347.

77. Davern, "The Case for Design Quality," 99–105; James M. Shanks, "Developers Want to Build Downtown," *Springfield Union*, August 16, 1974.

78. Davern, "The Case for Design Quality," 128.

79. Ransen, interview with GLH.

80. Mary Walton, "Bill Rouse's High-Stakes Gamble on Market Street," *Inquirer Sunday Magazine*, June 10, 1984.

81. Ibid.

82. Ibid.

83. Huffman, interview with GLH.

84. Ibid.; Walton, "Bill Rouse's High-Stakes."

85. Ibid.

86. Ibid.

87. Rouse & Associates, media release, April 5, 1984, AAUP, 292.II.B.2.242.

88. Walton, "Bill Rouse's High-Stakes."

89. Thomas Hine, "A Matter of Keeping Phila. Under His Hat," *Inquirer*, March 4, 1984.

90. ENB, "Gentlemen Don't Try to Top Billy Penn," *Inquirer*, March 11, 1984.

91. Ibid.

92. ENB, "Bringing Us Back to Our Senses."

93. Walton, "Bill Rouse's High-Stakes."

94. Meryl Levitz, interview with GLH, tape recorded, November 10, 2008, Philadelphia, GLH Papers.

95. ENB, Talk before Philadelphia Foundation for Architecture, April 25, 1984, AAUP, 292.II.B.2.246.

96. Gregory R. Byrnes, "The 9 Projects Planned West of City Hall," *Inquirer*, March 31, 1985.

97. Graham Finney, interview with GLH, tape recorded, April 30, 2008, Philadelphia, GLH Papers.

98. ENB, letter to Mayor W. Wilson Goode, May 12, 1984, AAUP, 292.II.B.2.242.

99. Mayor W. Wilson Goode, testimony on height limit legislation, City Council Rules Committee, May 15 1984, AAUP, 292.II.B.2.242.

100. ENB, interview with GLH, September 24, 2002.

101. ENB, letter to Mayor W. Wilson Goode, June 3, 1984, AAUP, 292.II.B.2.242; ENB, "A Protest of 'Intrusions' into our Skyline," *Philadelphia Inquirer*, June 7, 1984.

102. Gregory R. Byrnes, "The Leader in the Great Office Race," *Inquirer*, March 31, 1985.

103. Willard G. Rouse, III, letter to ENB, April 17, 1985, AAUP, 292.IV.A.7.

104. ENB, letter to Willard G. Rouse III, May 13, 1985, AAUP, 292.IV.A.7.

105. Kia Gregory, "Osage's Lingering Loss: Community," *Inquirer*, May 13, 2010.

106. ENB, letter to Mayor W. Wilson Goode, May 8, 1985, AAUP, 292.II.B.2.246.

107. ENB, "Put the Lid on Buildings," *Inquirer*, December 6, 1985.

108. ENB, "A 'Zone of Respect' for City Hall," *Inquirer*, February 26, 1987.

109. Paul Goldberger, "Giving New Life to Philadelphia's Skyline," *New York Times*, November 15, 1987.

110. Hank Klibanoff, "An Ominous Warning About an 'Endangered Fountain'," *Inquirer*, October 13, 1989.

111. James M. Ridenour, letter to Arlen Specter, December 27, 1989, AAUP, 292.II.B.2.122.

112. For Bacon's criticism, see ENB, "Bugs Bunny Ears in the Middle of Independence Mall?" September 12, 1989, AAUP, 292.II.B.2.122; for examples of support from public figures, see Maurice K. Goddard, letter to David Boldt, October 23, 1989,

AAUP, 292.II.B.2.122; also Arlen Specter, letter to ENB, January 3, 1990, AAUP, 292.II.B.2.122.

113. Thomas Hine, "Memorializing the Constitution," date unknown, AAUP, 292.II.B.2.123.

114. Alfred Branam Jr., letter to ENB, March 27, 1991, AAUP, 292.II.A.3.50.

115. Joseph R. Daughen, "$200M plan is unveiled," *Daily News*, August 10, 1995, 10.

116. Martha B. Aikens, letter to ENB, October 4, 1995, AAUP, 292.II.B.2.129.

117. U.S. Department of the Interior, National Park Service, "Draft General Management Plan, Environmental Impact Statement: Independence National Historical Park, Pennsylvania," 1995.

118. Barbara Faga, *Designing Public Consensus: The Civic Theater of Community Participation for Architects, Landscape Architects, Planners and Urban Designers* (Hoboken, N.J.: Wiley, 2006), 33.

119. Daniel Rubin, "Park Service Blasted over Independence Mall Plan," *Inquirer*, August 9, 1995.

120. Joseph R. Daughen, "His Role? 'Getting People to Think'," *Daily News*, October 18, 1995.

121. ENB, "You had every right to expect . . ." undated, GLH Papers.

122. Daughen, "His Role?"

123. "The Wisdom of Age," editorial, *Inquirer*, February 20, 1996.

124. Robert J. Butera, "Revitalizing the Mall," letter to the editor, *Inquirer*, November 8, 1995.

125. Martha B. Aikens, letter to the editor, *Inquirer*, date unknown, copy in AAUP, 292.II.E.142.

126. Janet Haas, letter to ENB, November 7, 1995, AAUP, 292.II.A.3.54.

127. W. Russell G. Byers, "Bacon's Proposals Mean Fun," *Daily News*, June 6, 1996.

128. Chris Satullo, "City and Region Should Be Looking Ahead to the Disasters That Await," *Inquirer*, June 18, 1996.

129. Stephan Salisbury, "Tentative Yes on Plan for Independence Mall," *Inquirer*, June 7, 1996.

130. Ibid.

131. ENB, "Keep the View, Revitalize the Mall," *Inquirer*, June 9, 1996; ENB, "Statement by Edmund N. Bacon on Plans for Independence Mall," July 1, 1996, AAUP, 292.IV.A.14.

132. Image accompanying: Thomas Ferrick, Jr., "Freeing Independence Mall from Its Own History," *Inquirer*, September 22, 1996.

133. "Change Sought for Landmark in Philadelphia," *New York Times*, July 5, 1996.

134. ENB, "What the Inquirer Refused to Print," unpublished ms., June 2, 1998, AAUP, 292.IV.B.32.

135. "A National Park Service," editorial, *Inquirer*, October 2, 1997.

136. ENB, "What the Inquirer Refused to Print."

137. Liz Matt, "Razing Mall Destroys History, Art," *Daily News*, July 3, 1998.

138. Thomas Ferrick, Jr., "Bacon's Bitter Final Fight," *Inquirer*, October 2, 1997.

139. Ibid.

140. ENB, "A Civic Center for Philadelphia," June 23, 1932, senior thesis plan, elevations, Class A plan study, Cornell University College of Architecture, Art, and Planning Records, 1905–1997, Coll. 15-1-512, Division of Rare and Manuscript Collections, Cornell University Library.

141. For history of skateboarding, see Iain Borden, *Skateboarding, Space and the City* (New York: Berg, 2003); "street skating" discussed 173–228.

142. Rick Valenzuela, "Love Jones," *Philadelphia City Paper*, April 25–May 1, 2002.

143. Independence Hall Association, "Love Park Timeline," http://www.ushistory.org/lovepark/timeline.htm.

144. Rick Valenzuela, "Bye Bye Love: A Eulogy for a Fallen Landmark," *City Paper*, May 2–8, 2002.

145. Philadelphia City Council, Legislative file 000147, 21 September 2000, http://legislation.phila.gov/detailreport/?key = 240.

146. Independence Hall Association, "Love Park Timeline."

147. See Christine Otto quoted in Daniel Brook, "I Can Fix Your City," *City Paper*, September 12–18, 2002.

148. Independence Hall Association, "Love Park Timeline."

149. Marty Bernoski, "Derailed at LOVE Park," EXPN.com, August 18, 2002, http://ushistory.org/lovepark/news/expn081802.htm.

150. Rick Valenzuela, "Love Jones," *City Paper*, April 25–May 1, 2002.

151. Brook, "I Can Fix Your City."

152. Ibid.

153. Urban Land Institute, *Understanding Cities: The American Urban Experience*, Urban Productions, 1984, distributed by Insight Media.

154. ENB, quoted on http://ushistory.org/lovepark/views.htm.

155. Howard Altman, "Love Burns Bacon," *City Paper*, October 31–November 6, 2002.

156. Ibid.

157. Ibid.

158. ENB, "Talk Given by Edmund N. Bacon, Former City Planner of Philadelphia at Love Park on October 28, 2002," copy in GLH Papers.

159. Altman, "Love Burns Bacon."

160. "Six Degrees of Edmund Bacon," *Skate*, date unknown, 40, copy in GLH Papers.

161. Kevin Bacon, statement submitted to Free LOVE Park website, http://ushistory.org/lovepark/views.htm.

162. Carla Anderson, "DN Poll: Show Some Love for Skateboarders," *Daily News*, May 23, 2003.

163. Dave Davies, "Katz: Give LOVE Park Back to Boarders," *Daily News*, May 21, 2003.

164. " 'LOVE' Requires Compromise," editorial, *Daily News*, August 4, 2003; "Wheel Deal," editorial, *Inquirer*, June 29, 2003.

165. According to the "City Council Scorecard" on Independence Hall Association, "Free LOVE Park," www.ushistory.org/lovepark.

166. Carla Anderson, "City to Boarders and Shoe $$: Keep Walking," *Daily News*, June 2, 2004.

167. Chris Satullo, "LOVE Park Remains a Test Case of Philadelphia's Will to Thrive," *Inquirer*, June 6, 2004.

168. Thomas Hine, "Just How Good Was Ed Bacon Really?" *Philadelphia*, March 1999, 87.

Conclusion

1. Robin Pogrebin, "Edmund Bacon, 95, Urban Planner of Philadelphia, Dies," *New York Times*, October 18, 2005.

2. Ibid.

3. Inga Saffron, "Grand Planner," *Metropolis*, January 16, 2006, http://www.metropolismag.com/story/20060116/grand-planner.

4. Inga Saffron, "An Appreciation: Flaws and All, Edmund N. Bacon Molded a Modern Philadelphia," *Inquirer*, October 16, 2005.

5. ENB, *Design of Cities*, rev. ed. (New York: Penguin, 1974), 301.

6. ENB, quoted in Steve Volk, "Bacon Bits," *Philadelphia Weekly*, October 19–25, 2005.

7. Center City District and Central Philadelphia Development Corporation, "Leading the Way: Population Growth Downtown," September 2011, 4, http://www.centercityphila.org/docs/CCR_Demographics2011.pdf; U.S. Census Bureau, 2010 Census Briefs, "Population Distribution and Change: 2000 to 2010," http://www.census.gov/prod/cen2010/briefs/c2010br-01.pdf.

8. Pew Charitable Trusts, Philadelphia Research Initiative, "A City Transformed," June 1, 2011, http://www.pewtrusts.org/uploadedFiles/wwwpewtrustsorg/Reports/Philadelphia_Research_Initiative/Philadelphia-Population-Ethnic-Changes.pdf.

9. Office of the Controller, City of Philadelphia, "Philadelphia's Poverty Rate Outpaces Largest U.S. Cities," September 28, 2010, http://www.philadelphiacontroller.org/page.asp?id = 613.

10. Center City District and Central Philadelphia Development Corporation, "State of Center City 2011," 56, http://www.centercityphila.org/docs/SOCC2011.pdf.

11. Liberty Property Trust, "1701 John F. Kennedy Boulevard," http://www.libertyproperty.com.

12. Natalie Kostelni, "Plans Unveiled for E. Market," *Philadelphia Business Journal*, December 10, 2010.

13. Ibid.

14. Labelscar, "PREIT Purchases Former Strawbridge's Flagship Store," July 21, 2006, http://www.labelscar.com/retail-news/strawbridges-sold.

15. Michael Callahan, "The Late Great Northeast," *Philadelphia*, January 2009.

16. Pew Charitable Trusts, Philadelphia Research Initiative, "A City Transformed," 5.

17. Joanna Zuckerman Bernstein, "Brazil on the Boulevard: Northeast Philadelphia Is Home to a Fast-Growing Brazilian Community," *Philadelphia Weekly*, August 30, 2006.

18. "Victory at Yorktown 40 Years Ago an Inner-city Community Was Born, and Today It's a Model for Urban Renewal," *Inquirer* (?), July 13, 1996.

19. Pennsylvania Department of Transportation, "Interstate 95 Revive.com," http://www.95revive.com/reviving-interstate-95-overview.aspx.

20. Joseph N. DiStefano, "Knock Down I-95," *Inquirer*, December 4, 2008.

21. John Kromer, *Fixing Broken Cities: The Implementation of Urban Development Strategies* (Philadelphia: University of Pennsylvania Press, 2010), 17–47.

22. For discussion of Center City District, see ibid., 49–75.

23. Barbara Faga, *Designing Public Consensus: The Civic Theater of Community Participation for Architects, Landscape Architects, Planners and Urban Designers* (Hoboken, N.J.: Wiley, 2006), 134–44.

24. For a discussion of Penn's programs, see ibid., 144–54.

25. ENB, "The New Paradigm for Design Education," talk at University of Michigan, February 19, 1987, AAUP, 292.II.B.2.77.

26. ENB, "A Fair Can Pace It," *Greater Philadelphia Magazine*, October 1959.

Index

Acknowledgments

This book has been a challenging undertaking, and I am fortunate that so many others shared my passion for this project. I want to convey my sincere thanks the following people who helped make this book possible:

Ruth O'Brien, who first suggested I meet Ed Bacon; Elizabeth Milroy for her tremendous support and encouragement; Prema Katari Gupta who initially recommended me to a publisher; the Bacon family, especially Karin, Elinor, Hilda, Michael, Kira, and Kevin, for their interviews and assistance in my research; my very good friends Ariel Ben-Amos, Daniel Brook, Andrew Dalzell, and Matthew Jakubowski for their help researching, reviewing, editing, and offering support and advice; William Whitaker and Nancy Thorne at the University of Pennsylvania Architectural Archives for going above and beyond the call of duty to assist me on this project, and for serving as wonderful stewards of Bacon's papers; Barry Seymour, Karin Morris, and others at the Delaware Valley Regional Planning Commission, who were flexible and patient with me as I worked a full-time job during the most difficult period of my research; Charles Cook for involving me in his film project on Bacon, and allowing me to take part in many of his interview sessions; Scott Gabriel Knowles, for involving me as a collaborator in the *Imagining Philadelphia* project, and for his confidence in me and my work; Audra Wolfe for her excellent developmental editing that helped me condense, adapt, and ultimately strengthen the manuscript; Robert Lockhart and the Editorial Board at University of Pennsylvania Press for the opportunity to finally see this book in print; Eugenie L. Birch, Susan M. Wachter, and the Penn Institute for Urban Research for including this book in Penn IUR's book series; in addition, special thanks to Dr. Birch for being a primary supporter of this project, for being extremely helpful to me over the years, and for encouraging other initiatives related to Bacon's work and legacy; Amy Montgomery (Penn IUR) and Kate Daniel (Penn Department of City and Regional Planning) for their assistance; Alexander Garvin for his endless encouragement of my work, and for helping me better understand Bacon's contributions to American urban planning; Rachel Aland, my talented research assistant, for helping me complete the manuscript; my extraordinary grandparents, Myra and Jack Heller for their love and support that made this book possible; all the members of my loving family, especially my parents Janis and Jonathan Schmalzbach, Doug and Nancy Heller, and brother Rob Heller, for believing in me and bearing with me over the course of this project; and of course Edmund N. Bacon, whom I had the great honor of getting to know and learn from in the final years of his life.

There are many other people, too many to name here, who assisted in this project. I want to offer my profound thanks to everyone who had a hand in producing this book; you know who you are.